OXFORD SHAKESPEARE STUDIES

*

SHAKESPEARE RESHAPED

OXFORD SHAKESPEARE STUDIES

Shakespeare Reshaped

1606–1623

GARY TAYLOR

AND

JOHN JOWETT

CLARENDON PRESS · OXFORD

Oxford University Press, Great Clarendon Street, Oxford OX2 6DP
Oxford New York
Athens Auckland Bangkok Bogota Bombay
Buenos Aires Calcutta Cape Town Dar es Salaam
Delhi Florence Hong Kong Istanbul Karachi
Kuala Lumpur Madras Madrid Melbourne
Mexico City Nairobi Paris Singapore
Taipei Tokyo Toronto
and associated companies in
Berlin Ibadan

Oxford is a trade mark of Oxford University Press

Published in the United States
by Oxford University Press Inc., New York

British Library Cataloguing in Publication Data
Data available.

Library of Congress Cataloging in Publication Data
Taylor, Gary, 1953– .
Shakespeare reshaped, 1606–1623 / Gary Taylor and John Jowett.—
(Oxford Shakespeare studies)
Includes index.
1. Shakespeare, William, 1564–1616—Stage history—To 1625.
2. Shakespeare, William, 1564–1616—Criticism, Textual.
3. Shakespeare, William, 1564–1616—Censorship.   4. Censorship—
England—History—17th century.   5. Editing—England—History—17th century.
6. Theatre—England—History—17th century.
I. Jowett, John.   II. Title.   III. Series.
PR3095.T39   1993   822.3′3—dc20   93–16328
ISBN 0-19-812256-X

Printed in Great Britain
on acid-free paper by
Ipswich Book Co Ltd,
Ipswich, Suffolk

PREFACE

The research which resulted in the writing of this book was undertaken as part of the preparation of an edition of Shakespeare's *Complete Works*, published by Oxford University Press in 1986–7, under the General Editorship of Stanley Wells and Gary Taylor. The research thus belongs to a period of close collaboration, when both authors were members of the Shakespeare department established by the Press in 1978. We are therefore most indebted to Oxford University Press itself, for its long and generous support of a unique research project, and to Stanley Wells, head of the department, who was an unfailing source of information, wisdom, criticism, and encouragement. Moreover, any insights in these essays cannot be disentangled from the larger investigation of which they form a part, an investigation to which many hands and minds contributed, over a course of almost a decade.

Act-scene-line references to Shakespeare are therefore keyed to the Oxford modern-spelling edition (1986); we routinely take for granted the hypotheses about individual texts explained in full in *William Shakespeare: A Textual Companion* (Oxford, 1987). Likewise, both versions of the Oxford *Complete Works*, and *Textual Companion*, act upon or refer to conclusions reached in the following essays, which were then described as 'forthcoming'.

A draft text of this book had in fact been finished by 1985, before completion of either edition or the *Textual Companion*; however, at that time the book was temporarily set aside, so that we could devote our entire energies to the preparation of final copy for *The Complete Works* and *A Textual Companion*. Our work on the *Companion* was not completed until 1987; we then found ourselves in new academic positions, with new commitments and demands upon our time, and we did not return to the manuscript until late 1989. We have made every effort to re-examine the entire text in the light of work published in the interim, and we have accordingly in a few places revised views expressed in the *Companion*. Any such changes of mind are noted. The only substantial changes are the extended examination of expurgation in *Measure for Measure*, at the end of the second essay, and the 'Post-Script'. Appendix 1—which belongs to Chapter 2—is the work of Gary Taylor; the remaining appendices—which belong to Chapter 3—are collaborative. The index was prepared by John Jowett.

Our thanks for the people who helped us with this project are long overdue, but no less genuine: they have, if anything, accumulated interest. The staff of the Bodleian, the Folger, and the British Libraries, in particular, were unfailingly patient and helpful; Trinity College let us examine Middleton's autograph *Game at Chess*. For specific details, we have drawn upon the expertise and generosity of R. E. Alton, Nigel Bawcutt, David Bergeron, A. R. Braunmuller, Lou Burnard, G. B. Evans, Charles Forker, R. V. Holdsworth, T. H. Howard-Hill, G. K. Hunter, MacDonald P. Jackson, Scott McMillin, Thomas Merriam, Kenneth Muir, Peter Saccio, David Sacks, F. W. Sternfeld, Robert K. Turner, Paul Werstine, and George Walton Williams. Without Christine Avern-Carr and Louise Pengelley, our thoughts could not have been translated into their present legible material form so efficiently.

J.J.
G.T.

TABLE OF CONTENTS

LIST OF TABLES

LIST OF ABBREVIATIONS

Beaumont and Fletcher Canon	*The Dramatic Works in the Beaumont and Fletcher Canon*, gen. ed. Fredson Bowers, 7 vols. (Cambridge, 1976–89)
Bentley, *Jacobean and Caroline Stage*	G. E. Bentley, *The Jacobean and Caroline Stage*, 7 vols. (Oxford, 1941–68).
Bentley, *Profession*	G. E. Bentley, *The Profession of Dramatist in Shakespeare's Time, 1590–1642* (Princeton, NJ, 1971).
Capell, *Notes*	Edward Capell, *Notes and Various Readings to Shakespeare*, 3 vols. (London, pr. 1779–80, publ. 1783).
Chambers, *Elizabethan Stage*	E. K. Chambers, *The Elizabethan Stage*, 4 vols. (Oxford, 1923).
Chambers, *William Shakespeare*	E. K. Chambers, *William Shakespeare: A Study of Facts and Problems*, 2 vols. (Oxford, 1930).
Division	Gary Taylor and Michael Warren (eds.), *The Division of the Kingdoms: Shakespeare's Two Versions of King Lear* (Oxford, 1983; repr. 1986).
Granville-Barker, *Prefaces*	Harley Granville-Baker, *Prefaces to Shakespeare*, 2 vols. (London, 1958).
Greg, *Bibliography*	W. W. Greg, *A Bibliography of the English Printed Drama to the Restoration*, 4 vols. The Bibliographical Society (London, 1939–59).
Greg, *Dramatic Documents*	W. W. Greg, *Dramatic Documents from the Elizabethan Playhouse*, 2 vols. (Oxford, 1931).
Greg, *Editorial Problem*	W. W. Greg, *The Editorial Problem in Shakespeare* (Oxford, 1942; rev. 1951).
Greg, *First Folio*	W. W. Greg, *The Shakespeare First Folio: Its Bibliographical and Textual History* (Oxford, 1955).

Hensman thesis   Bertha Hensman, 'John Fletcher's
                                     *The Bloody Brother, or Rollo Duke
                                     of Normandy*' (Ph.D. thesis,
                                     University of Chicago, 1947).

Hinman, *Printing and Proof-Reading* Charlton Hinman, *The Printing
                                     and Proof-Reading of the First
                                     Folio of Shakespeare*, 2 vols.
                                     (Oxford, 1963).

Holdworth   R. V. Holdsworth, 'Middleton and
                                     Shakespeare: The Case for
                                     Middleton's Hand in *Timon of
                                     Athens*' (Ph.D. thesis, University
                                     of Manchester, 1982).

Howard-Hill, *Ralph Crane*   T.H. Howard-Hill, *Ralph Crane
                                     and Some Shakespeare First Folio
                                     Comedies* (Charlottesville, Va.,
                                     1972).

Hunter   G. K. Hunter, 'Were there Act-
                                     Pauses on Shakespeare's Stage?' in
                                     Standish Henning, Robert
                                     Kimbrough, and Richard Knowles
                                     (eds.), *English Renaissance Drama:
                                     Essays in Honor of Madeleine
                                     Doran and Mark Eccles*
                                     (Carbondale, Ill., 1976), 15–35.

Jackson, *Attribution*   MacDonald P. Jackson, *Studies in
                                     Attribution: Middleton and
                                     Shakespeare* (Salzburg, 1979).

Jewkes, *Act Division*   W. T. Jewkes, *Act Division in
                                     Elizabethan and Jacobean Plays,
                                     1583–1616* (Hamden, Conn.,
                                     1958).

Lake, *Canon*   David Lake, *The Canon of
                                     Thomas Middleton's Plays*
                                     (Cambridge, 1974).

Mal. Soc. Repr.   Malone Society Reprint (Oxford)
N. & Q.   *Notes and Queries*
Nashe   *The Works of Thomas Nashe*, ed.
                                     R. B. McKerrow, 5 vols. (Oxford,
                                     1904–10; rev. 1966).

PBSA   *Papers of the Bibliographical
                                     Society of America*

RES   *Review of English Studies*
RORD   *Research Opportunities in
                                     Renaissance Drama*

SB	*Studies in Bibliography*
Smith, *Blackfriars Playhouse*	Irwin Smith, *Shakespeare's Blackfriars Playhouse: Its History and its Design* (London, 1964).
SQ	*Shakespeare Quarterly*
SS	*Shakespeare Studies*
Textual Companion	Stanley Wells and Gary Taylor (with John Jowett and William Montgomery), *William Shakespeare: A Textual Companion* (Oxford, 1987).
TLN	Through-Line-Number(s), keyed to Charlton Hinman (ed.), *The Shakespeare First Folio: The Norton Facsimile* (New York, 1968).
Walker, *Textual Problems*	Alice Walker, *Textual Problems of the First Folio* (Cambridge, 1953).

Introduction

An author's work can be reshaped in two ways: by the author, or by other people. Both kinds of reshaping affected the Shakespeare canon, and they are not always easy to distinguish. But although textual critics may differ over whether to attribute certain textual variants to Shakespeare revising or to someone else interfering, about other kinds of reshaping a greater degree of consensus is or should be attainable. No one imagines that Shakespeare was the secret author of the Parliamentary 'Acte to Restraine Abuses of Players' in 1606; everyone recognizes that every play performed during Shakespeare's working lifetime had to be licensed by the Master of the Revels, who had the power and the duty to censor whatever the government of the hour might find objectionable. Some of Shakespeare's plays must have been reshaped by such political interference, and some might also have been reshaped by major changes in theatrical conventions. In later periods, the introduction of actresses, of the proscenium arch, of elaborate stage scenery and lighting, and of large numbers of supernumerary actors, significantly affected the texts of revivals of some of Shakespeare's plays; if similarly basic changes of convention occurred between 1586 and 1634, they could have affected some of the early texts of Shakespeare. Shakespeare's plays were also, of course, adapted in later periods, by playwrights bent upon making them more attractive to contemporary taste; such adaptation also occurred during the Elizabethan and Jacobean period, and may have affected Shakespeare's plays, as it did other men's.

These kinds of interference, when they occurred, must have reshaped Shakespeare's plays much more drastically than the occasional errors of compositors or sophistications of scribes. For several decades textual scholars have concentrated upon the identification and evaluation of the scribes and compositors who transmitted the early texts of Shakespeare's works. Such studies have many uses, and will be referred to often enough in the following pages. But although the influence of such agents of transmission upon the spelling and punctuation of the early texts can hardly be overstated, even the most careless or overweening of them can have had—relatively speaking—only a minimal effect in corrupting the words and meaning of a work. A single stroke of the pen by the Master of the Revels could have caused the omission of more words than the carelessness of all the compositors who set into type the rest of the canon; a single paragraph of legislation in 1606 almost certainly caused more verbal substitutions, in any one affected text, than Ralph Crane perpetrated in all six plays which he transcribed for use by the printer of the First Folio.

The following essays deal with some of the kinds of macroscopic interference to which Shakespeare's texts were subjected: the imposition of
act-divisions, the expurgation of profanity, the late interpolation of
unShakespearian material. If the book were to be comprehensive, it
would need to include essays on political censorship and on *Macbeth* (the
only play, other than *Measure for Measure*, which seems to us to have
suffered from posthumous interpolation). We have omitted *Macbeth* simply because we have little new to say about it. We do have things to say
about the censorship of certain plays, but we have said them elsewhere.
The problem of expurgation, or of act-division, can hardly be discussed
without a consideration of the entire canon; each allegation of censorship,
by contrast, is a separate problem, most usefully considered in detail and
in isolation. Moreover, Shakespeare's plays began to be censored as soon
as he began to write, whereas the other kinds of interference we have
examined can all be conveniently located in the period between May 1606
and November 1623, and all reshaped plays years (rather than days or
weeks) after they had originally been written. Cumulatively, we believe
that such late reshaping has seriously affected subsequent understanding
of some plays, and—as a result—of Shakespeare's achievement, and his
nature as a writer.

I

The Structure of Performance
Act-Intervals in the London Theatres, 1576–1642
by GARY TAYLOR

MODERN criticism encourages us to read between the lines of Shakespeare's plays, but not between the acts: to pick out the local significance of pauses and silences in the texture of dialogue, but to ignore the four longer silences between the five acts; to probe the sub-text implicit in a character's failure to act or speak, but to disregard the un-text of those four intervals, when all the characters collectively stop acting and speaking, and the play itself hesitates. This double standard arises from the widespread belief that Shakespeare wrote all his plays for uninterrupted performance, and the corollary that act-divisions are meaningless literary status symbols, a bogus superstructure first tacked on to the plays by the editors of the First Folio, and then expanded by their eighteenth-century descendants.

These allied assumptions have been challenged by G. K. Hunter, who takes up arms in the defence of T. W. Baldwin.[1] Baldwin's work has been unjustly neglected because it is virtually unreadable. Yet his *William Shakspere's Five-Act Structure* (1944) compendiously demonstrated that any educated Elizabethan would have assumed that a play had five acts. Educated Elizabethan playwrights therefore, presumably, thought in terms of five sections, when they sat down to structure a play.[2] Unfortunately, of course, the intellectual models by which an author sets about constructing a play tell us little about how actors set about performing the finished product. On this issue Baldwin has waged an unequal battle against Harley Granville-Barker, whose criticism is as impressionistically brilliant as Baldwin's is indigestibly laborious.[3] Granville-Barker has, predictably, had greater success in the battle for

---

[1] G. K. Hunter, 'Were There Act-Pauses on Shakespeare's Stage?' in Standish Henning, Robert Kimbrough, and Richard Knowles, eds., *English Renaissance Drama: Essays in Honor of Madeleine Doran and Mark Eccles* (Carbondale, Ill., 1976), 15–35.

[2] For evidence that plays were indeed sometimes composed in this way, with collaborators writing different acts, see G. E. Bentley, *The Profession of Dramatist in Shakespeare's Time, 1590–1642* (Princeton, NJ, 1971), 227–34. It is noticeable, however, that in both the early examples drawn from the adult theatres the key figure is Ben Jonson. As Greg says, 'A plot by Jonson was sure to be carefully divided' (*The Shakespeare First Folio: Its Bibliographical and Textual History* (Oxford, 1955, 145). By 1613 and 1624, however, playwrights like Daborne, Tourneur, and Dekker were also using acts as units of collaborative composition.

[3] *Prefaces to Shakespeare*, 2 vols. (London, 1958).

hearts and minds. Yet this success probably depends not on his arguments (often highly subjective), but on his reputation, which encourages an unconscious syllogism: 'Baldwin is a scholar, and therefore competent to describe what went on in the writer's study; Granville-Barker is a director, actor, and playwright, and therefore competent to describe what went on in the theatre'. Granville-Barker's prejudices, moreover, are our own: like many modern playwrights, he envies and aspires to the fluidity of film, and admires Shakespeare because his plays possess an 'organic' rather than 'mechanical' structure. Such continuity and fluidity seem, to most of us, immeasurably more appealing, more 'natural', than the Renaissance formalism which would chop performances of *any* play into five chunks. But Shakespeare was, after all, a Renaissance playwright, not a modern one: what seemed pejoratively artificial to Granville-Barker might have seemed admirably 'artificeal' to him. Clearly, we must have grounds less relative than this.

Whatever may have been the practice earlier, by some point in the second decade of James I's reign plays produced by the London companies were being regularly performed with intervals between the acts. Every one of the 245 extant plays written for those companies between 1616 and 1642 (inclusive) is divided into five acts.[4] This applies equally to printed and manuscript texts, to plays from authorial or theatrical copy, to plays printed in octavo or quarto or folio, to plays written by at least fifty-six authors, printed by dozens of printers, and performed by a dozen London companies. Moreover, to these 245 plays may be added another four—Chettle and Day's *Blind Beggar of Bethnal Green*, Dekker's *Match Me in London*, Heywood's *1 Fair Maid of the West*, and Rowley's *A Shoemaker a Gentleman*—all originally written earlier in the century, but which only survive in texts apparently set from prompt-books of known revivals in the late 1620s or 1630s: all four, like the other 245, have regular divisions. Such unanimity can hardly be the result of chance, or even of the literary pretensions of playwrights and publishers: after all, some writers and some publishers, in any period, are less pretentious than others. Yet no one departs from the convention of dividing plays into five acts, and no one lambasts the fashion for printing plays in this way as artificial or pretentious.

The testimony of the manuscripts is particularly compelling. W. W. Greg describes eleven manuscripts from this later period as prompt-

---

[4] For dates and provenance of plays I have (unless otherwise specified, below) relied on Alfred Harbage's *Annals of English Drama 975–1700*, rev. S. Schoenbaum (London, 1964). I have not included masques, civic pageants, academic or closet plays. The only definitely unacted play included is Shirley's *The Court Secret* (1642), which was, according to the title-page, '*Never Acted,* | But prepared for the Scene at | BLACK-FRIERS', and which therefore remained unacted only by political accident. All quotations are from the original edns.; I have modernized the use of i, j, u, and v, ignoring long-s and ligatures.

books:[5] *The Second Maiden's Tragedy* (1611), *Sir John Van Olden Barnavelt* (1619), *The Two Noble Ladies* (1622–3?), *The Welsh Ambassador* (c.1623), *The Parliament of Love* (1624), *The Captives* (1624),[6] *The Honest Man's Fortune* (1624/5), *Believe As You List* (1631), *The Soddered Citizen* (1631?), *The Launching of the Mary* (1633), and *The Lady Mother* (1635). All have act-divisions. To these eleven may now be added both *The Faithful Friends* (1618–30) and *The Wasp* (1636–9), which Malone Society editors have identified as theatrical texts; both, again, have act-divisions.[7]

The treatment of act-divisions in these manuscripts is as significant as their mere presence. In *Believe As You List*, the theatrical scribe crossed through Massinger's own centred act-divisions, then 'proceeded to reinstate the act division by emphatic notes in the margin'; moreover, to the headings for Acts 2 and 4 'he appended the word "Long", which may be interpreted with some confidence as meaning a long interval'.[8] Although the provision for 'long' intervals is not very common, the placing of act-divisions in the margin (with other important theatrical business, like directions for entrances and props) is typical of all these manuscripts. In *The Launching of the Mary* the theatrical scribe duplicated one of the author's centred act-divisions in the margin, and provided for music in each of the four intervals. In *The Soddered Citizen*, *The Wasp*, and *The Lady Mother* the scribe moved act-divisions to a different location; this strongly suggests that these theatrical agents regarded act-divisions as of some importance to the intended function of the prompt-book. Moreover, in *The Lady Mother* the scribe 'added warnings in the left margin some twelve to twenty lines before all the entrances *except those following an Act interval*'.[9] *The Welsh Ambassador* and *The Wasp* also, less systematically, provide such warnings; neither marks them for entrances at the beginning of an act.[10] It is difficult to avoid the inference that warnings were not needed at the beginning of an act because the

---

[5] *Dramatic Documents from the Elizabethan Playhouses*, 2 vols. (Oxford, 1931), 239–308. For MSS generally I have relied on Mal. Soc. Reprs., or Greg, where possible.

[6] Arthur Brown, who edited the Mal. Soc. Repr. (1953), concluded that the MS was foul papers heavily annotated by a bookkeeper, as a preliminary to preparing a prompt-book proper (p. xii). (All Mal. Soc. Reprs. are printed by the Clarendon Press, Oxford).

[7] *The Wasp*, ed. J. W. Lever, Mal. Soc. Repr. (1976), and *The Faithful Friends*, ed. G. M. Pinciss and G. R. Proudfoot (1975), pp. xiv–xv. The latter MS seems not to have been the prompt-book itself, but it was clearly being prepared for such a purpose, by experienced theatrical agents, with an eye to possible censorship and with a definite company in mind. However, in the end it was either abandoned or copied. I here accept Pinciss and Proudfoot's dating of the play (see pp. xv–xvi) rather than Harbage and Schoenbaum's (1614).

[8] Greg, *Dramatic Documents*, 295.

[9] *The Lady Mother*, ed. Arthur Brown, Mal. Soc. Repr. (1958), p. viii; my italics.

[10] In *The Wasp* it appears that two of the warnings overlap act-intervals, but this is because the warnings were written before the position of the act-divisions was altered; see Lever, pp. x–xi.

action was not continuous: the prompter did not need to ensure that an actor arrived on the stage at an exact moment required by the dialogue. If someone was late for the first entrance of Act 2, they could always just prolong the interval.

Similar evidence of theatrical practice can be found in printed texts. The bookkeeper's 'Long' opposite two of the act-divisions in *Believe As You List* is duplicated in the printed text of Heywood's *1 Fair Maid of the West* (1631): the Chorus at the end of Act 4 tells the audience to 'sit patient', and then—between the Chorus's exit and the beginning of Act 5—the printed text tells the reader '*Act long*' (H3).[11] '*Act*' here clearly refers to the interval itself, not the five sections of dramatic action into which the play is divided. The same convention occurs consistently in the so-called Padua prompt-books, First Folio texts of *Macbeth*, *Measure for Measure*, and *The Winter's Tale*, which were annotated to regulate performances some time in the late 1630s or after: each interval in each of these texts is marked with the marginal direction 'Act'.[12] Another early prompt-book, a marked-up copy of Q2 of *Romeo and Juliet* now in the Elizabethan Club at Yale University, likewise marks acts and calls for music before them;[13] an early seventeenth-century hand also provided act-divisions in a copy of the 1612 Quarto of Webster's *The White Devil*, now in Edinburgh, which was apparently marked up for use as a prompt-book. The 1659 Quarto of Day and Chettle's *Blind Beggar of Bethnal Green*, clearly printed from the prompt-book of a revival which took place after 1630, has directions for music in the margin opposite each act-division.[14] Middleton and Rowley's *The Changeling* (1622) tells us at the beginning of Act 2 that '(*In the Act Time De Flores hides a naked Rapier.*)' (D3^v). This usage can also be seen in Massinger's *The City Madam* (1632), between Acts 4 and 5: '*Whil'st the Act plays, the Footstep, little Table, and Arras hung up*' (K1^v); likewise in Nathan Field's portion

[11] *1 Fair Maid* probably dates from the first decade of the century, but the text printed in 1631 was clearly prompted by and shows evidence of a very recent revival, in conjunction with the newly-composed *2 Fair Maid*. See Robert K. Turner's Regents Renaissance Drama edn. (London, 1968), pp. xi–xiii, xviii–xx.

[12] G. Blakemore Evans, *Shakespeare Prompt-Books of the Seventeenth Century*, 5 vols. (Charlottesville, Va., 1960–70), i–ii.

[13] Edmond Malone first drew attention to this copy of Q2 in his 1790 edn., and certified that the handwriting of the annotations was 'of a very old date' (iii, 111 n. 3). It is listed first for *Romeo* in Charles H. Shattuck's *The Shakespeare Promptbooks: A Descriptive Catalogue* (Urbana, Ill. 1965), 411. R. E. Alton and Peter Croft have confirmed for me that the hand responsible for the divisions dates from 1620 to 1660, more probably belonging to the latter end of this spectrum; the performance might have taken place during the Commonwealth, and would in any case almost certainly have been provincial. Neither Malone nor George Steevens (who owned the volume earlier) mentioned that the quarto's act-divisions differ from the standard editorial divisions, originating with Rowe: they fall after what modern editors identify as 1. 3, 2. 3, 3. 3, and 5. 2.

[14] For evidence of the revival, and the printer's copy, see Harold Jenkins, *The Life and Work of Henry Chettle* (London, 1934), 188, 199–201. (Jenkins does not adduce the act-divisions, or music directions, as evidence.)

of *The Fatal Dowry* (1617–19) at the end of Act 2: '*Here a passage over the Stage, while the Act is playing*' (F1).[15] In both these texts, '*the Act*' clearly refers to the music played during an interval; hence, '*while the Act is playing*' is synonymous with the direction '*While the musicke is playing*' (E1), which we find at the beginning of Act 3 of Shirley's *The Witty Fair One* (1628). Likewise, the Folger manuscript of Middleton's *Hengist* (1618) has directions for music at each act-break.[16] None of these directions for music survives into the printed text (1661), perhaps because the association of music with act-intervals became so strong that a specific call for music at such points came to seem redundant. Hence one finds a text like J. D.'s *The Knave in Grain* (1639), which places the direction '*sound Musick*' at the beginning of Acts 2 (D1ᵛ) and 3 (F2), clearly separate from the entrance direction. At the end of Act 2 of Shirley's *The Sisters* (1642), Paulina says 'Let me have Musick' (C2ᵛ); no stage direction for music is supplied, but the act-break immediately follows. In Shirley's *Hyde Park* (1632), Act 2 begins with '*Bonavent, Listening*', and then saying 'Musicke and revelles? they are very merry' (C3ᵛ); again, no direction for music appears in the printed text, nor has any been explicitly called for by the preceding action.

Calls for and references to music between the acts are supplemented by clear evidence of the kind of pause in playing implied by the treatment of entrance warnings in *The Lady Mother*, *The Welsh Ambassador*, and *The Wasp*. At the end of Act 4 of Heywood's *The Escapes of Jupiter* (1620–41), the Chorus tells us that 'after some small pause wee shall pursue' (l. 1869) the events of the plot;[17] likewise, at the end of Act 2 of William Hemming's *The Jews' Tragedy* (1626) the Chorus says, 'mean time we pray | Let pleasing musick charm the time away' (D4ᵛ). The Prologue to Thomas Nabbes's *Hannibal and Scipio* (1635) tells us that 'the Scene [. . .] is translated as the musick plays | Betwixt the acts' (A3ᵛ).[18] Implied evidence of pauses complements this explicit testimony. For instance, in Lodowick Carlell's *The Deserving Favorite* (1629), Jacopo and Clorinda are on stage alone together at the end of Act 3, undisguised; immediately after their exit, Act 4 begins with the direction '*Enter Clarinda in disguise, Iacopo.*' (I2). This direction certainly implies something other than immediate re-entry: elsewhere fifteen to twenty lines of

---

[15] *The City Madam* was set from the prompt-book, *The Fatal Dowry* from theatrically-annotated authorial papers. For dates, authorship, and textual provenance of Massinger plays I have relied on *The Plays and Poems of Philip Massinger*, ed. Philip Edwards and Colin Gibson, 5 vols. (Oxford, 1976).

[16] *Hengist, King of Kent; or, The Mayor of Queenborough*, ed. R. C. Bald (New York, 1938). The music directions do not appear in the printed text. Bald concludes that 'there is little doubt that' the MS is copied from 'an annotated prompt-book' (p. xxix).

[17] *The Escapades of Jupiter*, ed. Henry D. Janzen, Mal. Soc. Repr. (1978).

[18] This example was noted by Malone, iii. 111 n. 3. His only earlier example is from *Gammer Gurton's Needle* (a university play, c.1552–63).

dialogue, or prolonged onstage business, is needed to cover such a change of costume.[19]

Cumulatively, this positive evidence for regular act-intervals in the later Jacobean and Caroline theatre is overwhelming; nor can I find a particle of testimony to contradict it.[20] Moreover, the children's companies—as has been generally recognized—had been using act-intervals from at least 1599, and perhaps in the 1570s and 1580s as well. Only twelve plays from the earlier boys' companies survive; seven of these are Lyly's.[21] All have act-divisions. Act 3 of *Campaspe* (1584) and Act 1 of *Gallathea* (1585) end with a song; Act 2 of *Endymion* (1588) concludes with a dumb show and '*Musique*'. On the other hand, in *Sapho and Phao*, Acts 3 and 4 definitely, and Acts 4 and 5 possibly, are continuous. Though accepting the orthodox view that *Sapho and Phao* is 'almost certainly Lyly's second play' for the combined boys' companies, 'possibly following within weeks of his first', Reavley Gair notes that it 'shows no signs of the special influence of the Paul's repertoire or special talents of the company'— qualities *Campaspe* deliberately exploits.[22] With only the extant printed texts to go on, all we can note is that, in respect to act-intervals as in other things, *Sapho and Phao* does not seem perfectly suited to what we would otherwise most naturally infer about early children's practice. The most explicit evidence of that practice comes in the unfortunately corrupt text of *The Wars of Cyrus*. F. P. Wilson has argued convincingly that this dates from *c*.1577–80; in the extant text 'act divisions are confused, the prologue is misplaced, choruses are removed. The songs too have been left out, but enough indications survive to show that originally there were musical intervals between the acts'.[23] These 'indications' are extra-dramatic directions for music at the ends of Acts 1 and 4, and the Prologue's

[19] See Stanley Wells and Gary Taylor, *Modernizing Shakespeare's Spelling, with Three Studies in the Text of 'Henry V'* (Oxford, 1979), 73 n. 1.

[20] One MS play sometimes assigned to this period (*The Fatal Marriage, or A Second Lucretia*) lacks act-divisions; but though this play, in its current form, certainly dates from after 1600, only one dubious topical allusion would put it in the 1620s. See the Mal. Soc. Repr., ed. S. Brigid Younghughes and Harold Jenkins (1959): 'All that one can say with safety is that the play belongs to the early seventeenth century' (p. xi). Since the play originally belonged to the Admiral's Men, it might have passed to their descendant Palsgrave's Men, in which case it might have been performed without act-intervals as late as the 1620s. (See below, p. 34.)

[21] I include the anonymous *Publii Ovidii Nasonis Meleager*, noted by Harbage and Schoenbaum as 'Lost'; see A. Freeman, 'The Argument of *Meleager*', *English Literary Renaissance*, 1/2 (1971), 122–31.

[22] Reavley Gair, *The Children of Paul's: The Story of a Theatre Company, 1553–1608* (Cambridge, 1982), 99–100. I have accepted Gair's dates for the company's existence, thereby including *The Marriage of Wit and Science* (*c*.1568) but not Redford's *Wit and Science* (undivided, *c*.1545).

[23] F. P. Wilson, *The English Drama 1485–1585*, Oxf. Hist. of English Lit. (Oxford, 1968), 147–8.

promise—unfulfilled in the printed text—that 'of mournefull plaints our *Chorus* sings' (C3). The first editions of Lyly's plays also often omitted songs, though fortunately some of them were supplied in seventeenth-century editions. All in all, though, the evidence of early children's practice offers little clear testimony of the presence or absence of intervals.

When the choir companies resumed playing, however, they certainly did use intervals. E. K. Chambers, W. W. Greg, and Irwin Smith have noted explicit references to act-intervals in the stage directions of fourteen plays written for the boy companies between 1599 and 1607: *Histriomastix* (1599), *Antonio's Revenge* (1600), *Cuckqueans and Cuckolds Errant* (1601), *What You Will* (1601), *The Gentleman Usher* (1602), *The Faery Pastoral* (1603), *The Malcontent* (1603), *The Phoenix* (1604), *The Dutch Courtesan* (1604), *A Trick to Catch the Old One* (1605), *Sophonisba* (1605), *The Fawn* (1605), *Your Five Gallants* (1605), and *The Knight of the Burning Pestle* (1607).[24] Gair notes that all of the plays William Percy wrote for Paul's Boys use entr'acte music—and that, whether or not the plays were ever performed, they everywhere display a detailed knowledge of the company's theatrical practice (*Children of Paul's*, 63, 193). To the evidence of these plays may be added Machin and Markham's *The Dumb Knight* (1608), which calls for 'Musicke' opposite the beginning of Acts 2 and 4, and 'Musique' opposite the beginning of 3 and 5. Middleton's *Michaelmas Term* (1605) also calls for dramatically extraneous '*Musicke*' after the *Exeunt* at the end of Act 3 (G3); likewise, *Cupid's Whirligig* (1607) places a similarly extraneous 'Sound Musicke' after the *Exit* at the end of Act 3 and before 'Actus Quartus' (G2). In Nathan Field's *A Woman is a Weathercock* (1609–11), the dialogue itself clearly calls for music at the end of Act 1: 'Lowder still, | And the vast Ayre with your enchantments fill' (C4ᵛ), while Act 3 of *The Insatiate Countess* (1610) ends with the words, 'Your lust being quench'd, a bloudy act must follow' (F3). *Antonio's Revenge* (1600) had already combined both these elements in the conclusion to its Act 1: 'Sound lowder musick: let my breath exact, | You strike sad Tones unto this dismall act' (C2ᵛ). Finally, Dekker and Webster's *Northward Ho*, performed by Paul's Boys in 1605, envisages in its dialogue exactly the sort of musical interval implied by all these texts: Bellamont, anticipating the performance of his play, fantasizes that some nobles in the audience 'shall take some occasion about the musick of the fourth Act, to step to the *French* King, and' introduce the monarch to the playwright (E3; 4. 1. 55–6).[25]

[24] E. K. Chambers, *The Elizabethan Stage*, 4 vols. (Oxford, 1923), iii, 131–2; Greg, *First Folio*, 144 n. 3; Irwin Smith, *Shakespeare's Blackfriars Playhouse: Its History and Its Design* (New York, 1964), 224.
[25] Noted by Henry L. Snuggs, *Shakespeare and Five Acts: Studies in a Dramatic Convention* (New York, 1960), 45. Snuggs also calls attention to an added stage direction in Q2 (1640) of *A Mad World, My Masters*, between Acts 2 and 3: '*A Song, sung by the musitians, and after the Song, a Country dance, by the Actors in their Vizards to a new*

The statistical evidence of printed texts confirms the explicit testimony of stage directions and dialogue. As Wilfred T. Jewkes demonstrated, of sixty-one extant plays which can be confidently assigned to the children's companies, only two were printed without any act-divisions: Middleton's *The Phoenix* and Armin's *Two Maids of More-clack*.[26] *The Phoenix* was probably the first children's play written by Middleton, who had until then worked for Henslowe;[27] Armin's play, though performed by the Children of the King's Revels in 1607-8, was originally written much earlier, almost certainly for an adult company (Jewkes, *Act Division*, 284-5). The evidence of act-divisions in printed texts is thus almost as good for the children's companies up to 1613 as it is for the adult companies from 1616 to 1642.[28] Moreover, in 1611 Cotgrave's *Dictionary* gives 'Pause in a Comedie, or Tragedie' as one of the meanings of 'Acte'. Cotgrave's definition certainly suggests that someone in London before 1611 was performing plays with intervals, and the evidence of printed texts gives

footing. *Exeunt*.' (E2). This apparently represents Caroline staging: Q2's title-page notes that the play was revived at Salisbury Court (i.e. in or after 1637).

[26] W. T. Jewkes, *Act Division in Elizabethan and Jacobean Plays, 1583-1616* (Hamden, Conn., 1958), 61-79, 239-98. I exclude five plays which there is no good reason to assign to the children: *Wily Beguiled, Wit of a Woman, Every Woman in her Humour, Christian Turned Turk* (discussed below, p. 34), and *Summer's Last Will and Testament*. The latter was acted at Archbishop Whitgift's palace at Croydon in 1592, and in both date and venue clearly falls outside the scope of the regular children's repertoire; Chambers (*Elizabethan Stage*, III. 453) believes it was performed 'by members of Whitgift's household'. Gair, *Children* (see n. 22), argues that *Wily Beguiled* was not a Paul's play (p. 199 n. 27); he might have added that the Epilogue's references to 'this circled rounde' and 'this round' (K3) rule out the Blackfriars and (on Gair's reconstruction) Paul's (see p. 59), making a public venue almost certain. Jewkes discusses *Wit of a Woman* and *Every Woman* (pp. 294-5).

[27] Middleton first appears as a playwright in 1602, working on a lost unnamed play and then in collaboration with Dekker, Drayton, Munday, and Webster (*Caesar's Fall*); later in 1602 he wrote *Randall, Earl of Chester*, and in 1604 collaborated with Dekker on *1 The Honest Whore*. All this documented early playwriting is for Henslowe. At some time in 1604-5 Middleton clearly shifted to writing solely or primarily for the boys: *A Trick to Catch the Old One, Your Five Gallants, A Mad World*, and *Michaelmas Term* all date from 1604-7, and Harbage and Schoenbaum date none of them earlier than 1605. Middleton almost certainly had nothing to do with *Blurt, Master Constable* (Paul's, 1601-2); on its authorship, see Thomas L. Berger's edn. (Salzburg, 1979) and MacD. P. Jackson's *Studies in Attribution: Middleton and Shakespeare* (Salzburg, 1979), 109-13. This leaves *The Family of Love* and *The Phoenix*. Middleton's share of the former is much disputed, as is the play's original date of composition: all recent investigators conclude that it was revised by Lording Barry c.1607, and at least written in part, or subsequently revised, by Dekker. When and how the Children of the Revels came to possess the play is unknown, and its most recent editor (Simon Shepherd, Nottingham Drama Texts, 1979) concludes that the original composition is unlikely to be earlier than 1603-4 (p. iv). *The Phoenix* dates from the same period (1603-4), and raises no such problems of authorship or theatrical provenance. Whether or not *The Phoenix* was written first, its extant text is much likelier to preserve Middleton's original than is Q of *The Family of Love*, and I do not find it surprising that a playwright for the adult companies might write a play without act-divisions, which came to be (or, even, was intended to be) performed by the children.

[28] Chapman's *Tragedy of Byron* does not mark the beginning of Act 2, which is exceptionally short, but this is clearly because a scene was censored: Chapman himself, in the Preface, refers to the play as 'dismembered'. Day's *Isle of Gulls*—also the cause of a political scandal—lacks divisions for Acts 3 and 4.

us no reason to doubt that the boys' companies, at least, were already doing so.

For the children's companies, then, and for all the London companies in the later Jacobean and Caroline period, there can be little doubt that performances were regularly divided by four musical intervals between the five acts. This procedure seems as strange to modern critics as it seemed self-evident to Renaissance ones: most modern plays have only one interval, and diptychs provide obvious opportunities for 'natural' symmetries and contrasts, in a way that five fractions do not. It should therefore hardly surprise us that a modern theatre-going critic like Emrys Jones sees 'The Two-Part Structure' as a constant feature of Shakespeare's dramaturgy.[29] But, excluding early interludes like Medwall's *Fulgens and Lucrece* (before 1500) and Merbury's *The Marriage between Wit and Wisdom* (1571–7), only one ambiguous piece of evidence points to any play before 1642 being performed with a single interval. In a letter written on 24 May 1619, Sir Gerard Herbert described a Court performance of *Pericles* which took place before the visiting French ambassador and his retinue.[30] 'In the kinges greate Chamber they went to see the play of Pirrocles, Prince of Tyre. which lasted till two aclocke. after two actes, the players ceased till the french all refreshed them wth sweetmeates brought on Chinay voiders, & wyne ale in bottells, after the players, begann anewe.' As in *Fulgens and Lucrece*, the break in this performance gave the audience an opportunity to eat. But how did Herbert know that 'two actes' had already passed? He might have guessed this, on the evidence of Gower's appearances; but Gower's entrances break the whole play into six acts, rather than the usual five.[31] It is equally possible that the acts were marked by intervals throughout, and that the French embassy refreshed itself in what Heywood and Edward Knight identified, in other prompt-books, as a 'long' act-interval. Even if this were not the case, this Court performance was certainly not representative of practice in the London theatres in 1619, and probably not entirely representative of Court practice either—for if this were routine procedure, why did Herbert bother to single this incident out for description?

However natural a two-part structure may seem to us, until the twentieth century it was an anomaly. The choice, in the period of England's greatest drama, was between four intervals, or none. The children's companies, and the adults by c.1616, evidently opted for four.

[29] Emrys Jones, *Scenic Form in Shakespeare* (Oxford, 1971), 66–88. Hunter makes some pertinent criticisms of Jones's hypothesis (p. 32).

[30] Gerald Herbert to Dudley Carleton at The Hague, 24 May 1619, in *The Shakspere Allusion-Book*, ed. C. M. Ingleby *et al.*, 2 vols. (London, 1932), 277.

[31] Hunter believes that the modern five-act arrangement conforms to Shakespeare's intentions and is evident from the text (p. 27); but the 1664 Folio, which first printed a five-act division, adopted the alternative.

G. K. Hunter believes, with Baldwin, that the plays of Shakespeare and his Elizabethan contemporaries were, from the beginning, written to be performed with pauses between the acts. In order to defend this position, he must discredit W. T. Jewkes's monograph. Extending and elaborating upon an earlier survey by W. W. Greg,[32] Jewkes showed that

some seventy-five plays for the adult companies . . . survive from the period 1591–1607; not a single one of these is divided, except for the five by Jonson. Since the texts show every conceivable variety of textual history, it is clear, then, that neither playhouses, nor authors, nor printers, nor scribes paid any attention to act-divisions during this period, with the glaring exception of Jonson.[33]

But some time after 1606 a change apparently takes place: printed plays written for the adult companies began to appear more and more regularly with act-divisions. Jewkes concluded that the adult companies only began to adopt act-intervals at some time about 1607. Hunter denies the validity of these inferences, claiming that how a play is printed can tell us nothing about how it was performed.

Hunter's attempt to dismiss the testimony of printed texts in fact raises difficulties he does not exorcise; but before the pattern of the printed texts is re-examined, other evidence of theatrical practice in the adult companies should be considered. The testimony of the manuscripts can be quickly summarized. Of seven surviving manuscript 'plots', only one (*The Dead Man's Fortune*) provides for act-intervals: each act is separated from the others by a row of crosses, with a direction for music in the margin.[34] However, these act-intervals were supplied *after* the plot had been initially prepared, and supplied by another hand, who also added a new scene at the beginning of Act 5. Moreover, this plot is in other respects easily the most puzzling of the seven: though it apparently dates from the 1580s or early 1590s, we can only guess at the play's venue, and only two of the specified actors are identifiable ('Robert Lee' and 'Burbage'). The latter name is famous enough, and tantalizing enough; but we know little about Lee's or Burbage's early careers, and nothing about the circumstances of this anomalous production. A 'Robert Lee' entered into a bond with Edward Alleyn on 18 May 1593; on 22 February 1598 he sold an old play to the Admiral's Men; in March 1604 he began a long association with the Queen's Men, which lasted until at

---

[32] 'Act-Divisions in Shakespeare', *RES* 4 (1928), 152–8. Hunter never mentions Greg, confining himself to attacks on Jewkes and the less formidable Snuggs.

[33] Jewkes, *Act Division*, 98. This summary discounts plays printed after 1616: plays printed after that date may have been revived in performances with act-intervals, or printers may have provided act-divisions, knowing they had since become standard in the theatres.

[34] For the plots, see Greg, *Dramatic Documents*, 1–171, and particularly 94–104 (*The Dead Man's Fortune*). For Lee's career, see ibid. 19; Chambers, *Elizabethan Stage*, ii. 328; G. E. Bentley, *The Jacobean and Caroline Stage*, 7 vols. (Oxford), ii (1941), 496–7; for Burbage's beginnings, Chambers, ii. 307.

least 1623. Burbage's career may well have begun as early as 1584, and in the plot 'Burbage a messenger' suggests a decidedly humble part. The divergent careers of these two named actors clearly establish that the play dates from before 1604, and probably before 1593–8 (when Lee already had connections with Henslowe's operations); Burbage's minor part, together with what Greg called the plot's 'rather primitive character . . . as compared with that of *The Seven Deadly Sins*' (which Greg dates in 1589–90), encourage an early dating. I would myself conjecture that the play dates from the mid-1580s, and—for reasons I will explain in a moment—that both the new scene and the act-divisions were added for a Court performance.[35] In any case, though this single problematic exception cannot be entirely dismissed, the evidence of the plots does little to encourage, and certainly cannot be taken to demonstrate, the assumption that the public playhouses regularly provided act-intervals.

Likewise, of the six surviving public playhouse documents from the period in question, three (*John of Bordeaux*, *Sir Thomas More*, and *A Looking Glass for London and England*) do not indicate act-divisions, and in two (*Woodstock* and *Edmund Ironside*) such divisions were supplied only by a later hand; in only one (*John a Kent and John a Cumber*) were act-divisions supplied in the original manuscript.[36] However, the hand that supplied them in that one early manuscript was the author's own, and as such it provides highly dubious evidence for Hunter's hypothesis.[37] In the first place, Hunter attempts to dismiss the extensive evidence of the printed texts surveyed by Greg and Jewkes by asserting that play-

---

[35] Scott McMillin—in 'The Plots of *The Dead Man's Fortune* and *2 Seven Deadly Sins*: Inferences for Theatre Historians', *SB* 26 (1973), 235–43—conjectures that *The Dead Man's Fortune* belonged to Pembroke's Men in 1592–3; however, this hypothesis presumes that the added scene was an expedient to reduce doubling problems, in provincial performances. I do not see why entr'acte music should be provided for provincial performances when it was not for London performances; nor can McMillin legitimately cite Jewkes as evidence against the practice of pauses between the acts (p. 238 n. 5), when this document itself seems to support that practice. Moreover, the later provision of music between the acts would itself have solved the doubling problems allegedly solved by the same hand's addition of a new scene in Act 5. McMillin's late dating of the plot also creates difficulties.

[36] I exclude, as does Hunter, the MS of *Charlemagne, or The Distracted Emperor*, a play of uncertain date and provenance, which contains act-divisions. Harbage and Schoenbaum date the play '1584–c.1605', but in the Mal. Soc. Repr. (1938), J. H. Walter notes that the paper dates from 1605–32 (p. v), while the presence of George Buc's hand indicates a date between 1603 and 1622. One passage might allude to James I's 'coronation' in Mar. 1604 (pp. viii–ix), but this is admittedly tenous evidence. The stage reviser duplicates the direction 'Actus 2' in the margin, and provides boxes or rules around the other act-divisions, which suggests that the play was intended for performance with intervals; but this could be due to performance by one of the children's companies, or adult performance after c.1610. Jewkes dismisses *Charlemagne* as 'evidently a private company play probably written by Chapman' (p. 9); but Chapman is unlikely to be the author, and although I think the play probably comes from the private theatres, this probability largely depends upon the interpretation of its act-divisions.

[37] I. A. Shapiro's 'The Significance of a Date' (*Shakespeare Survey 8* (Cambridge, 1955), 100–6) showed that the play probably dates from 1589.

wrights would not have bothered to indicate act-divisions, in their own manuscripts; yet here is Anthony Munday supplying just such divisions in a fair copy of his work. Secondly, *because* the act-divisions here are authorial, they may well be literary rather than theatrical. Certainly, they have not been boxed, ruled, or moved into the margin (as happens in later prompt-books), nor have directions for music, or for 'long' pauses, been appended to them by the theatrical scribe who went over Munday's finished manuscript.

Munday reappears, in association with a different theatrical scribe, in the manuscript of *Sir Thomas More*; there, Munday was making a fair copy of what is presumed to have been a collaborative work, and he did *not* supply act-divisions; nor did the theatrical scribe, C.[38] *John of Bordeaux* was prepared by a theatrical scribe in the early 1590s, evidently with Shakespeare's own company in mind (since the scribe supplies the names of several actors associated with it); no act-divisions were marked.[39] At some time between 1603 and 1606, an exemplar of a quarto of *A Looking Glass for London and England* was marked up for use as a prompt-book, at least in part for London performances: though entrances and exits were systematically marked, no act-divisions were supplied.[40]

Edmund Ironside probably dates from the late 1580s or early 1590s; the surviving manuscript, of uncertain date and authorship, is probably scribal, but the acts are added by another hand, which also supplies the names of several actors; these clearly point to a performance in the 1630s.[41] *Woodstock* also survives in a scribal transcript; Hunter quotes the editor of the Malone Society reprint, who suggests that the owner of the hand which 'systematically inserted the act numbers, may be supposed also to have been concerned with the manuscript at an early stage'.[42] But the editor offers no evidence for this conclusion; indeed there is none, beyond the apparent assumption (shared by Hunter) that act-divisions *should* have been supplied for the first production. Since the distinctive hand and ink in question made no other divisions or alterations to the manuscript, his marginal act-divisions could have been added for the revivals in the 1620s and 1630s, for which other alterations to the

---

[38] For the evidence of collaboration, see W. W. Greg's Mal. Soc. Repr. (1911), rev. Harold Jenkins (1961), pp. xvi, xxxiv–xxxix. Hunter dismisses *More* as 'anomalous' (p. 24); anomalous it is in several respects, but it was submitted to the Master of the Revels once (and perhaps twice), thoroughly gone over by a theatrical scribe (C) and by several other professional dramatists (Chettle, Dekker, Heywood, and probably Shakespeare), none of whom provided act-divisions.

[39] See the Mal. Soc. Repr., ed. William Lindsay Renwick (1936). Hunter does not mention this MS.

[40] C. R. Baskerville, 'A Prompt Copy of *A Looking Glass for London and England*', *Modern Philology*, 30 (1932), 29–51.

[41] See the Mal. Soc. Repr., ed. Eleanore Boswell (1927), pp. vii–ix.

[42] *The First Part of the Reign of Richard the Second, or Thomas of Woodstock*, ed. Wilhelmina P. Frijlink (1929), p. xvi.

manuscript provide compelling evidence.[43] Since it is clear that act-intervals were normal practice in the later Jacobean and Caroline period, the addition of such divisions by a later hand is hardly surprising; their absence in the original text is much more significant.

To summarize: as originally written, five of these six early theatrical manuscripts, all scribal, have no act-divisions; the lone exception is an authorial fair copy, in which the author's inconspicuous act-divisions are completely ignored by the theatrical scribe. As with the plots, the manuscript prompt-books provide a reasonably clear picture of uninterrupted performance, with a single exception which is demonstrably exceptional or problematic on other grounds as well.

Eyewitness accounts tell the same story. No existing record explicitly refers to intervals in performances by the adult companies before 1616. Thomas Platter, describing his attendance at a performance of *Julius Caesar* (1599), noted that '*during the play* food and drink is carried around among the people, so that one can also refresh oneself for one's money' (my italics).[44] Though Platter describes the design of the theatre, the number of actors, the time of performance, the prices of admission, and the dining afterwards, he makes no reference to any interval, and the most natural (though not the only) interpretation of his reference to food and drink is that one bought these commodities while the play was being performed. Platter's testimony suggests that there were no intervals; at best, it is no better than ambiguous. But explicit references are made to intervals at the Blackfriars, before and after its acquisition by the King's Men, by Sir Richard Chomeley (*c.*1603), Francis Beaumont (*c.*1609), Ben Jonson (1616, 1631), and Thomas May (1657).[45] Moreover, Marston's *The Malcontent* (1603) contains a famous reference in the Induction (specially written when the play transferred from the Children of the Chapel Royal to the King's Men) to 'the not received custome of musicke in our Theater' (A4). As Hunter says in his edition of that play, this phrase is usually interpreted to mean 'that the boys gave further musical performances between the Acts, and that the men did not'.[46] Certainly, such an interpretation is attractive, especially given the overwhelming evidence now accumulated that the boys did perform music in intervals between the acts. However, Hunter himself interprets the phrase as a reference to the 'whole hour' of music preceding Blackfriars' performances. *The*

---

[43] A. P. Rossiter, in his ed. of *Woodstock* (London: Chatto, 1946), made the same point: 'Possibly C made the act-divisions next; but since his ink (VI) is used nowhere else, this is a mere guess, and he could equally well come in after Stage (7) [= theatrical revisions for later revival]' (p. 173).

[44] Ernest Schanzer, 'Thomas Platter's Observations on the Elizabethan Stage', *N. & Q.* 201 (1956), 465–7.

[45] Bentley, *Jacobean and Caroline Stage* vi (1968), 9–11.

[46] John Marston, *The Malcontent*, ed. G. K. Hunter, The Revels Plays (London, 1975), p. liii.

Malcontent Induction thus does not provide unambiguous evidence of a contrast between boys' and men's practice; but it certainly permits such an inference.

Of course, this might all be a coincidence, but it coexists with surprisingly similar coincidences in all of the other evidence. For the later period, and for the children's companies, the evidence is unanimous, unambiguous, and overwhelming; for the earlier period, there is only one (dubious) piece of manuscript evidence, one (dubious) plot, no explicit external references to act-intervals, no directions for 'long' intervals, no dialogue references to a break in the playing, no directions identifying 'the Act' as an interval between two stretches of continuous dramatic action, and only one play which calls for music between the acts: Ben Jonson's *Sejanus*.[47] Since the extant text of *Sejanus* consists of Jonson's own version, for publication, of the collaborative play earlier performed by the King's Men, this single exception clearly tells us nothing about how the play (which failed) had actually been performed.[48] The repertoire of the adult companies before 1610 conspicuously lacks all the features which enable us to identify the act-interval convention in the later adult and contemporaneous children's repertoire.

Printed play texts display the same contrast. Jewkes made the mistake of stopping his survey of printed plays at 1616, a date clearly chosen for its connection with a rather famous biographical *terminus ad quem*; but 1616 also saw a famous *terminus a quo* in the history of printing, the publication of Jonson's *Works* in Folio. This coincidence might lead one to attribute the increasing number of texts printed with act-divisions after 1616 to the influence upon printers and publishers of Jonson's First Folio, rather than to any change in theatrical practice. But the change in printing fashion clearly began long before Jonson's Folio appeared: well

---

[47] Chambers (*Elizabethan Stage*, iii. 125 n. 2) cited Robert Yarington's *Two Lamentable Tragedies* as another example of entr'acte music. The play is of unknown provenance, and dates from 1594–1601. However, in context it is clear that the dramatic action is continuous. Merry never exits, but remains on stage cutting up the body; Truth enters and says '. . . But though this sight bring surfet to the eye, | Delight your eares with pleasing harmonie, | That eares may counterchecke your eyes, and say, | Why shed you teares, this deede is but a playe: | His worke is done, he seekes to hide his sinne, | Ile waile his woe, before his woe begin' (E2ᵛ). The direction '*Exit Trueth*', and a speech by Merry, immediately follow. The music called for by Truth clearly accompanies the dramatic action, and is explicitly justified in terms of aesthetic distancing from a horrible sight; two characters remain onstage, acting or speaking, throughout. Another speech by Truth, earlier in the play, confirms the continuity of the action: the speech begins by addressing the departing characters with the words 'weepe, weepe poore soules' (I2), and ends by announcing another character's arrival with the words 'Heere comes the Duke . . .' (I2ᵛ).

[48] Jonson's reversion to music between the acts in the published and rewritten text of *Sejanus* is also easily explicable, since for the period 1600–5 all his other plays (*Cynthia's Revels, Poetaster*, and *Eastward Ho*) were for the boys' companies. For the influence on *Sejanus* of the children's repertoire and style, see R. A. Foakes, 'Tragedy at the Children's Theatres after 1600: A Challenge to the Adult Stage', in David Galloway, (ed.), *The Elizabethan Theatre II* (Toronto, 1970), 37–59.

over half the plays published between 1609 and 1616 contain act-divisions. One would also expect Jonson's Folio to have had the most influence upon its obvious successors, the 1623 Shakespeare Folio and the 1647 Beaumont and Fletcher Folio. Yet these two volumes between them contain eight plays, all written before 1620 at the latest, which do not have act-divisions.

Hunter attributes the change in printing fashion not to Jonson's *Works* but to

a general improvement in the social status of plays in the first quarter of the seventeenth century . . . larger margins and a more spacious layout became the rule. If the publisher or printer thought that the new audience would look for act-divisions, clearly stated, as a symptom of the classical status sought for modern plays, then he was perfectly capable of supplying them.

Hunter thus postulates that a gradual change in the 'social status' of plays had a dramatic effect on printing practice, and though this is not itself impossible it would surely be simpler to suppose that a change in theatrical practice had a direct effect on the manuscripts of plays which printers received. Moreover, although 'larger margins and a more spacious layout' did become the norm, exceptions exist, and plays printed between 1616 and 1642 vary greatly in the quality of the printing and paper, the layout of stage directions and speech prefixes, the treatment of verse lines split between two or more speakers, and the marking and method of scene divisions; the act-divisions themselves are sometimes in English, sometimes boxed or ruled, and sometimes indicate the end of one act as well as the beginning of the next. The only thing all these printed texts have in common is a division into five acts.

Moreover, if the act-divisions in these late texts were supplied by the printers, we would expect many of them to be unsatisfactory. Yet apparently bogus act-divisions occur only in plays written much earlier than 1616: in the Folio texts of *1 Henry VI* (1592?), *The Taming of the Shrew* (1590–1?), *King John* (1596?) and *Henry V* (1598–9), and perhaps also in *Richard III* (1592–3?)[49] and *Love's Labour's Lost* (1594–5?),[50] and in the

---

[49] Hunter (p. 22) quotes Jewkes (*Act Division*, 157) quoting Greg (*First Folio*, 197) to the effect that the act-division in *Richard III* is 'most likely introduced at the time of printing': but only the scene-divisions in *Richard III* are demonstrably defective, and an editorial origin for these by no means implies an editorial origin for the theatrically important act-divisions. However, Dr Johnson did question the dramatic wisdom of two of the Folio breaks, and since someone must have extensively annotated the quarto copy used by Jaggard, the same hand may have editorially provided his own conjectural act-divisions (as he clearly did scene-divisions).

[50] Jewkes (*Act Division*, 163) follows Greg (*First Folio*, 223) in attributing the 'monstrously disproportionate' acts in *LLL* to the printer; but Act 5 is monstrously disproportionate because of the length of the final scene, and Stanley Wells has recently shown that a theatrical MS was consulted in preparing the Folio text: see 'The Copy for the Folio Text of *Love's Labour's Lost*', *RES* 33 (1982), 137–47. However, act-divisions were provided for all Folio plays through *Henry V*, so they may be editorial here: see below, pp. 44–7.

1631 Quarto of Henry Chettle's *The Tragedy of Hoffman* (1602–3).[51]
Eighteen plays from the London theatres printed after 1616 also survive
in one or more manuscripts; in all but one of them the manuscript(s)
agree with the print on the placing of all the act-divisions.[52] Finally, if a
change in printing fashion accounts for the changed treatment of act-
divisions after 1616, we would expect that change in fashion to have had
a similar effect on reprints of earlier plays; yet plays originally printed
without act-divisions are, until after the Restoration, regularly reprinted
without them. Of 108 such quarto reprints between 1610 and 1660, 106
leave the plays undivided; act-divisions are added only in the 1629 reprint
of Wilkins's *Miseries of Enforced Marriage* and the 1639 reprint of
Heywood's *1 If You Know Not Me, You Know Nobody*.[53] The second of
these also includes a new prologue and epilogue, dating from a theatrical
revival of *c*. 1626–30; the act-divisions might come from the same source.
In other words, only one quarto reprint, out of 108, clearly shows us a
publisher imposing editorial act-divisions on his undivided copy.[54]

But the most damaging weakness in Hunter's argument is the absolute
unanimity of the testimony of plays printed after 1615, a unanimity
difficult to attribute to a mere conspiracy of fashion among London stationers. Of plays written in 1642 or before, but first printed in 1616 or
after, only nine are printed without a division into five Acts: the First
Folio texts of Shakespeare's *Contention* and *Duke of York* (1591), *Romeo
and Juliet* (1595), *Hamlet* (1600–1), *Troilus and Cressida* (1602), *Timon of
Athens* (1605), and *Antony and Cleopatra* (1606), with Dekker's *2 The
Honest Whore* (1604–5; printed 1630), and Fletcher's *Four Plays in One*
(1609–20; printed 1647).[55] Notably, all of these plays were *written* for the

---

[51] See John Jowett's Nottingham Drama Texts edn. (1983), and his unpublished Ph.D.
thesis (Liverpool, 1983).

[52] The anonymous *Nero*, Berkeley's *The Lost Lady*, Brome's *The English Moor*, Carlell's
1 Arviragus and Philicia and *2 Arviragus and Philicia*, Cavendish's *The Country Captain*,
Daborne's *The Poor Man's Comfort*, Killigrew's *Claracilla*, May's *Cleopatra Queen of
Egypt*, Middleton's *Hengist*, Shirley's *The Court Secret*, Suckling's *Aglaura*, and Fletcher's
Bèggar's Bush, Bonduca, Elder Brother, Honest Man's Fortune, and *Woman's Prize*. In
Fletcher's *Humorous Lieutenant*, the MS (foul-paper-based) and the print (annotated foul
paper based) disagree on the placing of Act 5: see *The Dramatic Works in the Beaumont and
Fletcher Canon*, gen. ed. Fredson Bowers (Cambridge), v (1982), 291–8.

[53] For act-divisions in reprints I have relied upon W. W. Greg, *A Bibliography of the
English Printed Drama to the Restoration*, 4 vols., The Bibliographical Society (London,
1939–59). It may also be worth recording that the three subsequent 17th-cent. edn. of the
Shakespeare Folio provide act-divisions for none of the plays lacking them in F1.

[54] The 1629 reprint of *Miseries* was printed by Augustine Mathewes for Richard Thrale;
both previous edns. were published by George Vincent.

[55] Jewkes overlooked *Four Plays in One*. Folio *Hamlet* marks the division for Act 2, but
not the remaining acts. Only one other printed play from this period—the anonymous
Swetnam the Woman-Hater Arraigned by Women (1615–19; printed 1620)—lacks any of its
act-divisions; but although *Swetnam*'s printed text lacks a division for Act 5, it does contain
a 'SCEN. II.' in Act 4 (G1ᵛ), and then another 'SCEN. II.' later (H4ᵛ), making it fairly
clear that the printer simply overlooked a MS act-division somewhere in-between, probably
at the beginning of a scene on H2ᵛ.

adult companies before, at the very latest, 1620; indeed, if we exclude *Four Plays in One* (of very uncertain date),[56] before 1609. Yet they were *printed* by three different printers, between 1622 and 1647—printers who, during the same period, provided act-divisions in all the other plays they published. The crucial variant, in determining the presence or absence of act-divisions in adult plays, seems clearly to be the date of *composition*, not the date of publication.

Hunter's attempt to dismiss the significance of the absence of act-divisions in early printed texts is no more convincing than his attempt to dismiss the significance of their presence in later ones. He first tries to discredit Jewkes's statistical conclusion by pointing to three anomalies: Robert Tailor's 'undivided' *The Hog Hath Lost His Pearl* (printed 1614), R. A.'s divided *The Valiant Welshman* (printed 1615), and R. W.'s *The Three Ladies of London* (printed 1584, with a 'confused act-notation'). Hunter points out that Tailor seems not to have been a theatrical professional, and so *should* have provided 'literary' act-divisions for his play, while R. A. and R. W. (whom he identifies as Robert Armin and Robert Wilson) were professionals, and so should *not* have divided theirs. But Tailor's play is in fact divided;[57] both it and *The Valiant Welshman* are late enough to be influenced by a change in public theatre practice; R. A. is almost certainly not Armin;[58] and the 'confused act-notation' of *Three Ladies* consists (as Jewkes notes, *Act-Division*, 24–5) of the standard 'Actus Primus' on the first page and 'Actus Secundus'—at the beginning of the second scene, on the same page—only 34 lines of dialogue later (in a play of approximately 1800 lines). To call this 'confused' is rather

---

[56] Harbage and Schoenbaum place *Four Plays* in 1612, with a range c.1608–13; this is based on Chambers, *Elizabethan Stage*, iii, 231, and its later limit assumes Beaumont as part-author. But Cyrus Hoy, in 'The Shares of Fletcher and his Collaborators in the Beaumont and Fletcher Canon (IV)', *SB* 12 (1959), 91–116, has shown that Nathan Field was almost certainly Fletcher's collaborator. Field's first play, *A Woman is a Weathercock*, cannot be dated earlier than 1609; this agrees well with the fact that antimasques established themselves in Court masques in 1608 (Chambers). Field died in 1619–20. After Beaumont's marriage and retirement from the stage in 1613, Fletcher was looking for other collaborators: about this time (1613–14), he collaborated three times with Shakespeare, and with Daborne, Field, and Massinger on an unknown play for Henslowe. Fletcher also collaborated with Field, Massinger, and Tourneur on *The Honest Man's Fortune* (1613), and with Field (and others) in three later King's Men plays: *The Jeweller of Amsterdam* (1616; lost), *The Queen of Corinth* (1616–17), and *The Knight of Malta* (1616–18). This pattern of collaboration suggests that *Four Plays in One* dates from 1613–19. See below, where this range is narrowed to 1613–15.

[57] Hunter here (p. 18) repeats an error in Jewkes (*Act Division*, 233).

[58] On the authorship of *The Valiant Welshman* see H. F. Lippincott, 'Bibliographical Problems in the Works of Robert Armin', *The Library*, 5/30 (1975), 330–3, and D. J. Lake, 'The Canon of Robert Armin's Works: Some Difficulties', *N. & Q.* 222 (1977), 117–20. Alexander S. Liddie, in the Preface to his edn. of *The History of the Two Maids of Moreclacke*, Garland Renaissance Drama Ser. (New York, 1979), concludes that the odds against Armin's authorship are 'three to one' (p. ii). The two chief pieces of evidence for Armin's authorship singled out by John Feather in his *Collected Works of Robert Armin*, 2 vols. (New York, 1972) are that the play has a Fool and a character who speaks Welsh.

generous: it is much less trustworthy, as evidence of R. W.'s intentions, than the solitary 'Actus Secundus' division provided at a reasonable point in the 1623 *Hamlet*. None of Wilson's other plays contain act-divisions. These anomalies are not in fact anomalous, and do nothing to endanger Jewkes's conclusions

Hunter's main difficulty is to explain the absence of act-divisions from various kinds of text. He begins by asserting that 'we could not expect' bad quartos to preserve such divisions (p. 22); yet I cannot see on what grounds this expectation is based. After all, 'bad quartos' supposedly represent a text of the play based upon seeing or participating in performances of it; if such performances always included act-intervals, why should the reporters not indicate them? As a striking interruption of the play's continuity, they would be easy enough for any actor or spectator to remember; if audiences and readers expected such intervals, if (like authors) they regarded them as significant pointers to the play's structure and meaning, then a 'pirate'—trying to make his text look authentic, full, and reliable—would have every incentive to include them. Yet none of the twenty extant bad quartos, dating from 1593 to 1608, indicate act-divisions.[59]

For the absence of act-divisions from 'good' quartos, set from prompt-books or authorial papers, Hunter relies upon two other lines of reasoning. He first conjectures that most authors would not have supplied such divisions in their manuscripts, because these were the bookkeeper's business, and would only be supplied at a very late stage in the play's development. In the first place, surviving manuscripts from 1611 on indicate no such authorial reticence; bookkeepers may, on rare occasions, have altered authorial divisions, but this possibility did not prevent authors from marking their own intentions clearly. Indeed, Hunter devotes much of his article to an explication of the dramatic significance of the act-breaks in certain early plays of Shakespeare; yet, having argued that such pauses were crucial to Shakespeare's design, he would then have us believe that Shakespeare did not bother to mark them.[60] As Greg remarked, a division into acts is (unless there are only five scenes in the play) arbitrary: 'An author may write without any such division in mind:

---

[59] For a list of recognized bad quartos see Leo Kirschbaum, 'An Hypothesis Concerning the Origin of the Bad Quartos', *PMLA* 60 (1945), 697. I have excluded *King Lear* and *Philaster*. *Philaster* (Q1) is only corrupt at the beginning of Act 1 and the end of Act 5, so that the act-divisions presumably derive from the authoritative portion of the MS: see Andrew Gurr's Revels edn. (London, 1969), pp. lxxiv–lxxxiv. *King Lear* (Q1) is not a bad quarto: see below. I have added *The First Part of Hieronimo*: see Andrew S. Cairncross's edn., English Renaissance Drama Ser. (London, 1967).

[60] Hunter in fact argues that no Shakespearean act-divisions are reliable, since all of those supplied in the Folio may be editorial intrusions; yet, of course, were this true, we would have no evidence on which to base pronouncements about Shakespeare's artistic use and placing of act-divisions.

if he intends a division, and wants it to be any way recognized on the stage, it is essential that he should indicate it in the manuscript.'[61]

Finally, Hunter conjectures that, even when early plays were printed from prompt-books which had been supplied with act-divisions, those divisions would have been 'ignored' by the printer, because he decided they were 'irrelevant to the reader' (p. 23). But why should a printer regard material in the margins as immaterial? Many stage directions would have been placed in the margins too. Why should printers after 1616 decide to stop ignoring such marginalia? Why should accident discriminate so consistently against plays written for the adult companies before 1616? Why should we seek three indirect and implausible explanations for the absence of act-divisions from the texts of such plays, when one explanation—a change in theatrical practice—is so readily to hand?

The presence or absence of act-divisions in early printed texts thus cannot be plausibly dismissed as evidence of theatrical practice. Moreover, the texts of the plays support the same conclusions in ways which no stretch of the most athletic critical imagination can dismiss. Records survive of a *Three Plays in One* acted in 1585, and a *Four Plays in One* acted in 1592; *A Yorkshire Tragedy* (1605–8) advertised itself as '*One of the Four Plays in One*', and Fletcher and Field wrote another *Four Plays in One*, probably between 1613 and 1616. As one might imagine, such amalgamations do not lend themselves to performance with four intervals between the acts; no record survives of the performance of any such play in London between 1616 and 1642.

Another convention of performances by the early adult companies is the so-called 'law of re-entry'. As usually understood, this law presupposes continuous performance: if no breaks or intervals interrupt the performance, then the immediate re-entry of the character(s) who have just left the stage, supposedly after an extended interval of time or extensive change of place, imposes some strain upon the comprehension, credulity, and goodwill of an audience. Potential or actual changes of locale are therefore indicated by a clearing of the stage, followed by the entry of a new set of characters. However, if sustained intervals in the performance itself do occur, then such a re-entry creates no problems of credibility.

Shakespeare's only flagrant violation of this convention occurs in *The Tempest*, when Ariel and Prospero exeunt together at the end of Act 4 and enter together at the beginning of Act 5. *The Tempest* was written between September 1610 and November 1611. Irwin Smith catalogues similar re-entrances, across act-breaks, in twelve children's company plays, and in sixty-two King's Men plays (including *The Tempest*) which date from the period of their occupancy of the Blackfriars Theatre,

---

[61] *First Folio*, 143. Greg is contrasting act-division with scene-division (which is based on mechanical rules, and so need not be indicated on the MS).

beginning with *Philaster* (May 1609–June 1610) and *The Alchemist* (1610). These sixty-two plays include ninety-four re-entries by a total of 157 persons. By contrast, such re-entrances occur only six times in early Shakespeare texts.[62] In addition, in eighteen non-Shakespearian plays performed by the Chamberlain's/King's Men between 1598 and 1607, the convention is violated only five times: in *Alarum for London* (1598–1600) between Scenes 1 and 2, in *A Warning for Fair Women* (1598–9) at Scenes 14/15, in *The Merry Devil of Edmonton* (1599–1604) at 2. 2–2. 3 and 3. 2–3. 3, and in Barnaby Barnes's *The Devil's Charter* (1607) at 2. 1–2. 2.[63] Moreover, in *Alarum for London* only Danila re-enters, and in doing so clearly moves from the upper to the lower stage, so that effectively no violation of the convention occurs. Noticeably, none of these eleven anomalous re-entrances occurs after an act-break, as marked in the original editions or subsequently understood by editors.[64]

Moreover, one play from this period—Marston's *The Malcontent*—survives in two texts, one representing it as performed by the Children of the Chapel Royal, another as adapted for the King's Men. In the original version there are two anomalous re-entries across act-breaks; in the adapted text both have been removed, by the interpolation of new material apparently written by John Webster.[65] Unless this is yet another coincidence, it suggests a difference between private and public theatre conventions—a difference most easily explained by the presence of intervals in the private, and their absence from the public theatres until *c*.1610.

The use of choruses reveals a similar disparity between early and late practice in the public theatres.[66] One must distinguish, first of all,

[62] Irwin Smith, 'Their Exits and Re-entrances', *SQ* 18 (1967), 7–16. Smith considers 16 possible exceptions, but only six seem likely: *3 Henry VI* 5. 6–5. 7, *Richard III* 3. 3–3. 4, *Taming* Induction i–ii and 5. 1–5. 2, and *All's Well* 5. 2–5. 3. Smith points out that the *Richard III* anomaly only exists in the Folio text, but the Quarto is itself anomalous at 2. 4–3. 1. *Titus Andronicus* and *Dream* are anomalous only in their altered Folio versions (see below). I am not persuaded by Smith's analysis of *Cymbeline* 5. 3–5. 4.

[63] I have included *Mucedorus* in its revised version (printed 1610), but excluded the re-entry between Acts 1 and 2 of Jonson's *Sejanus*. (See n. 48 above.) I have also excluded *The First Part of Hieronimo*; see Cairncross's edn. The re-entry in *Devil's Charter* should perhaps be excluded, as falling within the category of 'battle scenes'.

[64] *The Devil's Charter* is divided in the original edn. (1607), clearly supervised by the author himself (see n. 82, below). *All's Well* and *Richard III* are plausibly divided in the Folio; *Taming* has an unsatisfactory act-division (including a break between 5. 1 and 5. 2) which is emended by all editors. For the other plays, divisions are editorial (though *A Warning* could be arranged into four irregular acts, separated by appearances of the Chorus).

[65] *The Malcontent*, ed. Hunter, p. liii n. 1. Hunter concluded that the added material was 'not-certainly-Marston's'; D. J. Lake has since shown that it is almost certainly Webster's, in 'Webster's Additions to *The Malcontent*: Linguistic Evidence', *N. & Q.* 226 (1981), 153–8. Lake's case has been further strengthened by MacD. P. Jackson and Michael Neil in their edn. of *The Selected Plays of John Marston* (Cambridge, 1986), 190–3, 513–15.

[66] For appearances of a chorus in printed plays I have relied on Thomas L. Berger and William C. Bradford, jun., *An Index of Characters in English Printed Drama to the*

between one or more speaking presenters (like Gower in *Pericles*) and interludes of choric song (like those in Seneca). Ten of the 155 extant plays written for the adult companies before 1610 are divided into five natural acts by speaking presenters: *Soliman and Perseda, The Spanish Tragedy* (four acts), *Locrine, James IV, Alphonsus of Aragon, The Battle of Alcazar, 1 Tamar Cam, Henry V, Two Lamentable Tragedies,* and *The Devil's Charter.*[67] To these might be added *David and Bathsheba*[68] and *A Warning for Fair Women* (four acts). Some (though by no means all)[69] early presenters thus reinforce Baldwin's evidence that even early public theatre plays might be naturally perceived as five-act structures. Hunter concludes, ambiguously, that such presenters are evidence that the plays were 'clearly divided into five acts' in performance.[70] But such choruses might or might not have coexisted with actual breaks in performance: in fact, neither of the extant plots which includes such presenters specifically calls for breaks in the performance, before or after their entrance, and to an extent the consistent use of choruses in this manner would seem to make intervals redundant, and vice versa. As Shakespeare wrote in *Venus and Adonis*, 'all this dumbe play had his acts made plain, | With tears which Chorus-like her eyes did rain' (ll.359–60). If, in 1592–3, performances in the public theatres made regular use of intervals, a play would not need a chorus to make 'his acts . . . plain'. Moreover, in at least one of the printed plays (*Two Lamentable Tragedies*) the text in fact requires continuous playing; several others are most naturally understood in the same way.[71]

Restoration (Englewood, Colo. 1975). Berger and Bradford do not consider the 'Friar' in *The Ghost, or The Woman Wears the Breeches* (anon., 1640?) as a chorus or presenter, since he takes an active part in the play as a dramatic character; however he does begin the play, and end each act, with a rhymed, lyric soliloquy, in one of which he says: ' 'Tis the glory of the Frier | To be *Chorus* in this Quire' (F1–F1ᵛ).

[67] *1 Tamar Cam* survives only in a plot; see Greg, *Dramatic Documents*, 160–70. Robert Greene's *James IV* was printed with several 'additional choruses' whose exact relation to the text is disputed: see Norman Sanders's Revels edn. (London, 1970).

[68] The 1599 Quarto has only two of the four Chorus interludes necessary to divide the play into five acts; but the second of these is headed '5. Chorus.', which suggests that the original had a structure similar to *Henry V*, etc.

[69] The presenters in twelve other early adult plays would divide a play into fewer, or more, than five acts: *The Taming of A Shrew, A Looking Glass for London and England, Dr. Faustus, Romeo and Juliet, 2 Edward IV, The Downfall of Robert Earl of Huntingdon, The Death of Robert Earl of Huntingdon, Thomas Lord Cromwell, Four Prentices of London, Travels of Three English Brothers, Pericles,* and *Christian Turned Turk.* To these should probably be added the anonymous MS play *Tom a Lincoln* (BL MS Add 61745), though the date and provenance of this have not yet been confidently established.

[70] By means of this ambiguity he can cite two additional plots (*Alcazar* and *1 Tamar Cam*) as evidence for 'Act-Pauses on Shakespeare's Stage' (pp. 18–19). These plots indicate entrances and exits for the Chorus, but no break in performance.

[71] For *Two Lamentable Tragedies*, see n. 47. In *Alphonsus, King of Arragon*, the Act 4 Chorus begins 'Thus have you seene . . .' (F1) and ends 'as straight shall appeare' (F1ᵛ). In *The Devil's Charter* the Chorus at the end of Act 1 begins 'Thus', and ends 'and now his trumpets hard | Unto the gates of *Rome* give fresh allarms | Unto the Pope, who stirreth up

Plays written after 1610 provide a striking contrast. In four plays—*The Valiant Welshman* (1614?), *Hengist, King of Kent* (1618), *The Jews' Tragedy* (1627), and *The Seven Champions of Christendom* (1635)—presenters appear sporadically during, rather than between, the acts. In none of the earlier plays which have act-divisions do the appearances of a presenter conflict with those divisions in this manner. Moreover, although the text of at least one early play clearly requires that there be no interval before or after the presenter's speech, in two late plays—*The Jews' Tragedy* and *The Escapes of Jupiter*—the presenter himself refers to the interval which follows his speech (above, p. 7).

Before 1609, presenters were sometimes used to indicate the act structure of plays written for the adult companies; after 1612, they almost entirely ceased to do so. It is difficult not to attribute the change in practice to the fact that the structural function of such presenters had been usurped by musical intervals between the acts. Moreover, the practice of the children's companies again contrasts with early, and coincides with late, adult practice. Only one early children's play is divided into five acts by a chorus: Samuel Daniel's *Philotas*. Daniel himself tells us that this play was originally intended 'as a private recreation for the Christmas'; the '*Chorus of the vulgar*' who '*stand | Spectators here*' (B8) speaks—or more probably chants or sings—in rhymed lyric measures, between the acts. Clearly, *Philotas* brings us closer to *Seneca His Ten Tragedies* than to the presenters of Elizabethan popular theatre: the conventions of the closet play have invaded the Blackfriars. By 1611 they had invaded the adult companies as well: the classical choruses in Jonson's *Catiline* again divide the play into five acts by means of rhymed lyric stanzaic interludes. But the apotheosis of this dramatic experiment comes in Henry Killigrew's turgid tragedy *The Conspiracy* (1635), in which a 'CHORUS of *Priests* and *People*' ends each act with a stanzaic song, and the play itself concludes with a 'Scene consist‹ing› onely of Musick and Shew; on the one side . . . stands a Consort of Musitions, representing the Priests of the Land, and on the other side . . . another, representing the People' (R2). Unlike *Catiline* and *Philotas*, Killigrew's turgedy succeeded, being played before the King and then by the King's Men at the Blackfriars.

Pauses between the acts were filled with talk as well as music; as Beaumont complained in his commendatory verses to Fletcher's *The Faithful Shepherdess*, 'Nor wants there those, who as the boy doth dance | Betweene the actes, will censure the whole play'. Three plays written for the early private or later public theatres attempt to reproduce such entr'acte conversations dramatically, in what Jonson called an 'intermean': Beaumont's *The Knight of the Burning Pestle* (1607–10, Queen's

in armes.' These lines are immediately followed by 'Act. 2 SCAE. 1. | *Enter* Alexander *with a Lintstock in his hand*' etc. (C4ᵛ). Likewise, just before the direction 'Act. 4' the Chorus concludes Act 3 with the words 'What followes, view with gentle patience' (F4ᵛ).

Revels), Jonson's *New Inn* (1625, King's Men), and Jonson's *Magnetic Lady* (1632, King's Men). All these, as it happens, flopped, like *Philotas* and *Catiline*: spectators apparently preferred not to have their own dialogues interrupted in order to be mocked. Only one early adult play attempts to employ the same convention: Jonson's *Every Man Out of His Humour* (1599). But in this the onstage 'audience' speaks frequently during the play, not just between the acts—and the dialogues of the 'Grex' in printed texts of the play were, in any case, probably not performed.[72]

Plays written after 1615, and plays written for the children's companies, were printed with act-divisions; excepting those by Jonson, plays written for the public stage between 1592 and 1606 (inclusive) were not. For late and children's plays external testimony, explicit stage directions, explicit references in dialogue, and theatrical manuscripts all witness to the normality of pauses between the five acts; for adult plays from 1591 to 1610 no external testimony, no explicit stage directions, no explicit references in dialogue exist to confirm such a practice, and only two of the available theatrical documents include act-divisions at all—and both are clearly, for other reasons, dubious evidence of theatrical practice. Late and children's plays regularly allow 'immediate' re-entrances at the beginning of a new act; early adult plays do not. Late and children's plays almost never divide a play into five acts by the use of presenters; early adult plays often do. Late and children's plays instead sometimes made use of an intermean between the acts, or an interlude of choric song; early adult plays do not. All roads lead to Rome: before c.1607-10, the adult companies did not perform plays with intervals between the acts.

Public theatre practice can thus be established with as much confidence for the period 1592–c.1607 as it can (in a different way) for the period 1616–42. The transition between these two eras creates, as one might expect, some difficulties of interpretation, which I will consider in a moment. First, however, something must be said about the fifteen shadowy years before 1592.

Some of the difficulties with this earlier period arise from a simple diminution of evidence: far fewer plays survive, and often we know little about the date or provenance of those which do. Moreover, what we do know about the authorship of many of them merely compounds the problem: for many of those which reached print were written by the so-called 'University Wits'. The very strength of the academic tradition that proper plays had five acts—the tradition so painstakingly documented by Baldwin—makes it easy enough to understand why such writers would want their plays *printed* with act-divisions, even if they were performed

---

[72] Ben Jonson, *Works*, ed. C. H. Herford, and Percy and Evelyn Simpson, 11 vols. (Oxford, 1925–52), i. 373–4.

without them. The printed texts of such plays may well tell us more about the well-known pretensions of their authors than about the little-known practices of their theatres.

Certainly, one would expect public theatre practice in the fifteen years up to 1591 to coincide with public theatre practice in the sixteen or more years after. No major changes in the circumstances of the companies, or the conditions of public playing, would explain or could have caused such a change. Moreover, the adoption of act-intervals after *c.*1607 took (as we shall see) a decade or more to become universal: no such period of transition can be discerned in the years before and after 1591. Seven plays written before 1592—or eight, if we include *David and Bathsheba*—make use of presenters to divide the action into five sections, a practice typical of continuous performance; no public theatre play written before 1592 makes use of the kind of academic lyric chorus, or the intermean, which can be clearly associated with intervalled performances in the children's companies or the later London theatres. Nor does the disdain of the public stage so evident in the work of Sidney and other humanists seem compatible with the assumption that those stages put into practice the humanist division of plays into five acts: one would expect such a concession to humanist theory to have earned corresponding concessions from the humanists—even if they went no further than a grudging reference to the players' attempts to dress their vulgar fare in the trappings of a more noble culture. Certainly, the cultural establishment did give its dubious approval to the seventeenth-century children's companies, and to the later adult stage, and it increasingly accredited Jacobean and Caroline plays as 'literature', a legitimate pursuit for noblemen and courtiers like Killigrew, Suckling, and Carlell. If the public theatres before 1592 had anticipated these later institutions in so fundamental a cultural virtue as the provision of musical act-intervals, some measure of blessing (however niggardly) should have been accorded them. None ever was.

Finally, though the presence of act-divisions in some plays written by the University Wits proves nothing, their absence from other plays by the same authors strongly suggests something. These authors almost certainly designed their plays on a five-act plan, which they would want the printed text to reflect; consequently, the absence of such divisions from any of their plays indicates that some other agent of the texts' transmission disregarded those divisions. That agent might, theoretically, have been the printer, but we have already seen that, with rare exceptions, the presence or absence of act-divisions can seldom be attributed to the printer rather than his copy. Consequently, those who disregarded or removed such literary divisions most probably represented the playhouses. The eight plays written by the University Wits which were printed without any act-divisions therefore cast a strong shadow of continuous performance, out of the playhouse on to the page. (In fact, more of the Wits' plays were printed without divisions than with them.)[73]

Why, then, is Jewkes, with so much reason to suppose that early adult performances were continuous, so coy about whether adult performances before 1592 employed act-intervals?[74] In the first place, even if we ignore all of the work of the University Wits, six of the remaining twenty-seven extant plays written for the adult companies between 1576 and 1591 (inclusive) contain a regular division into five acts. Jewkes does not actually mention this proportion, but, given his fondness for figures, one suspects that he may have noticed it. Certainly, the ratio contrasts strikingly with that for 1592–1606 (21:6 vs. 70:5). Moreover, all five examples in the later period belong to Ben Jonson, whose idiosyncrasies need not be documented. Before 1592, texts divided into five acts include the work of Anthony Munday (a former stationer's apprentice) and a series of anonymous plays which must certainly boast more than one author (*The Rare Triumphs of Love and Fortune*, *Fidele and Fortunio*, *The Dead Man's Fortune*, *Locrine*, and *Jack Straw*). Moreover, *Jack Straw* (printed with act-divisions in 1593, and written between 1590 and 1593) may well be a 'bad' quarto.[75] If so, it constitutes the only memorial reconstruction ever printed with act-divisions, and the fact that it too comes from this early period must disconcert any investigator.

The disproportionately large number of early five-act plays itself causes uncertainty; but two explicit pieces of evidence turn these ambiguities into an inescapable contradiction. One is the printed text of *Fidele and Fortunio*, acted at Court at some time between 1579 and 1584, which contains the following stage directions:[76]

[73] The eight undivided plays are: *David and Bathsheba*, *Friar Bacon and Friar Bungay*, *George a Greene*, *A Looking Glass for London and England*, *The Old Wives' Tale*, *Soliman and Perseda*, *Orlando Furioso*, and *Edward I*. Only seven are divided: *Alphonsus*, *The Spanish Tragedy*, *1* and *2 Tamburlaine*, *The Wounds of Civil War*, *Alcazar* (imperfectly), and *James IV*.

[74] Jewkes never specifically discusses the period before 1592 as a distinct problem. In his conclusion he dismisses the evidence of five early divided plays because they are 'early' (*Act Division*, 98), without explaining what difference this makes. Elsewhere, he attempts to dismiss most of the anonymous plays by assigning them to various University Wits: *Jack Straw* to Peele, *Love and Fortune* to Kyd, *Locrine* to Peele and Greene (ibid. 53). Only the last attribution has any plausibility (see Baldwin Maxwell, *Studies in the Shakespeare Apocrypha* (New York, 1956), 67–71) and even it has been recently challenged by Peter Berek, in '*Locrine* Revised, *Selimus*, and Early Responses to *Tamberlaine*', *RORD* 22 (1980), 33–54.

[75] Kenneth Muir's Mal. Soc. Repr. (1957) unfortunately says nothing about the copy for or provenance of the play—though Muir does doubt that Peele, sometimes conjectured to be the author, could have written a play 'so destitute of poetry' (p. v). The destitution might, of course, be due to textual corruption, and the brevity of the text (only 1209 lines in Muir's edn., counting stage directions and centred speech prefixes) certainly arouses suspicion. On the other hand, the act-divisions might be part of Danter's thorough attempt to stretch the material: he also uses blank pages, generous leading, centred speech headings, and ornaments, all for the same purpose (Muir, p. v).

[76] Jewkes dismisses the evidence of this play because it is a translation (*Act Division*, 53); yet it was performed at Court, and the only edn. of Luigi Pasqualigo's *Il Fedele* (Venice, 1576), from which it was translated, contains no such directions for music between the Acts.

The first Act beeing ended, the Consorte of Musique
    Soundeth a pleasant Galliard. (C2)

The second Act beeing ended, the Consorte soundeth again. (D4^v)

The third Act being doone, the Consort sounds a sollemne Dump. (E3^v)

The fourth Act being ended, the Consort soundeth a pleasant Allemaigne. (G1)

Not until *The Fatal Dowry* (1617–19) and *Hengist* (1618) do we again find such explicit evidence of a musical interlude between the acts of an adult company's play. Even so, this might be dismissed as an authorial fancy, were it not for the manuscript plot of *The Dead Man's Fortune*. The earliest extant plot, and probably the earliest extant professional theatrical manuscript, *The Dead Man's Fortune* contains—added by a second hand—explicit directions for intervals between the five acts, with music during each interval. The fact that these directions, and an extra scene, were added by a later hand makes them dubious evidence of normal adult practice, especially given the contrary evidence of all the other plots; on the other hand, this plot undeniably demonstrates that, in at least one venue, at least one early company did perform at least one play with musical intervals between the five acts. The occasion of this subsequent performance can hardly have been a late Jacobean or Caroline revival (as with *Woodstock* and *Ironside*), for the only two actors named—Burbage and Lee—could not have collaborated after 1604 at the very latest, and probably not after 1593. Moreover, it can hardly have been a performance by a choir company, either: whatever Robert Lee's childhood occupation, Burbage's family background makes it impossible to believe that he ever exercised his talents in one of the boys' theatres. Nor is it easy to imagine that act-intervals were added for the backward provinces, when ignored in the sophisticated metropolis. This leaves us, of course, with only one likely special venue for such a subsequent performance: the Court. Not only were plays normally performed at Court after they had proven successful in public (which explains the later additions), but the Court might well have been provided with a certain cultural flourish considered unnecessary, or positively undesirable, for the vulgar (which explains the added act-divisions and music). Certainly, the Revels office sometimes saw fit to alter plays in order to make them more appropriate and more entertaining for their special audience.[77]

Only the hypothesis of a Court performance in the 1580s will account for the unique peculiarities of *The Dead Man's Fortune*, and the same explanation will also account, of course, for *Fidele and Fortunio*. It would also explain the directions for '*Musicke*' in two of the breaks between acts in the printed text of *The Rare Triumphs of Love and Fortune*, acted at Court in 1582, and printed from what seems clearly to have been a

---

[77] See Chambers, *Elizabethan Stage*, I. 78, 224.

theatrical manuscript. Finally, the scattering of early plays by a variety of authors which appear with act-divisions could result from the fact—or the expectation, or hope—of Court performance. Some of these exceptions, like *The Dead Man's Fortune*, might be due to an Inns of Court performance; but this would not account for *Fidele and Fortunio* or for *The Rare Triumphs of Love and Fortune*, nor can it plausibly be invoked for all the exceptions. Moreover, we know relatively little about Inns of Court performances, whereas the exceptional nature of early Court performances has been extensively documented. In particular, the Revels Office was responsible for maintaining a 'music-house', and employed musicians even during trial performances of plays being considered for a Court production.[78] Moreover, Italian practice had a strong influence on English Court drama, and five-act plays with musical *intermedii* had been *de rigeur* in Italy since early in the sixteenth century.[79]

This hypothesis—that performances at Court in the 1580s, and perhaps earlier, regularly used intervals to divide plays into five acts—forces us to assume that Court practice changed *c*.1590, for unknown reasons: if Court practice had remained the same, the comprehensive lack of evidence for the years after 1591 becomes difficult to explain. But although the exact reasons for such a change cannot now be discerned, other changes in the management of Court performances also occurred at about this time. As J. Leeds Barroll has noted, 'a curious kind of "anarchy" seems to have begun with the season of 1591–2 . . . whatever plan had been instituted for regulating court performance and performers seems to have been breaking down'.[80] The last surviving choir company—Paul's Boys—was suppressed at some time after 6 January 1590–1; this left the Court entirely dependent on the adult companies, who normally performed plays without musical intervals between the acts. Also, coincidentally, the detailed Revels Office accounts available for earlier years cease after 1589. Later in the 1590s a major reorganization of the Office was attempted, and there are signs that its finances had been disrupted since the beginning of the decade.[81] So there seems nothing unreasonable in the suggestion that certain performance practices may also have changed at about this time. Such an hypothesis accounts for all the peculiarities of *The Dead Man's Fortune* plot and *Fidele and Fortunio* and for the smattering of other early directions for act-intervals. Moreover, by making sense of the contradictory signals from this early period, it removes the only anomalies in the manuscript record of adult theatre

---

[78] Ibid. i. 224–5, 229–32.

[79] For Italian influence see ibid. iii. 1–46; for my knowledge of Italian intervals I am indebted to F. W. Sternfeld, whose study of the subject is forthcoming.

[80] Clifford Leech and T. W. Craik (eds.), *The Revels History of Drama in English*, iii. *1576–1613* (London, 1975), 26.

[81] *Elizabethan Stage*, i, 223 (records), 91 (delayed payment); Wilson, *English Drama* (see n. 23), 163.

performances before 1611: *The Dead Man's Fortune* and *John a Kent*. In one stroke this hypothesis removes all of the little evidence which could claim to contradict the conclusion that early adult plays were normally performed without act-intervals.

At some time between 1607 and 1615, conditions of performance by London's adult companies dramatically changed. In the years up to 1609, the King's Men performed *Timon of Athens* (1604–5?), *The Miseries of Enforced Marriage* (1605–6), *King Lear* (1605), *Antony and Cleopatra* (1606), and *Pericles* (1607–8); all five were originally published without act-divisions.[82] By contrast, no play known to have been written for the King's Men after spring 1608 is undivided. By 1609–10, *Philaster* and *The Alchemist* exhibit a new leniency in allowing 'immediate' re-entrances at the beginning of an act; in 1611 the scribal prompt-book of *The Second Maiden's Tragedy* contains prominent act-divisions; in 1611 Shakespeare has Prospero and Ariel exit together at the end of Act 4 and re-enter together at the beginning of Act 5; in 1611 Jonson's *Catiline* envisages a classical lyric chorus between the acts. For the King's Men, at least, the change almost certainly happened after the spring of 1608 (*Pericles*) and before the summer of 1610 (*Philaster*).[83]

The King's Men acquired the Blackfriars playhouse in August 1608; they probably began performing there in late 1609 or early 1610.[84] Hunter regards with 'scepticism' the idea that 'the entry of the King's Men into the private Blackfriars Theatre was a crucial event in theatrical history and altered the whole nature of Elizabethan play-performance' (p. 21). Others have expressed similar doubts.[85] One can sympathize with those doubts: minds raised on Darwin abhor abrupt disjunctions. But the entire tradition of continuous playing—inherited from the mystery and

[82] Jewkes and others have seized on 1607 as a significant date because of the publication in 1608 of two adult plays with act-divisions. But one of these—Barnabe Barnes's *The Devils Charter*—announces on the title-page that it has been 'more exactly revewed, corrected, and augmented since [its performance] by the Author, for the more pleasure and profit of the reader'; moreover, a 'large number of substantive variations indicates the hand of the author in the proofreading' (*The Devil's Charter*, ed. Jim C. Pogue, Garland Renaissance Drama Ser. (New York, 1980), 5). *The Devil's Charter's* act-divisions thus tell us little about public theatre practice in 1607. The other play is *The Revenger's Tragedy* (1606–7): already a notorious historical crux. Its divisions might confirm that the play is Middleton's, and originally written for Paul's; however we interpret them, one problematic text provides poor evidence of a shift in practice before 1609—especially as the undivided *Antony* and *Pericles* contradict it.

[83] Andrew Gurr, in his Revels edn. of *Philaster* (London, 1969), persuasively dates the play's completion some time in or soon after May 1609 (pp. xxvi–xxviii).

[84] Smith, *Blackfriars Playhouse*, 248; J. Leeds Barroll, 'The Chronology of Shakespeare's Jacobean Plays and the Dating of *Antony and Cleopatra*', in Gordon Ross Smith, ed., *Essays on Shakespeare* (University Park, Penn., 1965), 132–3.

[85] See especially J. A. Lavin, 'Shakespeare and the Second Blackfriars', in David Galloway (ed.), *The Elizabethan Theatre III* (Toronto, 1973), 66–81. Lavin does not actually discuss the limited issue of act-division, however.

morality plays, the Tudor interlude, and the rough-and-tumble of provincial touring—must at some time before *c.* 1616 have given way to the more academic Renaissance convention of a formal division into five acts, by means of four intervals. The building of the Theatre in 1576 could have prompted that change; but it apparently did not. The first acquisition of a private theatre by an adult company, in 1608, represents the next most significant development in the physical history of English Renaissance drama.

Given the evidence, now overwhelming, for a widespread change in practice at some time between 1607 and 1616, and the particular evidence for a change in the practice of the King's Men at some time between spring 1608 and summer 1610, one finds it difficult not to notice the purchase of the Blackfriars lease in August 1608, and the beginning of adult performances there in or soon after December 1609. Certainly, the acquisition of the Blackfriars is more likely to have influenced the theatrical practice of its purchasers (as Dover Wilson, Jewkes, Irwin Smith, and Richard Hosley assumed)[86] than to have had a far-reaching impact on the habits of printers (as Hunter instead suggests).

Moreover, the historical pattern of theatrical practice makes architectural sense. As Harbage noted, 'The roofed rectangular auditorium of the typical "private" theatre attested its descent from the banqueting halls of the wealthy or academic'.[87] We have already seen evidence that intervals were used at Court, at the Universities, and in the 'private' theatres, in the late sixteenth and early seventeenth centuries—in short, in all the architectural haunts of the 'wealthy or academic'. The decade after 1608 saw London's adult companies beginning to move into 'private' theatres, and also adopting the use of intervals.

No clause in the Blackfriars lease compelled the King's Men to perform plays with intervals between the acts, but a conjunction of incentives would have encouraged them to do so. It would be natural enough to adopt some of the conventions of the children's companies when moving into their theatre. For indoor performances candles would need to be trimmed; act-intervals provide a convenient opportunity.[88] The Blackfriars playhouse had better architectural facilities for musicians; plays written for the King's Men after the move testify to greater musical resources.[89] Most important of all, since 1599 the children's companies had been serious commercial rivals, and since 1603 a succession of outbreaks of plague had made life particularly difficult for anyone economically dependent upon

---

[86] J. Dover Wilson, 'Act and Scene Division in the Plays of Shakespeare', *Res* 3 (1927), 392; Jewkes, *Act Division*, 91–2; Smith, *Blackfriars Playhouse*, 249; R. Y. Hosley, 'The Playhouses and the Stage', in Kenneth Muir and S. Schoenbaum, eds., *A New Companion to Shakespeare Studies* (Cambridge, 1971), 33.

[87] *Shakespeare and the Rival Traditions* (New York, 1952), 41.

[88] Smith, *Blackfriars Playhouse*, 230.

[89] See Hosley, 'Playhouses' (see n. 86), 33, and Smith, *Blackfriars Playhouse*, 236–7.

receipts from the outdoor theatres. The adult companies were taking over
the children's playwrights, and assimilating some of their innovative dramatic techniques;[90] to appropriate some of their more attractive conventions of performance would be logical enough. The decision to purchase
the Blackfriars itself testifies to an intention to beat the competition at
their own game. And this intention was realized: for the years 1609–16
saw not only the adoption of act-intervals by the adult companies, but
also the complete collapse of their child rivals.

The other adult companies would have shared most of these motives
for adopting act-divisions, but with an added incentive, provided by the
King's Men themselves. The King's Men were, as their stability since
1595 and name since 1603 suggest, London's leading company; that predominance can only have been increased by their acquisition of a second
playhouse. If the King's Men successfully adopted some of the practices
of the children's companies in 1609, it would not be surprising if the
other adult companies eventually followed suit.

Lady Elizabeth's Men and the Prince's Men may have come next. Lady
Elizabeth's Men amalgamated with the Children of the Queen's Revels in
1613, and all their extant plays thereafter (beginning with *A Chaste Maid
in Cheapside* in 1613) have act-divisions.[91] In 1614–15 Prince Charles's
Men joined forces for a while with the expanded Lady Elizabeth's
company; after the new private playhouse at Porter's Hall ended its
short life, they moved into the new Hope Theatre. All of the company's
extant plays—*The Valiant Welshman* (1614–15), *A Fair Quarrel* (1615–17),
All's Lost by Lust (1619–20), and *The Witch of Edmonton* (1621)—are
divided.

The Queen's Men have left a more complicated history. They moved
into the Red Bull Theatre in 1606, and stayed there until 1617 when they
occupied the new Cockpit. *The Three English Brothers* (1607) and *The
Rape of Lucrece* (1606–8) are undivided: so are *Tu Quoque* (1611), *If This
Be Not a Good Play, the Devil is in it* (1611–12), and *The White Devil*
(1612).[92] In 1614 or early 1615 Wentworth Smith's *The Hector of
Germany* (entered in the Stationers' Register on 24 April 1615) was performed at the company's theatre, though not by the company; it too was
printed without act-divisions. Thereafter, beginning with *The Honest
Lawyer*, by 'S. S.' (*c.* 1614–15; Stationers' Register, 14 August 1615), all

---

[90] See Foakes, 'Tragedy of the Children's Theatres' (n. 48 above).

[91] By 1613 (at the latest) the Swan had a music room: *A Chaste Maid in Cheapside* calls
for 'a sad Song in the Musicke-Roome' (K2ᵛ). R. B. Parker, in his Revels edn. (London,
1969), convincingly dates this play's first performance between Mar. and Aug. 1613
(pp. xxviii–xxxv).

[92] Harbage and Schoenbaum date *The White Devil* to 1609–12; for the more precise dating see John Russell Brown's Revels edn. (London: Methuen, 1960), pp. xx–xxiii. Rowley's
A Shoemaker a Gentleman (1607–9) also probably belonged to Queen's, but the 1639 edn.
almost certainly owes its act-divisions to later revivals (Jewkes, *Act Division*, 309).

Queen's Men plays have act-divisions. Since we do not know who 'S. S.' was, it could be claimed that the divisions in his play testify to literary pretension rather than theatrical practice. However, Daborne's *The Poor Man's Comfort* can have been written no later than January 1616–17, and is probably earlier;[93] since the Queen's Men did not move into the Cockpit until that March, Daborne's play confirms the evidence of *The Honest Lawyer* that the company adopted intervals even before their move into an indoor theatre, presumably at some time in late 1614 or early 1615.

However, Heywood's *Ages* plays, written for the company between 1609 and 1613, disturb this clear chronological progression.[94] *The Golden Age* (1609–11; Stationers' Register, 14 October 1611) is divided into five acts, with Homer as chorus beginning each; *The Silver Age* (1609–11; printed 1613) has a similar arrangement of choruses, but Acts 4 and 5 are not marked in the printed texts, and Act 3 is wrongly marked;[95] in *The Brazen Age* (1609–11; printed 1613), only Act 1 and 2 are marked, though Homer again appears regularly. Moreover, the title-page of *The Brazen Age* divides the play's contents into acts ('The first Act Containing . . .' etc.), and Homer's speeches themselves refer to these divisions ('with whose sad death our first Act we conclude', 'Our mortals . . . to the Gods, for this Act, leave the Stage', 'Our last Act comes'). Finally, *1* and *2 Iron Age* (1612–1613; printed 1631) both have regular act-divisions but no choruses at all.[96] *The Golden Age* title-page tells us it was 'sundry times acted at the Red Bull, by the Queenes Majesties Servants'; neither *Silver* nor *Brazen* mentions a company, but we know that *Silver* was performed jointly by the Queen's Men and King's Men at Court on 12 January 1612; Heywood's Epistle to *1 Iron Age* tells us that 'these were the Playes often (and not with the least applause,) Publickely Acted by two Companies, upon one Stage at once, and have at sundry times thronged three several Theaters' (A4). Since the King's Men joined the Queen's Men in performing *The Silver Age* at Court, it would be

---

[93] *The Poor Man's Comfort*, ed. Kenneth Palmer, Malone Soc. Repr. (1955), pp. x–xii.

[94] Harbage and Schoenbaum give the limiting dates for *Silver Age* as 1610–12, and for *Brazen Age* as 1610–13; but the Epistle to *Golden Age* describes it as 'the eldest brother of three Ages, that have adventured the Stage' (A2), which implies clearly enough that the *Silver* and *Brazen* Ages were already written and performed by late 1611. *Silver*, moreover, was acted at Court on 12 Jan. 1612. The Epistle to *The Silver Age* announces that 'wee begunne with *Gold*, follow with *Silver*, proceede with *Brasse*, and purpose by Gods grace, to end with *Iron*' (A2); as Chambers says (*Elizabethan Stage*, iii. 345), this clearly implies that the *Iron Age* plays were not yet written.

[95] See Greg, *Bibliography*, i. 316–17.

[96] In the *Golden* and *Silver* Ages, Homer's Chorus begins each act; in the *Brazen*, he appears sometimes before the act-division, sometimes after; in both *Iron* Ages, he disappears altogether. I am tempted to see this uncertainty followed by surrender as evidence that the choruses, taken over from earlier adult practice, did not work particularly well with intervals, and so were experimented with and then abandoned.

natural to assume that the same two companies 'Publickely Acted' it 'uppon one Stage at once'.

The incomplete marking of divisions in the *Silver* and *Brazen Age*, and the error in the former, suggest that act-divisions may not have been marked in these plays; since Homer's appearances divide *The Golden Age* into five acts, the division there might be the printer's. (The divisions in the *Iron Age* plays could have been supplied at any time between 1612 and 1631.) *The Brazen Age* lays a heavy emphasis upon the 'Act' as an intelligible unit of the drama, but this would in any case be clear from Homer's appearances; Heywood and/or his publisher might be trying to exploit the fashion for 'Acts', created by the children's companies and the King's Men, without actually making use of intervals. On the other hand, since the King's Men were using intervals by this time, and collaborated in performing at least one and probably more than one of these plays, their practice might have been adopted on this occasion.[97] Whatever the correct interpretation of this conflicting evidence, Heywood's *Ages* plays probably represent an anomaly, which should not be taken as characteristic of Queen's Men's practice from 1608 to 1615.

Prince Henry's Men, who became Palsgrave's Men, apparently did not employ intervals before 1611: there are no divisions in *2 The Honest Whore* (1604–5), *The Whore of Babylon* (1606–7), or *The Roaring Girl* (1611).[98] The next company play to survive is Thomas Drue's *Duchess of Suffolk* (1624), printed with act-divisions in 1631; the change in company practice could therefore have taken place at any time between 1611 and 1624 (or even 1631).

There remain a few undivided plays of indeterminate provenance. The anonymous manuscript play *Tom a Lincoln* seems to me clearly a public theatre play by a professional dramatist; since it contains echoes of *King Lear* and *The Winter's Tale*, it can be no earlier than 1609–11 (depending on our dating of the latter), but could belong to any adult company other than the King's Men.[99] Harbage and Schoenbaum attribute Robert Daborne's *A Christian Turned Turk* (1609–12) to the 'King's Men (?)' or 'Queen's Revels (?)'; but no clear evidence supports either of these ascriptions. Both companies were using act-intervals at the time the play was written. In 1610 Daborne was a patentee for the Queen's Revels: in 1613

[97] It may not be impertinent to note that the only two companies clearly associated with the *Ages* plays—the King's and Queen's Men—were performing in 'three severall Theaters' at the time of their composition: the Red Bull, the Globe, and Blackfriars. One does not think of the *Ages* as Blackfriars material; but this may be our prejudice, not theirs. See Lavin, 'Second Blackfriars' (see n. 85), 76–81.
[98] Harbage and Schoenbaum date *The Roaring Girl* 1604–10, and place it in 1608; for the more precise later date, see P. A. Mulholland, 'The Date of *The Roaring Girl*', *RES* 28 (1977), 18–31.
[99] My thanks to G. R. Proudfoot, for lending me his transcript of the play, and to whom I also owe the evidence for its date.

he was writing for Henslowe, but threatening to sell a play to the King's Men; he also claims a share in *If This Be Not a Good Play, the Devil is in it* (1611–12, Queen's Men).[100] In these three years he was associated with four companies, and the play could belong to any of them. Harbage argued convincingly that the play clearly belonged to the adult, public theatre repertoire.[101] On the available evidence, *A Christian Turn'd Turk* was probably staged at the Red Bull or the Fortune. By contrast, the quarto-based prompt-book of *A Looking Glass for London and England* (without act-divisions) was probably used for provincial performances in the 1620s: the hand responsible for most of the late additions, and the consistent use of 'clear' at the end of scenes, reinforce each other in pointing to this period.[102] Whether or not the direction specifying 'Mr Reason' belongs to the early or late period of annotation cannot be determined, but Reason was leader of the provincial Prince's company from 1617 to 1625.[103]

Altogether more puzzling is Fletcher and Field's *Four Plays in One*, the only play without act-divisions in the Beaumont and Fletcher canon, and also the only Fletcher play whose provenance is a complete mystery.[104] Field's career, and the pattern of Fletcher's collaborations, strongly suggest that it dates from 1613–19; but from 1616 on both dramatists wrote exclusively for the King's Men, who had clearly adopted act-intervals years before. The absence of act-divisions therefore reinforces R. F. Brinkley's conclusion that the play belongs to the earlier period of their collaboration, writing for Lady Elizabeth's Men (1613–15).[105] But, as already noted, this company seems to have adopted intervals by 1613; in fact, on surviving evidence neither Field nor Fletcher ever wrote for a company which did *not* use intervals, since both of them began their careers with the children's companies, and only moved to the public theatres after the companies in question had adopted intervals. Consequently, even if *Four Plays in One* had been printed from foul papers, one would expect (from these authors) regular act-divisions. However, the play must in fact have been printed either from a prompt-book, or from a manuscript which had been very carefully prepared for performance, with full and professional stage

[100] Chambers, *Elizabethan Stage*, iii. 270–1.
[101] *Shakespeare and the Rival Traditions* (see n. 87), 86.
[102] C. R. Baskerville, 'A Prompt Copy'; *A Looking Glass for London and England*, ed. W. W. Greg, Mal. Soc. Repr. (1932), p. xxix.
[103] Bentley, *Jacobean and Caroline Stage*, ii. 541–3.
[104] Chambers added *Wit at Several Weapons* and *Faithful Friends* (*Elizabeth Stage*, iii. 217), but modern studies all assign the former to Middleton and Rowley, while the Mal. Soc. edn. (1975) dismisses Fletcher's claims to the latter. All of the others wind up in the possession of the King's Men or the Cockpit.
[105] Roberta Florence Brinkley, *Nathan Field, The Actor-Playwright*, Yale Studies in English, 77 (New Haven, Conn., 1928), 131–6.

directions.[106] One can only conclude, therefore, that the play was performed without intervals; indeed, its structure makes it difficult to imagine how an act structure could ever have been imposed on it.[107]
Moreover, it must have been written for Henslowe between March 1613
and 6 January 1616 (when he died), a period of less than three years during which Henslowe had 'broken and dissmembred five Companies', at
different times running operations at four different theatres (Swan,
Whitefriars, Porter's Hall, and Hope).[108] It would appear that, during at
least a part of this chaotic period, Henslowe's public playhouse was
offering plays without act-intervals. It may not be entirely coincidental
that one other Fletcher play written for Lady Elizabeth's Men at about
this time was printed with a confused act notation.[109]

Alternatively, one could conjecture that companies with both public
and private playhouses used intervals only in the private one.[110] But we
have no evidence of such a distinction. Until the 1630s, the Globe and
Blackfriars repertoires seem to have been almost identical; *The Winter's
Tale, Cymbeline, Macbeth*, and *All is True* (all with act-divisions) were
performed at the Globe; the Epilogue of *All is True* in fact refers to spectators who 'come to take their ease, | And sleepe an Act or two' (TLN
3451–2);[111] the second Globe (for which Field and Fletcher wrote, after
1615) already had a music room, and from 1609 on the company clearly
had the resources to provide music during the intervals of a play; plays
performed at the Globe after 1609 contain 'immediate' re-entries across
act-breaks, just as do Blackfriars plays. For the King's Men, at least, no
such schizophrenia between public and private playing seems ever to have
existed, and consequently *Four Plays in One* can hardly be theirs. Since it
therefore seems to belong to Henslowe, 1613–15, some fluctuations in the
practice of his companies must be assumed; what caused it, and how long
it lasted, we cannot guess.

Adult practice changed only gradually, perhaps over the course of as

---

[106] No one seems to have investigated the printer's copy for *Four Plays*, but F omits only
one necessary exit, and has complete and specific directions for entries, action, and props,
including many music cues and calls for entrances above. It also includes much trumpet
music but no evidence of cornetts (which at least suggests an outdoor theatre).

[107] The Induction is too short to constitute Act 1, and consequently the play could only
have had four acts, at best. But the King, Queen, and court remain onstage throughout;
moreover, their comments on each 'play' occur sometimes after and sometimes before the
culminating dumb show to each.

[108] Chambers, *Elizabethan Stage*, ii. 248–60.

[109] See Hans Walter Gabler's Introduction to *Monsieur Thomas*, in *Beaumont and
Fletcher Canon*, iv (1979), 417–20.

[110] See Smith, *Blackfriars Playhouse*, 227–8.

[111] This passage is in fact *OED*'s first citation for *Act* meaning 'One of the main divisions
of a dramatic work' (*sb.* 7). Though this sense of the word was clearly current earlier, one
may at least remark that the Epilogue assumes that even the sort of spectator who sleeps
through plays will know perfectly well, by 1613, what an act is. (Might Fletcher also mean
that the entr'acte music wakes him?)

much as a decade. The King's Men led the way when they moved into the Blackfriars (1609); Lady Elizabeth's Men probably followed when they amalgamated with the Children of the Queen's Revels (March 1613). The Prince's Men, in turn, probably adopted intervals when they amalgamated with the expanded Lady Elizabeth's Men (1614–15). The Queen's Men also systematically adopted the new practice at that time (1614–15), even before they moved into a private playhouse. On the other hand, Palsgrave's Men may not have done so until a decade or more after 1611. Though we cannot be sure, as Jewkes claims, that intervals were 'universal by 1616 at the latest' (p. 92), most established companies had adopted them by then, and all companies formed after 1616 used intervals as a matter of course.

With characteristic civil servant caution, E. K. Chambers opined that the introduction of four intervals in theatrical performances 'might well modify the methods of the dramatist'.[112] Some of these modifications we have already seen: an increased flexibility in providing for the 'immediate' re-entrance of characters, a decline in the use of presenters to demonstrate a play's five-act structure, a corresponding stimulus to 'classical' lyric choruses between the acts. Like the introduction of intervals, these changes brought adult plays closer to academic ideals.

As Suckling wrote, in the Epilogue to *Aglaura* for the Court (1638): 'Plays are like Feasts, and every Act should bee | Another Course, and still varietie' (p. 82). Whether or not late Jacobean and Caroline plays became more episodic or sporadic than their predecessors, they certainly became more sensational, and though this sensationalism (like the academic complacency with which it coexisted) no doubt had many causes, act-intervals can only have exacerbated it. Even though the proscenium arch has gone out of fashion, every theatrical professional still knows what 'a strong curtain' means, and why it matters: in order to sustain an audience's interest across an interval, dramatists endeavour to end each act with some measure of theatrical éclat. The structural bumpiness this produces will be familiar to anyone who has watched American television programmes on the BBC, where they have been stripped of their commercial 'intervals': the peaks and discontinuities of action usually make it all too evident where the commercials originally occurred. The scripts have been designed for interruption.

I do not propose to squeeze a full survey of the structure of late Jacobean and Caroline drama into the postscript of this essay; but its characteristic de-dum de-dum de-dum de-dum de-dum dramatic rhythm can be illustrated by Massinger's *The Roman Actor*. Act 1 ends with the triumphal entry of the Emperor Domitian; Act 2 with his order to 'take

[112] *Elizabethan Stage*, iii. 131.

[Philargus] hence | And hang him instantly'; Act 3 with Aretinus growing
suspicious of Domitia, and promising in an aside to 'find out' her
motives, while Domitilla in the last line of the act looks forward to her
'revenge'; Act 4 with Domitian stabbing Paris, then ordering his glorious
funeral. Likewise, in *The Picture* Sophia ends Act 3 with an impassioned
soliloquy in which she swears to revenge herself; in *The Emperor of the
East* Theodosius ends Act 1 with the transparently foreboding 'From
foule lust heaven guard me'. In *St. Patrick for Ireland*, '*The Devils rejoyc-
ing in a dance conclude the Act*' (E4ᵛ). Examples multiply under every
bush.

To a lesser degree, the beginning of an act also acquires a new impor-
tance. As Granville-Barker observes, 'one may prefer to begin a fresh act
upon a note of revived interest' (*Prefaces*, i. 48). So, in John Mason's *The
Turke*, Act 3 begins with the entrance of '*Timoclea like a Ghost*' (F2). Act
4 of Thomas Killigrew's *The Prisoners* ends with the characters, during a
'*Storme*' at sea, going off stage to enter 'The Long boate'; Act 5 begins
'*Enter Gallippus with Lucanthe tyed to his backe and the knot in his mouth*'
(C7). At the beginning of Act 4 of Shirley's *The Lady of Pleasure*, '*Enter
two men leading Alexander blinded, and goe off suddenly*' (G1ᵛ); Alexander's
pitiful soliloquy follows. Act 5 of Massinger's *The Guardian* brings on
'*Claudio, and all the Banditi (making a guard), Severino and Iolante (with
Oaken-leav'd garlands) and Singers*' (M2) who proceed to sing a song, the
'Entertainment of the Forests Queen'. Again, Act 4 of Dekker's *The
Virgin Martyr*, '*A bed thrust out, Antoninus upon it sicke, with Physitions
about him*'; or Act 3 of *The Witch of Edmonton*, '*Enter Cuddy Banks, and
Morice-dancers*'; or Act 4 of *The Wonder of a Kingdom*: '*Trumpets sounding. Enter Torrenti very brave, betweene the two Dukes, attended by all the
Courtiers, wondring at his costly habit. Enter a mask, women in strang
habitts, Dance. Exit. He gives jewells, and ropes of pearle to the Duke; and
a chaine of gold to every Courtier. Exeunt. Nicholetto and he stay.*' Anyone
casually perusing the late Jacobean and Caroline drama could add many
other anecdotal, impressionistic examples as characteristic as these.

In three extant late prompt-books, act-divisions have been moved, and
the principles behind these shifts of interval can be, in part, discerned. In
The Wasp, the alterations seem designed merely to compensate for the
heavy cutting of two scenes, which would have left the original Acts 2
and 3 disproportionately short. In *The Lady Mother*, though, the beginning of Act 2 has been rewritten; instead of a drunken soliloquy followed
by a drunken sleep, several comic characters enter before the drunk, plot
to play a trick on him, stand aloof when he enters, and speak scurrilous
asides during his soliloquy. The result resembles, in structure if not detail,
the famous gulling-of-Malvolio scene from *Twelfth Night*, and some idea
of how much more dramatic the revision has made the opening of the act
may be gleaned by trying to imagine how much poorer Malvolio's scene

would be without the onstage eavesdroppers. Later in the play, the original twenty-line dialogue between two minor characters at the beginning of Act 4 has been cut, so that the act begins with Lady Marlove's tortured soliloquy; then the beginning of Act 5 has been moved back a scene, so that it too begins with a (contrasting) soliloquy by Lady Marlove—herself the 'Lady Mother' of the title.

These last two, related changes in *The Lady Mother* illustrate the practical application of an obvious dramatic principle. By stopping and then restarting the play four times, a division of performances into five acts lends an extra-dramatic emphasis to each stop and start, and consequently makes it possible to contrast or compare these otherwise unrelated moments. Thus, in Clavell's *The Soddered Citizen*, the beginning of Act 5 has been postponed until one scene later. As a result, Brainwash and Miniona end Act 4, as they had Act 3. Equally important, in the revised structure Undermine and Mountayne begin Act 5, as they had begun Act 3, and ended Act 1; Undermine, moreover, ends Act 2 with a soliloquy, and is one of only two characters onstage at the beginning of Act 1. The moved act-interval simply reinforces Undermine's dominance of the strategic heights of the play's structure, while at the same time supplying the bonus of a link between the endings of Acts 3 and 4. Whoever added the act-divisions to the manuscript of *Woodstock* would seem to have had similar considerations in mind: Act 2 begins with the first entry of '*Richard, Greene, Baggott, Busshy, Scroope, Trisillion, and others*'; Act 3 with the same group '*Very Richly Attyrd* In newe *fashions, & Trissilion whispering wth the King*'; Act 4 with '*Trissilion* [. . .] *& a man wth baggs of money*'—money Trisillion has collected in the King's name, but most of which (as he immediately tells us) he plans to keep for himself.

Shakespeare, Heywood, and Dekker all straddled this revolution in performance practice. So too did Jonson, Middleton, and Fletcher, but these dramatists either wrote most of their early work for the children, or (in Jonson's case) always insisted upon advertising a five-act structure, so the change in practice must have affected them less. Nevertheless, most modern editorial practice unwittingly obscures the distinctions between and within the work of all these major figures. Fredson Bowers's influential edition of Dekker's *Dramatic Works* gives equal, centred prominence to the act-divisions in all the plays, even though those for the early work are editorial—hence obscuring the uninterrupted structure of the early plays and their contrast with the later.[113] His later edition of Marlowe's *Complete Works* relegates act-divisions to the margin, even in the case of *Dido, Queen of Carthage*, written for the children and hence probably performed with four intervals. The new Cambridge edition of

---

[113] See, by contrast, *The Shoemaker's Holiday*, ed. R. L. Smallwood and Stanley Wells (Manchester, 1979), 63–5; they more logically divide the play into scenes only. The Revels Plays are, in general, admirably flexible in the matter of act-division.

The Dramatic Works in the Beaumont and Fletcher Canon also reduces the act-divisions to modest marginalia, although all the works in that canon (except *Four Plays in One*) were written for intervalled performance. The Regents Renaissance Drama Series square-brackets divisions, and shunts them to the side, even when they occur in the copy-text. Most significantly, all previous editions of Shakespeare treat act-divisions in his canon consistently, giving them equal prominence in all the plays or (in most recent editions) marginalizing them all. But there now seems little doubt that, as Dover Wilson and W. T. Jewkes suggested decades ago, Shakespeare's late plays were written for a different convention than his early and middle ones.

Some late plays, in the Shakespeare canon as elsewhere, show less interest in the theatrical use of act-division than others. But most of Shakespeare's late work makes theatrically intelligent, and sometimes structurally subtle, use of the act-break. Modern readers and performers tend to overlook these divisions, and modern critics accept—for the most part silently—Granville-Barker's belief in the artistic advantages of continuous performance; but a brief rehearsal of the act-breaks in Shakespeare's late plays should make it clear that we ignore them to our critical peril.

Coriolanus (probably written in late 1608 or early 1609) may have been the first play Shakespeare planned with the new conditions in mind; certainly, its divisions are theatrically astute. Act 1 ends with Aufidius swearing to wash his fierce hand in Martius's heart; Act 2 with the Plebeians hurrying off to rescind his election as Consul; Act 3 with his banishment; Act 4 with Aufidius pronouncing 'When, Caius, Rome is thine, | Thou art poor'st of all: then shortly art thou mine'. Just as the end of Act 4 echoes the end of Act 1, so the beginning of Act 5 echoes the beginning of Act 2, with Menenius and the Tribunes jibing at each other, and receiving news of Coriolanus's military victories—against Rome, this time, instead of for her. Likewise, Act 3 opens with Coriolanus's entrance as newly elected Consul, surrounded by Menenius, Cominius, *'all the Gentry . . . and other Senators'*; Act 4 opens with him entering, again in the company of Menenius, Cominius, and *'the young Nobility of Rome'*, but now on his way to banishment.

Act 1 of *The Winter's Tale* (1609–11) ends with Polixenes and Camillo planning to flee the city in secret; Act 2 with Leontes awaiting the imminent arrival of the message from Delphi; Act 3 with the shepherds discovering the baby, and narrating the death of Antigonus and his crew; Act 4 (wholly devoted to Bohemian pastoral) with the exit of Autolycus and the shepherds to join the ship bound for Sicily (in which Act 5 takes place). Even Granville-Barker had to admit that, in *The Winter's Tale*, the division into acts is 'not . . . badly done'.[114]

[114] 'Preface' to *The Winter's Tale: An Acting Edition* (London, 1912), as collected in *Prefaces*, vi (1974), 19–25.

In *Cymbeline* (1609–11), Act 1 ends with Innogen's apparent vanquishing of Giacomo, Act 2 with Posthumus cursing her, Act 3 with Roman preparations for the move against Britain, Act 4 with Belarius and his boys preparing for the decisive battle. Granville-Barker concedes that 'This is a fairly well proportioned arrangement; each act has its own chief interest . . . and bears a just relation to the whole' (*Prefaces*, i. 488). He claims that the pauses are not very 'dramatically effective', but admits that the end of Act 1 'leaves us expectant' of Giacomo's trick while 'for a climax and a finish [to Act 2] we are shown its effect upon Posthumus' (p. 487); 'the third act does definitely and emphatically begin a new interest', Acts 3 and 4 both end 'expectantly' looking forward to imminent war or battle, and Act 5 has 'the repentant Posthumus to set it going' (p. 489). Given that Granville-Barker clearly sympathizes with Johnson's description of this play as an 'unresisting heap of imbecility', and wants to attribute as much as possible of it to anyone but Shakespeare, he spares more praise for the act-divisions than one has any reason to expect. Moreover, his fine analysis of the character of Cloten might have been even finer if he had noticed that Cloten begins Acts 2, 3, and 4: the second as an idiot, the third as a patriot, the fourth as a would-be rapist. On this last occasion he enters alone, dressed in Posthumus's clothes; the next act begins with Posthumus, alone—a parallel even more striking if (as has been suggested) one actor played both parts.[115]

In *The Tempest* (1610–11), Act 1 ends with Ferdinand under the control of an apparently hostile Prospero, Act 2 with Caliban's conversion to the worship of Stephano and liquor, Act 3 with Alonso, Sebastian, and Antonio rushing off in a desperate ecstasy, Act 4 with Prospero rejoicing that 'At this hour | Lies at my mercy all mine enemies'. And in *All is True* (1613), Act 1 ends with Henry's fateful meeting with Anne Boleyn, Act 2 with Henry breaking up the court after the aside 'I may perceive | These cardinals trifle with me', Act 3 with Wolsey's final exit, Act 4 with Katherine's. And Act 4 begins with the entry of '*two Gentlemen, meeting one another*', just as they had at the beginning of Act 2, as the characters themselves remark.

> 1 Y'are wel met once againe.
> 2 So are you.
> 1 You come to take your stand heere, and behold
>   The Lady *Anne*, passe from her Corronation.
> 2 'Tis all my businesse. At our last encounter,
>   The Duke of Buckingham came from his Triall.

---

[115] See for instance Stephen Booth, 'Speculations on Doubling in Shakespeare's Plays', in Philip C. McGuire and David A. Samuelson (eds.), *Shakespeare: The Theatrical Dimension* (New York, 1979), 123.

1 'Tis very true. But that time offer'd sorrow,
   This generall joy.

                                                    (TLN 2378–85)

Finally, *The Two Noble Kinsmen* illustrates the variety of uses to which act-divisions may be put. Act 1 ends with a funeral procession, a solemn exit which brings to a close the story of the three queens and their dead husbands, but which also anticipates the end of the play, with its funeral procession for Arcite. Act 2 begins with the first scene of the subplot, and ends with another subplot scene; moreover, in that Scene of Act 2 the audience first learns of the imprisonment of Palamon and Arcite, and in the final scene of Act 2 we learn that Palamon, like Arcite before him, has been freed, so that the entire narrative of their imprisonment and release is contained within the act. The entire action of Act 3 takes place in a few hours, beginning just before dawn on a day when the court ventures into the country to observe 'a solemn rite | They owe bloomed May' (3. 1. 2–3), and ending that afternoon when Arcite and Palamon are discovered by Theseus and his Maying party. Act 3 is also given a visible unity of place by the bush from which Palamon emerges in the first, third, and sixth scenes. Although this property bush might be thrust out before and removed after each Palamon scene, it would be more in keeping with the conventions of the Renaissance theatre to leave it in place from the beginning to the end of the act, where its presence helps to identify the forest locale of all six scenes, and even raises the tantalizing dramatic possibility that the gaoler's daughter may be wandering within a few feet of the man she is searching for. Act 4 resembles Act 1 in that neither Palamon nor Arcite appears onstage at all; it resembles Act 2 by beginning, and ending, with a subplot scene. And Act 5, like Act 1, begins with spectacular ceremonial solemnities—there a wedding procession interrupted by the sequencial appeals of three queens, here a series of three appeals to an onstage altar—and ends with a funeral procession. The artistic intelligence of these act-divisions does not, of course, prove their authenticity; but the divisions in *Kinsmen*, and in Shakespeare's other late plays, certainly do nothing to contradict the other evidence for a change of theatrical convention.

But while the active influence of this new convention creates new dramatic possibilities, which criticism has done little to explore, its retroactive influence creates vexing, and perhaps intractable, problems for editors. Any play of Shakespeare's first published after *c.*1610 may have had act-divisions imposed on it, in accordance with what had since become an accepted convention; moreover, most plays potentially so edited first appear in the Shakespeare First Folio, a volume which may have been particularly influenced by the example of Jonson's First Folio.

On the other hand, any play revived in or after 1609 should have had act-divisions introduced in it; later texts of such plays might easily have the authority of theatrical practice, and perhaps of authorial intention, for their divisions. Of course, most such texts appear—again—in the First Folio.

Before turning to Shakespeare, however, the editorial problem may be clarified by a brief examination of other plays written early but printed late. Jewkes devotes special attention to texts written before but printed after 1616, on the grounds that any divisions in these plays may have been subsequent additions (*Act Division*, 80–95, 299–335). But if we exclude (*a*) printed texts clearly set from a theatrical manuscript associated with a late revival, and (*b*) plays written at a time, between 1609 and 1616, when the company involved had already adopted the regular use of intervals, there remain, according to Jewkes's own analysis, only nine non-Shakespearian plays in which editors or printers may have 'faked' act-divisions: *Lust's Dominion, Grim the Collier of Croydon, Fortune by Land and Sea, The Jew of Malta, The Birth of Merlin, The Royal King and the Loyal Subject, The Wise Woman of Hogsdon, The Tragedy of Hoffman*, and *The Lovesick King*. For three of these (*Malta, Royal King*, and *Hoffman*) publication was prompted by a recent revival; even if the basic manuscript were non-theatrical, the division into acts might, in one or all of these cases, have come from a knowledge or recollection of the revival. Moreover, even if *Malta* were printed from autograph copy, the divisions could have been supplied by Marlowe (one of the University Wits) or by a later adapter (whose presence has recently been strongly supported).[116] The author was certainly responsible for the divisions in *Hogsdon*, for the printer misread them in a way only made possible by an idiosyncrasy of Heywood's handwriting.[117] For *Malta* and *Hogsdon*, at least, editorial interference seems an unnecessary or implausible assumption; it may or may not, on external evidence, have affected *Hoffman* and *Royal King*.

This leaves only five plays in which, on present evidence, editorial interference would *have* to be invoked. One of these is *Lust's Dominion*, a play printed in 1657 and then attributed to Marlowe, but which recent scholarship regards as a Dekker and Marston revision of a Marlowe original. Critics have usually identified it with *The Spanish Moor's Tragedy*, a Marlowe play revamped for Henslowe by Marston, Dekker, Day, and Haughton in 1599–1600. Scattered evidence of Dekker's and Marston's presence can certainly be found; Day and Haughton, however, are either not present or impossible to identify. Moreover, Cyrus Hoy argues, persuasively in my opinion, that a passage in *Satiromastix* (1602) suggests

[116] D. J. Lake, 'Three Seventeenth-Century Revisions: *Thomas of Woodstock, The Jew of Malta*, and *Faustus B*', *N. & Q.* 228 (1983), 133–43.
[117] W. W. Greg, *Collected Papers*, ed. J. C. Maxwell (Oxford, 1966), 161–2.

that Dekker had recently made two *different* adaptations of Marlowe's play, and supplied the second to the boys' company at Paul's. 'Could the Paul's revision have been called *Lust's Dominion*?'[118] I think it could have been, for the extant text not only contains act-divisions, but evidence of theatrical adaptation to allow for an interval. Act 1 closes with a soliloquy by Eleazar, who then apparently exits; Act 2 begins with a group entrance which includes 'Mendoza, *Eleazar with him*'. Yet Mendoza begins the scene talking about Eleazar:

> Why stares this Divell thus, as if pale death
> Had made his eyes the dreadfull messengers
> To carry black destruction to the world.
> Was he not banisht *Spain*?

This speech would clearly make better sense if the group entered while Eleazar was onstage, finishing his soliloquy; it reads awkwardly as it stands, constituting yet another piece of evidence that the extant text represents an incomplete state of the adaptation. But in this case the adaptation seems to have been made at least partly, and perhaps entirely, to accommodate a pause in the performance.[119] Like the difference in title, the apparent absence of Haughton and Day, and the 'lurid', 'rampant sexuality' which characterizes so many seventeenth-century 'children's' plays, this passage strongly suggests that *Lust's Dominion* was the adaptation made for Paul's, not for Henslowe.

If Hoy is right about *Lust's Dominion*, then only four non-Shakespearian plays remain in which editorial provision of act-divisions need be assumed: *The Birth of Merlin, Grim the Collier of Croydon, Fortune by Land and Sea*, and *The Lovesick King*. The first of these, moreover, is of very uncertain date, and should perhaps be excluded. The last two, however, were both printed in 1655 for Robert Pollard and John Sweeting, a coincidence which encourages suspicion: with the two late reprints which introduced unauthorized divisions (discussed above, p. 18), these two 1655 texts constitute our strongest evidence of editorial interference, and to this I would myself add *Hoffman*. Yet although this handful of examples encourages us to be cautious, the very rarity of interference permits us to be cautiously encouraged about the theatrical authenticity of the divisions in most printed texts.

Every play in the Comedies section of the Folio (which, bibliographically, includes *King John* and part of *Richard II*)[120] has act-divisions. Most of these plays were set from late transcripts, or from quartos which

---

[118] *Introductions, Notes, and Commentaries to Texts in 'The Dramatic Works of Thomas Dekker'*, 4 vols. (Cambridge, 1980), iv. 56–72.

[119] I am grateful to John Jowett for pointing out this anomaly.

[120] See Charlton Hinman, *The Printing and Proof-Reading of the Shakespeare First Folio*, 2 vols. (Oxford, 1963).

had been annotated with reference to a prompt-book; their divisions are, at least presumptively, theatrical in origin. Three early plays, however—*The Comedy of Errors, The Taming of the Shrew*, and *All's Well that Ends Well*—were set from what appear to have been non-theatrical early texts; in *Shrew* these divisions seem clearly mistaken, and presumably editorial. Though there is nothing obviously wrong with the divisions in *Errors* and *All's Well*, the evidence of editorial interference in *Shrew*, and the discernible initial desire to provide act-divisions for all the plays, gives us little reason to place much confidence in their authenticity.

The Comedy of Errors, however, was almost certainly performed at, and may well have been written for, Gray's Inn;[121] as with other indoor 'theatres', plays written for the Inns of Court are invariably divided into five acts.[122] Thus *Comedy*'s divisions might well be authoritative, without in any way reflecting early (or late) practice in the outdoor theatres. As for *All's Well*, it seems to me somewhat unlikely that Shakespeare would end Act 4 with Lavatch's 'Faith there's a dozen of em, with delicate fine hats, and most courteous feathers, which bow the head, and nod at everie man' (TLN 2588–90; 4. 5. 103–5), rather than with Helen's 'All's well that ends well, still the fines the Crowne; | What ere the course, the end is the renowne' (TLN 2479–80; 4. 4. 35–6). Not only would division at the end of 4. 4 rather than 4. 5 be more dramatic; it would also set Act 5 entirely in France (as Acts 1 and 2 had been). I therefore suspect that the division in *All's Well* is non-Shakespearian, while that in *Comedy* may result from special circumstances. However, *All's Well* is the only public theatre play written before 1609 which calls in its stage directions for cornetts, an instrument before then very strongly associated with the boys' companies.[123] This fact, and the presence of act-divisions, suggest that the

---

[121] See R. A. Foakes's new Arden edn. (London, 1962), app. II. In *William Shakespeare: A Study of Facts and Problems*, 2 vols. (Oxford, 1930), E. K. Chambers argued that the stage direction at 5. 1. 9, '*Enter Antipholus and Dromio againe*', shows that the action was meant to be continuous, since the two characters left the stage at the end of Act 4 (i. 307); Greg repeated this argument (*First Folio*, 201). But Antipholus and Dromio could never have been onstage for the first 8 ll. of the scene, and in an authorial MS the '*againe*' probably indicates continuous writing rather than continuous performance. Foakes finds no other evidence of editorial or prompter intervention in the text (pp. xi–xvi).

[122] The invariable division into acts might, however, reflect only the academic pretensions of the writers for such a 'theatre'. *Jocasta* and *Gorboduc* have dumb shows, accompanied by music, before each act; *The Misfortunes of Arthur* has, as well as such entr'acte dumb shows, a lyrical chorus at the end of each act. *Gismond of Salerne* also has such lyrical choruses. The only explicit evidence of act-pauses, however, is in the 1591–2 quarto of the revised version of that play, *Tancred and Gismund*: between Acts 2 and 3, but *after* the chorus, occurs the direction *Cantant* (C3ᵛ), which may refer to music during the act-break. However, this text itself represents a literary revision of that performed by the Gentlemen of the Inner Temple *c*.1567, and so constitutes dubious evidence of normal practice in the 1590s.

[123] W. J. Lawrence, *Shakespeare's Workshop* (Oxford, 1928), 48–74. For the cornett, see also David Munrow, *Instruments of the Middle Ages and Renaissance* (Oxford, 1976), 69–70, and Gair, *Children* (see n. 22), 64–5. For the MS behind the Folio text, see *Textual Companion*, 492–3.

foul papers may have been sketchily annotated by a theatrical professional at some later date, perhaps as a preliminary to preparing a new
prompt-book.[124]

After the Comedies, the next play set into type was *Henry V*, in which
the Folio act-divisions are grotesquely inappropriate.[125] At this point a
decision must have been taken not to continue imposing divisions on
manuscripts which had none: *2* and *3 Henry VI* stay undivided, and the
remaining history plays (with divisions) were all set from annotated
quarto copy or transcripts.[126] Four Tragedies are undivided: *Timon* and
Antony and Cleopatra were apparently set from undivided manuscripts,
Romeo was set from an exemplar of Q3 which had been edited minimally
if at all,[127] and *Troilus* was set from a quarto which had been systematically collated with an early prompt-book.[128] *Hamlet*, which marks the
first three scenes and the beginning of Act 2 only, was probably set from
an undivided manuscript, in which an early editorial attempt to provide
divisions was abandoned.[129] The remaining plays in the Tragedies section
are either late plays (*Coriolanus*,[130] *Cymbeline*), or set from theatrical
transcripts (*Caesar*,[131] *Macbeth, Lear, Othello*), or from a quarto annotated by reference to such a transcript (*Titus*). It would thus appear that
(with the exception of the abortive '*Actus Secundus*' in *Hamlet*) *Henry V*

[124] A new prompt-book might need to be prepared because the original had been lost, as
happened with Fletcher's *Bonduca*—for which see W. W. Greg's Mal. Soc. Repr. (Oxford,
1951)—and with Shakespeare's *Winter's Tale*—for which see *The Dramatic Records of Sir
Henry Herbert*, ed. J. Q. Adams (New Haven, Conn., 1971), 25. For another foul-paper text
annotated for a later revival, see Robert Kean Turner's introduction to *The Mad Lover*, in
Beaumont and Fletcher Canon, v. 8.
[125] For specific evidence that the Folio act-divisions in *Henry V* originated in the printing-house, see my Oxford Shakespeare edn. (Oxford, 1982), 15.
[126] For MS consultation in the preparation of Folio *1 Henry IV*, see *Textual Companion*,
331–2.
[127] See S. W. Reid, 'The Editing of Folio *Romeo and Juliet*', *SB* 35 (1982), 43–66.
[128] See Gary Taylor, '*Troilus and Cressida*: Bibliography, Performance, and
Interpretation', *SS* 15 (1983), 99–136.
[129] Most recent editors believe that the MS used or consulted in printing Folio *Hamlet*
was a transcript influenced by late theatrical practice: see for instance Harold Jenkins's new
Arden edn. (London, 1982), 53–74. I find this hypothesis wholly unconvincing, on many
grounds: see my '*King Lear*: The Date and Authorship of the Folio Version', in Gary
Taylor and Michael Warren (eds.), *The Division of the Kingdoms: Shakespeare's Two
Versions of King Lear* (Oxford, 1983; repr. 1986), 405–9, and *Textual Companion*, 399–402.
[130] Intended as the first play in the Tragedies section, *Coriolanus* might have been printed
with editorial divisions: *The Tempest* and *King John* clearly received special treatment, at the
beginning of the two other sections. However, the divisions in *Coriolanus* are so good that I
think they are unlikely to be editorial. Moreover, the provision for cornets in four stage
directions also suggests that the play was written with the new theatrical conditions in mind.
[131] Fredson Bowers has argued that *Caesar* was set from an 'intermediate transcript', mid
way between foul papers and prompt-book: see 'The Copy for Shakespeare's *Julius Caesar*',
Southern Atlantic Bulletin, 43 (1978), 23–36. But much of the evidence for this has been
undermined by John Jowett's 'Ligature Shortage and Speech-Prefix Variation in *Julius
Caesar*', *The Library*, 6/6 (1984), 244–53, and Thomas Clayton's 'Should Brutus Never
Taste of Portia's Death But Once?', *Studies in English Literature*, 23 (1983), 237–55.

is the last Folio play whose act-divisions need be suspected as editorial rather than theatrical in origin.

Of course, most of these plays were originally designed for continuous performance and, even if the Folio act-divisions can claim the uncertain authority of later theatrical revivals, editors would do well to accord them little prominence. It would nevertheless seem sensible and desirable somehow to distinguish divisions with such a claim to theatrical warrant from those in plays like *Timon* and *Antony*, where the standard divisions derive from eighteenth-century editors, whose criteria for act-divisions almost certainly owe nothing to Renaissance practice.

But the most interesting cases are not those where act-divisions were simply slotted in to an existing structure, but those where the structure itself was altered, perhaps in part to accommodate the new convention. *A Midsummer Night's Dream* provides a well-known example of this: the Folio, but not the Quarto, has the lovers '*sleepe all the Act*' (TLN 1507) between 3. 2 and 4. 1. Likewise, in *Titus Andronicus*, the Folio has Act 2 dramatically begin with Aaron's villainous soliloquy; the Quarto instead simply had him remain behind when the others left, making 1. 1 and what is universally called (following the Folio) '2. 1' into one long continuous scene of exposition. This change in staging has other advantages, too: during the resulting interval the monument of the Andronici, called for in 1. 1, could conveniently have been removed while a new set of clothes was set out for Aaron to put on during the soliloquy ('Away with slavish weedes, and idle thoughts, | I will be bright and shine in Pearle and Gold'). The Folio also adds the so-called 'Fly Scene' (3. 2), which provides a most memorable conclusion to Act 3 and which requires an 'immediate' re-entry of several characters across the act-break. The addition itself almost certainly dates from the 1590s,[132] but the Folio act-division (and the resulting re-entry) may well be later.[133]

Measure for Measure and *Othello* may also provide examples of textual revision. Alice Walker has recently argued that 'the song and the opening dialogue' of 4. 1 of *Measure* 'were an interpolation and formed no part of the play as Shakespeare wrote it', but were added soon after *The Tempest* was written.[134] To her arguments may be added the facts (*a*)

---

[132] See Eugene Waith's Oxford Shakespeare edn. (Oxford, 1983), 17–18.

[133] If the first 29 ll. of 4. 1 had been omitted (TLN 1541–72) when 3. 2 was added, then 3. 2 and 4. 1 could naturally have been played continuously. When, many years later, act-intervals became normal practice, this cut (signalled by a line in the left margin) could have been restored. The ending of 3. 2 ('*Lavinia*, goe with me, | Ile to my closset, and goe reade with thee [. . .] Come boy, and goe with me, thy sight is young, | And thou shalt read, when mine begin to dazell' (TLN 1535–9) easily prompts 'How now *Lavinia, Marcus* what meanes this? | Some booke there is that she desires to see' (TLN 1573–4), etc.; but the end of 3. 2 is not so easily reconciled with the apparent ignorance of Marcus and Titus about what Lavinia and the Boy have been doing, evident in the original opening lines of 4. 1 (TLN 1541–72).

[134] 'The Text of *Measure for Measure*', RES 34 (1983), 1–20.

that the same song appears in Fletcher's *Rollo, Duke of Normandy*, and
(*b*) that the alleged interpolation would make a much more striking introduction to Act 4. (For a fuller discussion, see the third chapter of this
book.) Likewise, the Folio text of *Othello* supplies a much more powerful
ending to Act 4 by its addition of Desdemona's famous willow-song.

But *King Lear*, here as elsewhere, presents the most striking evidence of
authorial revision.[135] Hunter's article in fact closes with a discussion of
the critical significance of the act-breaks in *Lear*, but as is usual he discusses the act-breaks in the conflated modern text, rather than the practice of either original.[136] Two of the act-breaks (after Acts 1 and 2) do
not contain significant textual variants—other than the act-breaks themselves, of course.[137] The Quarto of 1608 (*The History of King Lear*) has
no act-divisions: it may seem natural to assume that Shakespeare always
envisaged 'Act One' ending after the fifth scene, but the Folio text (*The
Tragedy of King Lear*) provides our only evidence for this supposition. If
the play was originally intended for continuous performance (as in the
Quarto), then the Folio act-divisions represent subsequent choices about
how to divide up the play, just as those in *Woodstock* do. For instance,
Shakespeare could have ended Act 1 with a direction for Kent to '*sleepe
all the Act*', as happens in Folio *Dream*, and in the Paul's plays *Marriage
of Wit and Science* (*c*.1568) and *Histriomastix* (1599), but he chose
instead to end the first two acts with Lear leaving Goneril's house (1. 5),
then Gloucester's (2. 2). Moreover, he chose to begin Acts 1, 2, 3, and 5
with dialogues referring to or illustrating political division within Lear's
sundered kingdom—a theme the Folio revision elsewhere makes more
prominent than it had been in the Quarto.[138]

But the Folio placing of divisions for the ends of Acts 3 and 4 coexists
with major textual variants. To begin with, the Folio cuts the dialogue of
the two servants at the end of 3. 7, thereby ending Act 3 with Cornwall's
wounded exit, Gloucester's blind exit, and the exit of servants carrying a
dead servant's corpse. One need hardly remark on the dismal effect of the
Folio act-division, when combined with the Folio cut—an effect demonstrated by Peter Brook's famous 1962 production. In another sense, however, the act-division makes the cut possible. If the Quarto text, designed

[135] For the many recent studies of revision in *King Lear*, see *Division*; *Textual
Companion*, 509–42; *The Complete King Lear*, ed. Michael Warren (Berkeley, Calif., 1989);
and Grace Ioppolo, *Revising Shakespeare* (Cambridge, Mass., 1991).
[136] Hunter also assumes modern scene-divisions, at one point (pp. 27–8) invoking the
'Folio' authority of the divisions for 2. 3 and 2. 4, which in fact derive from Steevens; the
Folio (correctly) marks the traditional 2. 2–2. 4 as one scene (as does the Oxford *Complete
Works*).
[137] The Folio-only direction '*Storme still*' at the beginning of Act 3 (TLN 1615) might
seem to suggest continuous performance across the act-break; but compare Heywood's
Captives, where 'Act: 2 Storme contynewed' has been written by the scribe in the margin
opposite 'Explicit Actus prˢ.'
[138] *Division*, 426–7.

for uninterrupted performance, had cut that dialogue at the end of 3. 7, then Gloucester would have had only eleven lines in which to exit, change clothes, put plasters on his eyes, and re-enter.[139] In the Folio, the interval intervenes, and no practical difficulty exists. The textual variant at the end of 3. 7 thus seems doubly related to the Folio's added act-division. Moreover, that act-division lends an extra-dramatic prominence to the soliloquy with which Edgar begins Act 4—thus compensating for the Folio omission of Edgar's soliloquy at the end of 3. 6, and contributing to the Folio's sustained magnification of Edgar's importance.

The end of 4. 6 presents an almost identical situation: the Folio adds an act-division, and cuts the preceding dialogue between Kent and the Gentleman. Just as the Folio had cut the low-key conversation of the two servants in 3. 7, so it cuts a similarly cool post-mortem here, instead ending Act 4 on the peak of emotion and meaning provided by the reunion of Lear and Cordelia. Instead of ending Acts 3 and 4 with two anonymous servants, Kent, and an anonymous Gentleman, the Folio instead contrasts dismal separate exits in 3. 7 with the loving exeunt at the end of 4. 6. Moreover, the act-divisions and the textual variants in concert strongly reinforce the structural parallel between Gloucester and Lear, by placing their contrasted exits at the end of adjacent acts. This is a parallel other Folio variants also underline. The Folio has Lear awaken in a chair, which he compares to being 'bound upon a wheel of fire', as Gloucester was literally bound in a chair and tortured; the Folio, by cutting Edgar's soliloquy at the end of 3. 6, more immediately juxtaposes Gloucester's rescue of Lear there with the 'reward' he earns for it in 3. 7; the Folio makes Lear's death closer (temporally and in kind) to Gloucester's.[140]

Finally, it is worth recalling that the interval between acts was not empty. Even if it were filled with nothing but silence, or the chatter of spectators, that silence or chatter would affect our experience of the play. The evidence suggests that the interval was usually filled with music; but we do not know what kind of music, whether music was always supplied, whether it varied between performances of the same play, whether it commented upon the action of the preceding act, or anticipated the action of the next. Near the end of Act 2 of *The Tragedy of King Lear*, a stage direction calls for '*Storme and Tempest*' (TLN 1584; 2. 2. 457. 1); at the very beginning of Act 3, a stage direction calls for '*Storme still*' (TLN 1615; 3. 1. 0. 1). Does the unusual form of this stage direction mean that the percussive sound effects for the storm continued through the interval? *The Tragedy* cuts eight of the Gentleman's lines, describing the storm, at the beginning of Act 3 (*History*, Sc. 8. 6–14); was the verbal description

---

[139] My attention was drawn to the difficulty of this re-entrance by Kenneth Muir, who played Gloucester to Wilson Knight's Lear in a University of Leeds production.
[140] See *Division*, 136–7, 412–13, 427.

unnecessary, because the audience had just heard a prolonged aural representation of the storm?

If the second interval performed the storm, the fourth was probably more harmonious. Critics have been puzzled by the fact that *The Tragedy*, quite deliberately, deletes the offstage instrumental music, which in *The History* accompanies Cordelia's reawakening of Lear (Sc. 21). This change in staging cannot be due to any paucity of resources in later performances by the King's Men; the company's musical capabilities actually increased after 1608. But what appears to be a cut was probably, in fact, merely a relocation. In *The Tragedy*, the exit of the reunited Lear and Cordelia ends Act 4; it was, in other words, immediately followed by an interval, and intervals were usually musical. If the harmonious music which *The History* supplied for scene 21 were transferred by *The Tragedy* to the succeeding interval, then that musical interlude (following Lear's exit with his good daughter) would have contrasted with a cacophonous 'storm' interlude after Act 2 (following Lear's exit from his bad daughters). And a soothingly musical fourth interval would have reinforced and prolonged the consoling mood of the reunion itself, a mood shattered by the reversals of Act 5.

In imagining the contents of the second and fourth interval, I am, of course, speculating. Speculation is inevitable, because for us the act-intervals in *The Tragedy of King Lear*, and other plays written or revised after 1608, are simply textual holes, performative lacunae, sites of meanings we can only guess at. But in *King Lear* the intervals themselves—which have in the past been simply dismissed, or simply accepted, and in either event taken for granted—are textual variants, and perhaps the variants most important to an understanding of the structure of the revised text.

The act-divisions in Folio *Lear* not only seem clearly related to adjoining textual variants; just as clearly, they seem intertwined with major changes of emphasis evident elsewhere in the Folio text. One can only conclude that the provision of act-divisions and the revision of the text flow from a single creative impulse, and hence that the revision of *King Lear* dates from after the introduction of intervals *c.*1609—a conclusion to which much other evidence also directs us.[141] More important, though, reading between the acts makes it clear that, at the end of his career, Shakespeare regarded act-intervals as elements of dramatic meaning, which we ignore to our cost.

---

[141] See '*King Lear*: The Date and Authorship of the Folio Version', ibid., 351–468.

'Swounds Revisited
Theatrical, Editorial, and Literary Expurgation

by GARY TAYLOR

For the preventing and avoyding of the great Abuse of the Holy Name of God in Stageplayes Interludes Maygames Shewes and such like; Be it enacted by our Soveraigne Lorde the Kinges Majesty, and by the Lordes Spirituall and Temporall, and Cõmons in this p^resent Parliament assembled, and by the authoritie of the same, That if at any tyme or tymes, after the end of this p^resent Session of Parliament, any pson or psons doe or shall in any Stage play Interlude Shewe Maygame or Pageant jestingly or pphanely speake or use the holy Name of God or of Christ Jesus, or of the Holy Ghoste or of the Trinitie, which are not to be spoken but with feare and reverence, shall forfeite for everie such Offence by hym or them cõmitted Tenne Pounde . . .

This 'Acte to restraine Abuses of Players'[1] is itself one of the most notorious abuses of players ever perpetrated by an English Parliament. By making it illegal for an actor to speak upon a stage words he could legally speak when off it, this single paragraph of legislation cut the dramatist off from a part of the language and a part of life. Not a very large part, admittedly: Parliament in 1606 did not yet see fit to cut off the playwright's right hand; only the tip of the index finger of his left. In 1642 Parliament did the logical thing and simply decapitated the offending institution. But although the ethical despotism of 1642 had more dramatic consequences for the health of English drama, the ethical despotism of 1606 did more harm to the works of Shakespeare. Because the 'Acte to restraine Abuses' applied to all future performances, it might apply, *ex post facto*, to all earlier plays, should they be so fortunate (or unfortunate) as to merit a theatrical revival. Parliament not only decreed how the dialect of the tribe should, in future, be transcribed; it also demanded that the past be rewritten. Most of Shakespeare's plays belonged to that unexpurgated past; but many of them were not printed until after 27 May 1606.

Editors have known all this for a long time, and in the confidence of that knowledge they have preferred profane early texts to reformed later ones. But although the validity of such editorial procedures can hardly be doubted, the apparently random expurgation of Folio texts has never been properly explained. As E. K. Chambers observed, more than half a

---

[1] 3 Jac. I, c. 21: 27 May 1606.

century ago, 'whatever degrees of profanity the Act covered, it clearly only related to words spoken on the stage, and not to words put into print. One does not see, then, why the publishers of the First Folio should have gone to the pains of expurgation.'[2]

If one did see, what difference would it make? It would make some difference, first of all, to our understanding of the Jacobean theatrical and publishing industries. Expurgation may result from interference in the theatre after May 1606, interference in the printing-house in 1622–3, or interference by particular scribes at any time up to 1622–3. Who interfered with the text matters, in this instance, as much as the mere fact of interference, for it may tell us a good deal about the transmission of several of the most problematic texts in the Shakespeare First Folio.

It would make some difference, also, to our understanding of several plays—most particularly *King John*, *The Merry Wives of Windsor*, and *Measure for Measure*. Editors have in the past tried to restore profanity removed from the Folio only where they already possess a 'good' early quarto, from which oaths and references to God can be transferred. But expurgation also affected Folio plays for which we possess no early text at all, or only a 'bad' early text; in such cases, the original profanity can be restored only by occasional resort to the 'bad' texts (which editors have been loathe to use) or by conjectural emendation (which editors have been even more loathe to use). The more clearly we understand the process of expurgation, and Shakespeare's own habits before passage of the Act, the more confidently editors can restore corrupted Folio speeches to the state of textual innocence, replete with Shakespearian profanation. Like most editorial piece-work, such restoration will have, in some cases, only a local effect; but in other cases it may enlarge or alter our understanding of characters, scenes, and the structure of dramatic meanings.

In 1953 Alice Walker conjectured that 'the removal of profanity from Folio plays was . . . editorial in inspiration'.[3] This conclusion depends upon an observation Walker had made two years earlier:

Broadly, the dividing line between plays from which profanity was not expurgated and those from which it was lies between the Comedies and the Histories. This corresponds with the break in the printing of the Folio, on which work was begun in 1621 and resumed with *Richard II* in the spring of 1623. In this interval Buc had resigned his office as Master of the Revels and it looks as if whoever prepared the copy for Jaggard anticipated a more rigorous attitude towards profanity in plays from Buc's successor.[4]

A combination of bibliographical and historical evidence thus appears to lend considerable credibility to Walker's hypothesis.

---

[2] Chambers, *William Shakespeare*, i. 329.
[3] Alice Walker, *Textual Problems of the First Folio* (Cambridge, 1953), 31.
[4] Alice Walker, 'Quarto "Copy" and the 1623 Folio: *2 Henry IV*', *RES*, NS 2 (1951), 225.

That hypothesis has, however, been fatally undermined by subsequent bibliographical research. Charlton Hinman in 1963 demonstrated that the interruption of Folio printing was actually much briefer than was once supposed, probably only lasting from mid-July to September of 1622. Buc was officially succeeded by Sir John Ashley on 2 May 1622, sometime in the middle of the printing of the Comedies. Ashley leased the office to Henry Herbert on 20 July 1623; by mid-August all of the Folio, except *Troilus* and the preliminaries, had been set into type.[5] Herbert's strict views about profanity can therefore have had little influence on editorial policy in the First Folio. In any case, although a change of editorial policy might have occurred during a gap of twelve to eighteen months, it is much more difficult to believe that such a change happened between July and September 1622. That break actually fell in the middle of work on *All's Well that Ends Well*. There was another, briefer interruption in December, after work had begun on *Richard II*; but in neither *All's Well* nor *Richard II* can one detect any differences of kind or degree in editorial intervention, in relation to profanity or anything else. Moreover, *All's Well* (which was not expurgated) was set before *King John* (which, as we shall see, was expurgated), but *King John* was set before *Twelfth Night* (which was not expurgated), which in turn was set before *Richard II* (which was expurgated). Neither the historical nor the bibliographical facts support Walker's division between the Comedies and the rest of the volume.

In the Comedies printed from extant good quartos, direct references to God are removed only a handful of times: *Love's Labour's Lost* 5. 2. 317 ('God' → 'Ioue'), *Merchant of Venice* 1. 2. 107 ('I pray God grant' → 'I wish') and 5. 1. 157 ('no Gods my Iudge' → 'but well I know'), *Much Ado* 4. 2. 17–20 (omitting 'Write down, that they hope they serue God: and write God first, for God defend but God shoulde goe before such villaines'), and *A Midsummer Night's Dream* 5. 1. 314–15 (omitting 'he for a man; God warnd vs: she, for a woman; God blesse vs'). The intrusive act-divisions in Folio *Dream*, and the added direction '*They sleepe all the Act*', suggest that the Folio text has been influenced by a manuscript reflecting later theatrical practice; certainly, the added direction specifying 'Tawyer', and the altered and added directions generally, have convinced most editors that the manuscript consulted by Jaggard was a prompt-book.[6] It has also been widely agreed that a number of variants in *Ado* derive from consultation of the prompt-book; since *Much Ado* was performed at Court during the winter season of 1612–13, the prompt-book consulted must have been in use after the passage of the 1606 'Acte to

---

[5] On the dating of Folio composition, see Hinman, *Printing and Proof-Reading*, ii. 520, 528; on Herbert's accession, Greg, *First Folio*, 170.

[6] See *Textual Companion*, 279–80.

restraine Abuses'.[7] The Folio variants in this instance might well reflect late theatrical practice, rather than late interference in the printing-house or by editors preparing copy for the printing-house. The same considerations apply with *Merchant* and *Love's Labour's Lost*. Among the Folio additions to the former is the direction '*Flo. Cornets.*' (2. 7. 77. 1; TLN 1055); as W. J. Lawrence has pointed out, cornetts seem to have been used by the King's Men only after their acquisition of the Blackfriars, late in 1608.[8] What evidence we have therefore suggests that the prompt-book consulted for *Merchant* included alterations made after 1606. In *Love's Labour's Lost* no such evidence is available; nevertheless, Stanley Wells has argued that Folio variants in that text do result from sporadic consultation of a late theatrical text.[9]

The situation in the last two sections of the Folio is more complicated, simply because the nature of Folio annotation fundamentally changed. In the four Comedies set from quarto copy, consultation of the manuscripts was sporadic, confining itself almost entirely to stage directions and speech prefixes, with only occasional emendations of dialogue. In these circumstances it should hardly surprise us that an occasional profanity has been removed, without any attempt to bring the text systematically into line with the 1606 Act: profanity has been treated no differently from any other dialogue variants. Beginning with *Richard II*, a much more thorough consultation of manuscripts began, at least for some texts, leading to the introduction of a good many more authoritative variant verbal readings. Where authoritative readings have been introduced, profanity has been expurgated; where the quarto dialogue has been reprinted without change, profanity too remains unaltered. In *Richard II*, the manuscript consulted must have been in use in 1615 or after, since it had apparently been patched in one place by reference to Q5, printed in that year; profanities are—as we would expect in a late prompt-book—systematically removed.[10] The same thing happens in *Titus Andronicus*. *Titus* was collated against a prompt-book less throughly than *Richard II* had been, but the original text of *Titus* also contained almost no profanity. The one 'Zounds' in Q1 has been removed in the Folio (4. 2. 71; TLN 1755). But the presence, elsewhere in the Folio text, of act-divisions (and of revisions of staging to accommodate such divisions) strongly implies that the prompt-book consulted

---

[7] For Jacobean performances of Shakespeare's plays, see Chambers, *William Shakespeare*, ii. 303–53 (*Ado* 1613, on p. 343).

[8] W. J. Lawrence, *Shakespeare's Workshop* (Boston and New York, 1928), 48–74.

[9] Stanley Wells, 'The Copy for the Folio Text of *Love's Labour's Lost*', *RES*, NS 33 (1982), 137–47.

[10] John Jowett and Gary Taylor, 'Sprinklings of Authority: The Folio Text of *Richard II*', *SB* 38 (1985), 151–200. This article also discusses, at some length, the general pattern of Folio annotation of printed copy.

had been used after 1609, when the King's Men began making regular use of intervals between the acts.[11]

Certainly in *Richard II*, and possibly in *Titus*, Folio expurgation seems to derive (as in the Comedies) from consultation of a late prompt-book. In most of the remaining Histories and Tragedies, expurgation has obviously not been attempted. The Folio texts of *King John*, *Henry V*, and all three *Henry VI* plays contain, between them, 201 instances of the Christian 'God'; *King John* and *Henry V* retain the Folio's only examples of the particularly offensive oaths 'zounds' and 'sblud'.[12]

'Zounds' has been removed in five lines of *Richard III* and *Romeo*. Though *Romeo* was probably collated against a manuscript, its dialogue and stage directions received exceptionally little annotation;[13] alone among Folio plays set from quarto copy it does not have act-divisions. If the manuscript consulted was of theatrical origin, it would thus appear not to have been used after 1609. We must therefore suspect that the removal of 'zounds' in *Romeo* may indeed be an example of purely editorial interference. Such interference is even more probable in *Richard III*, where the Folio text uses 'God' 105 times, yet omits all four examples of 'zounds' found in its quarto copy (1. 4. 122, 1. 4. 142, 3. 7. 209, 5. 5. 162). Such a pattern makes it clear that 'zounds' has been singled out for special treatment, and since the manuscript consulted for *Richard III* seems not to have been a prompt-book (or a copy of one), we can only conclude that the animus against 'zounds' was editorial, rather than theatrical.[14] Theoretically the editor in question could have been a scribe, who prepared the manuscript consulted by the Folio annotator; but since the same pattern (retention of 'God', removal of 'zounds') also occurs in the Folio texts of *Titus* and *Romeo*, it would be far simpler to suppose that the special treatment of 'zounds' is the work of a single editor, involved in the preparation of all three Folio texts.

Jaggard's compositors seem unlikely to have reformed the text on their own initiative, especially as three different workmen (A, B, and E) set the lines from which 'zounds' was omitted.[15] Of course, the compositors may have been given a general instruction to remove 'zounds'. But Compositor B left the word standing at *King John* 782 (2. 1. 467), set from manuscript copy; either the alleged general instruction had not been given, or Compositor B blundered, or (as seems more probable) the word was left standing because the manuscript had not been 'edited' in the printing-house, as marked-up quartos had to be.

---

[11] *Textual Companion*, 115, 209; see also Ch. 1, above. The Quarto of *Titus* was reprinted in 1611; it has been plausibly suggested that such reprints of play quartos might have often coincided with revivals.

[12] Francis A. Shirley, *Swearing and Perjury in Shakespeare's Plays* (London, 1979), 22.

[13] S. W. Reid, 'The Editing of Folio *Romeo and Juliet*', *SB* 35 (1982), 43–66.

[14] *Textual Companion*, 230.

[15] For compositor attributions throughout the Folio see *Textual Companion*, 148–54.

The setting of *Richard III* was interrupted by the beginning of work on the Tragedies: composition moved from *Richard III* to *Coriolanus*, *Titus*, and *Romeo*, then back to *Richard III*, *All is True*, and *Romeo*. *Coriolanus* and *All is True* were both set from manuscript copy, and should have received little editorial preparation. The copy for *Titus* and *Romeo* would, therefore, probably have been prepared for the compositors very soon after that for *Richard III*. It should hardly surprise us if the idiosyncratic censorship of a single editor has, minimally, affected all three texts. The same editor was presumably responsible for the Folio's omission of another line in *Richard III*, 'By Christs deare bloud shed for our grieuous sinnes' (1. 4. 185). Like 'zounds' (meaning 'God's wounds') this line refers not to God but to Christ, and in particular to Christ's crucifixion; it also occurs in the same scene as two of the uses of 'zounds' omitted by the Folio. 'Zounds', then, or any other specific reference to the crucifixion, may have fallen victim to editorial interference in the printing-house. Even in this very restricted instance, however, the danger of editorial interference seems to have been greatest in plays set from quarto copy, which would need to be specially prepared by an editor transferring readings from a manuscript to his quarto; in plays set from manuscript copy (*King John*, *Henry V*), such expletives are left standing. Moreover, no difference in the treatment of profanity can be discerned between the Comedies and the rest of the volume: the Histories and Tragedies contain numerous examples of profanity, and the removal of profanity in *Richard II* seems to be merely a function of more extensive collation against a late prompt-book.

Another, independent test of the incidence of profanity in Folio plays strongly confirms this analysis. In most of the Shakespeare quartos apparently set from authoritative manuscripts, 'God' (in various inflexions) heavily predominates over 'heaven(s)'. In Table 1 I have only counted instances of 'God' (or 'God's') which refer to the Christian deity, and instances of 'heaven(s)' which could substitute for 'God'. Three of the four apparent anomalies (asterisked in the table) have pre-Christian settings. Noticeably, even in the early *Titus* and *Dream* Shakespeare made much less use of 'God' than normal, and all his later classical plays are even more sparing (see Table 2).

Theoretically, the later texts in this group may have suffered posthumous theatrical or editorial expurgation, but the very consistency of the pattern for all nine plays makes it likely that Shakespeare made some effort at historical accuracy. At the very least, it would be unsafe to regard the use of 'God' in his late classical plays as characteristic of Shakespeare's practice elsewhere. If, therefore, we set the quartos of these plays aside, in only one of the eleven remaining good quartos does 'heaven' predominate over 'God'. The exception—*Othello*—is the latest of these quartos, and apparently set from a scribal transcript. The possibility

TABLE 1. *Profanity in Shakespeare quartos set from authoritative manuscripts*

Quarto	God('s)	Heaven(s)
Titus (1594)	7	6
Richard II (1597)	61	11
LLL (1598)	33	9
1 Henry IV (1598)	49	0
Romeo (1599)	34	8
Dream (1600)	6	1
Merchant (1600)	20	5
2 Henry IV (1600)	64	8
Ado (1600)	65	0
Hamlet (1604)	27	18
****Lear* (1608)	1?	8
****Troilus* (1609)	6	9
Othello (1622)	21	35
****Kinsmen* (1634)	2	8

TABLE 2. *Profanity in Shakespeare's late classical plays*

Text	God('s)	Heaven(s)
Caesar (1623)	0	0
Troilus (1609)	6	9
Timon (1623)	0	4
Lear (1608)	1?	8
Antony (1623)	1	1
Pericles (1609)	3	8
Coriolanus (1623)	2	3
Cymbeline (1623)	0	13
Kinsmen (1634)	2	8

of scribal or editorial substitution perhaps makes Quarto *Othello* suspect evidence of Shakespeare's normal practice; in particular, its date (1622) and provenance (scribal) bring it much closer to most First Folio texts than to any of the other good quartos.

In the ten quartos which do apparently constitute reliable evidence of Shakespeare's pre-1606 practice, 'God' predominates over synonymous uses of 'heaven(s)' by 366 to 66; even if we include the figures from *Othello*, the figures are 387 to 101. Except for plays with classical settings, no good quarto uses 'God' less than twenty times. The three Folio plays most probably set from foul papers mirror this pattern (see Table 3*a*).

These texts seem to have suffered no editorial expurgation in Jaggard's printing-house. The first tetralogy also emerges unscathed (see Table 3*b*). Most of the Folio Comedies were set from annotated quarto copy, or from transcripts made by Ralph Crane. I have already observed that the occasional expurgation in the former group probably resulted from sporadic consultation of late prompt-books, and the Crane transcripts raise potential difficulties of interpretation which I will discuss in due course. For the moment, I will simply exclude Crane's work. The remaining Folio Comedies all contain the usual Shakespearian preponderance of 'God' (see Table 3*c*). These Comedies betray no more evidence of editorial expurgation than do the Folio foul-paper texts, or the Folio texts of the first tetralogy.[16] Like the evidence already assembled, this test confirms that the printers or publishers of the Folio did little to expurgate their copy; instead, they reproduced profanity as they happened to find it in the materials available to them.

TABLE 3. *Profanity in some Shakespeare Folio plays*

		God('s)	Heaven(s)
(*a*)	*Comedy*	14	1
	All's Well	20	14
	Henry V	71	3
(*b*)	*1 Henry VI*	25	7
	Contention	61	7
	Duke of York	36	8
	Richard III	105	18
(*c*)	*As You Like It*	22	7
	Shrew	19	2
	Twelfth Night	17	4

Chambers had noted that 'In *King John* the examples of "Heaven" markedly outnumber those of "God"'.[17] This pattern obviously contrasts with the Shakespearian norm, and we have already seen that the discrepancy can hardly be due to printing-house interference. In fact, it can be demonstrated with some confidence that it results from scribal interfer-

---

[16] Chambers suggested that 'Sir Toby Belch swears less and more mildly than one would expect, and the use of "Jove" is common' (*William Shakespeare*, i. 241; see also 406), and Shirley repeats this claim (pp. 51–2); but in both cases this seems to derive from a belief that 'Sir Toby seems mild in comparison to Falstaff' (Shirley). But Shakespeare might have been anxious to make Toby *un*like Falstaff. Moreover, the allegedly suspicious 'Jove' occurs less often than 'God'.

[17] Chambers, *William Shakespeare*, 241.

ence. The spelling of the exclamation 'oh' and a number of other words, coupled with the unusual use of round brackets in stage directions, strongly suggest that the copy for *King John* was prepared by two different scribes ('X' and 'Y'), whose work can also be differentiated by their treatment of profanity.[18] The section by X (lines 1–1893) has 'God' 9 times and 'Heaven' 27 times, whereas Y (lines 1941–2729) has no instances of 'God' but 8 of Heaven. Both scribes expurgated the text, as is clear not only from the general figures but by two clear examples, one in the work of each scribe (my italics):

> But as we, vnder heauen, are supreame head,
> So vnder *him* . . .
>
>   (TLN 1082–3; 3. 1. 81–2)
>
> Where heauen *he* knowes how we shall answer him
>   (TLN 2670; 5. 7. 60)

In both cases the subsequent use of the personal pronoun makes it obvious that 'heauen' has been substituted for Shakespeare's 'God', and editors have confidently emended. But although both scribes expurgated the text, the first did so much less systematically than the second. Scribe X retained the only nine occurences of 'God' in the text and also left one 'Zounds' intact (TLN 782; 2. 1. 467); Scribe Y removed all traces of 'God', just as in other respects he imposed his personality on the text more systematically than did his colleague. The pattern of profanity in *King John* thus reinforces the existing evidence for mixed scribal copy, and exonerates the Folio compositors and editors of any responsibility for the text's expurgation.

But why was profanity removed from the manuscript? In 1955 Greg concluded that the manuscript might have been either foul papers or a prompt-book; more recent editors have inclined to describe it as foul papers.[19] The foul-paper hypothesis must now be rejected, but the new evidence of scribal interference by no means demonstrates that the resulting manuscript was a prompt-book: it might be a scribal transcript of Shakespeare's foul papers. That transcript would have to have been prepared in or after 1606, for the removal of profanity seems to have been the work of the two scribes: if a later hand had expurgated a pre-existing manuscript we should not expect that expurgation to vary so dramatically between the shares of the two scribes who prepared that manuscript. The copy for the Folio therefore can hardly have been a normal 'intermediate transcript', between the author's completion of the foul papers and the preparation of the original prompt-book, at some time in the 1590s; if it were such an intermediate transcript, it must instead have been prepared

---

[18] See App. II.

[19] Greg, *First Folio*, 248–53; in their eds. of *King John*, both E. A. J. Honigmann (New Arden, 1954) and R. L. Smallwood (New Penguin, 1974) argued for foul papers.

for a revival, after the original prompt-book had been lost. Alternatively, it may have been a private transcript, prepared between 1606 and 1622, either for a patron or for use in the First Folio. English history dictated that *King John* must be the first play in the Histories section of the Folio; given the prominence fortuitously accorded it by such chronological primacy, the publishers might have wanted to ensure that it was set from a suitably polished literary text. Both *The Tempest* (certainly) and *Coriolanus* (probably) seem to have been chosen to introduce their respective sections of the volume with some such considerations in mind. The manuscript from which *King John* was set was thus either (*a*) a prompt-book still in use after May 1606; or (*b*) an intermediate transcript, antecedent to the preparation of a new prompt-book after May 1606; or (*c*) a private transcript; or (*d*) a transcript especially prepared for use by the Folio printers. The first two explanations leave the expurgation as a natural corollary of changed theatrical practice after May 1606; the last two force us to assume a tradition of purely literary expurgation.

The first explanation can probably be ruled out. The Folio text contains an exceptional number of irregularities of reference, in both speech prefixes and stage directions; equally important, it does not contain any evidence at all of theatrical use, in the form of actors' names, specification of properties, or advance warnings for certain actors or entrances. In combination these confusions and lacunae do not encourage the hypothesis that a prompt-book was used. Nor do we have any evidence for late revivals of *King John*, which seems to have been one of the least popular of Shakespeare's plays. On balance, it seems probable that (as recent editors agree) *King John* was not set from a prompt-book; some sort of transcript of the foul papers is much more likely. But a late private transcript also seems relatively unlikely, given the play's apparent unpopularity. Of course, the play may have been revived at some time between 1606 and 1622, and as a result of that revival a suitably important somebody may have asked for a copy. But why copy the old foul papers? On this hypothesis the prompt-book must have been available. Why, if a handsome presentation copy were required, split the job between two scribes? Why does the resulting text bear so little resemblance, in its level of punctuation and care of presentation, to other Folio texts apparently set from special transcripts? Why should the play be partially expurgated for such a patron? In so far as a private transcript may be distinguished from other sorts of manuscript, the *King John* manuscript would appear not to have been one.

This process of elimination, if valid, leaves us with only two options: a late 'intermediate transcript' or a transcript especially prepared for Jaggard's use. In fact the manuscript could have been prepared to serve both purposes. In 1622 *King John* was a relatively unpopular play at least twenty-five years old; the company might, in the circumstances, no longer

possess the original prompt-book.[20] The publishers might reasonably prefer a new transcript in the place of foul papers a quarter of a century old;
nor may the company have wanted to part with their only manuscript.
But if such a transcript had to be made for Jaggard's compositors, then it
would be in the company's interest to prepare a transcript which could be
made the basis of a new prompt-book if they chose to revive the play. A
revival of *King John* may have seemed a particularly attractive possibility
in 1621–2: England was again, for the first time since 1604, deeply
engrossed in continental wars, particularly in a struggle dominated by (on
the English side) strong anti-Catholic feeling, prompted by (on the
Protestant side) an usurpation. Such a revival may in fact never have
materialized, but in the circumstances the company would have been
foolish not to consider the potential theatrical usefulness of the manuscript they supplied (and perhaps prepared) for Jaggard. In preparing a
transcript with such theatrical uses in mind, the scribes should have been
particularly concerned to regularize the messy stage directions and speech
prefixes which could have been expected in Shakespeare's foul papers, to
supply at least one feature presumably missing from the foul papers (act-
divisions), and to remove one feature presumably present in the foul
papers (profanity).

The act-divisions in the Folio text have in fact been bungled, but the
bungling probably originated—as Greg suggested—in the printing-house.
Certainly, no theatrical scribe would call for a first act of 874 lines, and a
second of only 74. All editors since Rowe have agreed that Act 2 should
begin with the play's second scene, rather than (as in the Folio) its third.
What the Folio identifies as '*Scaena Secunda*' (of Act 1) is in fact '*Actus
Secundus*'; what the Folio identifies as '*Actus Secundus*' could thus have
been '*Scaena Secunda*' (of Act 2). In these circumstances, any compositor
might have confused one '2' with the other. The Folio's '*Actus Secundus*'
was set by Compositor B (a4^v); soon afterwards Compositor C first set
'*Actus Tertius, Scaena prima*' (a5), then '*Scaena Secunda*' (a2).
Compositor B's error on a4^v may have been facilitated by the fact that
his block of copy for that page ended at the beginning of Act 3: *Actus* is
his catchword at the bottom of a4^v, and under its influence he may have
unconsciously substituted '*Actus*' for the '*Scaena*' of his copy. Even more
probably, the copy itself may have had nothing but the number, perhaps
but by no means necessarily with some abbreviation beside it ('sc.II',
'II.2.', 'ii.ii', or '2.2', which he might have misunderstood as an uninten-
tional repetition).

Compositor B could, one way or another, easily have committed the
original error of identifying 2. 2 as the beginning of '*Actus Secundus*'.

[20] The King's Men certainly had mislaid their prompt-book of *Winter's Tale* (a much
more recent play) by 1623: see *Textual Companion*, 601.

Compositor C, on the other hand, should not, in the normal course of human incompetence, have independently made the complementary error of identifying 2. 1 as '*Scaena Secunda*'. Admittedly, in his case, too, the error would have been easy enough, either because a marginal 'ii' was ambiguous, or because he mentally transposed numbers in his copy, or found them already physically transposed in the copy itself ('i.ii' instead of 'ii.i'). But one would expect Compositor B's original error somehow to have caused Compositor C's subsequent blunder. Before he set a2 and its forme-mate a5^v, Compositor C distributed the very first forme in *King John* set by Compositor B (a3^v and a4). These pages must, therefore, already have been machined before C set a2. The next forme set had been that which included a4^v, with the '*Actus Secundus*' error; this would probably have been machined while C was actually setting a2, if not somewhat earlier. Certainly, the third forme set (a2^v and a5) was distributed by C after he set a2 and a5^v. By the time Compositor C finished setting the forme which contained the beginning of the play's second scene, the first three formes had apparently already been run. This means that a foul proof of Compositor C's a2 (containing the correct '*Actus Secundus. Scaena prima*') would have been pulled not long after Compositor B's a4^v (containing the incorrect '*Actus Secundus*') had been printed, and a pressman or proof-reader might easily have noticed that *King John* now contained *two* pages graced with a prominent '*Actus Secundus*'. One of these pages had already been run, and the heading thus could only be altered by throwing away the thousand or so copies of forme a4^v:a3 already printed, and rerunning the (corrected) forme.[21] Alternatively, it would be possible to alter the heading on a2, which had not yet been run. Of course a conscientious modern editor would insist on the former course, but Hinman's study of Folio press-correction has amply demonstrated that Folio proof-correctors were more often concerned with appearance than reality. Even if the corrector did consult copy, he might have chosen the easier course. If Compositor C had originally set the correct '*Actus Secundus. Scaena prima*' on a2, that reading might easily have been deliberately miscorrected, in proof, in order to conform with Compositor B's earlier error, now already in print.

I have dwelt at such length upon the mechanics of this error because Greg offered a different explanation, which seems to me less satisfactory.[22]

---

[21] This account of the sequence of setting is based upon Hinman. A. R. Braunmuller, in his Oxford edn. of *King John*, offers a detailed bibliographical reconsideration of the act-division problem here (pp. 27–36), drawing in part upon a draft text of this essay; however, Braunmuller had not seen Ch. 1 (or the discussion of the dating of *John* in *Textual Companion*) when his edn. went to press. He therefore considers 'the imposer of act divisions' to have been 'a non-authorial, perhaps non-theatrical' agent.

[22] Greg, *First Folio*, 250.

All we need suppose is that in the manuscript handed to the printer the second act was accidentally headed 'Scaena Secunda' instead of 'Actus Secundus'. The printer would naturally reproduce the incorrect heading, and would next find himself confronted with 'Actus Tertius'. All he could do would be to convert this into 'Actus Secundus', and then alter III.ii to III.i and so on.

But this reconstruction presupposes seriatim setting, during which a2 would have been set before a4^v, a5, or a6. In fact, the erroneous identification of the play's third scene as '*Actus Secundus*' occurred long before the printer was 'confronted with' the alleged error 'Scaena Secunda' at the beginning of Act 2. Greg is thus probably right in attributing the confusion to the printer, but undoubtedly wrong in explaining how it arose.

Moreover, Greg's error makes considerable difference in editing the play. If Greg were right, editors would be justified in following Theobald, who rejected the Folio's identification of the beginning of Act 3: the position of '*Actus Tertius, Scaena Prima*' in the Folio is, according to Greg, a consequence of the original error on a2. But since Greg is wrong, R. G. White and E. A. J. Honigmann are almost certainly right in arguing that the confusion over Act 2 in no way invalidates the Folio heading for Act 3.[23] That direction by no means indicates that Shakespeare intended an interval (or even a scene-break) after TLN 996: he presumably intended no interval at all. But whoever prepared the manuscript from which the Folio was printed did intend Act 2 to end with Constance throwing herself upon the ground:

> here I and sorrowes sit,
> Heere is my Throne, bid kings come bow to it.

No one would deny the melodramatic effectiveness of such a conclusion to the act. The Folio division may not represent Shakespeare's intentions, but it does almost certainly correctly reproduce what stood in the manuscript.

If the Folio division for Act 3 *does* reflect a division in the manuscript, then that manuscript must have been influenced by late theatrical intentions (whether realized or not). All other evidence suggests that Shakespeare himself did not indicate act-divisions in his early

---

[23] Braunmuller nevertheless opts for the traditional arrangement, while admitting that the division for Act 3 certainly stood in the MS. His first reason for adhering to Theobald is that it 'permits easy cross-reference'—surely somewhat dubious, since the Arden and the Oxford *Complete Works* both revert to F; unanimity of reference is already impossible, and always a poor reason for emending a text. Second, he claims that 'either arrangement requires an important distortion of the Folio as printed'; but in fact Braunmuller reconstructs the staging in the same way as the Oxford *Complete Works*. Third, he argues that his division 'accepts less of what is demonstrably wrong, confused, or uncertain in the Folio'. I do not know what he means; the one thing demonstrably certain, and theatrically sensible, in F, is its division for Act 3. That division is probably not authorial—but then, neither are the other act-divisions in *John*, or in many other Folio plays, where editors preserve them.

manuscripts; even if he had done so, we would not expect him to mark the beginning of a new structural unit in the middle of a continuous scene. Nor should a literary scribe have committed such a blunder. Unauthoritative or mistaken act-divisions in Folio *Shrew*, *Henry V*, and *Hamlet*, all of which may be the work of Folio editors, at least have the elementary good sense to occur between scenes. We would hardly expect Shakespeare, a literary scribe, or a Folio editor to have placed an act-division where Folio *John* puts it. On the other hand, the Shakespeare canon itself contains three accepted examples of the interpolation of a late act-interval in what was originally a continuous scene (*Titus* Act 2, *Dream* Act 3 and Act 4). The Folio division for Act 3 only makes sense in a manuscript prepared for use in a late Jacobean playhouse, and this conclusion strongly encourages the suspicion that the Folio text was printed from a manuscript with strong theatrical connections.

The expurgation of profanity from *King John* was, if this reconstruction is correct, neither the work of Jaggard's shop, nor the work of scribes specially expurgating a manuscript for use by that shop; it instead arose because the manuscript was intended to serve a dual function as Folio copy and as the basis for a new prompt-book, should a revival be undertaken. The manuscript was an unusually 'late' transcript, which was sent to the printers before use as the new prompt-book of a projected revival. The expurgation of profanity could have been theatrical in intention, even if that intention never matured into practice.

So far, with the probable exception of the omission of 'zounds' in three plays set from annotated quarto copy, all of the Folio expurgation of profanity can be attributed to theatrical practice. This is, after all, very much what we should expect: profanity had been outlawed from public performances, not private manuscripts or printed texts. Editorial expurgation would not normally fall within the brief of Jacobean compositors and editors, and on the basis of thirty-two of the thirty-six plays in the First Folio we can confidently say that we have no evidence that ('zounds' excepted) Jaggard's shop was responsible for any of the expurgation of the texts it printed. This conclusion should be of the greatest importance in evaluating the evidence of the remaining four texts: *1 Henry IV*, *2 Henry IV*, *Hamlet*, and *Othello*.

All four plays were written before 1606, and all four survive in a good quarto as well as the Folio itself. In the Folio versions of all four much profanity has been removed, though in *Hamlet* the expurgation is considerably less thorough than in the other three. On the evidence of the rest of the Folio, this wholesale expurgation cannot have been performed by anyone in Jaggard's shop, nor does it seem likely that it was performed for Jaggard's benefit. Walker believed that all four Folio texts were set from annotated quarto copy; in these circumstances, an editor of some kind would have had to go through the texts carefully, collating the quarto against his manuscript, and he could easily make some editorial changes of his own.[24] But recent scholarship has produced forceful bibliographical evidence that neither *Hamlet* nor *Othello* was set from quarto copy;[25] similarly persuasive evidence can be adduced to demonstrate that Folio *2 Henry IV* was also set from manuscript copy. (See Appendix I.) These three plays should therefore have received only the usual minimum of printing-house preparation. For *2 Henry IV*, *Hamlet*, and *Othello* the hypothesis of printing-house expurgation has nothing to recommend it.

Even in the case of *1 Henry IV*, Alice Walker's bibliographical assumptions have been critically undermined. Walker attributed most of the substantive variation between Folio *1 Henry IV* and its quarto copy to compositorial error; Paul Werstine's more extensive examination of Compositor B's errors has rendered her thesis untenable.[26] Moreover, both Sidney Reid and John Jowett have independently concluded that, even if we disregard the excision of profanity, some consultaton of a manuscript source for variant readings in Folio *1 Henry IV* must be presumed.[27] One cannot easily determine, for *1 Henry IV*, what kind of manuscript the Folio editor consulted, but the availability and use of a manuscript simply increases the probability that the expurgation of profanity derives from the manuscript, rather than the Folio editors. If that expurgation originated in the printing-house, *1 Henry IV* would be, in terms of the First Folio, inexplicably unique.

I will not attempt to solve, in passing, all of the problems raised by the Folio texts of *2 Henry IV*, *Othello*, and *Hamlet*. But none of these texts appears to have been set directly from a prompt-book. The complete absence of necessary music cues from Folio *Othello* (including some present in the Quarto) makes it hard to believe that the printer's copy could have been the prompt-book itself. No editor since Dover Wilson has believed that Folio *Hamlet* was set from a prompt-book;[28] nor does the absence of regular act-divisions or the presence of scene-divisions encourage us to believe that the Folio text represents late theatrical practice.[29] In short, the expurgation of profanity in the Folio texts of those two

[24] Walker, *Textual Problems* (throughout).

[25] Gary Taylor, 'The Folio Copy for *Hamlet, King Lear*, and *Othello*', *SQ*, 34 (1983), 44–61, and 'Folio Compositors and Folio Copy: *King Lear* and its Context', *PBSA* 79 (1985), 17–74; MacD. P. Jackson, 'Printer's Copy for the First Folio Text of *Othello*: The Evidence of Misreadings', *The Library*, 6/9 (1987), 262–7.

[26] Paul Werstine, 'Compositor B of the Shakespeare First Folio', *Analytical and Enumerative Bibliography*, 2 (1978), 241–63.

[27] S. W. Reid, 'The Folio *1 Henry IV* and its Copy' (forthcoming); for Jowett, see *Textual Companion*, 331–2, and 'The Thieves in *1 Henry IV*', *RES*, NS 38 (1987), 325–33.

[28] See the edns. by T. J. B. Spencer (New Penguin, 1980), Harold Jenkins (New Arden, 1982), Philip Edwards (New Cambridge, 1985), and G. R. Hibbard (Oxford, 1987), as well as *Textual Companion*, 399.

[29] See Ch. 1 and 'Post-Script', pp. 239–41.

plays would appear not to have originated in the printing-house, but instead occurred in a manuscript which was not a prompt-book; it might therefore represent deliberate 'literary' bowdlerizing.

The problems of *Othello* and *Hamlet* may be resolved more easily if we begin with *2 Henry IV*. Everyone agrees that Folio *2 Henry IV* derives from an unusual private transcript, but that transcript could have been made from the prompt-book, and indeed most investigators have assumed that it was. Eleanor Prosser, however, has recently denied this assumption, claiming instead that the Folio text shows no evidence of familiarity with stage practice.[30] This assertion is a single but essential cog in a much more elaborate mechanism, designed to explain all of the variants between Quarto and Folio as the work of (*a*) error in the Quarto, (*b*) scribal interference, and (*c*) exceptional compositorial error and interference in the Folio. No one but Prosser seems to believe that all the parts of this mechanism work, but her denial of stage influence has been sympathetically received.[31]

Like everyone else, Prosser argues that the scribe who prepared the manuscript was unusually officious and, as with the plays set from Crane transcripts, this officiousness makes it unusually difficult to determine what the scribe himself was copying. The scribe consistently removes mutes, supernumeraries, offstage sound effects, and descriptive material from stage directions, even when these are specified in Q and hence, presumably, in the author's foul papers as well as the prompt-book. Such deficiences must therefore, as Prosser recognizes, be scribal in origin, and hence tell us nothing about the scribe's own copy. Likewise, the fact that the Folio text contains one 'unquestionable' massed entry, presumably of scribal origin, prohibits us from denying that other massed entries may be intended. Prosser alleges that another eight inaccurate entrances in the Folio text result from the scribe's misinterpretation of the action, a misinterpretation which would have been impossible if he were working from the prompt-book; in fact all eight could result equally well from a tendency to mass entrances at the beginning of a scene. Likewise, Prosser makes much of the fact (pp. 21, 46) that the Folio omits directions for three pairs of exits and re-entrances. But Greg noted the tendency of prompt-books not to signal such re-entrances, or the exits associated with them.[32] Hence, none of these deficiences in the Folio manuscript militates

---

[30] Eleanor Prosser, *Shakespeare's Anonymous Editors: Scribe and Compositor in the Folio Text of '2 Henry IV'* (Stanford, Calif., 1981), 19–50.

[31] See George Walton Williams, 'Textual Studies', *Shakespeare Survey 35* (Cambridge, 1982), 181, and Thomas L. Berger's review in *SS* 15 (1982), 369–80. Giorgio Melchiori's New Cambridge edn. of *2 Henry IV* (1989) accepts and amplifies Prosser's conclusion, in an extremely complicated textual hypothesis which seems to me quite mad. It is based upon principles which I have criticized elsewhere in relation to *Hamlet* (*Textual Companion*, 401–2).

[32] Greg, *First Folio*, 133.

against its derivation from a prompt-book, for they can all be explained as pecularities of the scribe or acceptable deficiencies in the prompt-book itself.

Several features of the Folio text support the orthodox hypothesis, that the transcript was influenced by and probably derives from a theatrical manuscript. At one point Prosser herself must conjecture that 'Silence may have been added [to the Folio entrance direction for 5. 1] because of the scribe's memory of a stage performance' (p. 23). Here theatrical influence has been admitted by the back door, and it would be altogether simpler to suppose that this theatrical feature of the Folio text results from normal manuscript transmission via the prompt-book. Prosser must also admit that five Folio corrections of Quarto speech prefixes are 'unquestionably valid' (p. 32). Three of these corrections Prosser attributes to the unaided acumen of the scribe; but even if we accept such arguments, two exceptions remain. For one of these (the penultimate line of 3. 1), Prosser must conjecture that the Quarto attribution of the speech to the Archbishop was a deliberate editorial alteration, in Valentine Simmes's printing-house; in addition, she conjectures that the scribe had access to the foul papers, from which Simmes had originally set the text. Neither of these conjectures can lay much claim to intrinsic probability, and if a manuscript in any case must be consulted then the prompt-book would have served the purpose rather more economically than the foul papers. (Prosser in fact asserts that, throughout, the scribe had access to and made use of both the printed Quarto and the foul papers.) Of the first three speech-prefix corrections Prosser claimed that 'Any alert editor should' have been able to infer the proper Folio reading; for the fifth, she thinks manuscript consultation possible, but believes that a 'really alert editor' could have done without it. Prosser must also dismiss two other Folio revisions, which have to most editors suggested stage practice. At 1. 1. 161 the Quarto gives a line to an otherwise non-existent 'Vmfr.', presumably Umfrevile; the Folio cuts the line. Prosser does not approve of this solution, but admits that no alternative is entirely satisfactory either (p. 36).[33] Likewise, at 3. 2. 55 Prosser approves of the Folio's insertion of a speech prefix, but again attributes it to scribal perspicacity and 'decorum' rather than access to a prompt-book. Of course, the possible intelligence of an unidentified scribe can be disproven no more easily than it can be proven, but Prosser requires an unusually intense collocation of stupidity and shrewdness. Moreover, it is hard to accept her claim that *none* of the verbal variation between Quarto and Folio results from authorial revision, or at least from consultation of a manuscript different in some respects from the foul papers. If access to such a revised manuscript must be postulated at any point, then at every

---

[33] Giorgio Melchiori gives the line, conjecturally, to Morton: see 'Sir John Umfrevile in *Henry IV*, Part 2, I. i. 169–79', *real* 2 (1984), 199–210; see Jowett's analysis in *Textual Companion*, 354–5.

other point it becomes likelier that Folio variants derive from the scribe's copy, not the scribe's mother wit.

Prosser has even more difficulty in discounting the theatrical origins of three major Folio changes in staging. First, in the rebel entry at the beginning of 4. 1, the Quarto includes Bardolfe, who has no role in the scene; the Folio replaces him with Colevile (who has no role either, but who is thus identified as an important party to the rebel cause, *before* his encounter with Falstaff in the next scene). Prosser believes that the Folio change cannot be right, asking, 'if [Colevile] accompanies the doomed rebels, how does he escape John's grasp to meet Falstaff on the open field?' (p. 41). But Colevile can conveniently exit at TLN 2175 (4. 1. 297), where the spoken instruction 'Hie thee, captain' is followed by the direction '*Exit*'. The captain in question never need return, and the 1964 Royal Shakespeare Company production in fact handled Colevile in exactly this way. In order to avoid this straightforward piece of staging Prosser must conjecture that the scribe first overlooked the necessary '*Exeunt*' at the end of 4. 1, consequently did not perceive the scene-break, consequently called for Colevile to enter at the beginning of 4. 1, then later corrected his original error, supplied the necessary '*Exeunt*', supplied a second entrance for Colevile, but did not remove the offending entrance at the beginning of 4. 1. This complex and unprovable hypothesis is necessary simply in order to dismiss *one* of the many Folio variants which suggest access to a theatrical manuscript.

At the opening of 2. 4, the Folio text 'does indeed solve three of the problems' in the Quarto's version of the dialogue of the drawers; 'By good luck' the resulting rearrangement solves yet another problem; 'Only incidentally' it also reduces the number of actors required from three to two (p. 43). Yet Prosser again attributes all of this careful rearrangement to the scribe's desire to solve 'logical, not dramatic problems'. She rejects the Folio solution because she finds it critically unsatisfactory: she prefers instead her own conjectural alteration of the Quarto. For similar reasons she resists a series of Folio alterations in the final scene, though in that instance even she admits 'a possibility that the revisions could reflect adaptation for the stage', admitting too that the Quarto text raises dramatic problems not easily resolvable in any other way (pp. 46–8).

Prosser's case against the Folio text's derivation from a prompt-book thus depends upon (*a*) misinformation about the treatment of re-entrances in contemporary prompt-books, (*b*) the assertion that some missed entrances are intentional, whereas others are mere errors, (*c*) the conjecture that at one point the scribe drew upon personal memories of a performance, (*d*) the belief that the scribe could have corrected a number of errors in Quarto speech-prefixes on his own initiative, (*e*) the assumption that the scribe had access both to the printed quarto and the foul papers from which it had been printed, (*f*) the conjecture that Colevile's

appearance in 4. 1 results from a complicated series of errors and miscor-
rections, rather than from intelligible theatrical practice, (*g*) the rejection
of Folio solutions to a number of recognized dramatic difficulties in the
Quarto, for which no other more attractive alternative is forthcoming,
and (*h*) the rejection of Folio solutions to recognized dramatic difficulties
in the Quarto, in favour of conjectural emendations of Prosser's own.
This wheelbarrow of conjecture does not seem to me to constitute a reasonable or credible alternative to the common-sense hypothesis that the
scribe of *2 Henry IV* was copying a prompt-book. Since most scholars
agree that *2 Henry IV* was performed at Court in the winter of 1612–13,
such a prompt-book was probably in use after 1606.

The Folio text of *2 Henry IV* may therefore derive from a transcript of
a late, expurgated prompt-book. That transcript almost certainly went
much further in the expurgation of mild profanity than the prompt-book
itself; it also cleaned the text of much vulgarity (sexual and otherwise)
and colloquialism. But if, as seems probable, the Folio derives, at one
remove, from the prompt-book itself, then we cannot responsibly distinguish between the expurgation undertaken in the theatre and the expurgation undertaken by the scribe. After all, even in the theatre some scribes
may have been more zealous than others about 'taking the name of the
Lord thy God in vain'. Even without the evidence of the two scribes in
King John, the light of mere common sense would guide us to such conclusions. Nor can we be sure that the scribe himself was responsible for
the removal of everything that has been removed. A private transcript
must have been owned and presumably read by a private reader, who
may himself have cleaned the text of language he considered offensive.

Finally, if we accept that certain variants between Quarto and Folio
represent deliberate alterations between the foul papers and the prompt-
book, then in *2 Henry IV* as in other plays the possibility of authorial
revision arises. In *Lear* almost certainly, and in *Othello* possibly,
Shakespeare appears to have revised the play at some time after its original composition and performance. We cannot rule out the possibility that
such revision may also have affected Folio *2 Henry IV*. If so, then the
thoroughgoing expurgation of the text might be Shakespeare's own
doing, during the course of a revision in 1606 or later. Certainly, the
nature of the substitutions in Folio *2 Henry IV* is often more characteristic of an author than a simple censor. Elsewhere in the Folio, expurgation
confines itself either to simple excision or to simple substitutions of
'Heaven' for 'God'. But in Folio *2 Henry IV* the process is more inven-
tive and conscientious (see Table 4). In several cases the expurgator has
attempted to ensure that the original function of the oath in Q has been
served, at least partially, by a weaker but acceptable alternative. Because
all of these substitutions occur in prose, they cannot have been caused
by the need to patch the metre of an expurgated line, and they reveal a

TABLE 4. *Substitutions in Folio* 2 Henry IV

	Quarto	Folio
2. 2. 57	By this light	Nay
2. 2. 62	by the masse	Looke, looke
2. 4. 17	By the mas	Then
2. 4. 52	By my troth	Why
2. 4. 271	By my troth	Nay truely
3. 2. 38	By my troth	Truly Cousin
3. 2. 82	by my troth	Trust me
3. 2. 172	Fore God	Trust me
3. 2. 189	by my troth	in good troth
4. 2. 46	by the Lord	I sweare
5. 2. 50	by my faith	to speake truth

sensitivity to the rhythms of prose which is elsewhere noticeably absent in the scribe's decolloquializing of Shakespeare's text.

If the expurgation of Folio *2 Henry IV* may derive, at one remove, from a late prompt-book, so may the expurgation of Folio *1 Henry IV*. Alice Walker suggested that the scribal transcript of *2 Henry IV* may have been half of a pair of manuscripts, prepared for a single patron, of both *Henry IV* plays. Walker identified the other half of the pair as the manuscript from which the Quarto text of *1 Henry IV* had been printed.[34] But the Quarto text of *1 Henry IV* shares few of the more remarkable and disabling features of Folio *2 Henry IV*. To take only the pertinent issue of profanity, the contrast between them is remarkable: 'God' has completely disappeared from Folio *2 Henry IV*, but shows up in Quarto *1 Henry IV* forty-nine times. But though Quarto *1 Henry IV* and Folio *2 Henry IV* can hardly be siblings, the idea of a matched set of *Henry IV* transcripts has much to recommend it, particularly if we seek the matching manuscript of *Part 1* behind the Folio rather than the Quarto text. Walker did not consider this possibility because she denied that any of the Folio variants in *1 Henry IV* had manuscript authority. We can now say with some confidence that the expurgation of profanity from Folio *1 Henry IV* was not editorial or compositorial, and that some manuscript source for variant readings was consulted. Unfortunately, the collation of variant readings was, as often elsewhere in the Folio, lamentably less than systematic. Nevertheless, from those Folio variants which do apparently derive from consultation of a second source, we can conclude that the manuscript Jaggard consulted had been thoroughly expurgated, contained

[34] Walker, *Textual Problems*, 109.

some clear corrections of erroneous Quarto speech-prefixes (2. 5. 174–81), contained stage directions which were somewhat sparser and less descriptive than their Quarto counterparts, contained at least one 'mass entry' (1. 2. 0; TLN 113–14), and tended to substitute *if* for *and* (2. 4. 21, 3. 3. 151). All of these characteristics the manuscript consulted for Folio *1 Henry IV* shares with the manuscript from which Folio *2 Henry IV* was directly printed.

Some or all expurgation of profanity from Folio *2 Henry IV* may be theatrical in origin, and the same conclusion applies with equal force to Folio *1 Henry IV*, whether or not the Folio editors consulted a companion manuscript of that play. We cannot prove that the expurgation in either play originated in the theatre; nor, however, can we prove that it did not.

The probability of authorial revision complicates the pattern in the two remaining Folio texts which have suffered some expurgation, *Hamlet* and *Othello*. Most editors have regarded the Folio as a superior text of *Othello*, and the textual variants there have been strongly defended as authorial revisions. (Whether these revisions were undertaken before or after the original performances we have, as yet, no way of knowing.) In *King Lear* a substantial authorial revision seems to have occurred in 1609–10, several years after the original composition. *King Lear* was probably originally written nor long after *Othello*, and one can easily imagine Shakespeare revising *Othello* for a revival in or after 1606. Any manuscript of such a revision would presumably take account of the profanity statute, and hence the Folio may have been set from a non-theatrical text of the revised version, written at some time after 1606. *Othello* may have been expurgated in the Folio because the play had been substantially revised after passage of the 'Acte to restrain Abuses'.

Alternatively, the Folio text of *Othello* may simply derive from a prompt-book in use after 1606. As noted earlier, the total absence of music cues makes it difficult to believe that Jaggard printed his text directly from the King's Men's prompt-book; but a scribe, preparing a 'literary' transcript, might have deliberately removed such directions from his copy. Like Folio *Othello*, Folio *2 Henry IV* contains no directions for offstage sound effects; nor do the Folio texts of *Two Gentlemen*, *Merry Wives*, *Measure for Measure*, *The Winter's Tale*, or *Cymbeline*. The last five plays were all apparently set from transcripts by Ralph Crane. Crane's hand also seems to lie behind the Folio text of *The Tempest*, which is—in a different way—equally anomalous in its treatment of sound effects.

2–3	*A tempestuous noise of Thunder and lightning heard*
45	*A cry within*
70	*A confused noyse within*

862	*playing solemne Musicke*
1038–9	*(a noyse of | Thunder heard)*
1223	*Sings drunkenly*
1535	*Solemne and strange Musicke*
1583	*Thunder and lightning*
1616	*He vanishes in Thunder: then (to soft Musicke)*
1716	*Soft musick*
1817–18	*a strange hollow and confused noyse*
1929	*A noyse of Hunters heard*
2018	*Solemne musicke*

Most of these directions are neither Shakespearian nor theatrical in form, and (like other peculiarities in the stage directions) they almost certainly represent the scribe's effort to provide a literary substitute for the theatrical effect.[35] But most other Folio texts apparently set from literary transcripts adopt the complementary alternative of removing such 'theatrical' cues from their texts altogether. Certainly, the absence of such directions from literary transcripts can tell us nothing about the manuscript underlying the transcript.

All of the printed texts apparently set from Shakespeare's own papers—the good quartos, and the Folio texts of *Comedy*, *All's Well*, *Henry V*, and *Timon*—contain directions for offstage sounds: alarum, chambers, flourish, knock, music, noise, sennet, and trumpet all occur. Unless we assert that each of these texts had been sporadically attacked by the bookkeeper, we must accept that Shakespeare, a deeply professional actor and dramatist, made some notes for sound effects in his own manuscript drafts. Consequently, the complete absence of such directions from *Two Gentlemen*, *Merry Wives*, *Measure for Measure*, *Winter's Tale*, *Cymbeline*, *2 Henry IV*, and *Othello* must result from deliberate scribal excision: it testifies to the active intervention of a scribe, rather than his passive reflection of the manuscript he set out to copy.

As with the two *Henry IV* plays, the expurgation of Folio *Othello* may derive, at one remove, from late theatrical practice: either the promptbook itself, or an authorial revision completed after May 1606. All the Folio texts which have suffered expurgation, except *Hamlet*, either certainly derive from late theatrical texts, or may have done so. We might, as in *Othello* and *Lear*, conjecture that the numerous textual variants between Quarto and Folio *Hamlet* result from a late authorial revision. But why should a number of the Folio verbal variants be reflected in Q1, a memorial reconstruction printed in 1603? In *Hamlet*, the hypothesis of late authorial revision creates more problems than it solves.

[35] See John Jowett, 'New Created Creatures: Ralph Crane and the Stage Directions in *The Tempest*', *Shakespeare Survey 36* (Cambridge, 1983), 107–20.

TABLE 5. *Profanity in Folio* Hamlet

Hamlet	TLN	Q2	Folio	Q1
1. 1. 54	70	God	God	God
1. 2. 132	316	o God, God	O God, O God	O God
1. 2. 150	334	**God**	**Heauen**	**God**
1. 2. 195	386	**Gods**	**Heauens**	**Gods**
1. 5. 24	708	**God**	**Heauen**	**God**
1. 5. 187	883	God	God	God
2. 1. 69	962	God buy ye	God buy you	Well
2. 1. 77	972	**God**	**Heauen**	–
2. 2. 45	1069	God	God	God
2. 2. 174	1209	God	God	×
2. 2. 223	1266	God	God	×
2. 2. 256	1300	×	God	×
2. 2. 418	1462	God	God	God
2. 2. 430	1472	God	God	God
2. 2. 469	1507	god	God	God
2. 2. 532	1570	God['s]	God[']s	O
2. 2. 551	1589	God	God	×
3. 1. 146	1799	God	God	God
3. 1. 148	1800	God['s]	God[']s	God[']s
3. 2. 119	1978	O God	Oh God	Who I
3. 2. 361	2243	God	God	God
4. 5. 43	2786	God	God	×
4. 5. 197	2948	**God a mercy**	**Gramercy**	**God a mercy**
4. 5. 198	2949	–	I pray God	I pray God
4. 5. 199	2950	**o God**	**you Gods**	–
4. 6. 6	2979	God	God	×
5. 1. 79	3271	God	God	×
5. 1. 270	3470	God	God	×
5. 2. 296	3830	**God**	**good**	**fie**

Even if we restrict ourselves to the issue of profanity itself, Folio *Hamlet* bears little resemblance to other expurgated texts. (In Table 5, possible examples of Folio expurgation are printed in bold type. When a text simply omits the offending word, the expurgation is signalled by a dash; 'X' means that it lacks the entire relevant passage.)[36]

The Folio provides substitutes for seven examples of Quarto 'God', while leaving nineteen intact, and actually adding another (TLN 2949; 4. 5. 198). The addition, however, occurs in the middle of two alleged cases

[36] In addition, the Folio changes Q2's 'God night . . . god night, god night' into 'Good night . . . good night' (TLN 2809–10; 4. 5. 71–2), but that almost certainly represents nothing more than a spelling variant. The opposite variant occurs at l. 2784, where Q2 'good dild' becomes 'God dil'd'. See *OED*, and *Titus* 4. 2. 51 'God night'.

of Folio expurgation, 'Gramercy' (TLN 2948; 4. 5. 197) and 'you Gods' (TLN 2950; 4. 5. 199). One would not expect an expurgator to add profanity in one line while removing it from the line before and after. In fact, 'gramercy' occurs four times elsewhere, all in apparently unexpurgated texts (Quarto *Merchant*, Quarto *Titus*, Folio *Timon*, Folio *Richard III*); it might easily represent an indifferent variant. Both texts of *Hamlet* have the imprecation 'you gods' again at l. 1533 (2. 2. 495), where expurgation cannot be suspected; consequently, this variant too may be authorial in origin. As for the change from 'O God *Horatio*' to 'Oh good *Horatio*' (TLN 3830; 5. 2. 296), not only do both readings make dramatic sense, but either could result from simple compositorial or scribal error (as at *Henry V* 4. 7. 113). In almost 3,000 lines from TLN 1069 to 3906, Quarto 'God' disappears from the Folio on only three occasions; none of the three can be confidently attributed to expurgation rather than error, or authorial revision. These lines also contain no act- or scene-divisions. They betray, in short, no symptoms of use in the theatre after 1606.

In the first part of the Folio text, by contrast, God is altered four times out of nine, and the Quarto oath 'By the masse' (TLN 944; 2. 1. 50) omitted. Of course, even here the expurgation has hardly been thorough; it does not begin to match the standards of *King John*, *Richard II*, *1 Henry IV*, *2 Henry IV*, or *Othello*. Moreover, this haphazard reformation of the text must reflect the manuscript itself. So long as Folio *Hamlet* appeared to have been set from a marked-up exemplar of Q2, an editor could allege that the Folio's failure to remove some profanity resulted from inefficient collation of Q2 against the manuscript. But the new evidence that Folio *Hamlet* was set directly from a manuscript rules out this explanation, leaving us with a little over a thousand lines of text which seem to have suffered some degree of expurgation. These lines also contain an act-division ('*Actus Secundus*', sensibly placed and followed by all editors) and three correct scene-divisions (for 1. 2, 1. 3, and 2. 2). These lines also contain most of the errors common to Q2 and F: 'designe' (Q2 'desseigne') for 'designd' (TLN 111; 1. 1. 93), 'Whereas' for 'Where as' (TLN 400; 1. 2. 209), 'wits' for 'wit' (TLN 730; 1. 5. 43). G. R. Hibbard has shown that almost all of the other suspected errors shared by Q2 and F are in fact legitimate readings or mere spelling variants.[37] The apparent distribution of shared errors may be coincidence, and it does after all depend upon editorial judgements about the authenticity of some shared readings. However, that distribution reinforces suspicions that the first thousand or so lines of Folio *Hamlet* may have been treated somewhat differently from the rest.

---

[37] G. R. Hibbard, 'Common Errors and Unusual Spellings in *Hamlet* Q2 and F', *RES*, NS 37 (1986), 55–61; see also *Textual Companion*, 397.

Nevertheless, the amount of deliberate expurgations even in the first 1,000 lines should not be exaggerated. The treatment of 'God' and 'heauen(s)' as virtual synonyms creates a situation which encourages substitution of one for the other, by scribes or compositors or even authors. Although such innocent substitution cannot reasonably account for the wholesale expurgation of texts, it may be sufficient to explain the scattering of variants in Folio *Hamlet. Richard III* offers three examples of such inadvertent substitution. 'God' occurs in the Folio text 105 times, proving that no deliberate expurgation of the word took place; yet 'heauen' has clearly been substituted for Shakespeare's word at least twice:

> *Rich.* Why, then, by Heauen.
> *Qu.* Hea[u]ens wrong is most of all:
> If thou didd'st feare to breake an Oath with him,
> (TLN 3165–7; 4. 4. 308)

On the other hand, the 1597 Quarto once elsewhere has 'heauen' where the Folio reads 'God' (TLN 2070; 3. 4. 97); since the Quarto cannot have been consciously expurgated, the variant presumably results from inadvertent substitution, by the Quarto reporter or compositor. Such substitutions would have been particularly easy for Folio Compositor B after he had worked on *Richard II* and *1 Henry IV*, where a good many examples of 'God' in his quarto copy must have been altered by hand to 'heauen(s)'. Compositor B was not only responsible for the double substitution of 'Heauen[s]' in *Richard III*; he may also have been responsible for two of the four substitutions of 'Heauen' in the first thousand lines of Folio *Hamlet* (TLN 334, 708; 1. 2. 150, 1. 5. 24).

Authorial substitution cannot be so easily demonstrated. Substantial authorial revision has been most widely suspected in *King Lear, Troilus and Cressida, Othello*, and *2 Henry IV*; the first two, having classical settings, seldom invoke a singular Christian 'God', while the last two have in the Folio been systematically expurgated. None of these four plays can provide us with clear evidence that Shakespeare, in revising a play before 1606, may have treated 'God' and 'heauen(s)' as synonyms, which he occasionally interchanged. But Shakespeare's good quartos do demonstrate his frequent use of 'heauen(s)' in places where 'God' would do just as well. In Q2 of *Hamlet* itself, he uses the strong 'God' only half again as often as the weaker 'Heauen(s)'. Given that the apparently pointless substitution of synonyms characterizes all the other revised plays, Folio *Hamlet* itself, and authorial revision in all periods, we can hardly rule out the possibility that Shakespeare himself, in copying out or revising *Hamlet*, changed 'God' to 'Heauen(s)' once or twice.

In conclusion, I think it more likely than not that the manuscript from which Folio *Hamlet* was set was an innocent transcription, faithful to the profanity it found, and that the text's very few apparent expurgations result from a combination of authorial revision, scribal inadvertence, and compositorial error, rather than any deliberate policy of sanctification. Four variants, however, almost certainly resulted from editorial interference. The Folio omits both Quarto instances of 's'bloud' (TLN 1422, 2240; 2. 2. 366, 3. 2. 357) and 's'wounds' (TLN 1616, 3471; 2. 2, 577, 5. 1. 272). Given the Folio's sensitivity to any such profane allusion to Christ's crucifixion, evident in the specific expurgation of such expressions in *Richard III*, *Titus Andronicus*, and *Romeo and Juliet*, one must suspect that these oaths in *Hamlet* were also deleted by an editor or proof-reader, one either working in or preparing copy for the printing-house. All four, noticeably, fall in the latter portion of the text, where the complete tolerance of 'God' gives us little reason whatever to suspect theatrical expurgation.

'But whatever degrees of profanity the Act covered, it clearly only related to words spoken on the stage, and not to words put into print. One does not see, then, why the publishers of the First Folio should have gone to the pains of expurgation.'[38] The answer to this conundrum, posed by E. K. Chambers half a century ago, is simple: the publishers of the First Folio only went to the pains of expurgation when they were setting directly from, or consulting, a manuscript which reflected theatrical practice after May 1606. With the exception of profane allusions to Christ's crucifixion, none of the expurgation of Folio texts seems to have originated in the printing-house—and even that restricted degree of editorial interference only began after the setting of both *Henry IV* texts, half-way through work on the volume. No Folio text apparently deriving from a late prompt-book contains any significant amount of profanity; no text apparently derived from foul papers, or an early transcript, has suffered any significant amount of expurgation; every text which has been expurgated either certainly did or might well reflect late theatrical practice. We can be reasonably confident that neither Jaggard, nor his partners in the publishing syndicate, set out to rid the First Folio of references to the Christian God.

Equally, unless we receive very strong evidence to the contrary, we must assume that heavily expurgated Folio texts (like *1* and *2 Henry IV*, and *Othello*), which *might* derive from late prompt-books, indeed *do* derive from late prompt-books. The fact that these texts show signs of having been set from literary transcripts does little to diminish the force of this fiat, for we have no evidence that literary transcripts in this period were purged of their expressive irreverence. W. W. Greg's earliest exam-

---

[38] Chambers, *William Shakespeare*, i. 329.

ples of purely editorial expurgation date from 1628–30, all the work of a particular publisher (not a member of the First Folio syndicate).[39] Greg also recorded, in a footnote, the fact that Fredson Bowers had noted some editorial expurgation in the 1618 and 1624 reprints of *The Shoemaker's Holiday*. But again, the publisher was not part of the Folio syndicate, and the alleged expurgation in fact consists of only two variants:[40] 4. 4. 40, 'as true as Gods in heauen' Q1–3, 'as true as you are L. Major' Q4 (1624); 4. 4. 111, 'Gods nailes' Q1–2, ''snailes' Q3 (1618). No reprint makes more than one change, and only the second occurs before the First Folio had been published. Noticeably, this single 1618 expurgation affects, as with 'zounds' and 's'blood', an allusion to Christ's crucifixion. *The Shoemaker's Holiday* does not provide any evidence for the early existence of a purely 'literary' tradition of expurgation. And the only other example of possible printing-house expurgation I have encountered occurs in the 1638 reprint of Massinger's *The Bondman*, which accidentally or deliberately omits the phrase 'Hell confound it' (2. 2. 142).[41]

Nevertheless, Folio texts set from private transcripts pose special problems, because those transcripts theoretically might have been affected by the requirements or preferences of the particular patron for whom they were prepared. George Walton Williams, for instance, suggested that the matching set of *Henry IV* transcripts was specially prepared for the Cobham family.[42] This particular hypothesis seems relatively unlikely, since Cobham was disgraced twenty years before the publication of the Folio, and spent the rest of his life in the Tower; his title died with him. Nevertheless, Williams's suggestion illustrates the potential influence of an unknown (and probably forever unknowable) patron.

Both *Henry IV* texts, *Othello* and *Hamlet* probably derive from private transcripts. In the case of *Hamlet*, the copyright to the extant Quarto text was held by a member of the Folio syndicate: the publishers could have reprinted Q2 or Q3 with little alteration, or could have set the Folio text from an annotated quarto, corrected and revised after consultation of the company's prompt-book. They chose to do neither, even though Q2 *Hamlet* was a good quarto, almost certainly set from Shakespeare's own papers, almost certainly officially released by the King's Men themselves in order to correct the false impression created by the 'bad' quarto of 1603. Why should they have gone to the trouble? Probably, in part,

[39] Greg, *First Folio*, 151–2.

[40] See the Historical Collation in *The Dramatic Works of Thomas Dekker*, ed. Fredson Bowers, 4 vols. (Cambridge, 1953), i. 98–104.

[41] *The Plays and Poems of Philip Massinger*, ed. Philip Edwards and Colin Gibson, 5 vols. (Oxford, 1978), i. 343. The only other changes to the reprint which may reflect an expurgating sensibility are subsitutions of 'Pox' for 'Plague' in imprecations at 1. 3. 374, 2. 2. 14, 2. 2. 143.

[42] George Walton Williams, 'The Text of 2 *Henry IV*: Facts and Problems', *SS* 9 (1976), 179–80.

because they knew that they had a later revision of the play, which might therefore be reasonably regarded as a better reflection of the author's final intentions; but perhaps also because the manuscript in their possession was tidy, elegant, and literary in format. Such a manuscript can hardly have been specially prepared for use by the Folio printers: they already had Q2. Equally, it can hardly represent an 'intermediate transcript', half-way between foul papers and prompt-book. If the many variants result from authorial revision, Shakespeare himself *must* have written out the intermediate transcript; yet the evidence of 'oh' spellings demonstrates that the manuscript behind Folio *Hamlet* was not in his own handwriting.[43] Of course, one might contend that the variants do not result from revision; but one can hardly imagine that Shakespeare or the company would have tolerated such massive incompetence or interference in a scribe instrumental in preparing the prompt-book of any play. We are thus driven to the conclusion that the manuscript must have been a private transcript. Since our earliest references to Shakespeare's *Hamlet* are Gabriel Harvey's note of its commendation by 'the wiser sort' and Q1's declaration that it had been performed at Oxford and Cambridge, the possible existence of such a transcript should astonish no one. Likewise, *Othello* was played at Court in 1604 and at Oxford in 1610; *1 Henry IV* was the most famous and popular of Shakespeare's plays. Manuscripts of all these plays might easily have been in some demand at some point before 1623.

It would be convenient to attribute the expurgation of profanity and colloquialism in *2 Henry IV*, *Hamlet*, and *Othello* to a single interfering scribe, who also probably prepared the manuscript consulted for Folio *1 Henry IV*. But any such hypothesis runs into formidable difficulties. *Othello* strongly prefers 'Oh'; *2 Henry IV* as strongly prefers 'O'; *Hamlet* prefers 'Oh', but much less consistently than *Othello*. *2 Henry IV* changes 'and' to 'if' more than two dozen times; *Hamlet* and *Othello* make the same change only six times between them. *Othello* has 31 exclamation marks, *Hamlet* only 17, and *2 Henry IV* only 8; *Hamlet* 44 round brackets, *Othello* 137, *2 Henry IV* 272. Neither *Hamlet* nor *Othello* comes anywhere near the exceptional number of hyphens in *2 Henry IV*. *Hamlet* preserves almost all of Shakespeare's profanity, contains many directions for offstage sounds, and lacks full act- and scene-divisions. The same scribe can hardly have been responsible for all three texts; nor, indeed, is one scribe likely to have been responsible for any two of the three. We seem to be confronted by three different scribes: one for *2 Henry IV* (and perhaps *1 Henry IV*), another for *Hamlet*, and a third for *Othello*. Of course, all of the transcripts may have been prepared for a single patron—but any such conclusion would be easier to accept if the texts

---

[43] See App. II.

had more in common than they do. We cannot prove that neither *Othello* nor *Henry IV* was expurgated for a particular patron; but we certainly cannot prove that they were, and the easy availability of an alternative explanation does not encourage me to try.

Why, after all, should a 'literary' transcript preclude profanity? Roman and Greek plays were full of indecent and pagan language; so were the plays of Ben Jonson. A scribe might provide the dignified accoutrements of Latin act- and scene-divisions, the sheen of elaborate punctuation; he might correct the grammar, modernize the spelling, even expand colloquial contractions to their full and decorous forms; he might mimic the presentation of classical texts, by removing directions for properties and sounds, or even by massing entrances at the head of a scene; he might try to make sense of apparent nonsense. But why should he remove oaths? All of his other massaging of the text affects only its presentation, what the modern bibliographer would call 'incidentals' (or 'accidentals'); when he tries to make sense of apparent nonsense he merely anticipates the modern editor, in seeking to restore the author's meaning. By removing profanity, he would be altering his author's meaning—and doing so in a way which brings his purely literary transcript into unnecessary and uncharacteristic conformity with a merely theatrical expedient.

God has been all but razed out of some of the King's Men's late theatrical manuscripts and their descendants; but we should expect him to survive in mere literary transcripts. The Act itself encourages such an assumption; no evidence exists to contradict it; logic, too, champions it. In particular, since the publishers of the First Folio indulged in little or no editorial expurgation, we should hardly expect expurgation to have been requested in any transcripts especially prepared for their use. Most scholars assume that the six plays apparently set from Crane transcripts were commissioned by the publishers, or by Heminges and Condell, primarily for use by Jaggard. This hypothesis cannot be definitely affirmed, but it seems a reasonable interpretation of the evidence. If we accept it, then these six plays represent a special category of 'private transcript', one for whom the intended recipient is known. Moreover, that recipient demonstrably had no desire to impose provisions of the 1606 statute upon the texts printed in 1623.

Three of the six Crane plays—*The Tempest*, *The Winter's Tale*, and *Cymbeline*—were written after 1606, and the almost total absence of profanity from these texts might reflect the influence of the new legislation, whether Crane was copying from Shakespeare's foul papers or a promptbook. But the other three were all written before 1606: *The Two Gentlemen of Verona* (1590–1?), *The Merry Wives of Windsor* (1597–8), and *Measure for Measure* (1603–4). All three texts have undoubtedly been purged (see Table 6). For *Merry Wives* the bad quarto provides corroborative evidence that the Folio text has in places fallen victim to moral

TABLE 6. *Purged texts copied by Crane*

	God	Heauen(s)
Two Gentlemen	0	8
Merry Wives	4	27
Measure	0	35

rectitude. On the evidence of the Quarto, G. Blakemore Evans restores 'God' in nine places where the Folio has removed it altogether, or altered it to something weaker.

Evans could in fact have gone considerably further. One of the favourite oaths of Shakespeare's comic Welshman in *Henry V* is 'by Jesu' (or 'jeshu' or 'cheshu'): Fluellen profanely invokes the name of Jesus six times (3. 3. 8, 15, 24; 4. 1. 66; 4. 7. 109; 5. 1. 38). Parson Evans, in the Folio, never does. But in the Quarto this is Evans's favourite oath: it occurs, in each case appropriately, at 3. 1. 11, 3. 1. 81, 3. 3. 162, 3. 3. 200, and 4. 2. 180, in well-reported passages, where F has no profanity at all. Not only would these oaths be appropriate to Evans as a character; they would be typical of Shakespeare's work in the period during which *Merry Wives* was written. In the other three plays in which Sir John figures, Jesus is named explicitly seventeen times; in the entire remainder of the canon, he is only named twelve times.

Sir John himself is another character who particularly suffers from the apparent expurgation of *Merry Wives*. In *I Henry IV* and its sequels, Sir John particularly, and his unsavoury entourage generally, are the most consistently profane characters in the canon. In *Merry Wives* the profanity disappears entirely, and its absence accounts for the dramatic lameness of some of Sir John's speeches. Consider how much more characteristic of Sir John all these speeches are, with the Quarto's profanity reinserted into the Folio text:

Mistress Ford A plaine Kerchief, Sir *Iohn*: my browes become nothing else, nor that well neither.
Falstaff [By the Lord] thou art a tyrant to say so

(TLN 1402–4; 3. 3. 45)

. . . what a thing should I haue beene, when I had beene swel'd? [By the Lord,] a Mountaine of Mummie.

(TLN 1694–6; 3. 5. 16)

. . . they conuey'd me into a bucke-basket.
Ford. A Buck-basket?
Falstaff [By the Lord]: a Buck-Basket:

(TLN 1754–6; 3. 5. 82)

And these are not Fairies: [By the Lord] I was three or foure times in the thought they were not Fairies

(TLN 2605–7; 5. 5. 120)

In the first and last of these speeches F has nothing in place of Q's profanity; in the second it lamely repeats 'I should haue beene' from the
foregoing question; in the third Falstaff's incredulous and indignant
confirmation is reduced—oh poverty of invention!—to a mere 'Yes'. But
in *1* and *2 Henry IV*, Sir John uses the very oath which Q gives her here
('By the Lord') eight times; in Folio *Merry Wives* it never appears. Since
explicit references to, or swearing by, 'the Lord', was as objectionable as
the words 'God' or 'Jesu', an editor who restores 'God' to Sir John's
mouth at TLN 793 (2. 2. 24) and 2563 (5. 5. 80), and 'Sblood' at 1687
(3. 5. 8), should also restore 'By the Lord' in these passages, which are all
well-reported in Q. And another, similar, profanity can be restored even
more simply. At 1392–4 (3. 3. 44–6) the Folio reads (Falstaff addressing
Mistress Ford):

Now shall I sin in my wish; I would thy Husband were dead, Ile speake it before
the best Lord, I would make thee my Lady.

In the Quarto this passage reads

> I would thy husband were dead.
> *Mistress Ford* Why how then Sir *Iohn*?
> *Falstaff* By the Lord, Ide make thee my Ladie.
>   (D4ᵛ)

The Quarto's interruption by Mistress Ford has no claim to authority,
and it seems highly unlikely that the Folio's elaborately unnecessary 'Ile
speake it before the best Lord' is an expurgator's substitution for 'By the
Lord'—after all, an expurgator could have solved the problem simply by
omitting the offending preposition. But in both texts some word-play
upon 'Lord' and 'Lady' takes place, and the Quarto suggests that the
word-play was originally profane. An expurgator could, by the simple
addition of 'best' before 'Lord', turn a profane affirmation into a rather
pointless, and certainly much weaker, social one. It seems to me likely
that Sir John originally said 'Ile speak it before the Lord, I would make
thee my Lady.'[44]

Evidence specific to *Merry Wives* thus confirms that the anomalous distribution of 'God' and 'heauen(s)' in that play results from expurgation,
and on this basis we may reasonably conjecture a similar explanation for
the similar anomalies in *Measure for Measure* and *Two Gentlemen*. About
Measure I will have a good deal more to say at the end of this chapter;
suffice it to say here that the text has clearly been censored. Likewise, at
least one other feature of the vocabulary of *Two Gentlemen* reinforces the
evidence provided by the distribution of 'God' and 'heaven'. In demonstrably expurgated texts, the weak asseveration 'trust me' often takes the

[44] *Textual Companion*, 345, mistakenly records this conjecture; read 'Ile speake it before
the Lord G. T. *conj.*'

place of a more profane original reading. 'Trust me' only occurs as an asseveration four times in good quartos (*Dream* 5. 1. 99, *Titus* 1. 1. 261, *Romeo* 2. 1. 142, 3. 5. 58); it also occurs four times in Folio texts which betray little evidence of expurgation (*Comedy* 1. 1. 142, 5. 1. 304, *Shrew* Ind. 1.23, *Duke of York* 4. 2. 1). All eight of these apparently authentic uses are early, and in verse. In vivid contrast to the rest of the canon, the asseveration occurs eleven times in Folio *Merry Wives* and *Two Gentlemen* alone, both of which have clearly suffered almost total expurgation; all the examples in *Merry Wives*, and one in *Two Gentlemen*, occur in prose. We may be reasonably confident that most of these asseverations in the two plays are sophistications.

TABLE 7. *Examples of 'Trust me' substituted for oaths*

		Quarto	Folio
2 Henry IV	2. 2. 1	Before God	Trust me
	3. 2. 82	by my troth	Trust me
	3. 2. 172	Fore God	Trust me
Othello	3. 3. 75	Birlady	Trust me
	3. 3. 219	Ifaith	Trust me
	4. 1. 235	By my troth	Trust me
Merry Wives	3. 1. 104	Afore God	Trust me
	3. 2. 45	By my faith	Trust me
	4. 2. 188	By my troth	Trust me

In *Merry Wives* comparison with an unexpurgated quarto is possible, and in three places it confirms editorial suspicion (see Table 7). One's confidence in the Quarto here is greatly strengthened by the fact that the alternatives it offers are all oaths for which 'Trust me' was substituted in Folio *2 Henry IV* and *Othello*. At *Merry Wives* 2. 1. 151 and 3. 3. 219 the Quarto, in paraphrasing the relevant speeches, offers no oaths, and hence tends to support the Folio; an editor should leave the Folio text alone. But the Quarto contains nothing comparable to the exchange at 2. 1. 31–3, and editors must evaluate the Folio text entirely on its merits.

> —*Mistris Page*, trust me, I was going to your house.
> —And trust me, I was coming to you:
>
> (TLN 579–81)

A strong oath seems inappropriate in this context for these characters, and would in any case make F's parallelism of phrase difficult to sustain; but 'by my faith' (or 'troth') would be appropriate, and easily answered with 'And by mine'. Either emendation is likely to approximate what Shakespeare wrote better than F's lame repeated 'trust me'.

In *Two Gentlemen* no second text can offer an editor guidance, and emendation must be based entirely on a judgement of the context and the evidence of patterns of expurgation elsewhere. In most of the examples context is of little help, and an editor must confess defeat; but one passage is, I think, legitimately emendable:

> Dare you presume to harbour wanton lines?
> To whisper, and conspire against my youth?
> Now trust me, 'tis an office of great worth,
> And you an officer fit for the place:
> There: take the paper: see it be return'd
> Or else returne no more into my sight

>   (TLN 195–200; 1. 2. 42–7)

'Trust me' is hardly of inspired relevance here; Shakespeare never uses 'now trust me' in any other play; and in context something stronger would be more characteristic and dramatic. Of phrases for which 'Trust me' is elsewhere substituted, the only one metrically attractive here is 'By'r lady' (for 'Now trust me'), which Shakespeare uses seventeen times elsewhere, usually at the beginning of sentences (as here).

We can now be reasonably confident that such expurgation was not undertaken by Folio editors or compositors; the alterations must have already been made in the copy supplied to the printer. Nor does it seem likely that Crane himself was copying a private transcript, for if such a transcript existed it might itself have been used as printer's copy; if the owner would not lend it for use by the printer, why should he lend it for use by Crane? In any case, why should Crane borrow a manuscript from some private party, when he could copy one already in the theatre's possession? We may thus reasonably assume that Crane was copying Shakespeare's foul papers, or an early intermediate transcript, or the company's prompt-book. Neither the foul papers nor the early intermediate transcript should have been expurgated; if Crane was copying either of these, he must have expurgated it himself. But the prompt-books might have been expurgated. *Merry Wives* was revived at Court in 1604 and 1638, and possibly in 1613; it was certainly popular in the seventeenth century; likewise, the extant music for the song in *Measure for Measure* makes it virtually certain that the play was revived at some time between 1612 and 1622.[45] The prompt-books of these two plays, at least, were in use after 1606, and may have been revised accordingly.

Crane's sophistication of his copy makes it extraordinarily difficult to

---

[45] For revivals, see *Merry Wives*, ed. H. J. Oliver, new Arden (1971), pp. ix–xi; for *Measure*, see Ch. 3, 125–6.

determine what he was himself copying. Trevor Howard-Hill conjectures that all five Crane Comedies were copied from Shakespeare's foul papers, but this seems to be a postulate rather than a proven conclusion.[46] In *Two Gentlemen*, Howard-Hill bases his conclusion entirely on the absence of directions for music and properties. But he admits that directions for music and properties may have been 'edited . . . out' by Crane himself;[47] this seems to me not only possible but virtually certain, given the presence of such directions in all the good quartos set from Shakespeare's foul papers. The unreliability of this evidence leaves us with no evidence at all for *Two Gentlemen*. Crane *may* have been copying foul papers, but equally he *may* have been copying a late expurgated prompt-book: the apparent expurgation of the Folio text is itself our only evidence. A judgement on Crane's copy for this play must therefore depend upon more reliable conclusions about other Crane texts.

Merry Wives supplies at least some corroborative evidence of the origins of the expurgation. Most editors have agreed that the alteration of Ford's pseudonym from Brooke (Q) to Broome (F) results from political interference. Since Cobham was disgraced two decades before the Folio text was printed, and died in 1619, this alteration could hardly have been made by Crane or the Folio editors; nor should it have been retrospectively imposed upon Shakespeare's foul papers. On the other hand, we would expect any such alteration to be made in the prompt-book; indeed it might very well have been made on the prompt-book by the Master of the Revels. Howard-Hill himself must, in order to explain this variant, conjecture that Crane's transcript was influenced by both the foul papers and the prompt-book, and yet he provides no evidence that the foul papers need have been used at all.

For *Two Gentlemen*, no evidence; for *Merry Wives*, evidence of the influence of a prompt-book; for *Measure*, the use of a prompt-book is implied by a variety of evidence, discussed by John Jowett and myself in Chapter 3 of this volume. Thus, for two of Crane's three expurgated texts, we have independent evidence that a late prompt-book existed, and that Crane was copying a prompt-book. It would be reasonable enough to assume, in the complete absence of other evidence, that the same explanation applies to the third.

In fact, as Jowett and I note below, none of Crane's surviving manuscripts gives us reason to believe that he would have personally expurgated his transcripts, or that he would have done so with the thoroughness noticeable in these three Folio plays (particularly *Measure*). The logical arguments against 'literary' expurgation as a general phenomenon in the early seventeenth century, and against the editorial expurga-

---

[46] T. H. Howard-Hill, *Ralph Crane and Some Shakespeare First Folio Comedies* (Charlottesville, Ill., 1972), 139-40.

[47] Ibid. 80.

tion of the First Folio in particular, are reinforced by the evidence of the extant work of this individual scribe. Crane can be seen expurgating a transcript on his own initiative only a single time in a single text—in preparing the King's Men's prompt-book for *Barnavelt*, in 1619.[48] This example simply confirms the common-sense principle that the law against profanity in performance affected the preparation of texts designed to regulate performance—affected those texts and, so far as we can judge, no others. If we accept that Crane's transcripts of *Two Gentlemen*, *Merry Wives*, and *Measure* all derive from prompt-books, then these texts fit the same pattern as the rest of the Folio.

Scribes copying a text for use in the theatre after May 1606 should have removed what profanity they found; scribes copying a text for use by a printer or patron after May 1606 should have left intact what profanity they found. But what if a scribe, preparing a text for use by a printer or patron, were copying a text which had already been expurgated for use in the theatre? Most scribes would, no doubt, simply copy the expurgated text—just as most scribes, confronted with an unexpurgated text, would simply copy that. In textual transmission, as in other jobs, most people do as little as possible. But since play texts were expurgated only for the sake of performance, some scribes, knowing that profanity was perfectly acceptable in a reading text, may have put back what theatrical expurgation had taken out. In other words, the fact of expurgation seems to be good evidence that a printed text derives from a theatrical manuscript, at one or more removes; but the presence of profanity in a printed text is certainly *not* good evidence of the ancestry of the manuscript the printer used.

Ralph Crane, obviously, did not go about reinserting profanities absent from the manuscript he was copying. But that other scribes may have done so is suggested by the Folio texts of *Macbeth* and *All is True*. *Macbeth* was almost certainly composed in the summer of 1606, just after passage of the 'Acte to restraine Abuses of Players', and the Folio text includes material apparently added in the second decade of the seventeenth century; we are clearly dealing, in this case, with a transcript of theatrical ancestry. *All is True* was written in 1613, and printed in the Folio from a scribal transcript. Nevertheless, in the Folio both plays are as profane as plays written before 1606. 'God' occurs sixteen times in *Macbeth* (to ten examples of synonymous 'heaven(s)') and thirty-three times in *All is True* (to twenty-seven of 'heaven'), in the scenes of both playwrights.

There are two possible explanations for these facts. The first explanation is the one I have already offered, that some scribes restored

---

[48] At l. 2425 of *The Tragedy of Sir John van Olden Barnavelt*, 'vpon my soule' is scribbled over by Crane: see the Mal. Soc. Repr., ed. T. H. Howard-Hill (1980), 76.

profanity; this possibility has, I think, never before been mentioned. The second explanation, which has hitherto prevailed, is that (in Greg's words) 'authors paid very little attention to the Act'.[49] Certainly, it can be easily demonstrated that the extant texts of some plays written by other authors after 1606 contain much profanity; some authors use more than others.[50] We might therefore suppose that Shakespeare, even after May 1606, continued to lace his plays with profane expressions, which happen to survive in *Macbeth* and *All is True*, but have been systematically expurgated by other hands in all his other late plays.

But Greg's explanation seems to me unlikely. Why would professional playwrights, committed to the theatrical realization of their work, write words which they knew could not be used on stage? Why would theatrical companies submit to the Master of the Revels manuscripts containing words to which they knew he would object? Why would actors memorize words for the speaking of which they could be heavily fined? Noticeably, the surviving prompt-books which postdate the Act contain very little profanity at all.

But although profanities could not be played, they could be printed, or circulated in manuscript. Beginning in 1600 with the title-page of Ben Jonson's *Every Man Out of His Humour*, some playwrights and publishers advertised the fact that the play they published was in various ways superior to the play that had been performed. Once authors and publishers recognize a distinction between the play as performance and the play as literary commodity, the door is opened to various literary embellishments of the theatrical text, including particularly the restoration of material cut in performance. This is, in fact, the very point made by the title-page of *Every Man Out of His Humour*, which offers readers a text '*Containing more than hath been Publickely Spoken or Acted*', giving them the play '*AS IT WAS FIRST COMPOSED* by the Author'. In the same vein, the publisher Humphrey Moseley said in his preface to the Beaumont and Fletcher collection of 1647, 'When these *Comedies* and *Tragedies* were presented on the Stage, the *Actours* omitted some *Scenes* and Passages (with the *Authour's* consent) as occasion led them . . . But now you have both All that was Acted, and all that was not; even the perfect full Originalls without the least mutilation.'[51]

In this historical and literary context, it would not be at all surprising if some authors and scribes supplied a certain amount of profanity when copying playtexts in which profanity had either been avoided or removed. In fact, the earliest demonstrable example of a private transcript of a

---

[49] Greg, *Editorial Problem*, 108.

[50] See the tables in David Lake, *The Canon of Thomas Middleton's Plays* (Cambridge, 1974), and Ch. 3 n. 34.

[51] *The Comedies and Tragedies of Francis Beaumont and John Fletcher* (London, 1647), sig. A4.

play—a manuscript of Beaumont and Fletcher's *A King and No King*, which belonged to Sir Henry Neville—is one of the texts which Greg cited as evidence that 'authors paid very little attention to the Act'.[52] It woud be safer to say that certain *reading texts* paid very little attention to the Act, or deliberately sought to undo the damage which the Act had done in the theatres. The simplest way of undoing that damage would be to insert 'God' on some occasions in place of 'heauen'. This procedure would have required no recourse to the author; it would also, inevitably, have done only part of the job. That something similar has happened in *Macbeth* and *All is True* is suggested by the fact that, although 'God' occurs far more often than in any other late or expurgated play, both plays contain a disproportionately high incidence of 'heauen', and a disproportionately low incidence of oaths.

If *All is True* had been printed from authorial foul papers, or if it were alone among the late plays in containing profanity, then we might simply conjecture that in his own manuscripts Shakespeare ignored the Act. But *All is True* was clearly printed from a transcript.[53] Moreover, *Macbeth*, though also a transcript, clearly derives from a late theatrical text. These two texts therefore compel us to conclude that, in practice, some transcripts reinstated profanity. That is, some Jacobean scribes, like some modern editors, supplied 'God' where the 1606 legislation had forced the theatre to put 'heauen'. In fact, the same scribe may be responsible for both texts. Both *All is True* and *Macbeth* contain scene-divisions; both make extensive use of round brackets;[54] both exhibit an anomalous, and statistically similar, preference for the spelling 'h'as'; both strongly prefer the spelling 'O'.[55]

Interestingly, all these features are shared by the 1622 Quarto text of *Othello*, which editors agree was set from a scribal transcript. (Indeed, Greg linked the transcript for *Othello* with that for *A King and No King*.) Moreover, although Quarto *Othello* contains a good deal of profanity, it also—by comparison with unexpurgated texts—makes disproportionately frequent use of 'heauen'. Twice, it has apparently been expurgated itself; on several occasions, it makes use of 'heauen' in phrases where Shakespeare consistently prefers 'God'.[56] It is at least possible that the

---

[52] Greg, *First Folio*, 153–4.

[53] *Textual Companion*, 618–19; *Henry VIII*, ed. Fredson Bowers, in *Beaumont and Fletcher Canon*, vii (1989), 3–20. The same conclusion was reached independently by both editors, using different evidence.

[54] For statistics on round brackets see Gary Taylor, 'Shakespeare and Others: The Authorship of *1 Henry VI*' (forthcoming in *Medieval and Renaissance Drama in England*), app. 1.

[55] For 'O', see App. II. Although the preference for 'O' in *Macbeth* and *All is True* could simply reflect Shakespeare's own preference, the tolerance for this spelling differentiates the scribe(s) in those two plays from the scribes who prepared copy for Folio *Coriolanus*, *Hamlet*, *Othello*, *Antony*, and parts of *John* and *Cymbeline*.

[56] *Textual Companion*, 481: nn. to 4. 2. 49, 4. 2. 152.

same scribe prepared all three manuscripts. This possibility has, of course, implications beyond the study of expurgation; but it would also help to explain the otherwise puzzling status of profanity in Quarto *Othello*.

If my reasoning about these three plays is at all convincing, then the presence of profanity is of dubious value in determining the nature of a printer's manuscript. Moreover, while some scribes were actively restoring profanity, other scribes may have passively permitted it. Although someone preparing a new prompt-book after May 1606 would have needed to respect the Act, it is by no means evident that scribes would always have gone to the trouble of expurgating the prompt-book of an old play, revived after May 1606. The actors would have needed to expurgate their own performances, or their own written parts; but the old prompt-book might have been left as it was. Or it might have been altered. We have no right to demand that the King's Men behave systematically in such matters: this kind of consistency is foreign to Renaissance thought and practice.[57]

But such inconsistencies should not bother us. After all, when profanity has been left intact, for whatever reason, Shakespeare's intentions have been preserved, and an editor need do nothing. Editors and interpreters only need worry when the text has been expurgated. It should therefore comfort us to discover that some of the texts which *should* have been expurgated were in fact *not*, and that some of the plays which were expurgated have had much of their original profanity restored in print. Moreover, such inconsistencies do nothing to disturb the consistency of the larger picture, a consistency mandated by the legislation itself: when a text *has* been expurgated, the source of that expurgation is almost always, apparently, the theatre.

Eleven plays in the First Folio were either written after May 1606, or have classical settings which minimize the use of profane references to the Christian God; in those texts no substantial post-authorial expurgation could or did take place. Of plays written before May 1606, nine seem to have suffered no expurgation whatever in the Folio (*Comedy, All's Well, Henry V, 1 Henry VI, Contention, Duke of York, As You Like It, Shrew, Twelfth Night*); three others were only trimmed of objectionable allusions to Christ's crucifixion (*Richard III, Titus, Romeo*). In none of these twenty-three texts (almost two-thirds of the Folio) do we need to suspect that late theatrical practice has affected the treatment of profanity. In another four texts—*Much Ado, Love's Labour's Lost, Dream,* and *Merchant,* four Comedies which were printed one after the other from

---

[57] For an excellent critique of the demand for consistency, see Marion Trousdale, 'A Second Look at Bibliography and the Acting of Plays', *SQ* 41 (1990), 87–96.

very similar copy—only a handful of profanities is altered; this accords with the treatment of dialogue in all four texts, which can have been collated only haphazardly with authoritative manuscripts. But in each case access to a manuscript is probable or certain, and in each case the manuscript consulted was probably or certainly a late prompt-book. The same situation recurs in *Richard II*, the first of the Histories to be set from annotated quarto copy—the only difference being that the manuscript was, throughout, more regularly consulted, with the result that more profanity was amended. All of the remaining plays which suffered expurgation seem to have been set from scribal transcripts, and in no case is the expurgation likely to have originated in the printing-house. Of the three relevant Crane transcripts, two (*Merry Wives* and *Measure*) were apparently copied from late prompt-books; *2 Henry IV* also seems likely to derive from a prompt-book; the expurgation of Folio *Othello* could derive either from the same source, or from late authorial revision. In *King John* the variation in the treatment of profanity between the apparent stints of two scribes makes it clear that expurgation took place in the underlying manuscript itself; this manuscript also seems to have been affected by late theatrical practice. In short, all ten of the foregoing Folio texts seem, on independent evidence, to betray the influence of theatrical practice after 1606, and for the expurgation of these texts we need seek no other explanation.

There remain only three Folio texts, in which our conclusions about the agents of expurgation must be based upon secondary evidence or inference. *Two Gentlemen* yields no clue to the nature of the text which Crane was copying; but on the basis of Crane's other Folio plays and other extant manuscripts, we may assume that what Crane copied in this instance had itself already been expurgated, and may have been a prompt-book. At least, nothing contradicts this assumption. The manuscript consulted when printing *1 Henry IV* cannot with any confidence be characterized; but it does seem clear that a manuscript was consulted. Neither of the compositors who set *1 Henry IV* was among the three who set *Two Gentlemen*; of the five compositors who worked on these two plays, only one reappears among the three engaged in setting *Hamlet*. At least seven different compositors worked on these three problematic texts, and as their work elsewhere in the Folio gives us no reason to believe that they were the primary agents of expurgation, it seems clear that the compositors themselves cannot be held responsible for the moralistic pruning of these three. Nor, on the evidence of the remainder of the Folio, does it seem reasonable to infer that a printing-house editor undertook the expurgation of *1 Henry IV*. It would therefore appear that the manuscript was itself expurgated; but about the manuscript's own derivation we can only confess ignorance. Finally, in the case of *Hamlet* late theatrical influence seems unlikely; on the other hand, very little expurgation took place, and could easily have resulted from a combination of authorial tinkering, scribal or compositorial substitution, and the demonstrable editorial sensitivity to any allusion to the crucifixion.[58] All three of these ambiguous cases are therefore best explained by the assumption that deliberate expurgation was limited to late theatrical texts, or derivatives of them.

For most of the sixteen Folio texts which have suffered minor or major expurgation, there has never been any doubt about what editors should do: the profanity of the available Quarto text has simply been—and should continue to be—restored. But it is now demonstrably obvious that the indecorous decency of *The Merry Wives of Windsor*, *The Two Gentlemen of Verona*, *King John*, and *Measure for Measure* also results from late interference.

For *Merry Wives* we can turn to the Quarto; as a memorially reconstructed text, that Quarto is not entirely reliable, nor does it solve all an editor's problems, but it does at least provide a contemporary source for profane variants. For the other three plays, we must rely entirely upon conjectural emendation. Editors have in the past not recognized the scale of the problem in these plays; the kind of emendation required and the principles of its application have never been discussed; accordingly, editors have done virtually nothing to repair the damage.

For *Two Gentlemen* the damage appears to have been minor, partly because Shakespeare's early plays make less dramatic use of profanity, partly because religious issues are not prominent in *Two Gentlemen* itself. *King John* is a more mature and more important play than *Two Gentleman*, and in part is concerned with religious matters; fortunately, one of the two scribes who expurgated the text did so less systematically than the other, so that some of the original profanity has been preserved and less needs to be recovered editorially. But in *Measure for Measure*, the most mature and most important of these three plays, religion is itself a central issue, and the expurgation of the text has been almost total.

In analysing the problems posed by such texts, it will be best to begin with the simpler case, *King John*, and with the simplest of editorial solutions, the reinstatement of 'God' for 'heauen'. I have already noted two cases where the Folio text has been emended by earlier editors, because the context itself seems to require the word 'God'.

> But as we, vnder heauen, are supreame head,
> So vnder him . . .
>
> (TLN 1082–3; 3. 1. 81–2)
>
> Where heauen he knowes how we shall answer him
> (TLN 2670; 5. 7. 60)

[58] Two more examples may occur in *Henry V*, where the Quarto has Fluellen swear by 'God's plud' at 3. 2. 19 and 4. 1. 76: however, these may be examples of authorial revision. See my discussion in *Henry V*, ed. Gary Taylor (Oxford, 1982), 316–17.

These lines have been emended by earlier editors. But in another line the context seems just as clearly to demand emendation:

> Arme, arme, you heauens, against these periur'd Kings,
> A widdow cries, be husband to me (heauens)
> Let not the howres of this vngodly day
> Weare out the daies in peace
>
> (TLN 1032–4; 3. 1. 33–6)

There is nothing demonstrably wrong with the first line, but in the second the metaphor of 'heauens' as a 'husband' is odd; in the imagery of Christianity Christ is the husband of the Church, and also specifically the husband of a woman entering a nunnery. Moreover, as scholars have recognized, Constance is alluding to Isaiah 54: 4–5: 'yea, thou shalt forget the . . . dishonour of thy widowhood. For he that made thee, shall be thy Lord and husband'. Under the influence of the preceding line, an expurgator could easily have substituted 'heauens' for some other word. That other word might have been 'God'; but 'Lord' would be even more attractive, because of the allusion to Isaiah, and because the collocation 'Lord . . . husband' occurs ten times elsewhere in Shakespeare's works.

In other cases, the Folio reading is suspect not because of any difficulty in the context, but because it violates Shakespeare's invariable practice, when his work has not been censored. Although we tend to regard 'God' and 'heauen' as synonyms, for some idioms Shakespeare consistently used 'God'. Consider, for instance, these two exclamations by Arthur.

> O heauen: that there were but a moth in yours,
>
> (TLN 1670; 4. 1. 91)
>
> O heauen! I thanke you *Hubert*.
>
> (TLN 1713; 4. 1. 13 1)

Surprisingly, Shakespeare never uses 'O heauen' in the unexpurgated text of any play written before the 'Acte to restraine Abuses of Players'. The only parallels are in four expurgated texts[59] and one late play (*Tempest* 3. 1. 68, 'O heauen, O earth'), where in any case the context explains the choice of 'heauen' instead of 'God'. By contrast, 'O God' occurs thirty-six times. Moreover, 'O God' was censored elsewhere, demonstrably, seven times.[60] We thus have a clear contrast between Shakespeare's unexpurgated practice and his expurgated texts, and clear evidence that a particular change was made. There seems no reason to doubt that Shakespeare originally wrote 'God' in both these lines.

The same principle casts suspicion on another exclamation, also used twice in *King John*.

[59] *Merry Wives* 1. 1. 190, *Two Gentlemen* 5. 4. 36, 59, 110, *Othello* 1. 1. 169, 3. 3. 373, 4. 2. 88 and 145, and *Measure* 5. 1. 163 (quoted below).
[60] *1 Henry IV* 5. 4. 50, *2 Henry IV* 3. 1. 44, 4. 3. 347, 5. 2. 19, 5. 4. 23, *Othello* 2. 3. 283, 5. 2. 224.

> I am not mad, I would to heauen I were,
> 			(TLN 1432; 3. 4. 48)
> No indeede is't not: and I would to heauen
> 			(TLN 1596; 4. 1. 23)

Again, this seems acceptable, and no earlier editor questioned it; but the only parallels for 'would to heauen' come from other expurgated texts.[61] Shakespeare uses the profane alternative, 'would to God', five times in early texts; on another eight occasions, his original 'would to God' was demonstrably censored.[62]

Three of these examples come from a single scene, which also affords another example:

> For heauen sake *Hubert* let me not be bound:
> 			(TLN 1654; 4. 1. 77)

Shakespeare uses 'God' in this phrase twenty-four times; 'heauen' never occurs in an unexpurgated text, but it is substituted for Quarto 'God' four times in expurgated Folio texts.[63]

In all the preceding examples we have been dealing with common phrases. In other cases Shakespeare prefers 'God' elsewhere, but he uses the idiom less often. An example is provided by Pandulph's first line upon entering:

> Haile you annointed deputies of heauen;
> 			(TLN 1063; 3. 1. 62)

Shakespeare four times identifies kings as divine 'deputies'; but they are always deputies of a personalized 'God' or 'the Lord', not an abstract 'heauen'.[64] Likewise, later in the same scene Constance appeals to the Dauphin to

> Alter not the doome fore-thought by heauen.
> 			(TLN 1245; 3. 1. 237–8)

Elsewhere, the agent of 'doom' is 'God' (*1 Henry IV* 3. 2. 4–6, changed to 'Heauen' by the Folio) or 'the gods' (*Coriolanus* 1. 8. 6).[65]

In all the cases discussed above, Shakespeare's usage is invariable in unexpurgated plays. In other cases in *King John*, Shakespeare's practice is

[61] 'Would to heauen': *Othello* 4. 1. 272, *Measure* 2. 2. 67 (quoted below).
[62] 'Would to God': *Shrew* 1. 2. 34, *Richard III* 1. 3. 139, 2. 1. 75, 4. 1. 58, *Ado* 2. 1. 256. 'Would to God' in Quarto, censored in Folio: *Richard II* 5. 3. 4, *1 Henry IV* 1. 2. 82, 4. 3. 34, 5. 4. 68, *2 Henry IV* 1. 1. 106, 1. 2. 222, 5. 4. 1, *Othello* 3. 4. 77.
[63] 'For heauen's sake': *Othello* 5. 1. 51; the examples at *All is True* 3. 1. 110 and *Kinsmen* 3. 6. 251 are both post-1606, and both by Fletcher. Examples of expurgation of 'for God's sake' occur at *Richard II* 3. 1. 37, 3. 2. 151, 5. 3. 72, *1 Henry IV* 5. 4. 15, *2 Henry IV* 2. 4. 175, 185.
[64] *Contention* 3. 2. 289–90, *Richard II* 1. 2. 37–8, 3. 2. 53, 4. 1. 116–17.
[65] This emendation of *King John*, unlike the others discussed here, was not made in the Oxford *Complete Works*; it is a later addition to this essay.

not absolutely consistent, but he does strongly prefer a profane expression, which expurgators regularly weaken. For instance:

> Heauen knowes they were besmear'd and ouer-staind
>
> (TLN 1267; 3. 1. 162)

'God knows' appears twenty-eight times in Shakespeare, and was altered by a censor three times (including once at *King John* TLN 2670; 5. 7. 60, quoted above); the only example of 'heauen knows' in an unexpurgated text is Sonnet 17.[66] Although the single example in the Sonnets makes it impossible to say that Shakespeare could not have written the line as it stands in the Folio, an editor can say that the probabilities are heavily weighted in favour of 'God'.

Similar calculations suggest that another line in *King John* should be emended:

> *Bast.* With-hold thine indignation, mighty heauen,
>
> (TLN 2595; 5. 6. 28)

In *Richard III*, 'heauen' is asked to send down 'indignation' (1. 3. 214–17), which would seem to support the Folio reading here. However, 'heauen' and 'indignation' are there separated by twenty-nine words, in the course of which Shakespeare seems to lose track of the singular subject of his sentence, referring instead to 'them' and 'their'; moreover, the Folio text of *Richard III* here carries over, verbatim, the text of its Quarto copy, a memorial reconstruction of uncertain reliability. By contrast, Shakespeare never describes 'heauen' as 'mighty', but does write of 'mighty' gods seven times, of 'mightful' gods once, of the 'might' of gods twice; he also calls God 'almighty' three times. In short, Shakespeare associates the whole family of words founded upon the noun 'might' with personalized gods, not with heaven. Moreover, Shakespeare nowhere else asks heaven to 'withhold' something, but does address the same imperative verb to 'God' (*Duke of York* 2. 2. 7) and 'gods' (*Antony* 4. 15. 69, *Pericles* 8. 3–4). All in all, it seems to me more likely that Shakespeare wrote 'God' than 'heauen' here.[67]

In considering the probabilities of these individual cases, one other set of figures should be considered. Even if all these conjectures were adopted, *King John* would still only contain twenty-one examples of 'God', to nineteen of synonymous 'heauen'. Comparison of these figures with any of Shakespeare's Elizabethan history plays makes it clear that

[66] For 'heauen knows' see *Two Gentlemen* 4. 4. 107 'heauen it knows', *Merry Wives* 3. 3. 80, *Othello* 3. 3. 298, 4. 2. 39 (where 'heauen' is in opposition to 'hell'), *Cymbeline* 3. 3. 99. The examples in *Two Gentlemen* and *Merry Wives* should have been emended in the Oxford edn. (which does emend *John* 3. 1. 162). 'God knows' was expurgated at *John* 5. 7. 60, *2 Henry IV* 3. 1. 67, 4. 3. 312.

[67] I here disagree with the text in the Oxford *Complete Works*; my discussion supplements the note in *Textual Companion*.

there are still too many 'heauen's and not enough 'God's. Consequently, an editor who is locally judicious in rejecting the less certain of these conjectures will also be globally injudicious, in offering readers a text which certainly contains too little profanity.[68] Since we are dealing with a demonstrably expurgated text, an editor should seize upon any evidence which justifies emending one example of 'heauen', rather than another. The standard of proof required here is much less than would be expected in justifying other sorts of emendation. In cases like this, the need for emendation is established by the overall pattern of the canon and the text; the kinds of probability I have described above are simply intended to help an editor choose which lines to de-expurgate.

The same kinds of criteria which have been illustrated in *King John* can also be applied to *Measure for Measure*.[69] But in *Measure for Measure* the extent of expurgation is greater, and its effect upon the play even more important. Just as *King Lear* provides the clearest demonstration of the importance of act-divisions, so *Measure for Measure* provides the clearest demonstration of the effect of expurgation upon a major play.

As in *King John*, in three passages of *Measure for Measure* some profanity seems required by the context.

> and neither heauen, nor man grieue at the mercy
> (TLN 798; 2. 2. 51)

> heauen hath my empty words,
> Whilst my Inuention, hearing not my Tongue,
> Anchors on *Isabell*: heauen in my mouth,
> As if I did but onely chew his name,
> (TLN 1004–7; 2. 4. 2–5)

> Their sawcie sweetnes, that do coyne heauens Image
> (TLN 1049; 2. 4. 45)

At 2. 2. 51, one would expect—and Shakespeare's usage elsewhere would require—a contrast between God and man, or heaven and earth, but not one between heaven and man. An allusion to the Eucharist seems unavoidable at 2. 4. 4, and if 'God' is supplied there it probably belongs in 2. 4. 2 also. Human beings are coined in the image of God, not heaven (2. 4. 45).

In other cases, the Folio reading is suspect because it violates

---

[68] See, as an example of this, Braunmuller's edn. of *John*, which does not adopt the conjectures at 3. 1. 34, 4. 1. 91, 4. 1. 131, or 5. 6. 28, nor explain why he rejects them; 4. 1. 91 he does not record, though he does record the identical emendation at 4. 1. 131. Braunmuller adopts the emendations at 3. 1. 62 and 162 (3. 1. 136 and 236 in his edn.), but does not record that he was anticipated by the Oxford *Complete Works*.

[69] Most of these examples of expurgation in *Measure* were only analysed and identified after publication of the Oxford *Complete Works* and *Textual Companion*. However, *Companion* does record (and the *Works* adopt) the emendations at 2. 2. 25, 2. 2. 167, 2. 4. 4, 2. 4. 45; it also records my conjecture 'By the Lord' at 4. 3. 56. ('God's will' is a later idea, which now seems to me much better.)

Shakespeare's invariable practice when his work has not been censored. *Measure* contains some examples of expurgator's phrases which we have already noticed in *King John*:

> Oh heauen, the vanity of wretched fooles.
>
> (TLN 2536; 5. 1. 163)
>
> *Isab.* I would to heauen I had your potencie,
>
> (TLN 817; 2. 2. 67)

No editor has ever challenged either reading, but Shakespeare's unexpurgated usage would require 'God' in both cases.

An equally clear discrepancy centres on the verb 'serve'. Again, no editor has questioned the following passage.

> euen for our kitchins
> We kill the fowle of season: shall we serue heauen
> With less respect then we doe minister
> To our grosse selues?
>
> (TLN 838–41; 2. 2. 86–9)

The only parallel in the Shakespeare canon for *Measure*'s phrase 'serue heauen' comes in another expurgated text (*Merry Wives* 4. 5. 125); by contrast, the biblical idiom 'serue God' occurs nine times elsewhere. If we include parallel phrases like 'serve the gods', 'serve the devil', 'whom I serve above', 'service of my god', the contrast in usage is even clearer: Shakespeare always imagines a personified object of service, never a generalized 'heauen'. Again it seems clear that Shakespeare originally wrote 'God' in this passage—and 'God' provides a much more striking image. In the culinary context created by Isabel's preceding words, the commonplace expression 'serve God' is literalized as the action of a servant waiting upon a master's table, serving God meat, in this case human meat. The Folio's vague 'heauen', by contrast, depersonalizes the image, and robs it of its profane horror.

It is appropriate enough for the novice Isabella to speak directly of God, and Shakespeare probably intended her to do so on three other occasions in her interviews with Angelo.

> I had a brother then; heauen keepe your honour.
>
> (TLN 790; 2. 2. 42)
>
> *Isab.* Heauen keepe your honour safe.
>
> (TLN 917; 2. 2. 157)
>
> *Isab.* Euen so; heauen keepe your Honor.
>
> (TLN 1038; 2. 4. 34)

Each of these speeches is a parting blessing (though after the first and third she is persuaded to postpone her departure); the similarity of situation and of phrasing makes the repetition notable and clearly conscious on Shakespeare's part. But in such phrases Shakespeare elsewhere always uses 'God', not 'heauen': 'God keep your worship!' (*Much Ado* 5. 1. 323), 'And so God keep your worship!' (*As You Like It* 1. 1. 162). Both of these examples are, like Isabella's phrase, used to signal a departure, and 'God keep' was demonstrably expurgated at least once elsewhere.[70]

Seven of the examples I have just cited occur in the speeches of Isabella; collectively, these individual restorations make more explicit her own religious vocation and the nature of her challenge to Angelo in Act 2. Another implicit rebuke to Angelo is spoken, in the preceding scene, by Escalus.

> Well, heauen forgiue him; and forgiue vs all:
> (TLN 491; 2. 1. 37)

Shakespeare, in reliable unexpurgated early texts, invariably says 'God forgive him', not 'Heaven forgive him'.[71] 'Heauen' is equally suspect in another line in the same scene:

> *Elb.* My wife Sir? whom I detest before heauen,
> (TLN 523; 2. 1. 70)

Shakespeare used the phrase 'before [or "afore", or "fore"] God' twenty-one times elsewhere; it was censored at least once (*1 Henry IV* 5. 3. 50); the only parallel for *Measure*'s phrase is in a post-1606 play (*Tempest* 4. 1. 7 'afore heauen').

Each of the following lines is spoken by Isabella at a moment when she is disappointed by the moral failure of a man in whom she had put her faith:

> Heauen shield my Mother plaid my Father faire:
> (TLN 1362; 3. 1. 142)
> In countenance; heauen shield your Grace from woe,
> (TLN 2487; 5. 1. 118)

The phrase 'Heauen shield' appears nowhere else in the Shakespeare

---

[70] *1 Henry IV* 5. 3. 34, Quarto 'God keep' becomes Folio 'Heauen keep'. This passage differs from the examples cited in the text, and the passages in *Measure*, because here 'God keep' governs a clause, a situation in which Shakespeare uses both 'God keep' and 'heauen keep': see *Richard III* 3. 1. 15 and 16, 3. 2. 56, *1 Henry IV* 5. 3. 34, *Ado* 2. 1. 109, *Henry V* 4. 7. 116 for 'God', and *Romeo* 4. 5. 70, *Othello* 3. 4. 163 for 'heauen'. Even in such circumstances, Shakespeare strongly prefers 'God', and the only clearly authoritative use of 'heauen' is in *Romeo*.

[71] 'Heauen forgiue' occurs at *Merry Wives* 2. 1. 26, 2. 2. 56, 3. 3. 201, 5. 5. 30 (Q has 'God'), *Othello* 3. 3. 378, 4. 2. 91, *Macbeth* 4. 3. 237, *All is True* 3. 2. 136, and in the reported text of *Pericles* 17. 40 ('Heauens', where the plural is anomalous, and should probably be emended); all of these examples occur either in plays written in 1606 or after, or in texts which have been expurgated (*Merry Wives, Othello*). By contrast, 'God forgiue' occurs at *Contention* 3. 2. 139, 3. 3. 29, *Duke of York* 5. 6. 60, *Romeo* 4. 4. 34, *John* 2. 1. 12, 2. 1. 283, *1 Henry IV* 1. 2. 92, 1. 3. 251, 3. 2. 130, *2 Henry IV* 4. 3. 347, *Ado* 4. 1. 282, *Henry V* 3. 6. 150, *Othello* 2. 3. 104 (expurgated by F), and *Macbeth* 5. 1. 72.

canon; the closest parallel is 'Heauens shield' at *Dream* 3. 2. 447 (a classical play, which generally avoids Christian oaths). By contrast, Shakespeare used 'God shield' three times, 'God 'ield' three more times, and the comparably personal pagan oath 'Joue shield' twice.[72] Likewise, Shakespeare never elsewhere used the phrase 'on my trust', which in the following line has probably been substituted for an original 'by my faith':

> And on my trust, a man that neuer yet
> (TLN 2518; 5. 1. 147)

'By my faith' is used by Shakespeare sixteen times elsewhere, and was removed by expurgators in *1 Henry IV*, *2 Henry IV*, and *Othello*.[73]

In all the cases discussed above, Shakespeare's usage is invariable in unexpurgated plays. In other cases—when the deity is being asked to 'save', 'bless', or 'give'—Shakespeare's practice is less consistent, but he does strongly prefer a profane expression, which expurgators regularly weaken. Consider two more passages in the first encounter between Isabella and Angelo.

> There shall be order for't.
> *Enter Lucio and Isabella.*
> *Pro.* 'Saue your Honour.
> (TLN 766–8; 2. 2. 25)

> *Isab.* 'Saue your Honour.
> *Ang.* From thee: euen from thy vertue.
> (TLN 923–4; 2. 2. 167)

In both cases, metrical regularity would require an extra syllable before the apostrophied ''Saue'. Outside of late classical plays (*Lear*, *Timon*, *Coriolanus*), Shakespeare used 'save' by itself in this way only five times; by contrast, he used 'God save' fifty-five times. In Crane plays 'God save' never appears; the apostrophied alternative occurs seven times, twice unmetrically (here in *Measure*), and twice contradicting Quarto evidence (*Merry Wives* 2. 3. 18, 3. 1. 39). Moreover, on another four occasions Quarto 'God saue' becomes Folio 'Saue', in a text which has been systematically expurgated.[74]

Two speeches by the Provost, one in the same pivotal scene, employ another suspect expression.

---

[72] 'God shield': *Romeo* 4. 1. 41, *Dream* 3. 1. 30, *All's Well* 1. 3. 168. 'God 'ield': *As You Like It* 3. 3. 75, 5. 4. 54, *Macbeth* 1. 6. 13. 'Joue shield': *Titus* 2. 3. 70, *Dream* 5. 1. 178.

[73] The Folio omits 'by my faith' at *1 Henry IV* 1. 2. 136, 2. 1. 88, 5. 4. 122, and *2 Henry IV* 2. 4. 74; F changes 'by my faith' at *2 Henry IV* 5. 2. 50 to 'to speake truth', and at *Othello* 3. 4. 184 to 'in good troth'. For other uses of the oath compare *Contention* 4. 2. 51, *Duke of York* 5. 1. 32, *John* 2. 1. 546, *1 Henry IV* 4. 1. 129, *Henry V* 3. 7. 107, *Ado* 2. 1. 219, *As You Like It* 3. 5. 39, 4. 1. 20, 5. 4. 62, *All's Well* 2. 1. 79, and *Pericles* 16. 131 (reported text).

[74] 'God saue' to 'Saue': *2 Henry IV* 2. 4. 110, 5. 3. 84, 5. 5. 43, and *Othello* 4. 1. 212.

Heauen giue thee mouing graces.
                    (TLN 782; 2. 2. 36)
Heauen giue your spirits comfort: by, and by,
                    (TLN 1926; 4. 2. 68)

In both cases, we would expect 'God giue'. In fact, 'God giue' occurs twenty-five times in the Shakespeare canon (and was censored at *1 Henry IV* 1. 2. 150 and *2 Henry IV* 1. 2. 95); by contrast, *Measure*'s 'Heauen giue' only occurs twice elsewhere, and both examples occur in an expurgated play (*Merry Wives* 5. 5. 236 and 240). 'God' should certainly be restored in both plays. And another use of 'giue' in *Measure* should also probably be emended.

Ang. The heauens giue safety to your purposes.
                    (TLN 82; 1. 1. 73)

There is no parallel at all for *Measure*'s 'The heauens give'. The closest any other plays in the canon come are *Othello*'s 'Heauens, giue him defense against the elements' (2. 1. 45) and *Lear*'s 'You heauens, giue me patience'; one of these is in an expurgated text, the other in a text which consistently eschews Christian allusions, and both passages are literally directed to the skies (as well as the gods). Metrically, restoration of the original text here is more complicated than the other examples; 'the gods' would correspond with Shakespeare's usage elsewhere, but as a pagan expression it does not suit Angelo and in any case should not have been censored. 'The Lord'—which would fit the metre equally well—is more likely to have been found unfit by an expurgator (as it was seven times in other plays).[75] It would also fit Angelo, especially since a fondness for references to 'the Lord' was thought characteristic of Puritans.

Another idiom where Shakespeare prefers 'God' to 'heauen' occurs three times in *Measure*.

Pro. Pray heauen she win him.
                    (TLN 883; 2. 2. 128)
                    pray heauen his wisedome
bee not tainted:
                    (TLN 2275–6; 4. 4. 3–4)
A businesse for your selfe: pray heauen you then
Be perfect.
                    (TLN 2245–6; 5. 1. 81–2)

Shakespeare uses 'pray God' twenty-six times (and 'pray the gods' another four times); it is demonstrably expurgated seven times. By con-

[75] *2 Henry IV* 2. 4. 295, 3. 2. 289, 3. 2. 298, 5. 4. 11, and *Othello* 5. 2. 62, 93, and 127.

trast, outside of *Measure* he uses 'pray heauen' only once in an unexpurgated text.[76] At least two of these passages from *Measure*, and quite possibly all three, are therefore suspect.

In unexpurgated texts, Shakespeare has the imperative '*X* bless *Y*' (where *X* is 'God(s)', 'Jesus', 'the Lord', 'heauen(s)', or 'Joue', and *Y* is pronoun or noun) thirty-five times; on at least nine occasions, this construction was expurgated by removing or weakening the sacred noun which preceded the verb,[77] and as a result the normal form of the expression does not appear at all in the expurgated texts of *Merry Wives*, *2 Henry IV*, and *Othello*. Nor does it appear in the expurgated text of *Measure*, where we get instead only the truncated form 'Bless you'

> *Elb*. Come your way sir; 'blesse you good Father
> Frier.
>
> (TLN 1500–1; 3. 1. 280)
>
> Blesse you Friar.
>
> (TLN 1566; 3. 1. 343)

Shakespeare uses this shortened version, outside of expurgated texts, only five times (*Shrew* 4. 2. 44, *Dream* 3. 1. 118, *Twelfth Night* 1. 3. 44, *All's Well* 1. 1. 119, 2. 4. 13), always mixing it with examples of the full form. It seems all but certain that at least the first example in *Measure*, and possibly both, have been censored.

Finally, metrical irregularity may point to expurgation. As already noted, metrical and lexical irregularity combine to cast suspicion on 'Saue your honour'. Elsewhere, there is no lexical or contextual reason to suspect expurgation, but the iambic pentameter norm would be achieved if we added 'God's'.

> Grace goe with you, *Benedicite*
>
> (TLN 996; 2. 3. 41)
>
> That brain'd my purpose; but peace be with him,
> (TLN 2783; 5. 1. 393)

Most editors will rightly find these last two cases less compelling than the others, but the possibility of censorship is nevertheless real, and should be recognized.

In all the examples considered so far, we have been dealing with simple cases where the word 'God' is either omitted, or replaced by 'heauen', in phrases where 'God' (or 'the Lord') would clearly be normal. It is much

---

[76] 'Pray heauen': *As You Like It* 1. 2. 197. It also occurs twice in *Othello* (2. 1. 34, 3. 4. 155), twice in Fletcher scenes of *All is True* (5. 2. 13 and 77), and once in a Fletcher scene of *Kinsmen* (4. 1. 16). 'I pray God' was expurgated in *Richard II* 3. 4. 102 ('I would'), *1 Henry IV* 2. 5. 190 ('pray heauen'), 3. 3. 152 ('let'), 4. 3. 115 ('pray heauen'), *2 Henry IV* 1. 2. 34 ('may'), 5. 4. 13 ('would'), and *Hamlet* 4. 5. 200 (omitted).

[77] *Merry Wives* 2. 2. 52, 2. 3. 17, *2 Henry IV* 1. 2. 221, 2. 4. 295, 3. 2. 289, 5. 5. 9, *Othello* 1. 1. 32, 2. 2. 10, 3. 4. 81.

more difficult, but equally important, to consider oaths. Oaths may
include the word 'God', but they are more varied, and consequently less
predictable. Moreover, oaths occur more frequently in prose than verse,
and so metre is usually of no use in awakening or guiding editorial
action. Nevertheless, it is important that editors make some effort to
locate passages where oaths might have been censored. For this play in
particular, the oaths of the prose characters are an important dramatic
and thematic counterweight to the serious religious imagery of Isabella,
Angelo, and the Duke. If we restore the 'high' profanity of the main plot,
we must also restore the 'low' profanity of the subplot, or we will leave
the play unbalanced.

Barnardine, unfit to live or die, absolutely rejects the Friar/Duke's
advice that he should 'Looke forward on the iournie you shall go'.

I sweare I will not die to day for anie mans perswasion.
(TLN 2138–9; 4. 3. 56–7)

An oath would be more dramatic, more in character, and more appropriate to the theme of the play than the weak asseveration 'I sweare'.
Moreover, at *2 Henry IV* 4. 2. 46 Folio 'I sweare' is a euphemism, replac-
ing an orginal profanity ('By the Lord'). On the evidence of his practice
elsewhere before 1606, Shakespeare is more likely to have had Barnardine
say something more colourful and offensive than the Folio's lame 'I
sweare'. Of course, it is less easy to be sure what oath Barnardine originally spoke. 'By the Lord' would do; 'God's will' would be stronger,
would retain the Folio's prose rhythm, and would introduce a characteristic contrast between God's will and man's persuasion. Shakespeare uses
the phrase 'God's will' ten times elsewhere, seven times in the same syn-
tactical situation as here; it was expurgated at least twice.[78]

If Barnardine's verbal politeness is implausible, so is Lucio's. Consider
this exchange between the disguised Duke and Lucio, on the subject of
'Lecherie':

Duke. It is too general a vice, and seueritie must cure it.
Luc. Yes in good sooth, the vice is of a great kindred;
(TLN 1588–9; 3. 1. 365–6)

Lucio's affirmative 'in good sooth' is one which Hotspur had elaborately
ridiculed, when his wife used it, as a protestation only fit for 'Sunday citizens' or 'a comfit-maker's wife' who had never walked 'further than
Finsbury' (*1 Henry IV* 3. 1. 242–52). Moreover, the expression is only
used by three of Shakespeare's characters before 1606: Lady Percy (provoking Hotspur's ridicule), Rosalind (*As You Like It* 3. 2. 378), and
Pandarus, in the scene which satirizes his effete courtly diction (*Troilus

---

[78] 'God's will': *Othello* 2. 3. 151 (Folio 'Alas'), 155 (Folio 'Fie, fie').

3. 1. 55). Both Hotspur's ridicule and the characters who use the oath elsewhere confirm that it is entirely inappropriate for Lucio. Moreover, we know that 'sooth' can be an expurgator's substitution for 'faith'.[79] So *Measure*'s 'in good sooth' could easily be a late substitute for Shakespeare's original 'in good faith' (which was expurgated twice in *2 Henry IV*). Shakespeare uses this alternative, profane expression ten times elsewhere; it is spoken by Feste, Lavatch, and the First Clown in the grave-digger scene in *Hamlet*.[80] Shakespeare is thus not only more likely, on statistical grounds, to have written 'in good faith' than 'in good sooth'; he is also much more likely, early in the seventeenth century, on dramatic grounds, to have given the profane expression to a cynical comic character like Lucio. He is particularly likely to have done so here, in this first encounter between Lucio the cynic and Vincentio the Friar/Duke.

The Folio text of *Measure* contains twelve examples of the word 'Yes'—more than all but two plays in the Shakespeare canon. The two exceptions are *All is True* and *Two Noble Kinsmen*, and in both cases the exception is clearly due to the presence of Shakespeare's collaborator, John Fletcher: the instances of 'yes' cluster in scenes assigned to Fletcher. Linguistically, Shakespeare strongly preferred 'I' (modern 'ay') to 'yes': if we exclude the work of his collaborators, outside of *Measure* the canon uses 'ay' 768 times, 'yes' only 172 times.[81] But in *Measure* 'yes' (thirteen) is used almost as often as 'ay' (fourteen).[82] These figures are suspect not only because they depart from Shakespearian norms, but more pertinently here because we know that expurgators elsewhere substituted a simple affirmative for a profane asseveration. There is no simple equation in Table 8 between the word used by an expurgator and the word used by Shakespeare; the affirmative replaces a variety of profanities. But what matters is that the affirmative is being used as a substitute for something else.

Given this pattern of expurgation, combined with the anomalous excess of 'yes' in the Folio text, it is virtually certain that some of the instances

[79] At *1 Henry IV* 2. 4. 78, *2 Henry IV* 2. 4. 35, Quarto 'faith' was weakened to Folio 'sooth'.
[80] *LLL* 5. 2. 280, *2 Henry IV* 2. 1. 15–16, 2. 4. 87, *Hamlet* 5. 1. 45, 5. 2. 105, *Twelfth Night* 1. 5. 26, *Othello* 4. 2. 116, *All's Well* 2. 2. 33, *Lear* 2. 2. 103, *Coriolanus* 1. 3. 55.
[81] In these totals for the canon as a whole I have excluded Fletcher's share of *All is True* and *Kinsmen*, Middleton's share of *Timon*, and the non-Shakespearian scenes of *I Henry VI*. It should also be noted, however, that the figures for 'ay' have certainly been depressed by two factors: the preference of the scribe who prepared the MS used as copy for Quarto *1 Henry IV* to substitute 'yea' for Shakespeare's 'ay' (see *Textual Companion*, 329), and the tendency of Valentine Simmes's compositors to substitute 'yea' for 'ay' (*Textual Companion*, 234). These factors have no doubt reduced the totals for 'ay' by at least 50.
[82] These figures exclude the opening lines of 1.2, which we believe to be a later, non-Shakespearian interpolation: see Ch. 3. Those lines contain three examples of 'ay', one of 'yes'.

TABLE 8. *Substitution of simple affirmatives for profane asseverations*

		Quarto	Folio
1 Henry IV	1. 3. 129	Zounds	Yes
Merry Wives	3. 5. 82	by the Lord	Yes
2 Henry IV	2. 1. 7	O Lord	I
	2. 1. 156	Ifaith I am	I
	3. 2. 293	Fore God	I
Othello	4. 1. 161	Faith	Yes
	5. 1. 91	O heauen	yes

of 'yes' in *Measure* are sophistications. Of the twelve examples, three are most suspect:

> *Isa.* Be readie *Claudio*, for your death to morrow.
> *Clau.* Yes. Has he affections in him,
> That thus can make him bite the Law by th'nose,
> (TLN 1325–7; 3. 1. 106–8)

Claudio's line is metrically anomalous, and earlier editors sought to emend it, without suspecting expurgation. But the metrical anomaly here coincides with a suspicious 'Yes', in a passage where it would be perfectly natural for Claudio to speak strongly. Since expurgators substituted the simple affirmative for a variety of profane expressions, an editor has some latitude for conjecture, and it seems to me the most attractive alternative to Claudio's lame 'Yes' would be 'As God's my judge'. This is a proverbial expression, which Shakespeare uses twice;[83] it is also, of course, a biblical sentiment central to the play as a whole. It could be spoken calmly, and with resolution; it need be no more overtly histrionic than the Folio's 'Yes'. But it is also a much stronger, and more ambiguous, affirmation than the Folio offers. It can mean either 'I will be ready, as surely as God is my judge' or 'I will be ready to die, if God [rather than this devilish Angelo] is my judge'. Moreover, the phrase would also be syntactically ambiguous, both answering Isabella's preceding speech and prefixing, as an oath, Claudio's following sentence. Finally, the idea of judgement follows naturally from the preceding 'death' and leads naturally to the following 'Law'. In terms of metre, linguistic preference, imagery, character, local and general dramatic meaning, 'As God's my judge' is more likely to represent what Shakeaspare wrote than 'Yes'.

Another instance of 'Yes' later in the same scene is no more convinc-

---

[83] R. W. Dent, *Shakespeare's Proverbial Language: An Index* (Berkeley, Calif., 1981), G198.1.

ing. Lucio again in his first encounter with the Friar/Duke has just claimed that the absent Duke had 'some feeling of the sport':

> *Duke*. 'Tis not possible.
> *Luc*. Who, not the Duke? Yes, your beggar of fifty:
> and his vse was, to put a ducket in her Clack-dish;
> > (TLN 1612–14; 3. 1. 388–90)

Surely we would expect something stronger here than 'Yes', from Lucio of all people. Part of the comedy comes from his insistent swearing to statements which we, and the Duke, know to be false; moreover, when addressing a man in a friar's habit, an oath would be in itself comically offensive. The stronger the oath, the more comic, for both reasons: 'Sblood', one of the strongest of oaths, has the further advantages of alliteration (with 'beggar'), and of an outrageously profane subterranean connection between God's blood and the slang sense of 'blood' as a synonym for 'lust'.

Finally, in his next encounter with the Friar Lucio mentions that he was once brought before the Duke for 'getting a Wench with childe':

> *Duke*. Did you such a thing?
> *Luc*. Yes marrie did I; but I was faine to forswear it,
> > (TLN 2263–4; 4. 3. 172)

An oath is structurally important here: Lucio must now swear before the Duke what he had before forsworn before the Duke, an oath binding enough to be used against him in the final scene of the play, when the Duke says 'I have heard him swear himself there's one Whom he begot with child' (5. 1. 509–10). Both the context and the later testimony of the Duke demand a strong oath—which 'Yes marrie' is not. Shakespeare could have put a number of different oaths in Lucio's mouth here; an editor can be sure that a strong profanity is required, but not sure which. I would be inclined to supply 'By Jesu' (since 'marry' elsewhere apparently replaced 'Iesu', and since 'By Jesu' has the same rythm as 'Yes marry').[84]

These three passages were called to our attention by the observation that expurgators sometimes substituted 'yes' for an oath; we can pinpoint other oaths by looking at other words used by expurgators for the same reason: *alas, away, come, fie, I pray, I protest, indeed, in troth, look, nay, oh, out, truly, what, why*. Like 'yes', these are all common words, which do not require much imagination on the censor's part; it is also difficult to prove that any particular instance of any of them is unShakespearian, because like all his contemporaries Shakespeare often used all these interjections. Again, as with 'yes', an editor must pay particular attention to words which are usually ignored, and isolate cases where stronger language would be more appropriate.

---

[84] See *Textual Companion*, 359: note on *2 Henry IV* 2. 4. 46.

The word 'come', for instance, is used three times elsewhere as a substitute for Shakespeare's original 'zounds'.[85] Most of the uses of 'come' as an interjection in *Measure* are clearly correct, expressing as often in Shakespeare a mild impatience. Only once is 'come' used by a character whose claims have been challenged—the sort of situation where a strong confirmatory oath would be appropriate:

> *Duke.* Loue talkes with better knowledge, & knowledge with deare[r] loue.
> *Luc.* Come Sir, I know what I know.
>
> (TLN 1637–9; 3. 1. 411–13)

This comes near the end of Lucio's first encounter with the Friar/Duke, and Lucio's speech finally provokes Vincentio to challenge him, and ask his name (3. 1. 414–19). Moreover, when Vincentio later declares, 'You'll for-sweare this againe' (3. 1. 426), he implies that Lucio has sworn to the truth of his slanderous statements, and the nearest opportunity for such an oath is here, where the Folio supplies only 'Come'. 'Swounds' would be far more appropriate.

In that same episode, there are several other suspect passages, which may be most usefully considered in the sequence in which they appear in the scene.

> *Luc.* No indeed wil I not *Pompey*,
> (TLN 1562; 3. 1. 340)

The innocent word 'indeed' is elsewhere a substitute for the objectionable oath 'i' faith' (or 'in faith').[86] Moreover, the Folio text of *Measure* does not contain a single example of 'In faith' (or 'i' faith'), though elsewhere Shakespeare uses it 108 times. Indeed, it appears at least once in every play Shakespeare wrote after *Richard II* (1595) and before *Antony* (1606). Here, 'in faith' would be particularly attractive, because 'No in faith . . . *Pompey*' would sardonically echo Pompey's earlier 'Yes faith sir' (3. 1. 329), and because Lucio is here, with his 'No in faith', breaking faith with Pompey.

> *Luc.* Why, what a ruthlesse thing is this in him, for the rebellion of a Codpeece, to take away the life of a man?
>
> (TLN 1602–3; 3. 1. 378)

'Why' is elsewhere substituted by expurgators for much stronger asseverations: *faith, fore God, 'sblood, 'swounds*. In a case like this, an editor not only has to choose which example of 'why' is most suspect, but which oath would most appropriately replace it. Most editors, in these circumstances, will do nothing, because nothing is certain. But if any 'why' in

---

[85] *Richard III* 1. 4. 122, *Hamlet* 5. 2. 272, *Othello* 5. 2. 225.

[86] 'Indeed' is used by expurgators at *1 Henry IV* 2. 4. 85 ('In faith'), *Othello* 3. 4. 55 ('ifaith'), 3. 4. 75, 3. 4. 168, and 4. 1. 111 ('faith'), and *2 Henry IV* 5. 3. 90 ('Birlady').

Measure is suspect, this is it, and if there is any pattern at all to Lucio's speeches in this scene it is a steady increase in outrageousness. It would be natural for Lucio's interjections to mirror this pattern, moving from the repetitions of 'what' and 'why' with which he initially taunts Pompey (3. 1. 311–42), to 'in faith' (3. 1. 340), then from the respectful 'God bless you, friar' (3. 1. 343) with which he first addresses Vincentio, to 'in good faith' (3. 1. 364), to 'Sblood' (3. 1. 389) and 'Swounds' (3. 1. 413). If this is right, then 'why' (3. 1. 378) should be replaced by an oath somewhere in intensity between 'faith' and 'sblood'; 'Fore God' would serve the purpose admirably.

There is another missed opportunity for swearing in Lucio's next speech.

> *Luc.* Oh Sir, you are deceiu'd.
> (TLN 1611; 3. 1. 387)

At *Merry Wives* 3. 5. 56 Quarto 'By the Masse' is reduced in the Folio to 'Oh'. In *Measure*'s context—addressing a friar—'By the masse' would be especially delicious, and the ambiguity ('you are deceived by the mass') would not be lost on a Prostestant audience.

This is as far as I think an editor can go in restoring the profanity which Shakespeare originally gave to his play. To some scholars it will, no doubt, already seem too far. But, as with *King John*, it is worth emphasizing that, even if all the changes proposed above were adopted, the ratio of 'God('s)' to 'heauen(s)' in *Measure* would still be only 22: 18. This proportion remains far short of the predominance of 'God' which Shakespeare's unexpurgated texts would lead us to expect. An editor who did this much would still not be doing enough; even if, in one or two cases, an editorial 'God' accidentally dislodged an authorial 'heauen', such excess of zeal would be more than compensated by the numerous cases where an expurgator's 'heauen' had deliberately dislodged an authorial 'God'. An editor is, in such cases, only attempting to provide measure for measure, de-expurgation for de-profanation; a more profane text of *Measure* is a text closer to the text Shakespeare professed, a text more likely to communicate the play's dramatic meanings, the religious intensity of its issues, the contrasts between its characters.

I am not proposing that this kind of intervention be undertaken everywhere. By looking at the problems of profanity globally, throughout the canon (and the period), it is possible for an editor to zero in on a small number of texts where expurgation is a major problem. A few editors, by contrast, have added profanity wherever they could find any contemporary warrant, drawing routinely upon memorial reconstructions to increase the amount of profanity in Folio texts which show no evidence of ever having been expurgated in the first place. On the other hand, most editors have made no attempt at all to restore profanities, even in texts which they believe to have been expurgated. Neither of these editorial habits is defensible. Editors should instead identify where the problem exists, and then do something to solve it. That is, after all, their only excuse for existence.

3

'With New Additions'
Theatrical Interpolation in *Measure for Measure*
by JOHN JOWETT and GARY TAYLOR

> a pox of yo[r] new additions, they spoile all y[e] plays
> that ever they Com in[1]

IF Ambrose Bierce had been a textual scholar, his *Devil's Dictionary*
might have defined an interpolation as 'a passage which the critic does
not admire, in the works of an author he does admire; which he therefore
determines editorially to excise (after the author's death), by pretending it
was editorially inserted (after the author's death)'. This facetious
definition would cover most of the passages in Shakespeare's works which
one critic or another has dismissed as interpolations. Thus, George
Steevens objected that a 'ha?' in one of Angelo's soliloquies in *Measure
for Measure* (TLN 927; 2. 2. 169) was 'certainly thrown in by the player
editors'; Grant White declared that Pompey's heroic couplet, just before
his exit (TLN 699–700; 2. 1. 244–5), was also 'probably an interpolation';
other words, phrases, and lines in the play have been similarly
impugned.[2] Such accusations transparently reflect the critical presump-
tions of the accusers; taste is the only evidence brought to the bar.

Scepticism about such claims is not only understandable, but admirable.
That Shakespeare *should* not have written certain lines could never prove
that he *did* not write them—even if agreement could be secured about that
'should'. Moreover, anyone who alleges that something has been interpolated has an obligation to explain who interpolated it, when, and how that
interpolation made its unsavoury way into a printed text. Most early critics paid no attention to such questions; even in the twentieth century,
respected editors like John Dover Wilson could base their theories of the
nature of a particular printed text on the assumption that it contained
interpolations, rather than evaluating the claims about interpolation in the
light of independent evidence about the nature of the manuscript being
printed. We would not expect a book printed from Shakespeare's own
working draft, his 'foul papers', to contain later theatrical interpolations;

---

[1] Thomas Middleton, *Hengist, King of Kent; or the Mayor of Queenborough*, ed. R. C.
Bald (New York, 1938), 5. 1. 325–6.
[2] See the New Variorum edn. of *Measure for Measure*, ed. Mark Eccles (New York,
1980). All our citations of earlier editors are taken from this edn., unless otherwise specified.
Quotations from *Measure* cite the Folio text itself, with emendations in square brackets; references supply both Through Line Numbers (TLN) and act–scene–line numbers.

we would not expect texts printed in Shakespeare's lifetime, apparently from good manuscripts, to contain material added without the author's consent. Moreover, although actors may occasionally have ad libbed the odd extraneous 'ha', or worse, these indiscretions should not have fouled the prompt-book, which was an official document, not to be lightly tampered with. Some recent editors have continued to operate on the assumption that 'actors' interpolations' have corrupted our texts of Shakespeare; none has yet provided a convincing explanation of how this corruption made its way into the early printed texts.[3]

But this does not mean that none of Shakespeare's plays have suffered from posthumous theatrical interpolation. We know that, whenever a play was revived, it might be supplied with 'additions'; Marlowe and Kyd both suffered, after their deaths, from this practice, and we have no reason to believe that Shakespeare's plays were immune to it.[4] Shakespeare himself seems to have provided such an 'addition' for *Titus Andronicus*, and for over a century almost all critics and editors have agreed that the Folio text of *Macbeth* has been corrupted by late, unShakespearian intrusions.[5] Henslowe's Diary records dozens of payments for such adaptations; Caroline legal documents take it for granted, as a part of a professional playwright's range of normal activities. The canon of a major dramatist is just as susceptible to such depredation as the canon of a minor one—indeed, perhaps more so, because the major dramatist's plays will probably be revived more often. But the psychological resistance to accepting the presence of such interpolation in the well-known, much-praised work of the language's most famous poet is, understandably, immense.

We have, despite that resistance, and as it were against the will of our own scepticism, come to the conclusion that two passages in *Measure for Measure* were added after Shakespeare's death, on the occasion of a late theatrical revival. This suggestion is not as extraordinary as it may appear: most other critics have conceded that the two passages in question create, in different ways, insuperable dramatic and textual problems. No one has, however, attempted to relate these separate difficulties to a single cause. Nor did we set out to do so. But we found ourselves led, inexorably, from what seemed the likeliest solution to one difficulty into what seemed the likeliest solution to another: something of great constancy seemed to emerge.

[3] For a criticism of this editorial procedure, particularly as it relates to *Hamlet* and *Lear*, see Gary Taylor, '*King Lear*: The Date and Authorship of the Folio Version', in *Division*, 405–10.
[4] On the whole topic of theatrical adaptation in this period, see Bentley, *Profession*, 235–63.
[5] For *Titus*, see Eugene Waith's Oxford Shakespeare edn. (1983), 9–11, 17–18; for *Macbeth*, Kenneth Muir's new Arden edn. (London, 1951; rev. edn. 1972), pp. xxxii–xxxv, *Textual Companion*, 129.

In what follows we have retraced our own steps, as intelligibly as we can. We begin with evidence for the kind of manuscript from which the Folio text was printed (I), and then look at a major textual crux, which most editors attribute to some unexplained variety of theatrical interference (II). Leaving this problem temporarily suspended, we offer our reasons for believing that one passage has been interpolated (III); removing this interpolation helps to solve the suspended crux (IV). This solution in turn leads to the examination of a second suspected passage (V), which seems to have been added at the same time as the first (VI). Finally, we offer our own candidate for the authorship of the 'additions' (VII) and a concluding interpretation of the effect of the interpolations on the tone and structure of the play (VIII).

I

All modern scholars agree that the Folio text was printed from a manuscript prepared by Ralph Crane, a professional scrivener. But Crane in all his work imposes his own scribal preferences so systematically that he obscures most of the evidence which might identify the kind of manuscript he was himself copying.[6] Hence, J. W. Lever, in the new Arden edition, conjectures that Crane was copying from Shakespeare's own papers; G. B. Evans, in the influential Riverside edition, conjectures that Crane copied from a prompt-book.[7] Either hypothesis could accommodate the conclusion that the Folio text contains late theatrical interpolations. If for any reason a prompt-book were lost, then the author's 'foul papers' would have to be used as the basis for a later revival, and might as a result be marked up by a prompter, or tampered with by a reviser; apparent examples of such dramatic texts survive, and we know that by 1623 the King's Men had somehow lost their original prompt-book for *The Winter's Tale*.[8] Nevertheless, a prompt-book would be likelier than Shakespeare's foul papers to contain such interpolations. We believe that Crane was copying from a theatrical rather than authorial manuscript. (We reached this conclusion before we suspected that the text contained any interpolations.)

Lever's argument for Crane's use of foul papers depends on the interpretation of several passages which appear to contain duplications or

---

[6] Crane's influence was first suggested as a possibility by F. P. Wilson in 'Ralph Crane, Scrivener to the King's Players', *The Library* IV/7 (1926), 194–215; many subsequent investigations have supported this conjecture. The most extensive study is T. H. Howard–Hill's *Ralph Crane*. Also see Eccles's edn., 293–4.

[7] *Measure for Measure*, ed. J. W. Lever (London, 1965), p. xxxi; The Riverside Shakespeare, ed. G. Blakemore Evans (Boston, 1974), 32.

[8] On 19 Aug. 1623 the Master of the Revels licensed *The Winter's Tale* again, 'without a fee'; it had been resubmitted because 'the allowed booke was missing' (*The Dramatic Records of Sir Henry Herbert*, ed. J. Q. Adams (New Haven, Conn., 1917), 25). More generally, see Ch. 1 n. 125.

inconsistencies allegedly characteristic of foul papers. Yet such duplications or inconsistencies only prove—even if we agree that they exist—that a change of intention has occurred. Shakespeare may have changed his mind (or forgotten what he had done earlier) in the course of writing the play, or someone else, years later, may have (as it were) changed his mind for him, by altering the action Shakespeare had envisaged. In extant prompt-books of the period, minor inconsistencies often stand uncorrected. In themselves, therefore, such anomalies cannot provide objective evidence for the kind of manuscript which Crane was copying.

Once we have discounted the value of such discrepancies, and also made allowances for all the ways in which Crane could be expected to regularize and normalize the text, precious little evidence remains. Stage directions, usually so valuable in differentiating foul papers from fair copies, are in Crane texts almost useless.[9] A detailed commentary on all the directions in *Measure* would be inappropriate and unavailing here; almost all of their questionable features are ambiguous, being attributable either to foul papers or a prompt-book, or to Crane rather than his copy. For instance, Lever cites, as typical of foul papers, the unnecessary elaboration of 'Enter Lucio and two *other* Gentlemen', 'Enter Duke and Frier *Thomas*', and 'Enter Isabell and Francisca *a Nun*' (TLN 96, 289, 348, I. 2. 0, I. 3. 0, I. 4. 0; our emphasis);[10] but W. W. Greg had already

---

[9] Crane could be responsible for anything from minor tinkering to radical restyling of stage directions (though the latter is not likely in *Measure*); he might also add directions. See Wilson, 'Ralph Crane' (see n. 6), 212–13; R. C. Bald, *Bibliographical Studies in the Beaumont and Fletcher Folio of 1647* (Oxford, 1938), 76–7; Howard-Hill, *Ralph Crane*, 21–7; and John Jowett, 'New Created Creatures: Ralph Crane and the Stage Directions in *The Tempest*', in *Shakespeare Survey 36* (1983), 107–20.

[10] Lever's emphasis on '*Frier Thomas*' at TLN 289 (1. 3. 0) stems from his belief that he should be the same character as '*Frier Peter*' elsewhere. If (as other scholars believe) two different characters were intended, then the Friar's name is not superfluous but essential. Even if (as we believe) Shakespeare intended only one friar, two alternative explanations of the Folio's distinction are possible, either compatible with derivation from the prompt-book. If Shakespeare gave the Friar different names in different parts of the play, then a scribe preparing a prompt-book might have perpetuated the inconsistency as easily as Crane did (*Textual Companion*, 470). Alternatively, the prompt-book might actually have created the inconsistency, for reasons of casting. Peter cannot be doubled by the Duke, Varrius, Angelo, Isabella, Mariana, Escalus, the Provost, Lucio, Barnadine, Claudio, or Juliet; Thomas cannot be doubled by the Duke, Lucio, Claudio, the Provost, Juliet, the two Gentlemen, Isabella, or Francisca. Hence, if Thomas doubled as Varrius, Escalus, Angelo, or Barnadine, or if Peter doubled as one of the two Gentlemen, then Peter could not be Thomas, and the role might have been deliberately split. The last scene makes heavier demands on the cast than any other, since it requires three speaking boys, eight speaking men, and '*Varrius, Lords … Citizens*' (plus, or including, Officers), the latter mute but essential to the scene. Splitting Shakespeare's single Friar into two would allow him to be played by two different actors, and hence permit much more flexibility of casting in the final scene. The otherwise redundant name '*Thomas*' in the entry for 2. 4 could therefore be a purposeful signal that another actor would play the part. In fact Shakespeare might himself have specified two friars for this very reason (anticipating the difficulties of the last scene). However individual editors and directors decide, '*Thomas*' is poor evidence for Crane's copy.

noted, long before, that prompt-books regularly duplicate such gratuitous details.[11] Lever alleges that 'directions for disguise or the sounding of trumpets', absent from the Folio text, would have been 'necessary in a prompt-copy' (p. xxiv). But the only possible use of trumpets in *Measure* would be at the beginning of 5. 1; like other editors even Lever does not find a flourish necessary there.[12] Moreover, Crane probably removed directions for offstage sounds deliberately: no such directions appear in the Folio texts of *The Two Gentlemen of Verona*, *The Merry Wives of Windsor*, or *The Winter's Tale*, and *Cymbeline* likewise has no flourishes. Only *The Tempest*, of all Crane's Folio texts, contains directions of this type, and in *The Tempest* they have been treated in a uniquely literary, untheatrical fashion.[13] As for disguises, authors were more solicitous than bookkeepers about marking them.[14] Lever's claim that '*The Letter*' at 4. 2. 122 (TLN 1985) 'is a customary heading in texts based on "rough drafts"' (p. xxvii, n. 2) is also misleading; it appears, for example, in Folio *Hamlet* (2. 2. 109; TLN 1136), for which no one believes the copy to have been foul papers, and in *Edmund Ironside* (Malone Society Reprint, l. 1275), a manuscript prompt-book. Entrance directions in *Measure* do not frequently occur 'where they might appear in prompt-copy, a few lines ahead as advance notice to the actors' (Lever, p. xxv); but Greg had already demonstrated that the absence of such early directions is poor evidence for the provenance of a manuscript.[15] Nor can we place any faith in the absence of some exit directions:[16] prompt-books, again, often leave actors to get themselves off the stage (and compositors could occasionally omit exit directions present in the manuscript).[17]

---

[11] Greg, *First Folio*, 132, and *Dramatic Documents*, ii. 208. See among many examples '*Enter L Anselmus the deposde kinges brother, wth his Frend Votarius*' in the King's Men's 1611 prompt-book of *Second Maiden's Tragedy* 257–8: Mal. Soc. Repr., ed. Greg (1909). The three examples Lever cites are in fact the only such directions in *Measure*, and Howard-Hill concludes that 'as Crane did not usually omit such descriptive directions . . . it is reasonable to assume that only the most necessary directions were present in his copy' (*Ralph Crane*, 122).

[12] According to Eccles, no editor has called for a flourish there (p. 234).

[13] For further discussion of this point, see Ch. 2.

[14] Greg, *First Folio*, 126–7. Greg also notes that in *Believe As You List* the bookkeeper substituted 'Ent: Antiochus: & Gard' for the author's specific 'Enter officers leading in Antiochus. his head shaude in the habit of a slave' (*Believe*, 2322; *First Folio*, 133), while in *The Parliament of Love* a marginal 'Ent Beaupre' duplicates the fuller 'Ent' Beaupre like a More' (*Parliament* 102; *First Folio*, 134).

[15] *First Folio*, 138; *Dramatic Documents*, ii. 219.

[16] Lever says there are 'about twenty missing exits' (p. xxv); however, this includes an '*Exeunt omnes*' at the end of the play, a direction hardly necessary in any text. Necessary exits are also missing at 2. 1. 263 (TLN 718) and 3. 1. 516 (TLN 1745); however, this last falls at the very beginning of what we regard as a major dislocation of the text, which may have obscured a direction present in the original prompt-book.

[17] Neither in *Second Maiden's Tragedy* (1611) nor in *Barnavelt* (1619) does the prompter for the King's Men add or duplicate a single exit direction—a sign of the indifference with which they were regarded. Anne Lancashire, in her Revels edn. of *Second Maiden's Tragedy* (Manchester, 1978), found it necessary to add 13 exit directions not present in the MS, this

Lever's account of the stage directions of the Folio text thus repeatedly attributes to foul papers features which are also demonstrably characteristic of prompt-books.

Lever also attributes the thoroughness and workability of the Folio stage directions entirely to Ralph Crane, rather than his copy. Undoubtedly, Crane could be counted on to sort out a good many inconsistencies and deficiencies in his copy. On the other hand, on the evidence of his work elsewhere, Crane cannot be credited with ironing out all the difficulties which Shakespeare's foul papers should have presented. One of Crane's last and most accomplished literary transcripts is the only extant copy of Middleton's *The Witch*. This transcript omits eight crucial entrance directions (TLN 199, 381, 933, 1687, 1801, 1817, 1988, 2050).[18] In a prompt-book, entrances (as opposed to exits) had to be marked, and Folio *Measure* omits only one such direction, the re-entrance of a servant at 2. 2. 17 (TLN 957), fifteen lines after his exit; there may be another example in the Duke's re-entrance at 3. 1. 154 (TLN 1375), if indeed he ever exits.[19] An exact parallel for such omissions occurs in the King's Men's prompt-book of *The Second Maiden's Tragedy* (1611), and Greg remarked on the general tendency for prompt-books to neglect calls for re-entrance.[20] In terms of its entrance directions, Crane's transcript of

does not include three cases where exit directions do not mention the necessary removal of bodies. Both *Measure* and *SMT* contain 35 marked exits. All of the missing exits in both texts occur within scenes, rather than at the end of them; this may or may not be significant. Certainly, texts set from foul papers do often omit exits at the end of scenes: see *Henry V* 2. 1, 2. 2, 3. 1; Quarto *Lear* 2. 1, 3. 2, 3. 4, 3. 6, 4. 1, 5. 2; Quarto *Troilus* 2. 1, 3. 3, 4. 2, 5. 1; Q2 *Romeo* 1. 2, 2. Chorus, 2. 6; Quarto *LLL* 3. 1, 4. 3; etc. Two of the missing exits in *Measure* might have been omitted deliberately because they would not fit on an already crowded line (TLN 658, 2494); at TLN 1574 the peculiar line-break in the middle of Lucio's prose speech suggests either that the MS contained an exit for Pompey, or that the compositor intended to set one (or both). Compositor D omits a copy exit direction at *Dream* 1384; B omitted them at *Merchant* 121 and *I Henry IV* 318 and 343 (both of the latter on one column of a single page).

[18] *The Witch*, ed. W. W. Greg and F. P. Wilson, Mal. Soc. Repr. (1949); see also Howard–Hill, *Ralph Crane*, 25 and 148 (n. 33). The entrance at 381 is technically a re-entrance, but occurs 90 lines after the character's exit, and hence constitutes a more serious omission than those in *Measure* or *Second Maiden's Tragedy*. The direction missing at 1687 is also a re-entry. No such extenuation applies for the other omitted entries. Crane also omits to mention Sebastian amongst the characters who enter at 2025 and the attendants necessary in the entrances at 603–4 and 1436, and he omits an *Exeunt* at the end of a scene (715). See, for comparison, the edited text in *Three Jacobean Witchcraft Plays: 'Sophonisba', 'The Witch', 'The Witch of Edmonton'*, ed. Peter Corbin and Douglas Sedge (Manchester, 1986).

[19] Editors since Theobald have also added 'Officers' to the entrance direction for '*Escalus, Prouost, and Bawd*' at 3. 1. 447 (TLN 1676); *Second Maiden's Tragedy* again offers a parallel, when the necessary soldiers are omitted from the group entrance to 4. 3 (ll. 1725–7). However, the presence of the Officers seems to us not only unnecessary but undesirable: see n. 79 below. At 5. 1. 0 (TLN 2346–7), we disagree with Lever, who doubts that one or more officers need enter with the rest; but they might be covered by '*Lords*' and '*Citizens*'.

[20] 4. 2. 56 (Lancashire), l. 1717 (Greg). On re-entrances generally see Greg, *First Folio*, 133; also Gary Taylor, '*Troilus and Cressida*: Bibliography, Performance, and Interpretation', *SS* 15 (1983), 112.

Measure is indistinguishable from a prompt-book; the same scribe's transcript of *The Witch* is not. Moreover, Crane's transcript of *The Witch*
also preserves a major confusion of character names (ll. 1767–71,
2025–7); this confusion affects two entrance directions and two speech
prefixes, and would be highly undesirable in a prompt-book. Again, the
Folio text of *Measure* contains no such lapses. Crane's transcript of
Measure is therefore demonstrably more regular than at least one of his
other literary transcripts, in the very features most important for a theatrical company. We can hardly, with this comparison in mind, claim
that Crane's copy must have been 'foul papers'.

The most distinctive repeated characteristic of the Folio stage directions for *Measure* is the centring, on a separate line, of a direction calling
for a character '*within*'. These appear at 1. 4. 13 (TLN 354), 4. 3. 23
(TLN 2101), and 4. 3. 103 (TLN 2191). The format cannot be discounted
as a compositorial trait, since two different compositors set these three
directions;[21] nor are such directions at all common elsewhere in the Folio.
The peculiarity in the printed text must therefore derive from some peculiarity in Crane's own manuscript. Similar directions occur in two Crane
transcripts: *Barnavelt* 2045, and Folger *Game at Chess*, p. 82. In the latter
example the direction occurs also in another Folger manuscript not prepared by Crane, and in the three printed editions. The relationship of the
superfluity of texts of *A Game at Chess* remains deeply problematic, so it
is hardly possible to be sure whether Crane took over the direction from
other texts, or himself transmitted it into them. This feature might therefore derive from Crane himself, though the number of examples in
Measure remains surprising.

It would be difficult to argue that the form of these directions originated in Shakespeare's foul papers. Stage directions of this type—'[name]
within', followed by a normal speech prefix on the next line—occur only
four times elsewhere in the Shakespeare canon: in Folio *Twelfth Night*
(TLN 2005) and *Richard II* (TLN 2535, 2573), and Quarto *Othello*
(M4ᵛ). None of these is believed to be a foul paper text. It is agreed that
Twelfth Night was set from some kind of scribal transcript;[22] the added

---

[21] *Measure* presents some of the most difficult problems of compositor attribution to be
found anywhere in the First Folio. Our own attributions are based on Hinman, *Printing and
Proof-Reading*, as modified by T. H. Howard–Hill, 'The Compositors of Shakespeare's
Folio Comedies', *SB* 26 (1973), 61–106; John O'Connor, 'Compositors D and F of the
Shakespeare First Folio', 28 (1975), 81–117; Eccles, p. 296 (drawing on unpubl. work by
Howard–Hill, also made available to us); and Paul Werstine, 'Cases and Compositors in the
Shakespeare First Folio Comedies', *SB* 36 (1983), 206–34. Compositor D set TLN 354;
Compositor B the two other examples. Howard–Hill cited as a parallel '*Cry within*' at
Comedy 1657 (*Ralph Crane*, 124), but this is not at all comparable, since it does not involve
a duplication of the speaker's name, or a specification of what was actually spoken from
within, or who spoke it (as do all three cases in *Measure*).

[22] For the fullest discussion of the evidence, see *Twelfth Night*, ed. J. M. Lothian and
T. W. Craik, new Arden Shakespeare (London, 1975), pp. xvii–xxv.

stage directions in Folio *Richard II* clearly derive from a prompt-book.[23] The status of Quarto *Othello* is more open to question, but most editors agree that it was set from a transcript, perhaps made for a private patron; it is alone among Shakespearian quartos in containing act-divisions.[24] Against these examples, all originating in apparently scribal manuscripts, we can set twenty-four cases where the specification '*within*' occurs on the same line as the words to be spoken within, and/or the character specified to speak them there.[25] Shakespeare himself therefore seems most unlikely to have contributed to the peculiar form and layout of these three directions in Folio *Measure*.

A prompt-book, on the other hand, might easily be responsible for the anomaly. Prompters usually duplicated important directions in the margin, and an actor who speaks offstage before going onstage in some sense 'enters' from the moment he is called upon to speak. Certainly, theatrical manuscripts show prompters duplicating 'within' directions in the margin, treating them effectively as though they were entrances. Thus, in *The Wasp* Hand B adds an anticipatory marginal direction '*Barrons within*' eight lines before an offstage noise is required in the text (TLN 2104). Closer to the situation in *Measure* is a marginal direction in the prompt-book of *Barnavelt* (1619), TLN 2045: '*Captaine w^{th}in*'. The following line is the Captain's speech, beginning with a normal speech-prefix 'Cap'. In Heywood's *The Captives* there are several prompt annotations for noises or speeches within which lead to duplication. Most pertinently, at ll. 2584–6, a speech prefixed 'Baker' in the transcript is annotated 'w^{th}in Baker' two lines above the speech prefix, and again 'Bak: w^{th}in' at the end of the line of his speech. In *The Two Noble Ladies*, too, the prompter duplicates '*w^{thin}*' directions three times in the margins (ll. 248–9, 798, 1147).[26]

The use of a prompt-book would likewise explain why, after 3. 1. 43 (at TLN 1248), the Folio has the direction '*Enter Isabella*' before a speech which is without doubt spoken within. A marginal prompt note could have called for Isabella to be available in time for this speech within, and Crane could easily have misinterpreted this direction as the cue for Isabella's actual entrance (in just the same way as another scribe misinterpreted similar prompt notes in preparing copy for Folio *2 Henry*

[23] For the fullest discussion see John Jowett and Gary Taylor: 'Sprinklings of Authority: The Folio Text of *Richard II*', *SB* 38 (1985), 151–200.

[24] Greg, *First Folio*, 357–62; *Othello*, ed. M. R. Ridley, new Arden Shakespeare (London, 1958), pp. xvi–xlv; E. A. J. Honigmann, *The Stability of Shakespeare's Text* (London, 1965), 112–20. On the importance of the act-divisions as a clue to provenance, see Ch. 1.

[25] See Marvin Spevack *et al.*, *A Complete and Systematic Concordance to the Works of Shakespeare*, 9 vols. (Hildesheim, 1968–80), vii. 430.

[26] All these examples are taken from Mal. Soc. Reprs.: *The Wasp*, ed. J. W. Lever (1976); *Sir John Van Olden Barnavelt*, ed. T. H. Howard–Hill (1980); *The Captives*, ed. Arthur Brown (1953); *The Two Noble Ladies*, ed. Rebecca C. Rhoads (1930).

IV). The Folio's misplaced direction represents a clear case of that species of 'warning direction' which characterizes prompt-books, directions which Lever claimed could not be found in *Measure*. Moreover, the misplacement cannot, in this instance, result from mere compositorial or scribal inadvertence.[27] Since stage directions were often placed (sometimes ambiguously) in the margins of dramatic manuscripts, a compositor could easily centre them in his printed text one or two lines before or after their proper position, and misplacements of such magnitude tell us nothing about his copy. But Isabella's entrance direction occurs in the Folio a full six lines, or four speeches, too early, and since the direction occupies a full type line the compositor can have had no incentive deliberately to misplace it after 1247 rather than after 1254. The error therefore cannot be compositorial, and the early texts apparently printed from Shakespeare's foul papers provide no evidence that Shakespeare would have called for a character to enter when in fact she was supposed to call from within. The Folio error therefore presumably reflects an error in Crane's manuscript, and that error makes better sense if Crane was himself copying a prompt-book.

The presence in *Measure* of the three distinctive '*within*' directions, combined with the related early entrance for Isabella at TLN 1248, suggest that Crane was working from a prompt-book; so does the complete absence of profanity. *Measure* was written, at the very least, one and a half years before passage of the 'Acte to restraine Abuses of Players', in May 1606, and no one supposes that Shakespeare prophetically anticipated that legislation. Yet, as previous editors have noted, 'God' never once appears in Folio *Measure*, despite his relevance to the story.[28] The text is also suspiciously free from objectionable oaths.[29] Clearly, the play has been systematically purged of its original profanity. (See Ch. 2, pp. 94–105.)

---

[27] Crane sometimes apparently added stage directions after writing out the text; consequently such marginal directions were sometimes slightly misplaced, as in printed texts: see Howard-Hill, *Ralph Crane*, 26–7. The entrance direction for Lucio at 1529 may, as Howard-Hill suggests (p. 123), be an example of this, since he is apparently not seen until one line later (after 1530). The error would in that case be scribal, compositorial—or no error at all. No '*within*' direction is involved here. But we find implausible Howard-Hill's suggestion that Crane was also responsible for the very different error at 1248, where the extent of misplacement is greater than any he cites from Crane's other work. Crane once added a marginal direction three lines too late, but that error was clearly due to eyeskip: both lines in question end with 'all' (*Ralph Crane*, 27). No such explanation could apply to the error in *Measure*.

[28] See Eccles, p. 295, and Ch. 2, above.

[29] None of the plays in F set from a Crane transcript is cleaner of profane oaths than *Measure*. We have noted only one instance in the play, a single 'By heaven' (5. 1. 105; 2473). Yet we have found five instances of the same expression surviving in *Demetrius*, as well as 'By this good light' (1131), 'By my crowne' (1604), 'By'r lady' (2871) and 'By this faire light' (2887).

Equally clearly, Crane himself might have performed such bowdleriza-
tions. The pattern of expurgation elsewhere in the First Folio, and in
other plays of the period, suggests that scribes preparing purely literary
transcripts did not expurgate dramatic texts. But even if we assume that
Crane did so, could Crane by himself have succeeded in removing *every*
trace of profanity? The evidence of his other transcripts suggests otherwise. Of the six Folio plays apparently set from Crane transcripts, only
Measure completely avoids 'God': *Two Gentlemen* and *Winter's Tale* have
one each, *Merry Wives* and *Cymbeline* manage two, *Tempest* boasts six.
Admittedly, few of these clearly allude to the Christian God; nor should
we expect such allusions in plays written after 1606.[30] But the two examples in *Merry Wives* clearly are Christian; moreover, that play also contains the Welsh mispronunciation 'Got' and the truncated oath 'od's'
(which also appears in *Cymbeline*). *Barnavelt*—where Crane was actually
preparing a prompt-book, which would have to pass the scrutiny of the
Master of the Revels—also contains a single 'od's' (l. 916). Thus, even if
we restrict ourselves to God/heauen(s) variation, leaving oaths out of
account, *Measure* is exceptionally clean. Moreover, in Fletcher's *The
Humourous Lieutenant*, which Crane transcribed under the alternative title
Demetrius and Enanthe, Crane's work can be compared directly with a
printed text, set from a different manuscript of the same play. Crane's
manuscript has fewer oaths and profanities than the printed text, but it
does not avoid such material consistently. Four instances of 'God' or
'god' are absent, but four remain; ' 's' appears in the place of printed
' 'Od's; 'Gods' appears where the printed text has 'Heaven'.[31] Even if we
assume that Crane himself is responsible for the reduction of profanity in
Demetrius (an assumption by no means certain), then the most generous
count would show him emending six instances of 'God' and leaving four.
Crane would certainly have found considerably more profanity in the
1603–4 foul papers of *Measure* than in the manuscript of a late play by
Fletcher. The entire absence of profanity in Folio *Measure* therefore
strongly suggests that Crane was working from a text with considerably
less profanity than his copy for either *Demetrius and Enanthe* (written
after 1606) or *Merry Wives* (which had probably been expurgated in the

[30] Eccles (p. 295) cites the absence of 'God' from all Crane's Folio Comedies, and from
The Duchess of Malfi (1623), apparently set from a Crane transcript. But *Malfi*, *Tempest*,
and *Winter's Tale* all postdate the profanity legislation, and are hence dubious evidence of
expurgation by Crane. Crane's Middleton transcripts are even less useful as evidence: 'asseverations, imprecations, and oaths straightforwardly naming the deity are entirely absent
from Middleton's undoubted plays—not even "the gods", classical deities . . . or Christian
saints are mentioned' (Jackson, *Attribution*, 75). Lake, *Canon*, 254–6, makes the same point
independently.
[31] *Demetrius and Enanthe*, ed. F. P. Wilson and Margaret McLaren Cook, Mal. Soc.
Repr. (1951); *The Humorous Lieutenant*, ed. Cyrus Hoy, in *Beaumont and Fletcher Canon*, v
(1982).

theatre). Such a text could only be an expurgated prompt-book, that is, a prompt-book carefully reformed for a revival after 1606.

The 'substantive' evidence of profanity thus reinforces the evidence of the stage directions for speech '*within*'; an important recurring spelling points to the same conclusion. Shakespeare's good quartos, printed by a variety of printers at widely separated dates, show an overwhelming preference for the spelling 'o' (or 'O') instead of 'oh' (or 'Oh'). These texts were set, with one or two debatable exceptions, from Shakespeare's own papers, and one can hardly avoid the inference that 'o' was Shakespeare's own decided preference. (See App. II.) The same spelling is likewise overwhelmingly preferred in Folio *All's Well* and *Henry V*, and in the Shakespearian parts of *Timon of Athens*—the three Folio plays most clearly set from foul papers, and hence most reliable as evidence of Shakespeare's own practice.[32] Moreover, most (perhaps all) Folio compositors consistently followed the spelling of their copy for this exclamation. The same Folio compositors who set *Measure* also set four other comedies from known quartos; they followed the copy spelling of the exclamation—usually 'o'—214 times, and changed it only three times.[33] We therefore have good reason to suppose that Shakespeare's own manuscript would have strongly preferred 'o', and equally good reason to believe that the Folio compositors would have reproduced whichever spelling was in the manuscript they were setting. Yet *Measure* contains fifty-eight instances of 'oh' to only seven of 'o'.

Again, Crane himself seems unlikely to be responsible for this discrepancy. In his own work he used 'o' twice and 'oh' once: he was thus either indifferent on the matter, or actually preferred 'o'.[34] In his transcripts he

[32] For Middleton's collaboration in *Timon*, see Jackson, *Attribution*; Lake, *Canon*; R. V. Holdsworth, 'Middleton and Shakespeare: The Case for Middleton's Hand in *Timon of Athens*' (Ph.D. thesis, Univ. of Manchester, 1982); *Textual Companion*, 127–8, 501–2. Jackson drew attention to Shakespeare's probable preference for 'o' (*Attribution*, 214–15), though he confined himself to the evidence from the good quartos of *LLL, Romeo, Dream, Merchant, 1 Henry IV, 2 Henry IV, Ado,* and *Hamlet*. See App. II.

[33] Only Compositor F—who set less of *Measure* than either of his three colleagues—did not participate in the setting of *LLL, Ado, Merchant,* or *Dream*; we therefore have no qualitative evidence of his practice. However, outside of *Measure* Compositor F preferred 'o' 28:14 (as against 1:18 in *Measure*); he therefore either tended actively to select 'o', or at the least had a high tolerance for it, and neither supposition would allow us to attribute the spellings in *Measure* to him rather than his copy. (In any case, in a forthcoming article Paul Werstine presents strong evidence that Compositors F and D may be the same workmen.)

[34] We are grateful to T. H. Howard–Hill for supplying us with detailed figures of Crane's spellings of 'o(h)' in the MSS he prepared. In *Ralph Crane*, he suggested that Crane's preference may have changed during the course of his preparation of the 5 Folio Comedies (pp. 136–7). But he admits that 'much work will have to be undertaken' before we can be confident about the order in which Crane prepared the 5 plays (p. 138). Howard–Hill's own order begins with *Measure* (Crane preferring 'oh') and ends with *Winter's Tale* (Crane preferring 'o'); but if Crane did have a preference, we should have expected him to begin preferring 'o' (as in *Barnavelt*, 1619) and end by preferring 'oh' (as in *Game at Chess*, 1624). It seems much more likely—as we argue above, and in App. II—that Crane simply reproduced the spelling of his copy.

seems simply to follow the spelling of his copy.[35] Middleton preferred
'oh'; Crane's Middleton transcripts prefer 'oh'. Fletcher and Massinger
both preferred 'o'; Crane's transcript of Fletcher and Massinger's
Barnavelt prefers 'o' (37:6). The Folio texts of *The Tempest* and *Merry
Wives*, which were set from Crane transcripts, strongly prefer the 'o'
spelling which Shakespeare himself seems to have preferred.[36] Both Crane
and the compositor(s) of Jonson's masque *Pleasure Reconciled to Virtue*
evidently follow copy in utilizing the short spelling. The situation is generally the same for Act 1 to 4.1 (inclusive) of *Demetrius and Enanthe*.
Both the Crane manuscript and the 1647 Folio (*The Humorous
Lieutenant*) observe a marked preference for 'o'; significantly both texts
depart from this preference in 3. 5, where both Crane and the compositor
spell 'oh' five times in succession. This gives a striking demonstration that
both Crane and the Folio compositors were primarily influenced by copy
spelling.[37] However, such correspondences make the situation in the later
scenes even more puzzling. The printed text continues in the same vein as
it begins, but after the end of 4. 1 the manuscript reverts to a consistent
use of 'oh'. The run of twenty-four 'oh' spellings can scarcely be dismissed as insignificant. As all other evidence points to Crane quite consistently following copy spelling, we can only conjecture that the spelling in
Crane's copy for *Demetrius and Enanthe* changed at this point, for
unknown reasons.[38]

Even if all twenty-four 'oh's in the later scenes of *Demetrius and
Enanthe* were Crane's unexplained departures from his copy, even if these
instances could be indifferently aggregated with the spelling distribution
found elsewhere in the play, and even if *Demetrius* was the only available
evidence, one would still have to conclude that Crane followed copy
sufficiently often to make it clear that the presence of fifty-six 'oh's to
only seven 'o's in Folio *Measure* cannot simply reflect any preference of
Crane's. Hence the copy for Crane's transcript must have shown a strong
preference for 'oh'. Crane's copy therefore cannot—on this evidence—
have been Shakespeare's own papers.

[35] For evidence of Middleton's, Massinger's, and Fletcher's preferences, see App. II.
[36] John Jowett has argued that Crane was working from foul papers in *The Tempest*, in
'New Created Creatures' (see n. 9), 115–19.
[37] Hoy identifies three compositors who set the 1647 text (*Beaumont and Fletcher Canon*,
v. 299–300); but the pattern of oh/o spellings bears no relation to their stints. Compositors
A and C both set pages at the end of the play, where F's spellings consistently diverge from
the MS; A elsewhere reproduced the run of 5 'oh' spellings in 3. 5, where F agrees with the
MS. It thus seems clear that the MS copy for F consistently preferred 'o'.
[38] The presence of a collaborator ought perhaps to be investigated, despite Crane's attribution of the play, in late 1626, to '*Iohn Fletcher gent*.' alone: Fletcher was dead, and the
play was 7 or more years old. Alternatively, Crane might himself have been copying a transcript, one in which two different scribes had been involved; but this would be easier to
believe without the cluster of anomalous spellings in 3. 5. See App. II.

All four kinds of evidence thus point to the same conclusion: Crane was not copying Shakespeare's foul papers. He had in front of him something which had been thoroughly expurgated, showed signs of prompter annotation, and was written throughout in a hand which (unlike Shakespeare's own) strongly preferred 'oh' in place of 'o'. Crane was himself transcribing a transcript. If Crane's copy had itself been a literary transcript, it should itself have been suitable for use by the Folio compositors: why bother to pay for another transcription? Logic therefore suggests that Crane's copy was a very particular kind of transcript, the prompt-book itself, which the King's Men may have been loath to let out of their hands. Both the thorough expurgation of profanity and the treatment of 'within' directions also suggest that Crane's copy was a playhouse manuscript.

This conclusion—that Crane was copying from a prompt-book—does not in any way depend upon interpretations of the staging, meaning, or authenticity of any passage in the play. It is founded upon purely mechanical criteria, the only such criteria we have been able to discover. The fact that our hypothesis about Crane's copy rests on objective evidence does not, of course, lend any special objectivity to our own interpretation of any of the play's critical-cum-textual problems. On the other hand, those who disagree with our interpretation of such passages must either offer an alternative interpretation which can be reconciled with the assumption that Crane copied from a prompt-book, or must themselves provide compelling objective evidence that Crane instead used foul papers. Interpretation must accord with the mechanical evidence; it cannot override it.

II

The way questions of copy intertwine with questions of theatrical botching is neatly demonstrated by a notorious crux in Act 4 scene 1. In her last, posthumously published work of textual criticism, Alice Walker concisely explained the problem:[39]

A further question is raised by the six lines on Place and Greatness spoken by the Duke while Isabella withdraws with Mariana [4. 1. 58–63]. It is generally recognized that these must have been removed from their correct position in III. [ii] and thrust inappropriately into IV. 1. In their original position they must have formed the introductory lines to the two couplets on Greatness which follow Lucio's exit (III. [ii.] 172 [=3. 1. 443]), since the ten lines, taken together, reflect in general terms on what has been said by Lucio in the preceding dialogue—the rumours concerning the Duke's whereabouts and Lucio's galling slander.

---

[39] Walker, 'The Text of *Measure for Measure*', *RES* 34 (1983), 5. We have bracketed Walker's references to 3. [2].

Something must have been lost to cause the makeshift substitution of the six lines from III.[ii].

This apparent transposition (first suggested by Warburton) caused Lever some difficulty. He had conjectured, for the text as a whole, that Crane was working from 'Shakespeare's own rough draft' (p. xxxi), but when considering the speech 'Oh Place, and greatness' he was forced to conclude 'that the book-keeper or some other member of the company' patched up a gap in the manuscript by transferring six lines (p. xxii). If this ever happened, it should have happened in the prompt-book, not the foul papers. At the very least, Lever's treatment of this crux presupposes that the foul papers had been drastically altered by theatrical personnel; as such, it critically undermines his overall hypothesis about Crane's copy.

Be that as it may, a major transposition does at first sight seem to have occurred. This alleged textual crime, if it took place, must have been perpetrated by the book-keeper, or Shakespeare himself, or another dramatist, or Crane, or a printing-house editor. A dramatist would surely write a few lines himself rather than cut up an earlier speech, with no obvious relevance to the context. Shakespeare, in particular, could not be expected in the normal run of affairs thus to mutilate his own play. Neither Shakespeare, nor any other regular dramatist, can be considered a likely suspect for the transposition. But the change is also (as Lever notes) utterly unlike any known procedures for preparing the text in, or (through Crane) for, the printing-house. The alteration looks like a desperate piece of theatrical patching performed by someone other than a dramatist. But if so, why did the bookkeeper (or whoever) not simply turn to Shakespeare (or whomever) and ask for a speech to repair the deficiency in the manuscript? And what happened to the speech that originally belonged here? Shakespeare must always have realized that he needed something to cover the dramatic interval while Mariana and Isabella talk, and any performance of the play must have filled that vacuum. Whether the bookkeeper had an early prompt-book or the foul papers in front of him, something must have been available in the gap which he filled with 'Oh, Place, and greatnes'.

Can we proceed beyond this apparent impasse? It will be well to begin by bringing together the two speeches:[40]

---

[40] The Folio 'these' at TLN 1836 strongly suggests that the Duke has Lucio's speeches in mind; the word makes little sense if its referent occurs over 150 lines earlier, and 'these' was in fact Warburton's prime reason for proposing that the speech had been transposed. However, almost all editors have agreed that the Folio's 'Quest', later in the line, must be emended to 'Quests' (F2) if 'these' is retained. We agree that both words seem unlikely to be correct; but if either is wrong, an editor must surely emend the one which conflicts with the context. 'Quest' as a noun is sensible in itself, and only questionable because of its apparent incompatibility with 'these'; 'these' on the other hand conflicts with 'Quest' and the speech's context. We would therefore accept Hanmer's emendation 'their' for 'these', an

Oh Place, and greatnes: millions of false eies
Are stucke vpon thee: volumes of report
Run with these false, and most contrarious Quest
Vpon thy doings: thousand escapes of wit
Make thee the father of their idle dreame,
And racke thee in their fancies. [Welcome, how agreed?]

(TLN 1834–9; 4. 1. 58–63)

No might, nor greatnesse in mortality
Can censure scape: Back-wounding calumnie
The whitest vertue strikes. What King so strong
Can tie the gall vp in the slanderous tong?

(TLN 1671–4; 3. 1. 444–7)

No one would deny some strong connection between these lines. But it should not too readily be assumed that they were originally written as a single speech.[41] There is no development from one set of lines to the next. Each speech is a discrete unit. Each rounds to its own conclusion. Each has a distinctive style of image-making. Either one would be appropriate to the context in Act 3, but the two are more convincing as discrete entities than they are as contiguous parts of a single soliloquy. Warburton's conjectural transposition produces one long repetitious speech in 3. 1 as a way of getting rid of one short inappropriate speech in 4. 1: nothing is gained to justify such a drastic dislocation—especially as the loss of Shakespeare's original lines for 4. 1 remains unexplained.

No one doubts that Shakespeare wrote both speeches. But almost all critics feel (and we agree) that Shakespeare did not intend the Duke to speak the lines on place and greatness during Isabella and Mariana's withdrawal in 4. 1. The speech is irrelevant to that context and unusually short to cover the unheard dialogue between the two women. On the other hand, Warburton's suggestion—that the lines originally formed part of a longer speech in 3. 1, and were transposed to fill a gap—seems untenable. Clearly a whole leaf of the manuscript was not missing. A manuscript could be damaged, but the extraneous material in *Measure* is neatly confined to a single speech.[42] If the passage had been revised, the

emendation made particularly plausible by the ease with which 'their' could be mistaken for Crane's usual spelling 'theis'. Hanmer's emendation makes the lines sensible in their larger dramatic context, and also makes the speech itself more intelligible, by removing the need to interpret 'Quest' (as Lever does) as a verb—a gloss which makes grammatical hash of the rest of the line. Whether or not other editors find this emendation compelling, it must be conceded that Warburton's case for transposition to TLN 1670–1 rests heavily upon a single word of doubtful authenticity, and a word which *should* have been altered by whoever undertook to transpose the material.

[41] E. K. Chambers, expressing doubts about Warburton's transposition, noted that, if the two speeches 'stood together, there would be a very awkward repetition of the word "greatness"'': see *William Shakespeare*, 455 (not recorded by Eccles).

[42] Walker conjectures (pp. 5–7) that the head or foot of a leaf had been damaged, and alleges that a similar 'botch', consequent upon a gap in the MS, can be detected in 4. 2; she conjectures that two adjacent pages were similarly damaged. We find her arguments for

revision would appear in F. If a revision appeared on a separate sheet, which was subsequently lost, then the original version of the speech could have been reinstated.

The hypothesis of a 'gap' in 4. 1 could only make sense if that gap were artificially created, by censorship: if the Master of the Revels objected to the original content of the speech, then the 'original' version would become unusable. Shakespeare would have to supply a new speech; at some point that substitute speech might have been lost. But in fact this scenario raises as many difficulties as the others. Even if the revised speech were lost, why not simply get Shakespeare or someone else to write another? Even if the prompter decided to transpose the Shakespearian lines about place and greatness from somewhere else, where did he find them? Moreover, what could Shakespeare have written here that would have provoked censorship? He had already written about hypocritical rulers in the Duke's soliloquy at the end of 3. 1; did he simply repeat himself, too explicitly? Are we to imagine that Shakespeare himself substituted the inappropriate lines, after being told that what he originally wrote was unacceptable? Why not just write a different speech on the same topic, less explicitly—or more explicitly making clear that no aspersions were being cast on the English ruling classes? One might conjecture that his heart wasn't in it: 'If I can't have what I wanted, I don't care what nonsense goes in!' Even if this were a practicable attitude for a practising Jacobean dramatist, why did he write the resulting lines in his most powerful and characteristic style? In short, censorship cannot explain the alleged gap either.

No one is satisfied with the speech in 4. 1 as it stands; almost everyone regards it as a striking example of the theatrical maladministration of Shakespeare's text. This accords well enough with, and indeed reinforces, the objective evidence that the manuscript from which the Folio was set had been copied from the company's prompt-book. But the lines are undoubtedly Shakespeare's and they do not seem to have formed part of a longer speech in 3. 1. We are left with a series of unanswered questions. Where did the lines originally belong? Why were they moved? What originally lay in the place they now occupy?

The clue to the answer to these questions lies, we believe, elsewhere in 4. 1. In offering that answer, we move from consensus to conjecture. But it must be stressed, before we do so, that all the mechanical evidence points to the Folio text's derivation from a late prompt-book, and that the Duke's soliloquy in the first scene of Act 4 itself seems to demonstrate (as has been almost universally accepted) that Shakespeare's origi-

---

corruption in this later passage unconvincing: see Eccles, p. 195, and Gary Taylor, '*Measure for Measure*, IV. ii. 41–46', *SQ*, 29 (1978), 419–21. But even if she were right, her reconstruction presupposes that new material was written to fill the gap in 4. 2; if in 4. 2, why not in 4. 1?

nal lines have been theatrically adapted. Moreover, *Measure for Measure* is one of only six Folio texts set into type from a manuscript which almost certainly postdated Shakespeare's death. Ralph Crane's first known work for the King's Men dates from January 1618, and the fact that the first four plays in the First Folio were all set from Crane transcripts suggests that those manuscripts were prepared even later, especially for Jaggard's publication. The Folio contains other texts probably set from scribal copy, but only the Crane texts can be confidently dated so late, on objective internal evidence. The Folio may also contain other texts, like *Macbeth*, which have suffered posthumous adaptation; but in those texts the argument for adaptation is itself our only evidence for giving the manuscript a late date. Only in *Measure for Measure* does a convincing instance of theatrical botching coexist with independent and convincing evidence that the Folio text derives from a manuscript prepared after Shakespeare's death—a manuscript, moreover, probably copied from the company's prompt-book.

III

Charles Gildon, in remarks attached to his 1710 edition of Shakespeare's poems, noticed that the song at the beginning of Act 4 also occurs, with a second stanza, in the 1640 Cotes-Benson edition of the poems; Gildon simply assumed that Shakespeare wrote both stanzas.[43] Lewis Theobald, in his 1733 edition of the play, drew attention to the fact that the song was (in his words) 'inserted in' another play, *Rollo, Duke of Normandy; or, The Bloody Brother*. He did not mention its appearance in the 1640 *Poems*. Edward Capell, in his *Notes* (published posthumously in 1783), made explicit Theobald's inference, asserting that 'Fletcher . . . borrow'd' the song from *Measure*, and 'join'd a second' stanza to it; like Theobald, Capell did not mention the *Poems*.[44] However, Capell had by 1766 already concluded (in an unpublished manuscript) that the 1640 edition had no authority, and in 1780 Edmond Malone publicly and conclusively disparaged that 'very incorrect' edition;[45] nevertheless, Malone was still ready, in 1790, to 'believe that both of these stanzas were written by' Shakespeare. James Boswell, in 1821, first questioned whether

---

[43] *The Works of Mr. William Shakespeare: Volume the Seventh* (London, 1710), 448–9. Gildon in fact takes the unargued authenticity of the song in *Measure* as 'yet another Proof' of the additional material in the 1640 edn. 'being *Shakespear*'s'. Eccles overlooks Gildon (p. 184); Peter J. Seng, in *The Vocal Songs in the Plays of Shakespeare* (Cambridge, Mass., 1967), misattributes his remarks to 'Rowe (ed. 1709)' (p. 180).

[44] *Notes and Various Readings to Shakespeare*, 3 vols. (London: pr. 1779–80, publ. 1783), ii. 50–1. Eccles (p. 184) ignores Capell, though he was the first explicit advocate of Fletcher's authorship of the second stanza, and the first critic to allege important differences between the style of the two stanzas (see below, n. 55).

[45] For an account of Capell and Malone's contributions to the editorial history of the *Sonnets*, see H. E. Rollins's New Variorum edn., 2 vols. (Philadelphia, 1944), ii. 38–9.

Shakespeare had written the stanza which appears in *Measure*; he suggested it had been 'introduced by the printer'. J. P. Collier, in 1842, more plausibly conjectured that the stanza, though by another hand, had been added in the theatre; yet he seems to have assumed, less plausibly, that Shakespeare had always intended to make use of a song here, but simply left someone else to write it. E. K. Chambers, in 1930, conceded that 'A musical interpolation in a Jacobean revival is always possible'.[46] In short, for over a century after the relationship between *Rollo* and *Measure* had been pointed out, only Capell doubted Shakespeare's authorship of *both* stanzas; it took another century before Chambers provided a plausible explanation for the possible interpolation of *one* of the stanzas in *Measure*.[47] Yet, until Frank O'Connor's book *The Road to Stratford* (1948), no one had gone beyond Capell's admission of doubt, or the concession that interpolation could have occurred.[48] O'Connor's intemperate and loosely argued speculation sank, almost without trace, for thirty-five years, until in 1983 Alice Walker independently made the same conjecture. Walker argued that the first twenty-three lines of 4. 1 were a later, non-Shakespearian addition. However, like O'Connor, she made her case entirely on the basis of the dramatic awkwardness of the material, never even mentioning the song's presence in *Rollo*.

The case for interpolation is, we believe, much stronger than O'Connor or Walker perceived; but before we can examine the evidence for or against Shakespeare's authorship of this passage, the relationship between *Measure* and *Rollo* must be clarified.

The date and authorship of *Rollo* have been the source of some controversy; Appendix III discusses these in detail. But everyone who has seen Bertha Hensman's detailed arguments, in her doctoral thesis of 1947, has agreed that the play was originally composed in, or not long after, the summer of 1617; like G. E. Bentley, Alfred Harbage, and S. Schoenbaum, we find Hensman's arguments convincing, and we offer additional evi-

---

[46] *William Shakespeare*, i. 455.

[47] *Macbeth* provides an interesting parallel. Because *The Witch* survives only in MS, discovery of its parallels with *Macbeth* had to wait until 1778. But for the next 90 years scholarly argument revolved around the priority of the two plays, everyone assuming that one dramatist had simply plagiarized the other; not until 1869 did W. G. Clark and Aldis Wright suggest—in their Clarendon edn. of *Macbeth*—that Middleton's songs had been interpolated in Shakespeare's play. However, Clark and Wright believed that the Folio text had been very heavily adapted throughout; they detect interpolations in 10 scenes. The despised F. G. Fleay, in his *Life and Work of Shakespeare* (London, 1886), was the first scholar to suggest that only 3. 5 and 4. 1 had been affected. This has since become the orthodox view.

[48] 'Frank O'Connor' is a pseudonym for Michael O'Donovan; the book was later revised and reissued with the title *Shakespeare's Progress* (New York, 1961). O'Connor—a novelist, playwright, and short-story writer, not a scholar—builds upon the revision theories of Dover Wilson, arguing that the play has been substantially replotted and rewritten by an incompetent hack. He makes similar claims about a number of other plays, and the scholarly neglect of his attack on 4. 1 is hardly surprising. (Eccles overlooks him.)

dence to support them.[49] The consensus of recent scholarship thus dates the composition of *Rollo* in a period after *Measure* had been written, and after Shakespeare had died, but before the First Folio was printed. The presence of the stanza in the Folio text of *Measure* thus *could* be the consequence of the theatrical interpolation of material originally written for *Rollo*. Certainly, as Chambers recognized, songs were often added to plays on the occasion of later revivals; the Hecate scenes in *Macbeth* provide a famous parallel.[50] Moreover, the two-stanza song in *Rollo* was, like the play itself, extremely popular, and survives in a large number of seventeenth-century song-books, printed and manuscript; the single-stanza version in the Folio text of *Measure* appears nowhere else.[51] The popularity of the *Rollo* song would, of course, easily account for its interpolation in Shakespeare's play. Finally, the extant music for the song was written by John Wilson, who was born in 1595, and whose earliest known compositions are for Campion's *The Masque of Flowers* (1614). Wilson also wrote music for at least fourteen other King's Men's plays between *c.*1612 and 1629: Middleton's *The Witch* (1612–17?), Ford's *Lover's Melancholy* (1628), Brome's *Northern Lass* (1629), and Fletcher's *Valentinian* (*c.*1612?), *Queen of Corinth* (1617), *Mad Lover* (1616–17), *Loyal Subject* (1618), *Women Pleased* (1619–23), *False One* (*c.*1620), *Pilgrim* (1621), *Wild-Goose Chase* (1621), *Beggar's Bush* (?1612–22), *Spanish Curate* (1622), and *Love's Cure* (*c.*1625).[52] By contrast, only one

[49] Bertha Hensman, 'John Fletcher's *The Bloody Brother, or Rollo Duke of Normandy*' (unpubl. Ph.D. thesis, Univ. of Chicago, 1947); Bentley, *Jacobean and Caroline Stage*, iii. 401–7; Alfred Harbage, *Annals of English Drama 975–1700*, rev. S. Schoenbaum (London, 1964), 108. Clifford Leech, in *The John Fletcher Plays* (London, 1962), also accepts Hensman's hypothesis, via Bentley (p. 91).

[50] Bentley, *Profession*, 135, 139–40. To his examples might be added the songs inserted in the 1640 edn. of Middleton's *A Mad World, My Masters*; for which see Standish Henning's edn. in the Regents Renaissance Drama Ser. (London, 1965), pp. xix–xx, 38, 102.

[51] For the play's popularity see Bentley, *Jacobean and Caroline Stage*, iii, 401–4, 407. The song survives independently in many MSS (see App. IV); it was chosen as the opening song in Playford's *Select Ayres and Dialogues* (1659) and *Treasury of Musick*, 3 vols. (1669).

[52] For Wilson's theatrical career, see *The New Grove Dictionary of Music and Musicians*, ed. Stanley Sadie, 20 vols. (London, 1980), xx, 443–4; Ian Spink there makes a strong case for identifying Wilson as the 'Iacke Wilson' mentioned in Folio *Ado*. Spink accepts the conventional date of *Valentinian* as '*c.*1614', but Robert K. Turner, jun., suggests it may have been written before Nov. 1612: see *Beaumont and Fletcher Canon*, iv (1979), 263. However, John P. Cutts thinks that Robert Johnson was the original composer of the songs in *Valentinian* attributed to Wilson: see *La Musique de scène de la troupe de Shakespeare* (Paris, 1959), 35–8, 140–2. Either Wilson began composing for the King's Men as early as 1612, when he was only 17, or *Valentinian* is later than Turner thinks, or Wilson wrote a later setting for compositions by Robert Johnson. The problem is complicated by two other plays of uncertain date, for which Wilson music survives. Spink accepts the traditional dating of *Beggar's Bush* (?1622), but Fredson Bowers and Cyrus Hoy think it may have been written as early as 1612: see Bowers's edn. in *Beaumont and Fletcher Canon*, iii (1976), 225–41. However, this early dating depends entirely on the alleged presence of Beaumont, who is believed to have given up playwriting in that year. Beaumont is notoriously difficult to identify, and Bowers himself sees serious obstacles to Hoy's attribution. Finally, the date of Middleton's *The Witch* remains disputed: some scholars date it as early as the King's

other song in the Shakespeare canon has been associated with Wilson. Wilson's authorship of the extant music for 'Lawne as white as driuen Snow', in *The Winter's Tale*, has been doubted; even if Wilson did compose this music, it could easily have been for a revival, since we know that *The Winter's Tale* was revived in 1623, and that a new prompt-book was prepared for that occasion, the original having been lost.[53] Of course, since the music for 'Lawne as white as driuen Snow' may well be by Wilson, we cannot rule out the possibility that he also composed the music for 'Take, oh take those lips away' for a late revival of *Measure*. This conjecture presumes, however, that *Measure* was, like *The Winter's Tale*, given a late revival; the conjecture that Fletcher's song has been interpolated into Shakespeare's play also presupposes a late revival. Consequently, a defence of the song's authenticity virtually presupposes the same late theatrical revival posited by a denial of the song's authenticity. We may therefore assume that such a revival did almost certainly take place.

The Folio text of *Measure for Measure* was therefore set into type from a manuscript transcribed after Shakespeare's death from a late prompt-book which contained at least one instance of theatrical botching, and which also appears (whatever our interpretation of the song) to have been used for a theatrical revival after Shakespeare's retirement and/or death. Wilson's setting by no means establishes that the song in *Measure* is a spurious addition; however, Wilson, whose ninth birthday would have been on 5 April 1604, could not have composed the extant music for the original production of *Measure*, but could easily have written it for the original production of *Rollo*—just as he composed the music for the original productions of many other late Fletcher plays.

The only modern editor of *Rollo*, John D. Jump, nevertheless concluded that Shakespeare's song came first, and his reasons are worth considering in some detail.[54] In the first place, Jump (whose edition went to press before he had heard of Hensman's thesis) dated *Rollo* in 1625; the arguments for this dating seem to us, as to other recent investigators, wholly inadequate, but Jump's dating forced him to place the composition of the song in *Rollo* after the publication of *Measure*. His arguments

Men's move into the Blackfriars (late 1609), others as late as *c.*1616. (See nn. 192 and 196, below.) Wilson's composition of music for one of the songs makes a date before 1612 virtually impossible: one could only defend an earlier date by denying Wilson's responsibility for the original setting. Moreover, in this case a later revival is out of the question, since Middleton's epistle testifies to the play's 'im-prisond-Obscurity'. To summarize: we cannot rule out a connection between Wilson and the King's Men as early as 1612, but equally we cannot be certain that the association existed before 1614. See also n. 192 below.

[53] Seng, *Vocal Songs* (see n. 43), 240; see also pp. 257 and 271, for the erroneous attribution to Wilson of two Robert Johnson melodies for *Tempest*; these lend some plausibility to the conjecture that Johnson wrote the original tune for *Winter's Tale*, too. The early setting of 'Get you hence', in the same play, is usually attributed to Johnson. For the revival of *Winter's Tale*, see n. 8, above.

[54] *Rollo Duke of Normandy, or The Bloody Brother* (Liverpool, 1948).

all depend upon allegedly significant differences between the two stanzas, which are printed as follows in his edition. (For a full collation and discussion of textual variants in printed and manuscript versions of the song, see Appendix IV.)

> Take o take those lipps away,
> That so sweetly were forsworne,
> And those eyes like break of day,
> Lights that doe mislead the morne,
> But my kisses bring againe,
> Seales of love though seal'd in vaine.
>
> Hide o hide those hills of Snow,
> That thy frozen bosome beares,
> On whose tops the pincks that grow,
> Are yet of those that Aprill wears,
> But first set my poore heart free,
> Bound in those Icy chaines by thee.

Jump finds the imagery of the second stanza 'less firmly controlled' and 'more mannered' than that of the first (p. 105). A number of modern scholars have expressed similar opinions; but only one critic in the eighteenth or early nineteenth century perceived any such difference of quality, and denigration of the second stanza only became popular after the possibility of interpolation had been raised.[55] Since one can only deny that possibility by asserting that different authors wrote the two stanzas, it seems to us more than a little likely that the desire to attribute the first stanza to Shakespeare has generated a desire to prove that the second is inferior. As Peter J. Seng concludes, in *The Vocal Songs in the Plays of Shakespeare*, 'Any arguments based on the qualitative merits of the two stanzas seem a waste of breath; they resolve themselves merely to subjective value-judgements' (p. 183). Moreover, even if those value-judgements were more reliable than they are, they would prove nothing about authorship; few poets can guarantee that their second stanzas will always be as good as their first. To us the first stanza seems no less conventional and mannered than the second:[56] lips are sweet, eyes are like heavenly lights, sealed lips are like sealed wax—just as breasts are like hills of

---

[55] 'Fletcher . . . to this stanza . . . has join'd a second the most unlike it that can be, this breathing sweets that are natural, the other conceits for Hurlothrumbo or Mr. Bayes in his attitudes' (Capell, *Notes*, ii, 51). As elsewhere, this denigration of the second stanza is part of an attempt to disintegrate the authorship of the song.

[56] See for instance two songs by Nathan Field, one in *Amends for Ladies* (1611)—'Rise Madame, rise and give me light, | Whom darknesse still will cover, | And ignorance darker than night, | Till thou smile on thy lover; | All want day till thy beautie rise, | For the graie morne breakes from thine eies.' (F2ᵛ)—and the other in *The Fatal Dowry* (1617–19)—'Set *Phoebus*, set, a fayrer sunne doth rise, | From the bright Radience of my Mistress eyes, | Than ever thou begat'st . . . | Fayre servant, come, the day these eyes doe lend | To warme thy blood . . .' (E1ᵛ). The first of these, incidentally, is sung by a boy, brought on for no other purpose; the second play was written for the King's Men by Massinger and Field, one

snow, and the lover is bound in chains.[57] The second stanza is of course prescribed by its rigorous patterning based on the first (for example the ambiguous dawn in ll. 3–4 and the ambiguous spring of ll. 9–10; the broken seals of ll. 5–6 and the unbroken chains of ll. 11–12). To raise eyebrows at the conceitedly descriptive/affective imagery of breasts where similar treatment of eyes is found poetic is surely to criticize the taste of the period, not the poem itself. Nor is the first stanza 'too good' for Fletcher to have written. As Hugh MacDonald observed in his Preface to *Songs and Lyrics from the Plays of Beaumont and Fletcher*, 'the poetical value of the songs in the plays of Beaumont and Fletcher varies greatly. A dozen or so are among the very best in English dramatic literature'.[58]

Jump cities, as evidence for Shakespeare's authorship of the first stanza, allusions to kisses as 'seals' in Sonnet 142 and *Venus and Adonis*, 511–12 (to which he might have added *Romeo* 5. 3. 113–15 and *Henry V* 4. 6. 26–7).[59] But no modern scholar would, in any other context, accept the value of such commonplaces as a test of authorship. Our own reading of only about half the plays in the Fletcher canon has turned up references to kisses as seals in *Monsieur Thomas* (1610–16), 5. 12. 91, *The Chances* (*c*.1617), 2. 3. 56–7 and 3. 1. 133, *The Loyal Subject* (1618), 5. 5. 13, *Women Pleased* (1619–23), 3. 4. 184 and 5. 2. 28, and *The Island Princess* (1621), 3. 1. 263. All scholars agree that Fletcher wrote the entirety of all five plays. Noticeably, a sample of Fletcher's work has turned up more parallels for this idea than all of Shakespeare; moreover, most of the Fletcher parallels come from the same period as *Rollo*, whereas all of Shakespeare's come from works of 1599 or earlier. The actual phrase 'seales of love' also occurs in Munday's *Amadis of Gaule* (*c*.1590) and Campion's 'Canto tertio' (1601); Middleton has 'seale a kisse of love' in *A Game at Chess* 2. 1. 51 (1624). Obviously, this image does not constitute reliable evidence of authorship, but even if it did, it would suggest Fletcher more strongly than Shakespeare.

Unless we wish to imagine that Shakespeare and Fletcher both independently happened to write the same stanza, we must 'disintegrate' either *Measure for Measure* or *Rollo Duke of Normandy*: either the Shakespeare play contains lines by Fletcher, or the Fletcher play contains lines by Shakespeare. No scholar can, in these circumstances, avoid

(and just possibly both) of whom contributed to *Rollo*, written at about the same time for the same company.

[57] We have run across the 'hills of Snow' conceit in Fletcher and Field's *Queen of Corinth* (1617?; 3. 2); in the Christ Church MS song-book which also contains a copy of 'Take oh take those lips away' (see App. IV); and in Middleton's *Ghost of Lucrece* 134–40.

[58] *Song and Lyrics*, ed. Hugh MacDonald, with contemporary musical settings ed. E. H. Fellowes (1928), p. v.

[59] Also in *Pericles* 2. 5. 85; but we can have little confidence in the text, authorship, or—if it is by Shakespeare—the date of this part of the play. See *Textual Companion*, 130–1 and 556–60.

entanglement in the thorny wood of attribution. The 'seales of love' conceit cannot decide the question; nor can verbal parallels for the rest of the stanza, which consists almost entirely of literary commonplaces. Both Fletcher and Shakespeare use the phrase 'breake of day' (*The Captain* 5. 4. 63, *Monsieur Thomas* 5. 2. 24, *Barnavelt* 2697, etc.); both describe kisses as sweet (*The Captain* 4. 3. 37, 5. 5. 118, *Valentinian* 3. 6. 75, etc). In *Love's Cure* (1606?), Piorata sings this song to his mistress Malroda, immediately after they kiss:

> Turn, turn thy beauteous face away,
> How pale and sickly looks the day,
>   In emulation of thy brighter beams!
> Oh envious light, fly, fly, be gone.
> Come night, and peece two breasts as one;
>   When what love does, we will repeat in dreams.
> Yet (thy eyes open) who can day hence fright,
> Let but these lids fall, and it will be night.
>
> (3. 2. 118–25)

All scholars attribute this song to Fletcher;[60] they also agree on Fletcher's authorship of the scene in *The Two Noble Kinsmen* (1613) which contains this passage:

>   thou shalt stay and see
> Her bright eyes breake each morning gainst thy window,
> And let in life into thee.
>
> (2. 3. 8–10; E2ᵛ)

But Shakespeare also compares the opening of a lover's eyes to the breaking of day (*Venus* 481–6; *Romeo* 2. 2. 20–2; Sonnet 132. 5–9). It may or may not be significant that all of these parallels—like those for 'seales of love' and 'breake of day'—occur early in Shakespeare's work. By describing the lover's lips as 'sweetly . . . forsworne' and the lover's kisses as 'Seales of love . . . seal'd in vaine' the song suggests that the kisses were like vows and the vows like kisses; similar amalgamations of the two functions of the lover's lips occur in Shakespeare's *Troilus* (1602?) 1. 3. 270 and Fletcher's *Cupid's Revenge* (1607–12) 1. 2. 9–10. In this case, unlike the others, the Shakespeare parallel is closer in date. But Shakespeare's works contain no examples of the idiom 'bring againe', which occurs in Fletcher's acknowledged work at least six times: *The Captain* (1609–13) 5. 2. 81, *Monsieur Thomas* (1610–16) 4. 3. 10, 5. 12. 91, *Barnavelt* 2909, 2921, *French Lawyer* 3. 2. In searching for parallels in

---

[60] The extant text of *Love's Cure* was revised by Massinger *c*.1626, but he seems to have interfered little with this scene. See George Walton Williams's introduction, in *Beaumont and Fletcher Canon*, iii (1976), 3–7. However, a John Wilson setting of this song survives (Bodleian MS Mus. b. 1, fo. 28ᵛ). This must have been written for the 1626 adaptation, and the song might have been added then (though Wilson could, alternatively, have been called in to write new music for a 20-year-old song lyric).

Shakespeare we can employ computer-generated concordances; in exploring Fletcher's vocabulary we are forced to rely upon the less reliable (and slower) progress of a human reader. It seems to us likely that a computerized search of the entire Fletcher canon would turn up more examples of this idiom than our manual search of half of it; even so, further parallels would not allow us to dictate that Shakespeare *could not* have used this idiom. Individually and collectively, mere verbal parallels cannot determine for us whether Fletcher wrote something attributed to Shakespeare or Shakespeare wrote something attributed to Fletcher. But what verbal evidence exists associates the stanza rather more closely with Fletcher's work *c.*1619 than with Shakespeare's *c.* 1603–4.

Jump's metrical arguments for Shakespearian authorship are no more convincing than his single verbal parallel. He notes that the second stanza 'in two lines . . . departs from the regular metrical form of the first'; but this is true of many other songs in the Fletcher canon.[61] Besides, the two offending syllables could easily have been avoided: neither 'yet' (in the fourth line) nor 'those' (in the last) is necessary to the sense, and several early texts of the song omit one or both. Whoever wrote the second stanza must therefore have deliberately introduced the syllabic variation in the second stanza: it cannot result from mere ineptitude. Jump also notes that in *Measure* the Folio repeats 'bring againe' and 'seal'd in vaine'; in *Rollo* 'the second stanza is so written that the repetition of the final words of its last two lines . . . would be both cacophonous and non-sensical' (p. 105). But this proves only that one text or the other has been adapted. As sung in *Measure*, 'bring againe' and 'seal'd in vaine' alone are repeated, immediately; as sung in *Rollo*, the last two lines of each stanza were probably repeated in their entirety (as the musical settings require). Jump seems to assume that Fletcher suppressed the repetitions which Shakespeare wrote because he was so incompetent that he could not write a second stanza which permitted similar repetitions; though possible, this does not seem to us very plausible, and it is certainly not inevitable. Whoever added the song to *Measure* could, just as easily, have called for the Folio's repetitions because they, as much as anything else, create the impression that the song fits Mariana's situation: her bonds with Angelo were 'seal'd in vaine', and she wishes he would 'bring againe' his kisses. The Duke has already told us as much. Either Fletcher changed the first stanza because he was inept, or whoever added the song to *Measure* was familiar with the plot of the latter, and made some small attempt to emphasize the affinities between Fletcher's first stanza and Shakespeare's play.

---

[61] As well as 'Drink to day' in *Rollo* itself (2. 2), see 'Go, happy heart' (*The Mad Lover*, 1617), 'Dearest, do not you delay me', and 'Let the bells ring' (*The Spanish Curate*, 1622), etc. Fletcher's songs may be conveniently sampled in A. H. Bullen's *Lyrics from the Dramatists of the Elizabethan Age* (London, 1901), 96–147.

Nothing in the two stanzas permits us to arbitrate, objectively, between these two possibilities; the extant music could easily be altered to accommodate a repetition of 'bring againe' and 'seal'd in vaine', or might easily have been altered to replace those repetitions with a repetition of the last two lines instead. But one may legitimately wonder why Fletcher would have borrowed a song of only one stanza, if he had in any case to write another.[62] Why not write a new song altogether, of one or two stanzas? Fletcher had no writer's block about composing songs, as even a glance at his pre-eminent position in A. H. Bullen's *Lyrics from the Dramatists of the Elizabethan Age* makes clear. Mariana's first words—'Breake off thy song'—suggest abbreviation of a longer song. Of course, Grant White may have been right in saying that 'Her command to the boy to break off his song . . . is but a dramatic contrivance to produce the effect of an intrusion upon her solitude' (1854, p. 166); one might go further and claim that this contrivance in turn stimulated Fletcher to add another stanza of his own.[63] But this is, as sceptics are fond of reiterating, 'mere conjecture'. One might expect interpolated songs to be abridged (as is one in *Macbeth*); the 1623 text of *Measure* claims that its only song is abridged; another King's Men's play, written before 1623, contains three songs, one of which is a longer version of the same song. In these circumstances, not to be somewhat sceptical about the integrity of the song in *Measure* amounts to wilful negligence.

Though most of the evidence so far examined points to the priority of *Rollo*, in isolation the song(s) in *Rollo* and in *Measure* cannot tell us which came first. Both songs are, though to different degrees, appropriate to their dramatic contexts. In *Measure*, 'the dramatic effect of the song

---

[62] E. F. Hart suggested that Fletcher's additonal stanza was an example of a special category of 'answer-poem', a category in which poems have stanzas added which 'develop or amplify some idea, image, or characteristic feature of rhythm or style in the original poem': see 'The Answer-Poem of the Early Seventeenth Century', *RES* 7 (1956), 25. But this song is in fact Hart's key example of the alleged category. In two others, the author of the original poem may himself have written the additional stanzas (p. 26). 'Probably the best and clearest example' is 'Like as the Damaske Rose you see', first printed in 1628, which inspired extensions by King, Quarles, William Browne, Strode, and others (p. 26). Not only is this example a decade later than *Rollo*; it also, crucially, differs in genre and context. As Hart observes, the whole tradition of the answer-poem 'centred on the court' or on the great aristocratic 'country houses', two environments which provided the 'peculiar blend of intimacy and formality' which fostered this essentially 'precious' art-form (p. 21). A song in a public play hardly constitutes a characteristic venue for this sort of activity. Fletcher's second stanza significantly departs from the 'characteristic . . . rhythm' of the first stanza; it does not amplify or develop the imagery of that stanza. It does not advertise itself as an extension, either; instead, the stanza in *Measure* declares itself an abridgement. The 'answer-poem' provides a poor explanation for Fletcher's alleged addition to Shakespeare's song.

[63] F. W. Sternfeld, in *Music in Shakespearean Tragedy* (London, 1963), alleges that 'The "Willow Song" in *Othello* is interrupted in a similar way' (p. 90 n. 1). But this parallel if anything casts further doubt on the authenticity of the song in *Measure*, for the Willow Song was 'An old thing' with many more stanzas than Desdemona sings (ibid. 31). Moreover, the dramatic situations are not strictly comparable, since Desdemona interrupts herself (several times).

seems to be aimed at an immediate characterization of Mariana upon
her entry. [She is] an addition to Shakespeare's gallery of melancholics
. . .Thus, from the effect of the song and the knowledge presumably
given us of Mariana's plight, our sympathies are instantly drawn to
her'.[64] This description seems accurate to us, and we cannot accept Alice
Walker's judgement that 'the song is an artistic blunder', inappropriate
to 'a consistently ironic comedy, which makes no concession to the sentimental or romantic' (p. 3). Nevertheless, the play contains no other
songs, no other passages of romantic poetry, and (rather surprisingly)
not a single kiss, called for or implied by the dialogue; Mariana's melancholy serves no further function in the plot, and does not characterize
her speeches or her conduct hereafter; Mariana's plight, and the sympathy she deserved, have already been made abundantly clear to us by the
Duke; the modesty and good will of her speeches when she enters later
in 4. 1 would make an equally favourable first impression upon an audience. In short, the song in *Measure* cannot be called necessary to its context, and critics may reasonably disagree about the value or aptness of
what it adds to the play.

In *Rollo* the song contributes to the climax of the plot. Edith has
appeared in two previous scenes. The first (3. 1) establishes Rollo's pas-
sion for her, and her own motive for revenge; in the second (4. 3), she
plots to make use of his infatuation in order to kill him. To assist in this
seduction, she asks to borrow jewellery and clothes; Matilda agrees to
this, and suggests that she use make-up too. When Edith enters, at the
beginning of 5. 2, she is presumably dressed to kill; 'a banquet' and 'a
boy' are also present. The banquet serves no direct purpose in the plot,
and is never even referred to by the characters; but it was clearly used,
for it is specified in both the 1639 and 1640 quartos (both deriving from
the prompt-book, and printed independently).[65] Like Edith's jewelry, her
make-up, and her clothes, the feast is part of the 'Banquet of Sense' with
which she hopes to lure Rollo to his death. The boy's song is the final
ingredient in this sensual stew: Edith specifically calls for it to 'entertaine'
Rollo (5. 2. 20). Sung by a boy, addressed to a woman, the song deliberately titillates, dwelling first upon the lips, eyes, and kisses, then the
exposed breasts and nipples, which the woman 'beares' (and 'bares'); the
male lover, 'bound in . . . Icy chaines', asks the woman (ambiguously) to
'return' his kisses, and to set his poor heart free. As a dramatic device,
the song allows Edith to tempt Rollo without explicitly offering herself to
him: she can maintain the modesty and reluctance essential to our dra-

[64] John H. Long, *Shakespeare's Use of Music: The Final Comedies* (Gainesville, Fla.,
1961), 20.
[65] *Rollo*, ed. Jump (see n. 54), pp. ix–xviii. Hensman agrees, though she claims that the
copy for 1640 was 'a Massinger autograph' prompt-book (thesis, 233)—an hypothesis decisively refuted by Cyrus Hoy's linguistic evidence. (See Apps. III and IV.)

matic sympathies (and her plot), while at the same time inflaming Rollo's lust.

The song in *Rollo* could be omitted, just as the banquet could; but it seems to us essential to the dramatic method of this climatic scene—and typical, too, of the melodramatic titillation of so many plays in the Fletcher canon.[66] Moreover, the song's imagery seems more appropriate to the situation in *Rollo* than to that in *Measure*. In *Venus and Adonis*, and also incidentally in *All's Well that Ends Well*, Shakespeare ironically puts the usual Petrarchan hyperboles into a woman's mouth, addressed to or of a man; in *Venus* this contributes to the 'preposterous' sexual comedy, while in *All's Well* it adds to the sense of shock and reversal occasioned by Helen's first soliloquy (and is pertinent to the plot and themes of the whole play). And Helen, though she dwells lovingly on the particulars of Bertram's face, describes his eye as 'hawking' (1. 1. 93), which is conventionally masculine enough. But the song in *Measure* employs its Petrarchan commonplaces with no sense of ironic or significant dislocation; Angelo, moreover, strikes few readers or actors as an effeminate Adonis. If the song originally belonged to *Rollo*, then the employment of such romantic diction (in a song sung by a boy, about a woman) occasions no surprise. In order to adapt that song for *Measure*, the second stanza would (as Gildon realized) have to be omitted, for although men have eyes and lips their breasts usually do not inspire much romantic sentiment.[67] But the first stanza seems, even so, more obviously appropriate if addressed to a female lover, as in *Rollo*. Moreover, in *Rollo* as in *Measure* that song is sung by a boy, at the request of a woman. In *Rollo* this distinction of gender accords with the song's own point of view, sung by a man to a woman; in *Measure* it does not, for if the song has any appropriateness to Mariana we must imagine it being sung by a female to a male, rather than—as we see before us—by a male to a female.

Outside this passage, Shakespeare nowhere begins an act with a song; only twice in non-collaborative plays, and only four times altogether, does he begin a scene with a song.

Enter, Amyens, Iaques, & others.
Song.

(*As You Like It* 2. 5; 889–90)

[66] Leech, in *John Fletcher Plays* (see n. 49), 125, draws attention to the similar climatic scene in *The Maid's Tragedy*; Hensman had noted the similar reversals of a romantic wooing in *Valentinian* and *Wife for a Month* as well (thesis, 51).
[67] 'The Reason why this Stanza was left out in that Place of *Measure for Measure*, where the first is, is this—it is plain that the second makes the Song to be from a Man to a Woman; whereas in the Play it is from a Woman to a Man. From *Mariana* to *Angelo*. For to have brought in *the Hills of Snow which his frozen Bosom bears*, had here been highly ridiculous' (Gildon, *Shakespeare* (see n. 43), 448–9).

Enter Autolicus singing.

(*Winter's Tale* 4. 3; 1668)

Enter Hymen *with a Torch burning: a Boy, in a white Robe before singing, and strewing Flowres: After* Hymen, *a Nimph . . . Then* Theseus *. . . Then* Hipolita *. . . After her* Emilia *. . .*

The Song.

(*Two Noble Kinsmen*, I. 1)

Enter the Queenes with the Hearses of their Knightes, in a Funerall Solempnity, & c.

Vrnes, and odours, bring away, . . .

(*Two Noble Kinsmen*, I. 5)

The last two examples are processions, which the song naturally accompanies; Autolycus is a pedlar, singing as he walks along the road; Amiens and the others, introduced in a previous scene, are exiled courtiers, and sing as they walk through the forest. None of these entries need occasion any surprise about *why* the characters sing, or *when* they started; nor would these entries create any difficulties of staging. In *Measure for Measure*, by contrast, two new characters 'enter', one of them apparently singing to the other. Should the boy be singing as they walk in? If so, why is he doing so? Or should they both arrive on the stage, silently, without explanation, and then the boy begin singing, again without explanation? One can only defend the Folio staging by indulging in 'speculative' reconstruction: '*Mariana drifts in, moodily, the boy discreetly following her; then at a gesture of her hand he begins to sing*'. But though such an entrance cannot be called impossible, it can be called uncharacteristic of Shakespeare's practice elsewhere. Mariana, moreover, almost immediately tells us that she has 'sat here all day' (TLN 1789–90; 4. 1. 19–20), surely a rather surprising statement, if she and the boy have just entered in the normal way.

In short, both the awkwardness of the entrance, and Mariana's explicit statement, suggest that Mariana and the boy do not in fact 'enter' at all, but are discovered. The wording of the Folio direction does not contradict this assumption, because 'enter' was used elsewhere of discoveries.[68] The outdoor theatres did, on occasion, make use of entrances by discovery, but these almost always involved the creation of a definite location, by means of large props: discoveries of one or more characters in a 'shop', or in bed. In Globe plays discoveries always involve corpses, sleepers, or a person 'studying', usually alone in a study.[69] No Globe play provides a parallel for Mariana's entrance here. Shakespeare himself makes very sparing use of such discoveries until his late plays, which include the revelations of Hermione as a statue, Miranda and Ferdinand

---

[68] Smith, *Blackfriars Playhouse*, 346–7.
[69] See Bernard Beckerman, *Shakespeare at the Globe 1599–1609* (New York, 1962), 82–7.

at chess, and Innogen in her bed beside Giacomo in his trunk. In this respect, as in many others, Shakespeare's late work reflects the increasing use of theatrical techniques associated with the private theatres. Discoveries in the outdoor theatres would apparently be managed by drawing a curtain across the central stage recess: the props were thus either revealed or thrust out, and the playing space thereby metamorphosed into a shop or bedroom or study. This method of entrance was necessarily limited by the size of the recess itself. But the indoor Blackfriars theatre, which the King's Men acquired in 1608 and began using for performances in late 1609 or early 1610, had curtains which could be drawn across the entire width of the stage, thereby dividing its area into an open forestage and a closed rear-stage. This arrangement permitted much more elaborate discoveries, and a more frequent, less specialized use of discoveries naturally resulted.[70] In the case of *Measure for Measure*, the opening of 4. 1 requires no recognizable generic setting, like a shop or a bedroom, which might have called for large or special props: none of the conventions of the outdoor theatres would call for a discovery here. On the other hand, the discovery does require enough space for Mariana to be revealed, sitting, and for a boy to be revealed, singing. In short, though we cannot prove that the beginning of 4. 1 in the Folio text presupposes performance in the Blackfriars, it certainly does fit the conventions of that theatre better than it fits those associated with the Globe, in 1603–4. The Folio text thus seems to envisage a type of staging associated with a theatre which the King's Men did not begin using until five or more years after *Measure* had originally been written— a staging here used for the introduction of a song which appears in another King's Men play of *c*.1617–20.

Moreover, this peculiar entrance begins an act. Before they began performing at the Blackfriars, the King's Men made no use of intervals between the acts; the adoption of this practice coincides with their move into an indoor theatre. The consistent use of intervals gave the beginning and end of an act much greater theatrical prominence, which dramatists predictably made some effort to exploit. As Granville-Barker suggested, 'one may prefer to begin a fresh act upon a note of revived interest'.[71] This song, at the beginning of Act 4, admirably serves just that purpose. Of course, this does not prove that the song *must* have been added after intervals became normal practice; on the other hand, early plays were sometimes altered, on the occasion of post-1609 revivals, in order to provide effective act-breaks—just as they were sometimes supplemented with new songs.[72] Given the probability that Mariana's entrance reflects later performance conditions, one can hardly avoid the suspicion that the entire beginning of Act 4 likewise reflects those conditions.

---

[70] Smith, *Blackfriars Playhouse*, 343–52.   [71] *Prefaces*, i, 48.   [72] Ch. 1.

The boy's presence raises similar doubts. The boy makes no other appearance; he enters, sings his song, and is immediately dispatched, without saying a word. The character is transparently introduced simply in order to sing a song. Shakespeare usually arranges matters more adroitly. Except for the boys in the two processions in *The Two Noble Kinsmen*, he introduces anonymous singers only five times elsewhere. In *The Merchant of Venice* 3. 2, *Much Ado* 5. 3, *As You Like It* 5. 3, and *All is True* 3. 1, songs are sung by one or more of a train of attendants, attached to someone of high rank. In *Merchant* the train has appeared in earlier scenes; in *Much Ado* they form part of the ceremonial procession, '*with tapers*', at Hero's tomb; in *All is True* Queen Katharine and her women enter '*as at worke*', until she tells them to 'leaue working' and sing to her. Only in *As You Like It* do the two pages in 5. 3 have no other dramatic function; yet they carry on a witty dialogue with Touchstone, as well as singing, and are in any case natural adjuncts to the court party in Arden. None of these examples affords a parallel for *Measure*. *Antony and Cleopatra* 2. 7 comes closer: the banquet on Pompey's galley begins with a direction for music, then a dialogue between '*two or three seruants*', then the entrance of the principals; the servants clearly remain on stage, and near the end of the scene we are told that 'the Boy shall sing' while they dance 'the Egyptian Backenals'. We hear no more of this boy, but his unobtrusive presence among the other servants is as natural as the song and dance which form the climax of these revels: he enters and exits with others, and only attracts our attention when called upon to sing. Uniquely in the Shakespeare canon, the singer in *Measure* both enters and exits awkwardly.[73]

The presence of this song in *Rollo* inevitably raises doubts about its presence in the 1623 text of *Measure*, doubts only increased by a comparison of its context in the two plays; moreover, *Measure* introduces the song, its singer, and its audience in an awkward, dubiously Shakespearian manner, which seems to depend upon a method of staging not in use until years after Shakespeare wrote the play. Finally, if the lines following the song are Shakespeare's, they are not Shakespeare at anywhere near his best:

> *Enter Duke.*
> *Mar.* Breake off thy song, and haste thee quick away,
> Here comes a man of comfort, whose aduice
> Hath often still'd my brawling discontent.
> I cry you mercie, Sir, and well could wish
> You had not found me here so musicall.
> Let me excuse me, and beleeue me so,
> My mirth it much displeas'd, but pleas'd my woe.

---

[73] As O'Connor says, 'The [adapter] has not the remotest idea of how to get people on and off the stage . . . Mariana's exit . . . is the low-water mark of dramatic incompetence', *Shakespeare's Progress* (see n. 48), 155, 159.

> *Duk.* 'Tis good; though Musick oft hath such a charme
> To make bad, good; and good prouoake to harme.
> I pray you tell me, hath any body enquir'd for mee here
> to day; much vpon this time haue I promis'd here to
> meete.
> *Mar.* You haue not bin enquir'd after: I haue sat
> here all day.
> > *Enter Isabell.*
> *Duk.* I doe constantly beleeue you: the time is come
> euen now. I shall craue your forbearance alittle, may be
> I will call vpon you anone for some aduantage to your
> selfe.
> *Mar.* I am alwayes bound to you.   *Exit*
> > (TLN 1776–96; 4. 1. 7–24)

Alice Walker pertinently observes that Mariana's first speech creates a real difficulty, 'since the "man of comfort" had assumed the role of Friar so recently' (p. 4). This contradiction might, of course, be Shakespeare's fault; but the presence of such an anomaly in a passage otherwise suspect does little to encourage confidence in the text's authenticity. Walker also opines that these lines

are clearly the work of an inexpert hand (probably a bookkeeper's) with a few tricks of the trade and a store of stage commonplaces—'I cry you mercy, sir', 'I do constantly believe you', 'I am always bound to you'. Tags like these occur anywhere and are common enough in Shakespeare's plays, but in the opening dialogue of 4. 1 they are so artlessly strung together that they reveal only too clearly its lack of matter (pp. 3–4).

Anyone would have to admit that the lines are, at best, undistinguished. Some critics, of course, feel that the second half of *Measure* falls lamentably short of its beginnings, and such critics might explain the weakness of the language here as no more than a specimen of the more general malaise. But the passages immediately before and after 4. 1. 1–24 spring with an unmistakably Shakespearian verbal life:[74]

> Craft against vice, I must applie.
> With *Angelo* to night shall lye
> His old betroathed (but despised:)
> So disguise shall by th'disguised
> Pay with falshood, false exacting,
> And performe an olde contracting.   *Exit*
> > (TLN 1762–7; 3. 1. 533–8)

[74] R. G. White (1857) and others since him have claimed that the soliloquy ending 3.1 is itself a non-Shakespearian interpolation. This view has not been taken very seriously in recent years (for a defence of this speech, see N. Bawcutt, ' "He Who the Sword of Heaven will Bear": The Duke versus Angelo in *Measure for Measure*', *Shakespeare Survey 37* (1984), 89–98); but it is worth recording that our own examination has revealed nothing that casts doubt on, and plenty that suggests, Shakespeare's authorship.

What is the newes from this good Deputie?
   Isab. He hath a Garden circummur'd with Bricke,
Whose westerne side is with a Vineyard back't;
And to that Vineyard is a planched gate,
That makes his opening with this bigger Key:
This other doth command a little doore,
Which from the Vineyard to the Garden leades,
There haue I made my promise, vpon the
Heauy midle of the night, to call vpon him.
            (TLN 1798–1806; 4. 1. 26–35)

In other words, those who would defend the beginning of 4. 1 must contend that Shakespeare's verbal wit abruptly and temporarily abandoned
him during the very passage which appears—on a variety of quite independent evidence—to be a posthumous interpolation.

This passage also, coincidentally, contains a number of phrases for
which Shakespeare's extant works provide no parallel. The redundant
locution 'haste . . . quick away' never occurs elsewhere; nor does the
awkward 'Let me excuse me'; nor does anything comparable to 'believe
me so'; nor does the construction '[*noun*] of comfort'. Capell, who did not
doubt Shakespeare's authorship of this dialogue, nevertheless remarked,
of the line 'Let me excuse me, and beleeue me so' and the line that follows it, that 'Here, for the only sake of a jingle and a foolish antithesis,
we have in this line a boldness of expression scarce matchable,—"believe
me so," and in the other, an enigma scarce solvable.'[75] Moreover,
although hundreds of greetings occur in Shakespeare's plays, nowhere
else is the greeting *well come* (TLN 1797; 4. 1. 25) expressed as two
words.

We would not wish to attach undue weight to such evidence: in itself it
amounts to little. But it does coexist with much else that causes suspicion.
For instance, the nine lines of verse in this passage contain not a single
metrical licence: every line consists of exactly ten syllables ploddingly disposed. By 1603–4, Shakespeare's verse had become increasingly open to
the use of part-lines, hexameters, tetrameters, and missing or extra syllables at the caesura and the beginning of the line; he had always admitted
an unusually high proportion of feminine line-endings. Of the fifty verse
lines in the remainder of this scene, eighteen contain more or less than
the regulation ten syllables. Of course, this means that thirty-two are regular, so that a run of nine regular lines cannot in itself constitute proof
that someone else wrote the lines; but, like much else at the beginning of
this scene, the rhythmical monotony of those nine verse lines is atypical
of Shakespeare.

The odd mixture of prose, blank verse, and rhyming couplets also
raises doubts about Shakespeare's authorship. Dover Wilson, in a series

---

[75] Capell, *Notes*, ii, 50.

of early conjectures about types of revision in Shakespearian texts, laid great and unwarranted stress upon mixtures of prose and verse as evidence of redaction; those conjectures have (rightly) been almost wholly rejected, and as a result few editors or critics pay much attention to such collocations. But the mixture in 4. 1. 7–25 deserves scrutiny—not as evidence of early material revamped, but as possible evidence of another author's intervention. Rhyming couplets occur elsewhere in *Measure*, as often in Shakespeare, at the end of scenes, or just before a character exits (or clearly intends to exit); or in asides or soliloquies. Outside such passages, however, the rest of the play uses couplets only twice: once at the end of a speech by the Duke

> whiles I
> Perswade this rude wretch willingly to die.
> (TLN 2162–3; 4. 3. 77–8)

and once in the middle of a speech

> Haste still paies haste, and leasure, answers leasure;
> Like doth quit like, and *Measure* still for *Measure*:
> (TLN 2798–9; 5. 1. 407–8)

The use of rhyme in the second instance requires no defence; the first serves a less obvious purpose, though it may be intended as a kind of 'false' exit line. In any case, the remainder of the play offers no parallel for such an isolated pair of rhyming couplets, split between speakers, as are found in 4. 1; nor are parallels easy to find elsewhere in Shakespeare's middle and late plays. Both characters then switch to prose, for no discernible reason; Mariana speaks verse everywhere else, and this scene itself continues, after Mariana's exit, in verse.

The theme of one of these two odd couplets is equally surprising: music, the Duke tells us, 'oft hath such a charme' to 'prouoake' good 'to harme'. In Shakespeare's works, the effects of music are almost always beneficial; only discreditable characters like Richard III and Shylock speak ill of it.[76] Nor is music provoking goodness to any discernible harm in this scene, or this play. Yet in the scene from *Rollo* which also makes use of 'Take, oh take those lips away', music is exploited in order to encourage lust. The Duke's comment is, in short, more appropriate to the song's use in *Rollo* than in *Measure*.

The presence of a longer version of the song in *Rollo*; the popularity of *Rollo*, and its song; the composer of the music for *Rollo*'s song; the dating and theatrical provenance of *Rollo*; the fact that *Rollo* contains the longer version of the song, and the fact that *Measure*'s shorter version is interrupted by the words 'Breake off thy song'; the song's superfluousness

---

[76] For contemporary beliefs about the ethos of music, see Sternfeld, *Music* (see n. 63), 79–92.

in *Measure*, and dramatic exploitation at the climax of *Rollo*; the greater appropriateness of the song's sexual imagery to *Rollo*; the unusual entrance of Mariana and the boy, which seems to presume the use of stage techniques not much exploited by the King's Men until late 1609 and after; the song's proximity to an act-break, itself presumably not introduced until 1609 or after; the awkward introduction and dismissal of the singer, and the uncharacteristic opening of the scene with an unexplained song; the plot-contradiction in Mariana's first speech, and the flatness of the writing until Isabella's entrance; the presence of several phrases found nowhere else in Shakespeare's work; the metrical monotony of the blank verse, the atypical and unexplained mixing of rhymed couplets with blank verse and prose, and the uncharacteristic criticism of the effects of music: everything about the beginning of 4. 1 points to its being a late theatrical interpolation. In the aggregate, this evidence seems to us irresistible—as good, at least, as the evidence which has led almost all scholars for over a hundred years to dismiss the Hecate scenes in *Macbeth* as such interpolations.[77]

IV

Without this alleged interpolation of Mariana's song and the dialogue which immediately follows it, the play runs without interruption from the Duke's great speech of admonition to Claudio ('Be absolute for death') until his exit with Mariana and Isabella, at the end of what the Folio calls Act 4, Scene 1: a single scene of over 600 lines (TLN 1202–1854), the fulcrum of the play's plot, which begins in the nadir of Claudio's acceptance of death, his plea to Isabella, and her blistering repudiation, carries through the Duke's first intervention, his persuasion of Isabella, his encounter with Elbow and Pompey, and his first taste of Lucio's defamations, and ends with the united exit of Isabella, Mariana, and the Duke, after they have resolved upon the counterplot against Angelo. The satisfying wholeness of this sweep of action makes it all the more apparent that the Folio interpolation breaks the back of an originally uninterrupted transition from tragicomedy to comedy. In the Folio adaptation, the critical central scene ends, not with the cementing of a virtuous counter-conspiracy, but with the Duke's extended series of encounters

[77] The conviction that the Hecate passages are interpolations has been based on (1) the presence of the songs in *The Witch*; combined with (2) the evident dependence of the songs on a source, Reginald Scot's *Discovery of Witchcraft*, much used for Middleton's play but not elsewhere relevant to *Macbeth*; and (3) the fact that both the Hecate scenes and *The Witch* require Hecate herself and at least six witches, as against Shakespeare's three witches for the rest of *Macbeth* (the Folio specifically calling in addition to the three witches for 'Hecat, and the other three Witches' at TLN 1566, and voices 'within' to sing 'Come away, come away' at TLN 1467). But most critics have probably been more influenced by (4) the felt inferiority and superfluousness of the material. For further discussion of *Macbeth*, see *Textual Companion*, 128–9.

with the characters of the subplot, followed by a long soliloquy which makes no reference to them. This rhyming soliloquy, and the Duke's exit, strongly create the sense of an ending—an impression reinforced by the beginning of the next scene with a song, the introduction of two new characters, and a marked change of locale. Yet, in terms of the play's plot, nothing has ended; we are smack in the middle of things; the impression of closure has been, in the Folio, created artificially, rather than arising unforcedly from the material.

The Duke's long soliloquy, 'He who the sword of Heauen will beare', directly contributes to this trumped-up ending. Just as the song on one side of the act-break creates the sense of a new beginning, so this formal soliloquy on the other side creates the sense of an action summed up and rounded off. The placing of this soliloquy reinforces the very effect introduced by the interpolation. This can be seen even more clearly if we imagine the outlines of the action as Shakespeare must have plotted it.

After Isabella's exit, under the Duke's instruction, to agree to Angelo's corrupt proposal, the Duke himself remains onstage. Elbow and the officers come on, leading Pompey to prison. Editors since Capell have marked a new scene here, because we have evidently shifted locale, from inside to outside the prison; but this shift takes place, in the usual Jacobethan manner, unobtrusively, and the Folio marks no new scene, nor does the action require a cleared stage.[78] Shakespeare calls for continuity; editors fragment it, thereby intensifying the damage done by the interpolation in 4. 1. The Duke is again, 180 lines later, left alone on stage after Lucio's exit; in a brief speech of 4½ lines he reflects that 'No might, nor greatnesse in mortality | Can censure scape'. This short speech covers the gap between Lucio's exit and the entrance of Escalus, Overdone, and the Provost—otherwise the departure and arrival would seem altogether too pat. After another 70 lines, Escalus departs, and the Duke is again alone.[79] If we remove the interpolated material, then after

---

[78] Eccles (p. 157) attributes this scene-division to Pope, pointedly correcting D. Wilson's attribution of it to Capell in his New Shakespeare edn. (Cambridge, 1922). But Pope consistently marked a new scene with any entrance of another character, after the French convention; he begins 'SCENE IV' here. Capell, by contrast, established the modern convention of scene-division, and identified this as the beginning of 'SCENE II'. All scholars since Wilson have agreed that Shakespeare's stage would have required no scene-break here (though all until the Oxford *Complete Works* continued to mark it).

[79] Capell also initiated the practice, followed in all modern edns., of calling for the Provost and Escalus to '*Exeunt*' at TLN 1745 (3. 1. 516). F1 does not mark any exit at all; F2 adds an '*Exit.*' only, after Escalus's speech at TLN 1744 (3. 1. 515). F2's arrangement seems preferable to Capell's: from the moment that Escalus first addresses the Duke (1700; 3. 1. 472) the Provost takes no part in the scene, and the intervening dialogue looks like an entirely private conversation between Escalus and the Duke. At 1692–3 Escalus says, 'Away with her to prison: Goe too, no more words' (3. 1. 464–5); editors since Rowe have naturally interpreted this as an instruction for Overdone to be escorted off immediately. However, according to the Folio no one but the Provost could perform this function: as the Provost continues to be addressed and replies to Escalus at 1698–9 (3. 1. 470–1), editors follow Theobald in interpolating '*and Officers*' in the entrance direction at 1676 (3. 1. 44–7).

Escalus exits the next thing which happens is Isabella's entrance; but again, as after Lucio's exit, we would expect a speech by the Duke to create a brief theatrical interval, before the new entrance. Isabella talks to the Duke, and he calls Mariana. Not until Mariana's entrance do we have any clear idea of the location of this dialogue: Shakespeare has carefully but unobtrusively shifted the locale out of the prison into the unlocalized outdoors, and by means of a series of encounters has created the impression that the Duke has moved. He probably knocks on the door when (at TLN 1823; 4. 1. 49) he calls 'what hoa, within; come forth'—a form of address appropriate enough if he has just arrived outside a house, and might expect a servant to answer, but unexpectedly undignified if Mariana has already appeared on the stage, and is known to be waiting for his signal.[80] The Duke introduces Mariana to Isabella, and the two women withdraw for an expository dialogue; the Duke is again alone on stage, and must cover the interval with a soliloquy. The women then return, and, after another ten lines of dialogue, the whole long sequence comes to a close.

Without the interpolation, Shakespeare would have needed, within the space of just over thirty lines, two soliloquies for the Duke. Presumably these should reflect on different topics. The first is a simple filler between one character's exit and another character's entrance; like most such fillers, it could be as short as Shakespeare chose to make it; moroever, it could deal with almost any issue, for it has no particular dramatic context, being spoken on a neutral unlocalized stage in a lacuna of emotion and action. The second soliloquy, by contrast, must cover an extended offstage conversation; it follows and precedes dialogue about Angelo and the plot against him, while covering an offstage dialogue on the same topic. This second soliloquy must also serve as the culmination of the

---

This may be correct, but if so 1676 is the only defective entrance in the entire text. It seems to us more likely that the Provost himself exits with Overdone, only six lines after the Duke's injunction (3. 1. 471; 1699). Overdone herself does not speak in this interval, but this should hardly surprise us after Escalus tells her 'Goe too, no more words'. The next word Escalus himself speaks is 'Provost' (3. 1. 465; 1693); in performance there would be no difficulty in a final brief exchange between Escalus and the Provost before the latter exits with his prisoner. In the Oxford text we therefore leave the entrance at 3. 1. 447 (1676) unemended, follow F2 in calling for Escalus alone to '*Exit*' at the end of his dialogue with the Duke, and have Overdone led off (by the Provost) at 3. 1. 471 (1699) instead of 3. 1. 465 (1693).

[80] Walker objects that 'This is no way to address a lady' (see p. 4, n. 39)—which seems true enough, if the Duke knows that the lady is waiting inside for his signal. Walker's further suggestion, that the line was added after the composition of *Tempest*, is frivolous. She bases the claim solely on the fact that 'What ho', 'within', and 'Come forth' occur within four lines (and three speeches) in *Tempest* (1. 2. 316–18; TLN 449–52). But 'ho' and 'within' are juxtaposed at least four times elsewhere in the canon (*Merry Wives* 1. 4. 131, *Comedy* 3. 1. 38, *Contention* 1. 4. 78, *Othello* 5. 2. 85); in the first of these examples 'Come near' recurs in the next line; 'what ho' and 'come' are also juxtaposed at *Merry Wives* 4. 2. 166, *Romeo* 5. 1. 57, and *Antony* 4. 14. 129; 'what ho' and 'forth' at *Romeo* 4. 2. 43.

whole uninterrupted 600-line sequence which begins with 'Be absolute for death'.

Obviously, 'He who the sword of Heauen will beare' fulfils the requirements of this second soliloquy as perfectly as 'Oh Place, and greatnes' fulfils the requirements of the first. Leon Kellner, in 1931, conjectured that the long rhyming soliloquy at the end of Act 3 should take the place of the short unrhymed one in 4. 1; Kenneth Muir, in 1966, independently tendered the same conjecture.[81] But neither could explain how such a drastic dislocation might have accidentally occurred; nor could either suggest a plausible motive for deliberately transposing them. Muir guessed that 'The audience may have been puzzled by the identity of the woman who listens to the song at the beginning of IV i', and notes that 'she is not referred to by name until' 4. 1. 48 (TLN 1821). Muir here isolated (without realizing it) another reason for suspecting the authenticity of TLN 1769-95 (4. 1. 0-25): it never even names the new character, Mariana, who is instead carefully identified immediately before her entrance, later in the scene, to meet the Duke and Isabella.[82] But we cannot credit Muir's proposal that someone altered the text so drastically simply in order to identify Mariana more clearly. 'He who the sword of Heauen will beare' does not even name her; it would have been simpler and more effective to give the Duke a short speech like 'Now I must speed to meet poor Mariana'. Muir supposed that the printer, rather than inventing such an obvious stopgap, transposed one speech (of dubious pertinence) from 4. 1 to 3. 1, and then transposed part of another speech (of even more dubious pertinence) from elsewhere in 3. 1, in order to fill the gap he had created in 4. 1. The Kellner/Muir transposition, itself implausible, presupposes Warburton's transposition of 'Oh Place, and greatnes'—which is, as we have already seen, indefensible.

Kellner and Muir proposed that the speech which in the Folio ends 3. 1 belongs in 4. 1, and that the soliloquy which the Folio places in 4. 1 belongs in the middle of 3. 1. We instead propose, more simply, that 'He who the sword of Heauen will beare' and 'Oh Place, and greatnes' have been transposed. Kellner and Muir conjecture that Shakespeare originally wrote the play without giving the Duke a speech before his exit at the end of Act 3, and in such a way that audiences would easily be confused about Mariana's identity on her first appearance; we conjecture that Shakespeare did give the Duke a speech after Escalus's exit, and that he carefully named Mariana just before her entrance. Kellner and Muir, like

---

[81] L. Kellner, *Erläuterungen und Textverbesserungen zu vierzehn Dramen Shakespeares*, ed. Walther Ebisch (Leipzig, 1931), 259; K. Muir, 'The Duke's Soliloquies in *Measure for Measure*', N. & Q. 211 (1966), 135-6. Eccles (p. 179) does not mention Muir, who offers a more detailed defence than Kellner.

[82] As O'Connor noted: 'in this extraordinary scene not one word indicates who the strange lady is, or for what purpose the Duke has visited her' (*Shakespeare's Progress* (see n. 48), 159).

others, have presumably overlooked this simple solution partly because of the currency of Warburton's conjecture, but more particularly because it depends on the recognition that Shakespeare did not write the beginning of 4. 1. In the structure created by the Folio's interpolation of Mariana's song, the proposed restoration of the speeches to their true positions would look, in itself, unconvincing. Why should Shakespeare write 'Oh Place, and greatnes'—which doesn't even end with a couplet—as the Duke's last speech before he exits at the end of Act 3? And why should he then revert to the subject of Angelo in a long speech which breaks the continuity of the opening scene of Act 4?

If we remove the interpolation, these objections to the transposition disappear. The long soliloquy convincingly brings to a philosophical conclusion the play's long central scene; the short soliloquy, by contrast, need not sustain the exaggerated emphasis given to an exit-line at the end of such an important series of scenes as those the Duke has witnessed and participated in throughout Act 3. The once-unfortunate lines on place and greatness no longer look so lost, when fitted between the Duke's dialogue with Escalus and Isabella's entry. After his encounter with Lucio, the Duke speaks a brief soliloquy on the subject of scandal-mongers (3. 1. 444–7; TLN 1671–5); in the middle of his conversation with Escalus he again brings up the subject of his own reputation, in two otherwise irrelevant questions (3. 1. 488–9 and 492; TLN 1715–16, 1720); the answer to the second of these ends just twenty-four lines before the Duke's soliloquy preceding Isabella's entrance—the soliloquy, we believe, on the subject of 'Place, and greatnes'. That the Duke continues to reflect upon calumny here need not surprise us; he has not, as in the Folio text, left the stage, returned after a passage of time and a change of place (and mood), talked with Isabella, dispatched the two women to discuss the plot against Angelo—and then, while they are doing so, inexplicably reverted to the annoyance caused him by Lucio. But there would be nothing unnatural about the Duke reverting to that subject after Escalus and the Provost leave. The significance of the similarity of 'Oh Place, and greatnes' to the soliloquy after Lucio departs is not that the two speeches are in any sense one, but that they mark similar moments of reflection linking sequences of dramatic action in an unbroken scene, the second characterized by the recurrence of a thread of thought established in the first.[83]

The Duke's reflections upon place and greatness not only make better dramatic sense at the end of 3. 1 than in the middle of 4. 1; they also acquire, in their new position, a new layer of secondary meaning. This

---

[83] As Ann Pasternak Slater remarks, 'the play's secondary theme, that of reputation, is a natural extension of the central concept of the dangers of *judgment*'; the Duke's speech on place and greatness is 'a formal meditation on the play's second most important theme': *Shakespeare the Director* (Brighton, 1982), 151–2.

ambiguity can be clearly seen if we again compare them with TLN
1671–4 (3. 1. 444–7):

> No might, nor greatnesse in mortality
> Can censure scape: Back-wounding calumnie
> The whitest vertue strikes. What King so strong,
> Can tie the gall vp in the slanderous tong?

Even if these lines did not immediately follow Lucio's defamations, 'censure' and 'calumnie' and 'gall' and 'slanderous' make it clear enough that
the Duke is reflecting upon libellous misrepresentations of 'whitest
vertue'. Ever since Warburton suggested that TLN 1834–9 (4. 1. 58–63)
should from part of this earlier speech, critics have interpreted it as a repetition of the same theme. So it would have to be, if the speeches were
conflated; but in isolation the second speech is decidedly less explicit:

> Oh Place, and greatnes: millions of false eies
> Are stucke vpon thee: volumes of report
> Run with the[ir] false, and most contrarious Quest
> Vpon thy doings: thousand escapes of wit
> Make thee the father of their idle dreame,
> And racke thee in their fancies.

Explicitly, these lines only say that persons in power are continually
watched, continually talked about, and continually misrepresented and
misinterpreted. Given that the Duke speaks them, given too his earlier
soliloquy on Lucio's slanders, one can hardly avoid taking these comments as, in part, a meditation on calumny; both 'escapes of wit' and
'racke' encourage the memory of Lucio. But, in contrast to his earlier
speech, the Duke here does not say that the 'Place, and greatnes' in question are 'strong' or of 'whitest vertue'; nor does he say that the misrepresentations of popular judgement defame their object. If these lines were
spoken immediately after Escalus exits, we could hardly avoid seeing
that—in a secondary sense—they apply as well to Escalus's mistaken
judgement of Angelo as to Lucio's of the Duke:[84]

> . . . my brother-Iustice haue I found so
> seuere, that he hath forc'd me to tell him, hee is indeede
> Iustice.
>   *Duke.* If his owne life, answere the straitnesse of his
> proceeding, it shall become him well: wherein if he chance
> to faile he hath sentenc'd himselfe.
>   *Esc.* I am going to visit the prisoner[.] Fare you well.
>   *Duke.* Peace be with you.
> [Oh Place, and greatnes . . .]

(TLN 1737–45; 3. 1. 509–16)

---

[84] The Folio prints the Duke's first speech as verse; all editors since Pope re-line as prose.

In this context we may apply 'Oh Place, and greatnes' at least in part to the exemplar of place and greatness they have just been discussing. The Duke and the audience realize that Escalus is as deceived about Angelo as, in a very different way, Lucio is about the Duke. Escalus, just before this exchange, supplied a corrective to Lucio's view of the Duke, a corrective which the disguised Duke had himself prompted ('of what disposition was the Duke?'); in contrast with his correct answer to the question about the Duke, he not only continues to see Angelo as 'Iustice' personified, but refuses to rise to the bait of the Duke's following speech. At the end of 3. 1, Shakespeare juxtaposes Escalus's misjudgement of Angelo with a clear reminder of Lucio's misjudgement of the Duke; the speech which we would transpose to follow that dialogue can allude to both those diametrically opposed misjudgements, subsuming them within the terms of a more general meditation on the fallibility of popular judgement.

The imagery of the speech encourages an audience to interpret it as an allusion to Angelo as well as the Duke. The 'millions of false eies . . . stucke vpon thee' seems, as H. C. Hart noticed, to echo Virgil's description of Fame (or Jonson's translation of it, in *Poetaster*); in context, Virgil's description is prompted by a ruler's illicit sexual liaison. Shakespeare had already dramatized a similar figure in the Induction of *2 Henry IV*, where '*Rumour*' enters in a costume '*painted full of Tongues*' and speaks of her 'false reports'; in this instance, he brings good reports which are not true, rather than unfounded defamation. Finally, a similar image occurs in *Timon of Athens*: Timon, describing the time of his prosperity, speaks of 'The mouthes, the tongues, the eyes, and hearts of men, | At duty . . . | That numberlesse vpon me stucke' (4. 3. 262–4; TLN 1888–90). All these parallels fit Angelo's situation better than the Duke's: Angelo has arranged an illicit sexual liaison, the eyes of others tend upon him duteously and admiringly rather than maliciously, and Fame falsely speaks well of him. Likewise, the noun 'Quest' strongly suggests judicial proceedings, appropriate to both Escalus and Angelo: 'Make thee the father' recalls the situations of Claudio (whom Escalus and the Duke have just been discussing) and Lucio (whom Overdone earlier in the scene had accused of fathering Kate Keepdown's child). And although 'racke' may remind us of Lucio torturing the Duke's reputation, that particular instrument of torture worked by stretching its victim, to make him bigger than he was. In *Much Ado about Nothing*, Shakespeare speaks of those who 'rack' [i.e. inflate] 'the value' of a thing (4. 1. 222), and he often uses 'fancy' in the sense of 'liking, love'; those who 'racke thee in their fancies' might well be interpreted as those who 'magnify you, out of all just proportion, in their love'.

One other difference between this soliloquy and the one earlier in 3. 1 should be noticed. After Lucio exits, the Duke speaks of '*the* slanderous tong', the generalizing singular adjective and noun suggesting the single detractor who has just left the stage, and encouraging us to understand, as at least a secondary implication of the speech, that 'no matter how great a man is, *someone* will defame him'. In the later soliloquy, by contrast, the Duke speaks of '*millions* of false eies', '*volumes* of report', '*thousand* escapes of wit'. This difference coincides with the difference between Lucio's misjudgement and Escalus's. Lucio libels a man whom everyone else deservedly respects, and hence at the end of the play he will be singled out for punishment; Escalus, by contrast, simply concurs in the praise which the whole world gives to the undeserving Angelo, and as a result his misjudgement will be forgiven. And the Duke's own change of emphasis, from the single detractor to the popular misconception, arises naturally from the earlier progress of the dialogue; asked for 'newes abroad i'th World', he had replied,[85]

> Noueltie is onely in request, and it is
> as dangerous to be aged in any kinde of course,
> as it is vertuous to be [in]constant
> in any vndertaking. There is scarce truth
> enough aliue to make Societies secure, but
> Securitie enough to make Fellowships accurst
>   (TLN 1709–14; 3. 1. 481–6)

It is no great leap from such reflections on the topsy-turvydom of human nature to the soliloquy on 'millions of false eies'. The dual interpretation we suggest for the latter may well be anticipated in the balanced rhetorical contrasts of the earlier speech, especially as its exemplars of constancy and inconstancy recall the styles of government of the Duke himself and Angelo.

If 'Oh Place, and greatnes' is a meditation on misjudgement in general rather than calumny in particular, might its Folio position be defended? Hardly, for this interpretation of the speech heavily depends upon the dramatic context in which we propose to place it. At the end of 3. 1 the lines are naturally understood as in part a reference to Angelo; but none of the characters in 4. 1 is deceived by Angelo's seeming integrity, nor does anything in the preceding dialogue there encourage an audience to relate Lucio's slander to Escalus's *naïveté*. The universal interpretation of the lines as a meditation on calumny itself strongly suggests that, in their Folio position, an audience will not grasp their secondary significance. The brevity of the speech still seems inept, if it must cover for the women's offstage dialogue—an ineptitude the more remarkable if the Duke has a long, formally distinctive speech less than thirty lines earlier. The speech is not dramatically satisfactory where it stands, or where Warburton proposed to transpose it; if moved instead to the end of 3. 1,

---

[85] F1 reads 'and as' in 1709; like most editors we follow F3 in omitting 'as'.

it not only serves its dramatic function naturally and economically, but by virtue of its context takes on a meaning relevant to much wider issues than can be discerned when it stands forlornly in the middle of 4. 1.

We do not mean to recoil to the opposite of orthodoxy, by suggesting that the Duke's soliloquy *only* or even primarily refers to the world's mis-judgement of Angelo; we stress that side of the speech's meaning because the other side has monopolized interpretation. Moving the speech to the end of 3. 1 restores to it a range of meanings which its imagery seems to require, meanings which would be inappropriate immediately after Lucio's exit, and inappropriate in 4. 1, but which arise spontaneously from the context after Escalus's exit. 'Oh Place, and greatnes' actually makes better sense at the end of 3. 1 than it does anywhere else.

Equally important, whereas the transpositions advocated by Warburton, Kellner, and Muir leave the Folio's misplacement unex-plained or unsatisfactorily explained, the transposition we propose comes complete with its own obvious explanation. As in Folio *Titus*, Folio *Dream*, and Folio *King John*, Folio *Measure* divides a long continuous scene into two, by interpolating an act-break. On one side of this interpo-lated pause in the performance, a popular song from another play has been intruded (as in *Macbeth*). On the other side is a soliloquy by the Duke. But the original soliloquy would hardly have served the new pur-pose: it provides a poor exit line for the Duke, and an even poorer con-clusion to Act 3. All the features which made 'He who the sword of Heauen will beare' a fitting culmination to the original uninterrupted scene 4 (its length, its subject-matter, its formal distinctiveness) make it even more attractive as the culmination of the newly created Act 3. Soliloquies by a plotter are, indeed, a favourite expedient for bringing an act to a thumpingly dramatic conclusion. The deliberate transposition of these two speeches would arise as a necessary corollary of the interpola-tion of the song. The independent conclusion that the song in 4. 1 was interpolated thus handsomely resolves the otherwise inexplicable difficulty which all critics have felt about the Duke's soliloquy in 4. 1.

Readers familiar with the Folio text may have difficulty in imagining what the original sequence looked like. If we remove the interpolated matter, and transpose the two speeches, the scene continues like this, from the exit of Escalus and the Provost:[86]

[86] Except for the rearrangement of the last three lines of Isabella's first speech (conjec-tured by Tennyson) we have bracketed all substantive alterations of the Folio text other than the transposition of the Duke's two speeches and the omission of the suspected inter-polation. For '*Exit Escalus*' and 'their' see n. 79 above and n. 40 above; like all editors since Rowe we have moved Mariana's entrance down one line, and called for both women to '*Exeunt*' where F simply puts '*Exit.*' after Mariana's speech; we follow Walker (pp. 2–3) in substituting 'Make my' for F's 'Making', and Lever in adding 'so' to Mariana's unmetrical first speech. In addition to these emendations of F we have also omitted F's 'and well come' in the Duke's initial address to Isabella. Without these three words, the Duke's speech would be metrically regular, except for the (common) licence of an extra unaccented

    Esc. I am going to visit the prisoner, Fare you well.
    Duke. Peace be with you.   [*Exit Escalus*]
Oh Place, and greatnes: millions of false eies
Are stucke vpon thee: volumes of report
Run with the[ir] false, and most contrarious Quest
Vpon thy doings: thousand escapes of wit
Make thee the father of their idle dreame,
And racke thee in their fancies.
    Enter Isabell.
Very well met:
What is the newes from this good Deputie?
    Isab. He hath a Garden circummur'd with Bricke,
Whose westerne side is with a Vineyard back't;
And to that Vineyard is a planched gate,
That makes his opening with this bigger Key:
This other doth command a little doore,
Which from the Vineyard to the Garden leades,
There haue I made my promise,
Vpon the heauy midle of the night,
To call vpon him.
    Duk. But shall you on your knowledge find this way?
    Isab. I haue t'ane a due, and wary note vpon't,
With whispering, and most guiltie diligence,
In action all of precept, he did show me
The way twice ore.
    Duk. Are there no other tokens
Betweene you 'greed, concerning her obseruance?
    Isab. No: none but onely a repaire ith' darke,
And that I haue possest him, my most stay
Can be but briefe: for I haue made him know,
I haue a Seruant comes with me along
That staies vpon me; whose perswasion is,
I come about my Brother.
    Duk. 'Tis well borne vp.
I haue not yet made knowne to *Mariana*
A word of this: what hoa, within; come forth,
    [*Enter Mariana.*]

syllable before the caesura. As noted above (p. 138), Shakespeare never elsewhere uses 'well come' as a greeting; the probable author of some or all of the interpolations in *Measure* does use it (p. 226, below). Whoever interpolated the unShakespearian opening of 4. 1 would have had to copy out (at the very least) the Duke's first words to Isabella, which serve as the necessary bridge between the addition and the original text. In these circumstances, the words 'and well come' must be regarded with some suspicion. Moreover, 'Very well met' does not give any clue as to the whereabouts of their meeting, and this neutrality accords perfectly with our reconstruction of the original staging; by contrast, 'and well come' does suggest that Isabella has *arrived* at the place to which she was sent, and this implication fits the adapted text much better than it does the original. Finally, the three words turn the Duke's words into prose, like the preceding interpolated speeches. In editing the play as Shakespeare originally wrote it we would therefore be strongly predisposed to omit 'and well come'.

I pray you be acquainted with this Maid,
She comes to doe you good.
    Isab. I doe desire the like.
    Duk. Do you perswade your selfe that I respect you?
    Mar. Good Frier, I know you do, and [so] haue found it.
    Duk. Take then this your companion by the hand
Who hath a storie readie for your eare:
I shall attend your leisure, but make haste
The vaporous night approaches.
    Mar. Wilt please you walke aside.   [*Exeunt Women*]
    Duk. He who the sword of Heauen will beare,
Should be as holy, as seueare:
Patterne in himselfe to know,
Grace to stand, and Vertue go:
More, nor lesse to others paying,
Then by selfe-offences weighing.
Shame to him, whose cruell striking,
Kils for faults of his owne liking:
Twice trebble shame on *Angelo*,
To weede my vice, and let his grow.
Oh, what may Man within him hide,
Though Angel on the outward side?
How may likenesse made in crimes,
[Make my] practise on the Times,
To draw with ydle Spiders strings
Most ponderous and substantiall things?
Craft against vice, I must applie.
With *Angelo* to night shall lye
His old betroathed (but despised:)
So disguise shall by th'disguised
Pay with falshood, false exacting,
And performe an olde contracting.
       Enter Mariana and Isabella.
Welcome, how agreed?
    Isab. Shee'll take the enterprize vpon her father,
If you aduise it.
    Duke. It is not my consent,
But my entreaty too.
    Isa. Little haue you to say
When you depart from him, but soft and low,
Remember now my brother.
    Mar. Feare me not.
    Duk. Nor gentle daughter, feare you not at all:
He is your husband on a pre-contract:
To bring you thus together 'tis no sinne,
Sith that the Iustice of your title to him
Doth flourish the deceit. Come, let vs goe,
Our Corne's to reape, for yet our Tithes to sow.   *Exeunt*

No doubt this looks radically different from the familiar Folio text, but it in fact depends on only two emendations: the omission of TLN 1769–96 (4. 1. 1–25) as an interpolation, and the transposition of the Duke's two soliloquies (a consequence of that interpolation).

The Folio transposition of these two speeches gives an exaggerated prominence to the Duke's preoccupation with Lucio. But what seems to us a disadvantage of this arrangement may well have seemed, to whoever perpetrated the transposition, an advantage. For the evidence of interpolation and dislocation in 4. 1 can be supplemented by independent evidence of another major interpolation, involving Lucio, earlier in the play.

V

In the Folio text of the play's second scene, Mistress Overdone enters and informs Lucio and his two companions that Claudio is being taken to prison, and will soon be executed, for getting a woman pregnant; the hearers express their concern and exit, leaving Overdone briefly alone onstage; Pompey then enters and tells her what she has just told the departing gentlemen. Overdone is first the all-knowing transmitter and then, twelve lines later, the ignorant receiver of the same piece of news. This can hardly be defended as an unsuspected subtlety of characterization, nor does there seem any reasonable doubt that both passages refer to Claudio; most editors agree that the two passages essentially duplicate one another, and hence that one was intended to replace the other.[87] In short, one of the two passages was written *after*, and as a substitute for, the other. In the broadest sense, editors already agree that this scene contains 'a later interpolation'; how much later, and by whom, may be disputed. Most investigators have assumed—reasonably enough—that Shakespeare wrote both passages, one soon after the other, and that they coexisted in his foul papers, like the duplicate passages in *Romeo and Juliet* and *Love's Labour's Lost*. But the same duplication could easily occur in a prompt-book, where an addition for a later revival had been interleaved with or superimposed upon an existing transcript.[88] Even if

[87] Lascelles (1953) and Nosworthy (1969) seem to be the only editors who have defended the duplication (Eccles, p. 28); both assert that 'yonder man' is not Claudio. If the text as it stands is correct, this is the only possible defence or interpretation of it; but it seems to us— as to most others—that this would be pointless, confusing, and inept, and that the confusion in fact results from the Folio's preservation of two different versions of the same report.

[88] For instance, in *The Lady Mother* 2. 1 it was decided to alter the staging of the scene's opening from a soliloquy followed by a group entry to an overheard soliloquy with comments spoken aside. To this end, ll. 619–40 following the soliloquy were marked for deletion. If a scribe had accidentally or deliberately retained the material marked for deletion, a duplication would result. Confusion would have been possible as the original deletion mark extended well beyond l. 640, but the latter part of it was subsequently cancelled. In *Sir Thomas More* (not a prompt-book, but certainly a theatrical MS) an uncancelled 5-line speech appears at the end of Add. vi which is actually a draft for the beginning of Add. v, where it is duplicated.

Shakespeare wrote both passages, he might have written one for a revival. Therefore the bibliographical evidence (that Crane was probably transcribing a prompt-book, rather than Shakespeare's foul papers) does not in itself rule out Shakespeare's responsibility (at different times) for both passages; one might simultaneously accept that Shakespeare wrote both, and that Crane was copying a prompt-book. On the other hand, editors and writers have no right simply to assert that Shakespeare wrote both passages; if one passage is (as agreed) a later addition, then someone else may have added it. The authenticity of both passages must be tested, not assumed.

The second of these two passages, Pompey's revelation, is only seven lines long:

> *Clo.* Yonder man is carried to prison.
> *Baw.* Well: what has he done?
> *Clo.* A Woman.
> *Baw.* But what's his offence?
> *Clo.* Groping for Trowts, in a peculiar Riuer.
> *Baw.* What? is there a maid with child by him?
> *Clo.* No: but there's a woman with maid by him:
> (TLN 176–82; Add. A 1. 2. 1–9)

We would not wish to assert that 'only Shakespeare' could have so brilliantly characterized promiscuity as 'Groping for Trowts, in a peculiar Riuer'; but no one would doubt the imaginative alertness of this snatch of dialogue, or feel any compunction about assigning it to Shakespeare. Moreover, it hardly constitutes attractive material for theatrical interpolation, short and unobtrusive as it is. Nothing in the language or dramatic content of this passage falls outside normal Shakespearian practice. Because of its brevity, its authenticity cannot be conclusively demonstrated, but nothing about it gives any excuse for suspicion—except its duplication of material in TLN 153–71; 1. 2. 56–79.

When the copy for F was cast off, it was probably envisaged that the seven lines would be omitted in the printed text, just as they could here have been marked for omission in the manuscript. In *Malfi* Crane included material excluded from performance; the manuscript may have marked this material as dispensable. As Lever pointed out:

The suspicion that the anomalous lines were not meant to be printed is strengthened by the abnormally crowded appearance of sig. F1ᵛ where the passage occurs, with its extremely compressed spaces for stage directions, and scene headings. It is clear that the compositor found he had too much material for his page: a fact which rather suggests that he was including some six or seven lines which the caster-off had not taken into account (p. xx).

Indeed the compositor can be seen to take deliberate space-saving measures which would allow precisely for an extra seven lines.

1. At TLN 137 and 175 entrances share a type-line with words of text instead of being set on lines of their own.
2. At TLN 170–2 three successive speech-prefixes are indented less than is usual. This expedient, combined with the use of a tilde, allows *procla-matiõ* to be accommodated on l. 170 without a line-break. (The two following prefixes are probably set in line with the first to make it less conspicuous.)
3. The scene-box for '*Scena Tertia*' is cramped, so saving another two lines of type.
4. The abbreviated form in the following entry direction, '. . . & *2. Gent.*', allows the direction to be set on a single type-line.
5. At TLN 214–5 the compositor introduced a turn-up.

There are further indications of squeezing, particularly in TLN 135 and 207, but it is doubtful whether these instances actually save a type-line.

Of course compositors find themselves short of space elsewhere in the Folio. But F1^v is a particularly marked example of such shortage, and has been used by both Hinman and Eleanor Prosser to illustrate its symptoms.[89] It is difficult to believe that this particular and exemplary space shortage is unconnected with the evident confusion as to whether a passage should be printed which was commensurate with the amount of space the compositor saved.

If we omit TLN 153–71 (I. 2. 58–79)—Overdone's announcement about Claudio, and the reaction to it—then Overdone takes no part at all in the gentlemen's conversation: she only appears in order to make this announcement. If we remove her, then we must not only remove 151–2 (I. 2. 56–7: the question which prompts her revelation about Claudio) but also 138–50 (I. 2. 43–55) prompted by her entrance:

> *Enter Bawde.*
> *Luc.* Behold, behold, where Madam *Mitigation* comes. I haue purchas'd as many diseases vnder her Roofe, As come to
> *2. Gent.* To what, I pray?

The whole of the intervening dialogue concerns these diseases, contracted under Overdone's roof; if Overdone's entrance goes, so must it. But if all of this goes, the remainder of the conversation between Lucio and the two Gentlemen stands suspended in perfect isolation from the rest of the play, without any indication of why they enter, why they leave, or what relation they can claim to the developing plot. As a result, in order to remove the duplicate revelation of Claudio's crime and arrest we must omit either TLN 176–82 (a passage nothing else requires us to suspect) or

---

[89] C. Hinman, 'Cast-off Copy for the First Folio of Shakespeare', *SQ* 6 (1955), 265; Prosser, *Shakespeare's Anonymous Editors* (see Ch. 2, n. 30), 61.

the whole of TLN 96–171, from the entrance of Lucio and the two
Gentlemen until their exit:

> *Enter Lucio, and two other Gentlemen.*
>
> *Luc.* If the *Duke*, with the other Dukes, come not to composition with the King
> of *Hungary*, why then all the Dukes fall vpon the King.
>
> *1. Gent.* Heauen grant vs its peace, but not the King of *Hungaries*.
>
> *2. Gent.* Amen.
>
> *Luc.* Thou conclud'st like the Sanctimonious Pirat, that went to sea with the
> ten Commandements, but scrap'd one out of the Table.
>
> *2. Gent.* Thou shalt not Steale?
>
> *Luc.* I, that he raz'd.
>
> *1. Gent.* Why? 'twas a commandement, to command the Captaine and all the
> rest from their functions: they put forth to steale: There's not a Souldier of vs all,
> that in the thanks-giuing before meate, do rallish the petition well, that praies for
> peace.
>
> *2. Gent.* I neuer heard any Souldier dislike it.
>
> *Luc.* I beleeue thee: for I thinke thou neuer was't where Grace was said.
>
> *2. Gent.* No? a dozen times at least.
>
> *1. Gent.* What? In meeter?
>
> *Luc.* In any proportion: or in any language.
>
> *1. Gent.* I thinke, or in any Religion.
>
> *Luc.* I, why not? Grace, is Grace, despight of all controuersie: as for example;
> Thou thy selfe art a wicked villaine, despight of all Grace.
>
> *1. Gent.* Well: there went but a paire of sheeres betweene vs.
>
> *Luc.* I grant: as there may betweene the Lists, and the Veluet. Thou art the
> List.
>
> *1. Gent.* And thou the Veluet; thou art good veluet; thou'rt a three pild-peece I
> warrant thee: I had as liefe be a Lyst of an English Kersey, as be pil'd, as thou
> art pil'd, for a French Veluet. Do I speake feelingly now?
>
> *Luc.* I thinke thou do'st: and indeed with most painfull feeling of thy speech: I
> will, out of thine owne confession, learne to begin thy health; but, whilst I liue
> forget to drinke after thee.
>
> *1. Gen.* I think I haue done my selfe wrong, haue I not?
>
> *2. Gent.* Yes, that thou hast; whether thou art tainted, or free.
>
> > *Enter Bawde.*
>
> *Luc.* Behold, behold, where Madam *Mitigation* comes. I haue purchas'd as
> many diseases vnder her Roofe, as come to
>
> *2. Gent.* To what, I pray?
>
> *Luc.* Iudge.
>
> *2. Gent.* To three thousand Dollours a yeare.
>
> *1. Gent.* I, and more.
>
> *Luc.* A French crowne more.
>
> *1. Gent.* Thou art always figuring diseases in me; but thou art full of error, I
> am sound.
>
> *Luc.* Nay, not (as one would say) healthy: but so sound, as things that are hol-
> low; thy bones are hollow; Impiety has made a feast of thee.
>
> *1. Gent.* How now, which of your hips has the most profound Ciatica?

Bawd. Well, well: there's one yonder arrested, and carried to prison, was worth fiue thousand of you all.

2. Gent. Who's that I pray'thee?

Bawd. Marry Sir, that's *Claudio*, Signior *Claudio*.

1. Gent. Claudio to prison? 'tis not so.

Bawd. Nay, but I know 'tis so: I saw him arrested: saw him carried away: and which is more, within these three daies his head to be chop'd off.

Luc. But, after all this fooling, I would not haue it so: Art thou sure of this?

Bawd. I am too sure of it: and it is for getting Madam *Iulietta* with childe.

Luc. Beleeue me this may be: he promis'd to meete me two howres since, and he was euer precise in promise keeping.

2. Gent. Besides you know, it drawes somthing neere to the speech we had to such a purpose.

1. Gent. But most of all agreeing with the proclamatiõ.

Luc. Away: let's goe learne the truth of it [*Exeunt Lucio and Gentlemen*]
(TLN 96–171; 1. 2. 0–79)

Whether or not the beginning of the scene was interpolated at a later date, there can be little doubt that it fulfils the qualifications of a later interpolation much better than TLN 176–82. The codpiece of a revival was often artificially padded out with extra comic material, and this episode, prominently situated near the forefront of the play, is suitably bulky and suitable bawdy.[90] Suitably gratuitous, too. The two Gentlemen take no further part in the action: they reappear with Lucio, at 1. 2. 105 (TLN 206), but there have—awkwardly—nothing to say. Like the Boy in 4. 1, like Hecate in the two suspected scenes in *Macbeth*, like Captain Albo and Meg and Priss in the 'new Additions' to *A Fair Quarrel*, like Passarello in QC of *The Malcontent*, these two Gentlemen have no part to play, except that given to them by this questionable episode. Moreover, like those interpolated characters, these Gentlemen clearly exist only as adjuncts to another and more important role: Lucio's. Lucio is described, in the Folio list of 'The names of all the Actors', as *'a fantastique'*, a word which might pass judgement on his imagination but which also, more practically, might describe his appearance, as a 'Young Gallant' or 'One given to fine or showy dress; a fop'.[91] The same list describes his companions as '*2. Other like Gentlemen*'; since we are given less taste of mental extravagance in these roles, the reference in this case must be (and therefore in Lucio's case may be) primarily to costume. Crane himself may have prepared the character list, but whatever its authority it confirms that the Gentlemen are mere appendages and reflections of Lucio, and that all three were, in performances, 'showily habited'. In a play so concerned with the distinction between seeming and

[90] For comic additions in adaptations, see John Kerrigan, 'Revision, Adaptation, and the Fool in *King Lear*', *Division*, 195–205, 217.

[91] The probability that theatrical practice influenced Crane's description of the characters would be even greater if (as suggested below) the revival dates from 1621.

being, we cannot claim that such extravagant dress is irrelevant; but certainly the dialogue here draws no attention to its relevance. On the other hand, the entrance of three ridiculously overdressed gallants would be an attractive titbit of stage spectacle. Modern directors, certainly, have often seized on the comic visual opportunity here. Without the suspected passage at the beginning of 1. 2, Lucio first enters in the middle of a serious scene, intruding upon Claudio's escorted journey to prison. Certainly any eccentricity in his appearance could be effective there, but it would have to compete against other potent and contrasting effects, and it could easily unbalance the scene, if carried too far. As introduced in the Folio, however, Lucio and his two companions first appear on an empty stage. Nothing can detract from the visual joke—which has in any case been tripled, just to be sure. Moreover, the opportunity to enter alongside two other similar gentlemen makes it possible for Lucio to distinguish himself as the fop of fops, the quintessential dandy: Lucio will, almost inevitably, be even more extravagantly dressed than the others. In their costume as in their conversation, the two Gentlemen simply multiply the effect already created by Lucio. In this passage itself, Lucio speaks half of the added lines; he both begins and ends the passage; he monopolizes the best ripostes. The episode which begins Folio 1. 2 therefore not only dishes up an extra helping of bawdy comedy, but more particularly expands the part of Lucio, the play's most memorable and important comic creation.

Dover Wilson argued, in 1922, that Lucio's role had been generously 'fattened' at some point in the play's transmission; Blakemore Evans, in 1974, agreed (citing Lucio's role in 1. 4, 2. 2, and 5. 1 as particularly suspicious).[92] But although a few speeches elsewhere may have been added or expanded, outside this episode in 1. 2 all Lucio's appearances are astutely and dramatically integrated in the plot. (See Appendix VI.) Only Lucio's first appearance, at the beginning of 1. 2, does not directly contribute to his involvement in Claudio's case, or the Duke's.

Moreover, the suspect episode in 1. 2 actually weakens the parallel between Lucio's encounters with Claudio and with Pompey, as each is escorted to prison. In 3. 1, Lucio meets Pompey unexpectedly, as he crosses the stage alone; so he would apparently meet Claudio in 1. 2 if his opening conversation with the Gentlemen were omitted. That conversation makes it clear that Lucio seeks Claudio out, knowing in advance of his predicament; it also makes it necessary for the Gentlemen to re-enter with him. Probably as a consequence, all three enter at the same time as the penal procession, watching and waiting as Claudio makes his way across the stage, rather than several lines later—as both the dialogue

[92] *Measure for Measure*, ed. Wilson, 97–113; G. Blakemore Evans, *Riverside Shakespeare* (Boston, Mass., 1974), 585.

itself, and the parallel with 3. 1, would suggest.[93] And in his conversation with Claudio, Lucio is specifically named in the first line addressed to him (TLN 216; 1. 2. 117) and three times again thereafter (TLN 234, 269, 285; 1. 2. 130, 164, 180). In other words, in the dialogue with Claudio Shakespeare has taken pains clearly to identify Lucio, by his name and his relationship to Claudio—just as Shakespeare clearly identified Mariana before the Duke calls her on to the stage, late in 4. 1. But in the Folio text of 1. 2 Lucio has already appeared in a 75-line conversation in which he is never named, and is identified only vaguely by allusion to his commercial relations with Mistress Overdone—just as, in the interpolated beginning of 4. 1, Mariana appears without being named. This observation is hardly in itself conclusive, for Shakespeare himself sometimes delays the naming of characters. Nevertheless, in terms of Lucio's dramatic identity and his part in the plot, the end of 1. 2 looks likelier than the beginning of 1. 2 to have been his first appearance in the play.

When Lucio meets Claudio he appears ignorant of his friend's fate— oddly so, as Mistress Overdone has, in the Folio text, just given him the information he seeks. His persistent and apparently perverse attentions go beyond any need to verify Overdone's story. If Overdone's own progress from knowledge to ignorance betrays a duplication in the text, such an inconsistency cannot determine which passage was supposed to replace which. But if Lucio follows the same course, it becomes clear that of the two revelations of Claudio's predicament only that involving Lucio can be the revised passage. It is true that few readers have been alarmed by Lucio's insistence on asking Claudio questions to which he knows full well the answer. Indeed, if a reviser wished to paint a darker picture of Lucio—as the tone of the conversation with the two Gentlemen suggests he did—then he may have been happy to create the implication that Lucio deliberately and unnecessarily discomforts Claudio. But 1. 2 is not 3. 1, and Claudio is not Pompey: Lucio, especially at the beginning of the play, is open and generous towards Claudio. When he first meets Claudio his attitude, like Overdone's when quizzing Pompey, looks suspiciously like a genuine quest for information he does not possess. The text as it stands in F is certainly workable, even, in its way, dramatically effective, but Lucio's and Overdone's joint oblivion of their exchanges at TLN 153–71 (1. 2. 58–79) reinforces the impression that those exchanges are not integral to the text.

---

[93] Davenant (1673) delayed Lucio's entrance until just before he spoke, and many modern editors follow Dyce (1844) in thus postponing the re-entrance for all three gentlemen. For a full discussion see Charles B. Lower's 'Separated Stage Groupings: Instances with Editorial Gain', *Renaissance Papers 1970* (1971), 62–3. (Not recorded by Eccles, either in his bibliography or on pp. 31, 33.) However, Lower seems mistaken in his attempt to dismiss the Folio direction as a 'massed entry'. None of the alleged parallels from foul-paper texts involve so extended a delay, and since there are no other examples of this practice in *Measure* it seems unlikely that Crane was responsible.

One cannot deny that the conversation between Lucio and the two Gentlemen is thematically relevant. But any discussion of sex and sin could claim as much, and an interpolator may be credited with enough intelligence to contrive some relationship between what he adds and what is already there. The Hecate additions in *Macbeth* are equally relevant to the theme of witchcraft, and the added scene in *Fair Quarrel* to those of roaring and whoring. In terms of the state of morality in Vienna, the immediate entrance of a bawd and a tapster-pimp, after the exit of the Duke and ministers at the end of the first scene, would be at least as telling as the conversation of Lucio and his companions. Shakespeare's primary source, George Whetstone's *Promos and Cassandra*, begins its second scene in exactly that way: with the entrance of a courtesan, then her man, bringing news of the arrest of Claudio's equivalent. If we omit the suspected interpolation in *Measure*, Shakespeare's play would exactly duplicate the progress of events in his source.

In F, Overdone's entrance is itself odd. She comes on at TLN 137 (1. 2. 42), is immediately seen, recognized, and spoken of; but she does not speak, or do anything inferrable from the text, nor is she addressed until TLN 151 (1. 2. 56) eight speeches later.[94] Perhaps in the interim she makes her own contribution to the Department of Funny Walks; the first words addressed to her enquire, facetiously or not, about the sciatica in her hips. Nothing else in the play requires or alludes to this, however; nor does the dramatic technique of the entrance seem Shakespearian. Shakespeare's characters sometimes enter unseen, several lines before they join the dialogue; they sometimes speak asides, to the audience or another character, before addressing another group of onstage characters; but we have found no real parallels in Shakespeare's works for an entrance like Overdone's.

Two other peculiarities of dramatic technique also separate the opening of 1. 2 from the rest of the Shakespeare canon. Shakespeare's plays contain a fair number of anonymous gentlemen. Such gentlemen are sometimes speechless attendants (as in *All is True* 1. 4, Quarto *Hamlet* 2. 3, *Othello* 3. 2, etc.), or extras who briefly speak (like the gentlemen who fill out the drinking party in *Othello* 2. 3, the one who stays behind briefly at the end of *Contention* 4. 1, the one who tries to stop an entrance in *All is True* 5. 1, etc.). Otherwise such anonymities are invariably used—except here in *Measure*—as messengers, communicating some news important to

---

[94] David Rosenbaum has suggested that 146–7 ('Thou art always figuring . . .') belongs to Overdone instead of '1. *Gent.*': see 'Shakespeare's *Measure for Measure*, I.ii', *Explicator*, 33 (1975), item 57. Collier gave it to '2. *Gent.*'; editors have also reassigned speeches at 108, 123, 138, 139, 142, and 155. It seems clear that the author of this passage made no attempt to differentiate the two gentlemen, so long as a steady flow of repartee was maintained. The overall carelessness might be Shakespeare's or someone else's, but reattribution of 146–7 seems dangerous. Even if Overdone did speak this, there would still be a noticeable delay before her entrance and her participation in the dialogue.

the developing plot. These two Gentlemen in *Measure* tell us nothing; they exist, instead, to be told.

The scene's position in the economy of the play is as anomalous as the role of the Gentlemen in it. Shakespeare almost always begins the second scene of a play with something immediately important to the developing plot. Often, such scenes begin with the first entrance of a major character: Hamlet, Othello, Caesar, Hal and Sir John, Henry V, Henry VIII and Wolsey and Katharine, Viola, Rosalind, Cressida, Portia, Prospero and Miranda, Palamon and Arcite, Leontes and Hermione and Polixenes. Only a handful of scenes is even remotely similar to the relaxed, free-floating conversation at the beginning of 1. 2 in Folio *Measure*. *Troilus* 1. 2 begins with a conversation about Hector and Ajax, between Cressida and her servant; what he tells her bears little relation to the rest of the play, but the delineation of Cressida's own character is itself crucial, and of immediate dramatic interest. *Richard II* 1. 2 consists of a conversation between Gaunt and the Duchess of York; this does not contribute directly to the plot, and the Duchess never appears again, but it strongly establishes the King's own guilt for Woodstock's death, and Gaunt's knowledge of this (both important to what follows), while filling the necessary gap before the trial by combat at Coventry. *Antony* 1. 2 introduces Enobarbus, Charmian, Iras, Mardian, and the Soothsayer, and although their dialogue has little direct bearing upon the plot, it does establish the character of the Alexandrian court, in the necessary interim between the exits of Antony and Cleopatra and their re-entrance; it also prepares for the Soothsayer's later, much more important, appearance. Finally, *Cymbeline* 1. 2 memorably introduces Cloten, the play's anti-hero, to the accompaniment of alternating flattery and abuse from the attendant lords. None of these scenes can be properly compared with the extended extraneous dialogue which begins the second scene of Folio *Measure*, in defiance of Shakespeare's source as well as his practice elsewhere.

All of the foregoing considerations suggest that the first section of 1. 2—from TLN 96 to 171—is an unShakespearian interpolation. Dover Wilson came to this conclusion as early as 1922. Wilson's contention has been, as it were, discredited by association—for it was advanced as part of an elaborate hotchpotch of conjectural rewriting, elaboration, and cutting throughout the play, a mixture too lamentably similar to his speculations about many other plays. As evidence for interpolation in 1. 2 he offered only three arguments: the fundamental contradiction in Overdone's speeches (with which we began), a topical allusion (to which we will soon turn), and a subjective judgement of style: 'It is sheer mud, dreary, dead; not even a maggot stirs. Let the reader consider these 57 lines [TLN 96–150; 1. 2. 1–55] of prose in isolation, and ask himself if Shakespeare could have written them, at any period of his career' (p. 107). Like E. K. Chambers, we hesitate to concede that the passage is as bad as all that,[95] nor need it be. Interpolations by a professional Jacobean dramatist may be as good as that dramatist's work elsewhere, so far as the actual writing goes; they identify themselves as interpolations not by exercrable badness, but by superfluousness, by bad joins, and by unShakespearian dramatic technique. Moreover, prose may be acceptable prose without being Shakespearian prose.

The suspected first section of 1. 2, from the entrance of Lucio and the Gentlemen to their exit, contains no distinctive Shakespearian image-clusters.[96] It contains no nouns or adjectives used as verbs, no past participles formed from nouns, no agent nouns in -er, no coinages from Latin stems, no words with the prefix un-, and no words which according to *OED* first occur here—verbal characteristics which are exceptionally common in all Shakespeare's work.[97] It boasts only one unusual compound ('promise keeping', TLN 166-7; 1. 2. 73-4) and, to our judgements, only one striking phrase ('Impiety has made a feast of thee', TLN 150; 1. 2. 55). The same deficiencies characterize the suspect passage in 4. 1, except that it altogether lacks both compounds and impressive phrases. Moreover, Shakespeare's acknowledged work always contains a very high proportion of *hapax legomena*, words which he uses only once. Though this seems paradoxical, one of the best tests of Shakespeare's authorship of a work is the presence in it of a large number of words which appear nowhere else in his canon; conversely, the absence of such words is strong evidence *against* Shakespeare's authorship.[98] For instance, in the approximately 120 lines unique to Folio *King Lear*, eleven such nonce words occur.[99] The approximately 110 lines of the suspect passages in 1. 2 and 4. 1 of *Measure for Measure* do not contain a single example.

Another widely recognized feature of Shakespeare's style, particularly in the period after 1600, is a fondness for doublets, like 'Within the booke and volume of my brain' or 'the dark backward and abysm of time'.[100] Such couplings abound in the first scene of *Measure*: 'speech &

[95] *William Shakespeare*, i. 454.

[96] See E. A. Armstrong, *Shakespeare's Imagination: A Study of the Psychology of Association and Inspiration*, rev. edn. (Lincoln, Nebr., 1963), and Caroline Spurgeon, *Shakespeare's Imagery and What it Tells Us* (Cambridge, 1935). Neither finds examples of Shakespearian images in these passages.

[97] Alfred Hart, 'Shakespeare and the Vocabulary of *The Two Noble Kinsmen*', *RES* 10 (1934), 274-87; see also Hart's articles on Shakespeare's vocabulary in *RES* 19 (1943), 128-40, 242-54; and his essay on *Edward III* in *Shakespeare and the Homilies* (Melbourne, 1934), 219-42.

[98] See (in addition to n. 97) Alfred Hart, *Stolne and Surreptitious Copies: A Comparative Study of Shakespeare's Bad Quartos* (Melbourne, 1942), 28-40; G. Sarrazin, 'Wortechos bei Shakespeare', *Shakespeare Jahrbuch*, 33 (1897), 121-65, and 34 (1898), 119-69; Jackson, *Attribution*, 148-58. Such evidence about Shakespeare's fondness for *words* which he uses only once should not be confused with the evidence (offered elsewhere in this essay) about his use of certain images, phrases, or senses of a word.

[99] Taylor, 'Date and Authorship' in *Division*, 400.

[100] Among many discussions of Shakespeare's use of this device, see Granville-Barker, *Prefaces*, i. 169, and George T. Wright, 'Hendiadys and *Hamlet*', *PMLA* 96 (1981), 168-93.

discourse', 'Art, and practise', 'such ample grace, and honour', 'Thy selfe, and thy belongings', 'Mortalitie and Mercie', 'tongue, and heart', 'so noble, and so great a figure', 'a leauen'd, and prepared choice', 'time, and our concernings', 'loud applause, and Aues vehement', 'strength and nature'. There are none in the opening lines of 1. 2, but the habit resumes after Claudio's entrance: 'the fault and glimpse of newnes', 'the drowsie and neglected Act', 'a prone and speechlesse dialect', 'reason, and discourse'. The absence of this verbal tic from the beginning of 1.2 may result from the switch to prose, or the descent into the lower orders of morality and class; but such couplings do occur elsewhere in Lucio's speeches, and elsewhere in the prose dialogue of the play's unseemlier characters.[101]

In all these respects the opening of 1. 2 and the opening of 4. 1 are of a piece, an unShakespearian piece. Another test, which can be statistically evaluated, points to the same conclusion. Eliot Slater has demonstrated that the distribution of words which appear ten times or less in the Shakespeare canon shows a highly significant correlation with the agreed chronology of that canon; according to such tests *Measure for Measure* as a whole was written after *Troilus*, before *All's Well*, and at about the same time as *Othello*; it has very strong links with *All's Well*, as does *All's Well* with it.[102] All of this agrees well enough with what we know, or all believe, about the play's place in Shakespeare's development.[103] But the relevant vocabulary of the two suspect passages strikingly differs from this picture of the play as a whole. The suspect passage in 1. 2 contains ninety-two words which occur ten times or less in the canon; these same ninety-two words can be found fifty-six times in plays written in 1600 or before, sixteen times in the plays of 1601–7 (up to but not including *Pericles* or *Coriolanus*), and twenty times in the plays of 1608 and after.

[101] In Lucio's speeches, compare: 'Gentle & faire' (374), 'a thing en-skied, and sainted' (384), 'fewnes, and truth' (389), 'his full Tilth, and husbandry' (394), 'The wanton stings, and motions' (411), 'rebate, and blunt' (412), 'Studie, and fast' (413), 'use, and libertie' (414). All of these come in the verse of 1. 4, but Lucio's later prose scenes also contain: 'your fresh Whore, and your pouder'd Baud' (1548), 'eating and drinking' (1591), 'the teeth and the lippes' (1623), 'browne-bread and Garlicke' (1669), 'dine and sup with water and bran' (2246). From Pompey in 2. 1 we might cite: 'gelde and splay' (676), 'flesh and fortune' (698).

[102] 'The Problem of *The Reign of King Edward III*, 1596: A Statistical Approach' (Ph.D. thesis, Univ. of London, 1981). Several published articles by Slater deal with the distribution of such vocabulary evidence for specific works: 'Shakespeare: Word Links Between Poems and Plays', *N. & Q.* 220 (1975), 157–63; 'Word Links with *The Merry Wives of Windsor*', *N. & Q.*, 220 (1975), 169–71; 'Word Links with *All's Well that Ends Well*', *N. & Q.* 222 (1977), 109–12; 'Word Links Between *Timon of Athens* and *King Lear*', *N. & Q.* 223 (1978), 147–9; 'Word Links from *Troilus* to *Othello* and *Macbeth*', *The Bard*, 2 (1978), 4–22. Specific data for *Measure* are taken from his thesis, p. 305.

[103] Most scholars place *All's Well* before rather than after *Measure*, but no hard evidence for such an order exists: it depends almost entirely upon a critical judgement that *Measure* treats many of the same themes more successfully. Walker argues for *Measure*'s priority (pp. 19–20); see *Textual Companion*, 126–7.

Even if the distribution of vocabulary links was purely random, and did not have (as Slater shows it does) a strong relationship to chronology, we should expect almost twenty-five such links with the 1601–7 group of plays (instead of only sixteen); in other words, this passage has exceptionally few links with the very plays with which *Measure* as a whole has exceptionally high links. The same discrepancy recurs in the vocabulary of the suspect passage in 4. 1: three links with the 1601–7 group, instead of an expected seven. If we combine the vocabulary for both suspect passages, the difference between the expected and the actual links with the plays of 1601–7 is 13.4; this discrepancy has a chi-squared value of 5.54, and would occur by chance less than one time in fifty. In itself this evidence suggests that, if these passages were written by Shakespeare, they were *not* written between 1601 and 1607. Even more particularly, they should *not* have been written at the same time as the rest of the play, which shows a positive association with the plays of 1601–7. On the basis of the rare vocabulary in the rest of *Measure*, we should expect the suspect sections of 1. 2 and 4. 1 to have over forty-one links with the 1601–7 group, instead of only nineteen; this discrepancy has a chi-squared value of 12.13, and would happen by chance only about once in ten thousand times. On the basis of vocabulary, the two suspect passages do not belong to the same statistical population as the rest of the play: they must have been written either at a different time, or by a different hand— or both.

Stylometric evidence also casts doubt on Shakespeare's authorship of this passage. Stylometry assumes that an author unconsciously associates certain words with certain others, and that the frequency of such collocations is a reliable measurement of an author's style. The method of enquiry is still in its infancy, and no full-scale stylometric 'portrait' of Shakespeare is available. However, we have been able to provide a complete account of Shakespeare's habits with one such collocation: *with* (or *wi'*) followed by *the* (or *th'*). A computer programme developed by Mr Lou Burnard of the Oxford University Computing Service tracked occurrences of *with* throughout the First Folio, identifying the following word; these occurrences of *with* were divided into consecutive sets of ten, with a note of the number of times the word is followed by *the* or *th'*. This procedure enables us to trace the relative frequency of the collocation *with the* throughout the First Folio, over suitably small areas of text.

For the Folio as a whole, less than one *with/wi'* in twelve is followed by *the/th'*. Of the 739 possible full units of ten occurrences of *with* or *wi'*, only seven (= 0.9 per cent) could be constructed which would have as many as five collocations with *the* or *th'*; moreover, one of these seven occurs in a passage traditionally attributed to John Fletcher (*All is True* 4. 1). Only two possible full units of ten in the entire Folio (= 0.2 per cent) have six or more such collocations. One of these occurs at *Taming of the Shrew* 3. 2. 50–5, and is in context easily explicable as the result of special circumstances: Grumio is describing the desperate condition of Petruchio's horse, afflicted 'with the glanders . . . with the Lampasse . . . with the fashions . . . with the Yellowes . . . with the Staggers . . . with the Bots'. Since in this instance the entire statistical anomaly results from a rhetorical repetition which is clearly conscious and deliberate, it offers poor evidence of authorship, or indeed of Shakespeare's normal unconscious practice.

If we exclude this example, there remains only one full set of ten, out of 738, which contains six or more collocations (= 0.1 per cent); this passage in fact contains seven such collocations, and is therefore easily the most anomalous passage in the entire First Folio in respect to this stylistic trait. The suspicious passage is, as the reader will have already guessed, *Measure for Measure* 1. 2. 1–84 (TLN 97–174). Moreover, the anomaly does not there reside (as in *Shrew*) in a single five-line passage of one speech, or in a deliberate rhetorical repetition (as in *Shrew*), or in the repetition of a single idiom (as, for example, in *All's Well* 4. 3, where the 50 per cent collocation is entirely due to the repeated phrase 'with the Duke'). Instead, all seven prepositional phrases have different objects, and they are distributed from beginning to end of the passage: 'with the other Dukes' (TLN 97), 'with the King of *Hungary*' (98), 'with the ten Commandements' (104), 'with the proclamatiõ' (170), 'what with the war' (173), 'what with the sweat' (173), 'what with the gallowes' (174). One might object that the last three examples represent deliberate repetition— but the author might just as easily have written 'what with the war, and the sweat, and the gallowes, and pouerty'. If we removed Overdone's last speech entirely, the proportion for the remainder of the suspect material would still be four collocations out of six, or 67 per cent—still higher than any of the control units. In any case, such *ad hoc* explanations for part of the discrepancy do nothing to diminish the fact that, for this collocation, this passage is demonstrably less 'Shakespearian' than anything else in the First Folio.

Like the suspect passage in 4. 1, this suspect passage at the beginning of 1. 2 is inextricably bound up with a textual crux, one which any responsible editor must face. The duplicate revelation of Claudio's fate, first by and then to Overdone, can only be avoided by assuming—as editors have done—that one passage was meant to replace the other. Timidity might tempt an editor to believe that the longer passage is the original: this belief would allow as little as possible of the Folio text to be relegated to the bottom of the page or back of the book, in an edition seeking to restore the text as Shakespeare wrote it.[104] But in fact the

---

[104] All previous editors in fact abnegated their responsibility entirely, by simply printing both passages (just as they do the duplicate passages in *LLL*). Lever at least concluded (p. xx) that the shorter passage was 'not meant to be printed', but he printed it none the less.

shorter passage seems clearly to be Shakespeare's, while the longer shows all the marks of unauthorized theatrical interpolation: extraneous to the plot, it fattens the part of an attractive comic character, introduces two superfluous characters, intrudes an opportunity for a peacocking display of wardrobe vanity, uses anonymous gentlemen in a manner unparalleled in Shakespeare's work, begins the play's second scene in a manner unexampled in Shakespeare's work, brings on Mistress Overdone by means of an equally 'unShakespearian' dramatic technique, displays none of the many idiosyncratic verbal hallmarks of Shakespeare's vocabulary, and verbally seems not to have been composed at the same time as the rest of the play. All of this evidence argues against Shakespear's authorship of the passage; yet it is just the sort of material which, on the evidence of other plays, might well have been interpolated in a revival.

If the suspect passage is not a late unShakespearian interpolation, then it must have been a duplication in Shakespeare's own foul papers, or a later interpolation by Shakespeare himself. But the available evidence argues against the hypothesis that Crane was copying from Shakespeare's foul papers; one cannot invoke that hypothesis here, without overthrowing all the contrary evidence. Moreover, like other scholars we believe that the recognized textual difficulties at the beginning of Act 4 are only explicable in terms of theatrical adaptation on the occasion of a posthumous revival. It would obviously be simplest to assume that all the alterations to the play were made for this one revival. Conjecturing that the passage in 1. 2 is a late Shakespearian addition not only complicates the hypothesis unnecessarily; it also leaves unexplained the variety of evidence that the passage differs substantially, in style and dramatic technique, from Shakespeare's other work. Thus, neither alternative can be plausibly reconciled with the evidence that the Folio text derives from a late, adapted prompt-book, and we are again driven back to what seemed, intrinsically, the likeliest explanation for the peculiarities of 1. 2: late unShakespearian interpolation. This conclusion would seem to us inevitable even if 1. 2 were the only scene of the play where theatrical interpolation was suspected. But if one concedes that the beginning of 4. 1 is indeed a posthumous 'new addition', then it becomes even more difficult to deny that status to the opening of 1. 2. If a text already contains one interpolation, we may legitimately suspect that it might contain another.

Our collective psychological resistance to the textual demotion of any passage in the accepted Shakespeare canon is, as we have already remarked, enormous. Moreover, in the late twentieth century this reluctance probably influences our responses to 1. 2 more strongly than to 4. 1. For a Victorian, the suggestion that anyone but Shakespeare wrote the 'exquisite' stanza 'Take, oh take those lips away' must have seemed outrageous; on the other hand, it might have appeared a work of charity to deprive Shakespeare of the authorship of the scurrilous first half of 1. 2. For a modern, these prejudices are apt to be reversed: we may willingly jettison the romantic sentiment, but we cling to the robust cynicism. Besides, the suspect passage comes so close to the beginning of the play, is so much longer, so much better written than the interpolated dialogue in 4. 1, that it has deeply influenced our view of what *Measure for Measure* is. It seems to us Shakespearian at least partly because we have always assumed it was written by Shakespeare. If we restrain these emotional allegiances, if we attempt to make objective judgements of the probabilities, the evidence against Shakespeare's authorship of the beginning of 1. 2 is as compelling as the evidence against his authorship of the beginning of 4. 1.

If we regard as an interpolation everything from the entrance of Lucio and his two companions until their exit, then we will also need to reconsider two other passages in this scene. Immediately after the three men exit, and before Pompey enters, Mistress Overdone, alone on stage, delivers a short speech to the audience:

> *Bawd.* Thus, what with the war; what with the sweat,
> what with the gallowes, and what with pouerty, I am
> Custom-shrunke.
>   [*Enter Clowne.*]
> How now? what's the newes with you.
>   (TLN 172–5; 1. 2. 80–3)

This joke depends upon an audience's knowledge of Overdone's occupation—a knowledge which presumes the existence of the previous conversation. Moreover, although Shakespeare twice has Gower, or the Chorus in *Henry V*, begin a speech (and hence a 'scene') with 'Thus', in each case that adverb clearly refers to something we have just seen or heard. This also applies on the rare occasions, as at the beginning of *Henry V* 2. 4, when a 'Thus' begins a normal scene; furthermore, that scene clearly begins in the middle of a conversation.[105] None of these criteria would apply in Overdone's case, and if Shakespeare did originally begin the scene at this point, then he began it in an awkward manner unparalleled in his extant work. On the other hand, Shakespeare begins at least six other scenes with the question 'How now?' Five of these (*Richard III* 3. 7, *2 Henry IV* 5. 2, *Ado* 1. 2, *Henry V* 3. 6, and *Antony* 3. 5) begin

---

[105] *Henry V* 2. 4, 'Thus comes the English with full power upon us'; see also *Contention* 2. 4, 'Thus sometimes hath the brightest day a cloud' (entrance in mourning); *Duke of York* 5. 3, 'Thus far our fortune keeps an upward course' (entrance in triumph); *Titus* 5. 2, 'Thus, in this strange and sad habiliment'; *John* 5. 1, 'Thus have I yielded up into your hands | The circle of my glory'; *1 Henry IV* 5. 5, 'Thus ever did rebellion find rebuke'; *2 Henry IV* 1. 3, 'Thus have you heard our cause and known our means'. In none of these is the speaker alone onstage; none is a comedy, and none was written after 1599.

with the simultaneous entrance of two characters, like Overdone and Pompey; two of them (*Contention* 4. 5, *Richard III* 3. 7) make it explicitly clear, in the stage directions, that the characters enter from different directions, and editors have assumed such a staging for all six. Cumulatively, this evidence suggests that the first sentence of Overdone's speech belongs to the suspect passage, and that Shakespeare began the scene with Pompey and Overdone entering from separate doors, and Overdone enquiring 'How now? what's the newes with you.'

After Overdone's Shakespearian conversation with Pompey, Claudio enters, being led to prison by the Provost and his officers; he encounters Lucio, carries on an extended conversation with him, and then departs for prison, while Lucio exits in the other direction, to report to Isabella. This sub-scene in itself creates no difficulties of staging or interpretation. But the Folio also calls for Juliet and the two Gentlemen;

> *Bawd.* What's to doe heere, *Thomas* Tapster? let's withdraw?
> *Clo.* Here comes Signior *Claudio*, led by the Prouost to prison: and there's Madam *Iuliet.*   *Exeunt.*

Scena Tertia.

Enter Prouost, Claudio, Iuliet, Officers, Lucio, & 2. Gent.
(TLN 201–6; I. 2. 104–7)

Juliet, like the Gentlemen, is silent, and is at no point directly implicated in the conversation. Many editors have considered this presentation of a new character dramatically inept.[106] Of course it does have a theatrical purpose in testifying to the consequences of the couple's misdeed; otherwise (from the point of view of our hypothesis) no adapter would bother to introduce Juliet in this way. But if there are two textual strata to the scene—an original text, and material introduced later by way of adaption—the unusual presentation of Juliet can be explained as a consequence of its belonging to the second major stage of the scene's textual history.

Obviously, the last four words of Pompey's speech could easily be omitted (or could easily have been added at a later date). Just as obviously, Pompey does not mention Lucio, his two companions, or the Officers. Consequently, the end of the Folio entrance direction could be omitted (or could have been added) as easily as the end of Pompey's adjacent speech. The Officers are particularly interesting. These silent characters are only necessary in order to accompany Juliet; Claudio is guarded by the Provost (as Pompey notes) and at the end of the scene he

---

[106] A reconstruction of the staging required by the Folio text here can be found in Lower's 'Separated Stage Groupings' (see n. 93); however, this reconstruction does little to establish the authenticity of the staging, or to answer Chambers's objection that 'Juliet is unexpectedly dumb on her first appearance' (*William Shakespeare*, i. 231).

addresses his escort in the *singular* ('Come Officer, away': TLN 287;
1. 2. 182). Moreover, the Folio only twice elsewhere calls for the entrance
of Officers—both times in the company of Elbow (TLN 495, 1490), who
is himself four times called an Officer (TLN 512, 622, 635, 1520). When
the Provost appears elsewhere, taking Juliet (2. 3) and Overdone (3. 1)
away, the Folio does not call for attendants, nor are any required.[107] In
short, all the characters named after Claudio in the Folio stage direction
may well not have entered at this point in the original text. Juliet, the
Officers, and the two Gentlemen are all silent and, in the sense that any
added material must be to its recipient text, superfluous. We have already
noted that the entrance of Lucio seems originally to have been intended
to occur later in the scene; the change of position seems a consequence of
the interpolation of Lucio's new introduction, earlier in 1. 2. As originally
written, therefore, Pompey's announcement that 'Here comes Signior
Claudio, led by the Prouost to prison' could easily have been immediately
followed by the entrance of (as announced) the Provost and Claudio
alone.[108] All the problems of staging in this episode could thus be solved
by the removal of the last half of two adjacent lines.[109]

In these circumstances, no one can deny that Juliet *could* be an addition to this scene, and her addition would have had several attractions
for the adapter. Her pregnant presence turns Lucio's otherwise innocent
and serious question, 'With childe, perhaps?' (TLN 248; 1. 2. 144), into a
snide joke, likely to gain a cheap laugh for the comic character most
inflated by the earlier addition. Juliet's entrance also requires the addition
of the extra Officers, her guards: these contribute to the Folio's expansion
of a simple entrance for two characters (Claudio and the Provost) into a
major procession. Juliet provides, in the crudest as well as the etymologi-
cal sense, spectacle: her pregnant condition 'With Character too grosse, is
writ on *Iuliet*'. Claudio may well have been made to wear a garment of
penance, as was Elizabethan and Jacobean practice; the introduction of a
second character thus visibly shamed would, like that character's

---

[107] For the superfluousness of editorial officers in 3. 1 (sometimes added by editors), see
n. 79 above. At least one officer is required in 5. 1, where the Provost also appears (though
the Folio direction identifies neither); they may there appear together, in the crowd.

[108] Claudio's first line—'Fellow, why do'st thou show me thus to th' world?' (TLN 207;
1. 2. 108)—would, in that case, refer to the theatre audience. Alternatively (but less plausibly), in the original staging Pompey and Overdone might have remained onstage.

[109] More radically, one might omit Pompey's speech in its entirety, as well as Overdone's
preceding question (which prompts it), thus ending 1. 2 with Pompey's consolatory 'you will
be considered' (TLN 199–200; 1. 2. 102–3). Shakespeare never elsewhere uses 'What's to
doe' (TLN 201; 1. 2. 104) in the sense required here, and Overdone's address to Pompey as
'*Thomas* Tapster' is potentially misleading, since the clown has not yet been named. But if
all four lines were added primarily in order to identify the silent Juliet, then why was the
actual identification of Juliet so lamely tacked on to the tacked-on addition? An almost
identical scene-bridge occurs in *Cymbeline* 1. 1. 69–70 (TLN 80–1), and '*Thomas* Tapster'
can be accepted as a generic title (Eccles, p. 30), so we see little reason to suspect seriously
anything but Pompey's last four words.

pregnancy, add to the visual impact of the entry.[110] Moreover, Juliet's entrance gives the two Gentlemen something to do: they can stand on one side of the stage miming conversation with her, while Lucio converses with Claudio. In the adapted text these two characters have left with Lucio, in search of Claudio, only twenty-five lines before; it would be rather odd if he entered without them, or pretended to encounter Claudio accidentally. The adapted Folio staging lets all three enter together to meet the procession, then split into two parties to talk with the two prisoners. Finally, the dramatic technique of Juliet's entrance—seen, and referred to, but silent, and not engaged in either the dialogue or the action—exactly mimics the technique of Overdone's entrance, in the suspected passage.

The same dramatic technique is used once again when, for the third and final time in the play, Juliet enters at 5. 1. 476 (TLN 2875). Again she exists only by virtue of her pregnant silence; as J. D. Wilson argued long ago, 'We . . . think it very unlikely that she was intended to appear here in the received text, since she has nothing to say' (p. 155).

Wilson conjectured that Shakespeare originally gave Juliet a speaking part in 5. 1 and that her speech was cut out because the actor who originally played Juliet was needed here to double Mariana. This suggestion does not stand up to scrutiny. In the Folio text a minimum of three boys are required: Isabella, Mariana, and the boy who sings the song. The boy and Isabella appear in quick succession while Mariana remains on stage, all within the first twenty lines of 4. 1. Mariana could double as Overdone and the boy as Juliet. The boy may have been primarily a

---

[110] See E. R. C. Brinkworth, *Shakespeare and the Bawdy Court of Stratford* (London, 1972), 73–92. In *Promos and Cassandra*, 'Andrugio, | For loving too kindlie, must loose his heade, | And his sweete hart, must weare the shamefull weedes: | Ordainde for Dames, that fall through fleshly deedes' (B2; Eccles, p. 311). The public humiliation of Claudio is a detail Shakespeare introduced, and the episode has no parallel in the source play. Given *Measure*'s emphasis on the man's predicament, it is unnecessary (though possible) to suppose that the presence of Juliet in 1. 2 is a detail deriving from *Promos*, especially as public penance would have been a familiar enough spectacle. The 'shamefull weedes' of *Promos* refers to the penitential blue gown worn by convicted prostitutes; this blue gown is also mentioned in *2 Honest Whore* 5. 1. 10 and 5. 2. 301, and in Massinger's *City Madam* 4. 2. 98. Nashe (?) describes the white sheet as a penitential garb for lechery in *A Prognostication* (D2; *Works*, ed. McKerrow, iii. 393, pp. 26–7): 'diverse spirites in white sheetes shall stand in Poules and other Churches, to make their confessions'. William Harrison, in his *Description of England*, ed. Georges Edelen (Ithaca, NY, 1968), noted that 'harlots and their mates, by carting, ducking, and doing of open penance in sheets, in churches and marketsteads, are often put to rebuke' (p. 189); it is this practice that the scene in *Measure* probably portrays. There are further references to the custom in *Northward Ho* 4. 1. 269 and Chapman's *All Fools* 4. 1. 243–9. Shakespeare himself staged the spectacle of an enforced and humiliating penance in a white sheet at *Contention* 2. 4. 17 (TLN 1188): '*Enter the Duchesse in a white Sheet*', etc. Dover Wilson doubted Shakespeare's authorship of this scene: see his edn. of *2 Henry VI*, New Shakespeare (Cambridge, 1952), 128. Most recent scholars assume Shakespeare's authorship of the entire play, but the whole question needs careful re-examination: see *Textual Companion*, 111–12. References to the penitential white sheet by the probable reviser of *Measure* are catalogued below (n. 219).

singer, but as Juliet is mute in two out of three scenes and speaks only sixty-three words in the entire play, the part of Juliet would have made little demand on his acting skills. If, however, the original text had no song, and so no boy to sing it, the need for a third boy actor disappears: the only point in the whole play which requires a third boy is the very end of 5. 1 when Juliet enters. Considerations of doubling suggest that, if anything, Juliet's original role was not pared down but bolstered for a late revival. And this is, after all, what we should expect: late revivals generally can count on more sumptuous theatrical means.

Wilson in fact retained Juliet in 5. 1. He believed that Juliet had originally acted as the crucial arbitrator between Claudio and Isabella, and he left her in the text so that she could perform this function—though the mediator's role in the Folio text must be played silently. If we are right in assuming that Juliet's presence in 1. 2 is an unauthorized addition, then the two lovers would not appear on stage together until 5. 1; even if we are wrong about 1. 2, the Folio text itself clearly requires the two to be effectively separated in that scene. The Folio's call for Juliet in 5. 1 thus requires that the only real onstage encounter of the two lovers should take place in total silence, without even a comment from anyone else. At the same time, Juliet must also mime the role of mediator between Claudio and Isabella—if we assume, as Wilson did, that such mediation is necessary. Even if (as seems to us more likely) Isabella is happy enough to see her brother alive, Isabella and Juliet (despite their noted friendship) never address each other, on this their first and only encounter. Even in the discourse of gesture we find Juliet stranded. In the dialogue itself she is most pointedly ignored. After she enters with Barnardine, the Provost, and Claudio, the Duke asks the Provost 'Which is that *Barnardine?*' (2876; 5. 1. 477), establishing the presence of the Provost (whom he addresses) and two men (one of whom must be Barnardine). Having dealt with Barnardine, he asks 'What muffeld fellow's that?' (2885; 5. 1. 485). To Juliet he remains blind. As the play concludes, though he alone has discoursed with Juliet earlier in the action, the Duke turns from character to character without hinting at her presence. It is true that he says to Claudio, somewhat abruptly, 'She Claudio that you wrong'd, looke you restore' (2924)—but this is equally or more appropriate as a reference to an absent character.

Juliet's presence in the Folio text of 5. 1 balances that in 1. 2. They are linked by the dramaturgy of silence; they mark Claudio's first and last appearances. The episodes themselves are parallel: the Provost shows Claudio to the world, first on his way to the prison, second on his way to release. If Juliet was added in 1. 2 as part of a late adaptation, so she may have been added to 5. 1.

Juliet is the last named character in the direction for her entry at 2875. This permits the conjecture that her name was a late annotation on to the list of characters who enter (though women characters often follow in the wake of the men in stage directions). The form of her name used in the direction is of greater interest: '*Iulietta*' is found elsewhere in *Measure* only in I. 2. While she is on stage (according to the Folio) the anomalous -*eta* appears in a genitive in a metrically ambiguous line: 'I got possession of *Iulietas* bed' (TLN 238; I. 2. 134). Earlier, in the suspected interpolation itself, is the only occurrence of '*Iulietta*' apart from this stage direction in 5. I (TLN 164; I. 2. 67). Presumably either the annotator of '*Iulietta*' in the 5. I stage direction had just looked at the earlier scene, or the author of the interpolation himself made the late alteration. Unlike Juliet's introduction in I. 2, that in 5. I is accompanied by no attempt to reorganize the dialogue or stage grouping, and she could have been brought into 5. I through simple imitation of the earlier scene. There is no way of determining whether the individual responsible was a functionary (such as the bookkeeper) or the dramatist who originally decided to expand Juliet's role in I. 2. What does seem clear is that Juliet's awkward entrance in 5. I can hardly be dissociated from her awkward entrance in I. 2, and that the awkward entrance in I. 2 can hardly be dissociated from the suspected interpolation earlier in that scene.

The text in 5. I has apparently been changed simply by this addition of Juliet to a stage direction. The changes in I. 2 are more complex and wide-ranging. We postulate that before these changes were made, the scene, to TLN 215, would have looked as follows.[111]

> [*Enter Clowne and Bawde, meeting.*]
> *Bawd.* How now? what's the newes with you.
> *Clo.* Yonder man is carried to prison.
> *Baw.* Well: what has he done?
> *Clo.* A Woman.
> *Baw.* But what's his offence?
> *Clo.* Groping for Trowts, in a peculiar Riuer.
> *Baw.* What? is there a maid with child by him?
> *Clo.* No: but there's a woman with maid by him:
> you haue not heard of the proclamation, haue you?
> *Baw.* What proclamation, man?
> *Clo.* All howses in the Sububs of *Vienna* must bee
> pluck'd downe.
> *Bawd.* And what shall become of those in the Citie?
> *Clow.* They shall stand for seed: they had gon down
> to, but that a wise Burger put in for them.
> *Bawd.* But shall all our houses of resort in the Sub-
> urbs be puld downe?

---

[111] The form of the opening direction is defended above (p. 166); for Lucio's late entrance, see p. 156. Editors agree in ignoring the Folio's scene-division, after Pompey's last speech; it seems only logical to have Claudio and the Provost become visible before (rather than after) they are identified.

> *Clow.* To the ground, Mistris.
> *Bawd.* Why heere's a change indeed in the Common-
> wealth: what shall become of me?
> *Clow.* Come: feare not you: good Counsellors lacke
> no Clients: though you change your place, you neede
> not change your Trade: Ile bee your Tapster still; cou-
> rage, there will bee pitty taken on you; you that haue
> worne your eyes almost out in the seruice, you will bee
> considered.
> *Bawd.* What's to doe heere, *Thomas* Tapster? let's
> withdraw?
>   [*Enter Prouost, Claudio.*]
>   *Clo.* Here comes Signior *Claudio*, led by the Prouost
> to prison.   *Exeunt* [*Bawde and Clowne.*]
>   *Cla.* Fellow, why do'st thou show me thus to th'world?
> Beare me to prison, where I am committed.
>   *Pro.* I do it not in euill disposition,
> But from Lord *Angelo* by speciall charge.
>   *Cla.* Thus can the demy-god (Authority)
> Make vs pay downe, for our offence, by waight
> The [bonds] of heauen; on whom it will, it will,
> On whom it will not (soe) yet still 'tis iust.
>   [*Enter Lucio.*]
>   *Luc.* Why how now *Claudio*? whence comes this restraint.

As reconstructed, the scene is both dramatically intelligible and demonstrably Shakespearian in structure and detail. By contrast, the suspect
material is markedly anomalous, in terms of its verbal style and dramatic
technique; vocabulary evidence suggests that it cannot have been written
at the same time as the rest of the play; and it fulfils all the dramatic
requirements of an addition made for a late revival. Among other things,
this passage gratuitously enlarges the role of a character whose importance is also magnified, rather awkwardly, by the suspected rearrangement of soliloquies in 3. 1 and 4. 1. It also, as we shall see, apparently
alludes to events much later than the composition of Shakespeare's play.

VI

Dover Wilson's claims about interpolation in 1. 2 relied heavily upon his
interpretation of an alleged topical allusion. Naturally, if a suspect passage clearly alludes to events which took place long after the play was
written, the passage must be a later addition. But before such claims can
be properly evaluated, the original composition of *Measure* must itself be
firmly dated.

Measure for Measure was performed at Court on 26 December 1604.
How new it was we have no means of knowing: during the previous

winter season at Court (1603–4), the only identifiable play performed by the King's Men was *A Midsummer Night's Dream* (1594–6), and during the same season as *Measure* they also performed *Henry V* (1599). Metrical and vocabulary tests strongly and independently suggest, as does the play's verbal style, that it belongs to Shakespeare's middle period, apparently postdating *Hamlet*, *Twelfth Night*, and *Troilus*, all of which had clearly been written by the end of 1602.[112] Such internal evidence allows us, with some confidence, to restrict the play's composition to the two years preceding its recorded Court performance. All efforts to date the play more specifically than this depend on the interpretation of alleged allusions to events of 1603–4.

Francis Tyrwhitt, in 1766, first suggested that a passage in the first scene alludes to, and flatters, King James I's distaste for crowds:

> I loue the people,
> But doe not like to stage me to their eyes:
> Though it doe well, I doe not rellish well
> Their lowd applause, and Aues vehement:
> Nor doe I thinke the man of safe discretion
> That do's affect it.
>
> (TLN 76–81; I. I. 67–72)

This allusion seems as probable to us as it has to all subsequent editors, and it apparently establishes that the passage in question must have been written after Queen Elizabeth's death, in March 1603. How soon after Elizabeth's death James's antisocial disposition became discernible has been disputed. Lever contends that complaints about James's attitude towards crowds only surfaced after his long-delayed official entrance into London, in March 1604.[113] But John Nichols, as early as 1828, quoted a letter by Thomas Wilson, written on 22 June 1603: 'The people, according to the honest English nature, approve all their Princes actions and words, savinge that they desyre some more of that generous affabilitye wch ther good old Queen did afford them.'[114] An entry in the journal of Sir Roger Wilbraham, written between April and July 1603, similarly contrasts James and Elizabeth: 'the Queen would labour to entertayne strangers sutors & her people, with more courtlie courtesie & favorable speeches than the King useth'; moreover the King's neglect of those ordinary ceremonies 'made common people' conclude that he lacked 'true benignitie & ingenuous nature'. Later that summer Wilbraham referred to

---

[112] For the vocabulary evidence, see n. 102 above; for a summary of the metrical evidence, see Karl Wentersdorf, 'Shakespearean Chronology and the Metrical Tests', in W. Fischer and K. Wentersdorf (eds.), *Shakespeare Studien* (Marburg, 1951), 161–93. (Like the vocabulary evidence, these tests put *All's Well* after *Measure* and *Othello*.) See also *Textual Companion*, 126.

[113] See Lever's edn., p. xxxiii, and his 'The Date of *Measure for Measure*', *SQ* 10 (1959), 381–4.

[114] Eccles, p. 18.

'the thronge at Courte (which evermore swarmed about his maiestie at every back gate & privie dore, to his great offence)'.[115] Even during the King's progress south, from Scotland to London, earlier in the year, the press of people wanting access to him became so objectionable that a proclamation was issued restraining 'the concourse of ydle and unnecessary posters'.[116] The coronation, in August, was a hole-and-corner affair, and though the plague was to blame for the restrictions on attendance, those restrictions may also have seemed to confirm an attitude already apparent.[117]

Clearly, James's distaste for crowds became visible, at least to discerning observers, very early, and TLN 76–81 could have been written any time in or after the summer of 1603. However, the lines in question could also easily have been added between the original composition of the play and the Court performance. As Wilson observed, the lines could be omitted without loss, and they have the effect of making the Duke bid farewell twice. Lever, committed to the belief that Crane had copied Shakespeare's foul papers, would not concede this possibility; but if Crane was copying from a prompt-book, or even if Crane's copy cannot be determined, then a special insertion to please the King cannot be ruled out. In particular, the severe outbreak of plague soon after Elizabeth's death closed the London theatres, probably without respite, from 19 May 1603 to 9 April 1604.[118] Therefore, even if the play had been written in the autumn or winter of 1603, its London première seems most unlikely to have occurred before April 1604; the play might well have had one or two special additions supplied on that occasion—or for the Court performance itself. In these circumstances, the apparent allusion in 1. 1 does nothing to narrow the limits of the play's composition, which might have occurred at any time in 1603 or 1604.

Lever himself laid great stress on a parallel he discerned between TLN 1030–3 (2. 4. 27–30) and *The Time Triumphant*, a pamphlet entered in the Stationers' Register on 27 March 1604. The parallel seems plausible enough, but can be interpreted in diametrically opposed ways. Lever assumes that the pamphlet influenced Shakespeare, and hence that *Measure* was written after 27 March 1604 (pp. xxiii–xxv). However, Alice Walker quite reasonably objects that *The Time Triumphant*, written in whole or part by Robert Armin, could just as easily have been influenced

[115] Robert Ashton (ed.), *James I by his Contemporaries* (London, 1969), 7, 63.
[116] William McElwee, *The Wisest Fool in Christendom: The Reigh of King James I and VI* (London, 1958), 109.
[117] *State Papers Venetian, 1603–7*, 74–5 (letter from the Venetian ambassador in London, 6 Aug. 1603).
[118] For a useful summary of the evidence for the effect of the plague on theatrical performances see J. Leeds Barroll's 'The Chronology of Shakespeare's Jacobean Plays and the Dating of *Antony and Cleopatra*', in Gordon Ross Smith (ed.), *Essays on Shakespeare* (Pennsylvania, 1965), 115–62.

by *Measure* (pp. 19–20). Indeed, we have no particular reason to suppose that Shakespeare would take a keen interest in the pamphlet; on the other hand, Armin—a popular actor and a sharer in the King's Men—clearly must, at some time in 1604, have taken part in performances of *Measure*. The parallel thus establishes that *Measure* was either finished before 27 March 1604, or after; but in itself the parallel cannot determine which limit applies. If anything, probability marginally favours Walker's interpretation, that *Measure* antedates 27 March 1604.

One other possible topical allusion points (if accepted) to composition no earlier than autumn 1603. Pompey, in a passage of 1. 2 to which no doubts cling, tells Overdone of 'the proclamation' that 'All howses in the Suburbs of *Vienna* must bee pluck'd downe' (TLN 185–6; 1. 2. 87–8). In *Promos and Cassandra* a prostitute and her servant are threatened with eviction; though Shakespeare's plot does not require this more sweeping proclamation, it seems a logical enough extension of Angelo's principles. In such circumstances, no extradramatic reference for the proclamation seems necessary, though one might nevertheless exist. Lever, following Fleay, relates Pompey's announcement to a proclamation, issued on 16 September 1603, which 'called for the pulling down of houses and rooms in the suburbs of London as a precaution against the spread of the plague by "dissolute and idle persons"'.[119] 'The measure, which was strictly enforced during the following months, bore heavily upon the numerous brothels and gaming houses which proliferated on the outskirts of the city' (Lever, p. xxxiii). This seems to us a somewhat misleading account of the proclamation, which was entirely aimed at the protection of health, not morals. It specified that 'no new Tenant or Inmate, or other person or persons, be admitted to inhabite or reside in any such house or place in the saide Citie, Suburbes, or within foure miles of the same, which have bene so infected', and that offending buildings 'be rased and pulled downe accordingly'.[120] Brothels receive no special mention. Furthermore, Elizabeth also had issued a proclamation for the pulling down of houses in the suburbs, in June 1602. James's wish to establish minimum building standards, expressed in a series of proclamations spanning his entire reign, was enforced by pulling down houses which failed to conform.[121] In 1619 he himself noted 'that order hath bene given for

[119] F. G. Fleay, *A Biographical Chronicle of the English Drama, 1559–1642*, 2 vols. (London, 1891), i, 132. Neither Lever (pp. xxxii–xxxiii) nor Eccles (p. 29) credits Fleay; nor does Eccles mention it in his synopsis of evidence for the play's date (pp. 299–301). The actual wording of the proclamation is 'the great confluence and accesse of excessive numbers of idle, indigent, dissolute and dangerous persons', which combines a reflex response to the general problem of the poor as a threat to law and order with a particular concern about overcrowding in insanitary houses as a cause of the spread of plague.
[120] *Stuart Royal Proclamations*, ed. James F. Larkin and Paul L. Hughes, 2 vols. (Oxford, 1973–83), i, proclamation no. 25.
[121] *Stuart Royal Proclamations*, i, nos. 51 (1605), 78 (1607), 87 (1608), 120 (1611), 175 (1618), 186 (1619), and 255 (1624).

demolishing the houses of divers offenders in that kinde'.[122] If the issue were not topical at a number of dates from 1602 onwards, if Shakespeare's source and his plot did not so easily explain Pompey's announcement, and if the London proclamation more closely paralleled the Viennese, we might have more confidence in this alleged allusion; as matters stand, it seems to us highly uncertain evidence. Even if accepted, it only establishes a date of composition in or after September 1603.

Malone, in 1790, called attention to the fact that four of the ten prisoners itemized by Pompey in 4. 3 (TLN 2078–95) are 'stabbers or duellists', and that Parliament passed a statute to deal with an outbreak of stabbings, at some time between 19 March and 7 July 1604 (1 Jac. I, c. 8).[123] But the legislation had been preceded (as Malone himself notes) by a proclamation on the same subject. In any case the four 'duellists' in Pompey's speech seem to us very dubious evidence of date: duelling was a recurrent problem, one would expect a prison to contain a few violent men, and the disturbances that prompted government action had been going on for some indeterminate time.

We are similarly unimpressed by Eccles's argument that *Measure* must date from 1604 because it belonged to a group of 'disguised ruler' plays written in that year (pp. 300–1). The most thorough examination of the most famous of these plays, Marston's *The Malcontent*, concludes that 1604 (the date Eccles quotes) is 'too late to be plausible'; the play probably dates from 1603, and even 1602 cannot be ruled out. *The Fawn* may well date from 1604, but could have been written in 1605.[124] Middleton's *The Phoenix* was almost certainly acted at Court on 20 February 1604, and probably written in the six months before that performance. Eccles's apparent clustering of disguise plays in 1604 must in fact, by more considered and cautious estimates, be spread out over 1602–5; as such it cannot help to limit the possible dates of *Measure*'s composition. However, Pendleton has argued plausibly that the resemblances between *Phoenix* and *Measure* suggest that *Measure* was the debtor;[125] if his arguments are accepted, then *Measure* cannot be earlier than the second half of 1603, and was probably not completed until March 1604, or later.

A handful of possible allusions, all ignored by Eccles in his discussion of the play's date, suggest that the play was probably not completed until

---

[122] *Stuart Royal Proclamations*, i, no. 186.
[123] Malone's summary presumes (as do almost all editors) that the Folio's 'Pots' represents a person, and so should have been italicized, in the phrase 'wilde *Halfe-Canne* that stabb'd Pots' (TLN 2093–4); otherwise there would only be three duellists.
[124] *The Malcontent*, ed. G. K. Hunter, Revels Plays (London, 1975), p. xlvi; *The Fawn*, ed. David A. Blostein, Revels Plays (Manchester, 1978), 32–6.
[125] *The Phoenix*, ed. John Bradbury Brooks (New York, 1980), 5–24; Thomas A. Pendleton, 'Shakespeare's Disguised Duke Play: Middleton, Marston, and the Sources of *Measure for Measure*', in John W. Mahon and Thomas A. Pendleton (eds), *'Fanned and Winnowed Opinions': Shakespearean Essays Presented to Harold Jenkins* (London, 1987), 79–98.

mid-1603 at the earliest. At 4. 3. 7–8, Pompey explains that 'then, Ginger was not much in request, for the olde Women were all dead' (TLN 2084–5). The belief in ginger's medicinal properties has been well documented, and its use by old women makes obvious sense. But why should Pompey specify that 'the olde Women were all dead'? Lever suggests that this is 'probably a reference to the plague in 1603', and we can see no other plausible explanation. Certainly, the plague could be expected to take an exceptionally heavy toll among the old and infirm. Since the plague did not become serious until mid-May, Pompey's enigmatic line would seem to date the play's composition in June or later (unless some other convincing explanation of its meaning is forthcoming). James I had, by this time, already succeeded Elizabeth, and the emphatic punishment of Lucio for 'Slandering a Prince' might easily be a bow in the direction of the new monarch, who held strong opinions on such defamation.[126] If the play cannot be earlier than summer 1603, then it was written suspiciously close to the time when the compliment to James in 1. 1 might have been a part of the original composition, and suspiciously close to the time when the proclamation of 16 September might have been alluded to. In themselves such straws would hardly be sufficient to break even the scrawniest camel's back, but if the choice has been narrowed to composition after May or after August, they perhaps tilt the balance towards the later date.

H. C. Hart, in his note on Lucio's 'Is't not drown'd i'th last raine' (TLN 1538–9; 3. 1. 316–17) detected an allusion to what Dekker called in March 1604, 'the late mortally-destroying Deluge' (*Magnificent Entertainment*, l. 106); he thought there might also be a pun on 'the last reign'.[127] Rain is, of course, lamentably common in English winters, but the line would have been exceptionally pertinent in the winter of 1603–4, or soon after. This period would also have supplied an unusually pertinent stimulus for the play's disguised ruler plot. Although James arrived outside London on 3 May 1603, his official entrance into the city had to be delayed, because of the plague, until March 1604. During these months, Londoners had a new ruler, whom they had not seen and would not recognize, who was apparently deprived of any opportunity to get to know his new subjects. The idea of James visiting his people in disguise might have occured to more than one mind, and it does not seem to us coincidence that both *The Malcontent* (probably) and *The Phoenix* (almost certainly) date from 1603 or very early 1604. Although the 'disguised ruler' plays as a group do not enforce a date of 1604 (an Eccles

---

[126] See Eccles, p. 273.

[127] *Measure for Measure*, Arden Shakespeare (London, 1905), 80. See also Eccles, p. 163, and Walker, p. 20. Hart also noted some probable indebtedness to Jonson's *Sejanus* (1603), in which Shakespeare acted, at the beginning of 4. 4; but this link does not help to narrow the limits of composition.

argued), the relationship of the earliest of these plays to the political situation does suggest that *Measure* probably dates (at the earliest) from the second rather than the first half of 1603. If so, some significance might be discerned in Overdone's reference to Lucio's bastard: 'his Childe is a yeare and a quarter olde come *Philip* and *Iacob*' (TLN 1687-9; 3. 1. 460-1). '*Philip* and *Iacob*' alludes to the feast of Philip and James, the apostles, on 1 May; Overdone's specification of the child's precise age 'indicates that Lucio's child owed its origin to a more pagan way of cele-brating May Day' (Lever). But if Shakespeare had been writing in June or July, one might have expected him to say that the child *was* fifteen months old *last* May Day; the chosen mode of expression suggests (how-ever frailly) that Shakespeare was writing in the eight months before May rather than the four after. Lever, the strongest advocate for a 1604 date, argues that composition took place between May and August.

Cumulatively, these hints and inferences make it seem more likely than not that *Measure for Measure* was written no earlier than September 1603. It may not have been finished until late 1604, but we have found nothing which would require composition later than March 1604.

The interpolations, by contrast, must have been written after the com-position of *Rollo*, which most probably dates from mid-1617. (See Appendix III.) Moreover, *Measure for Measure* was probably set into type—according to the bibliographical researches of Charlton Hinman—as early as April 1622;[128] in order to have been included in the manu-script from which the Folio text was printed, any theatrical additions to *Measure* must have been written by the winter of 1621-2. Any apparent topical allusions in the suspect portion of 1. 2 must be evaluated in the context of these two widely separated dates of possible composition: autumn 1603 to December 1604, or late 1617 to very early 1622. To which of these two dates is the alleged allusion most appropriate?

We can begin with the very end of the suspect passage, Mistress Overdone's short speech to the audience:

> *Bawd.* Thus, what with the war; what with the sweat,
> what with the gallowes, and what with pouerty, I am
> Custom-shrunke.

> (TLN 172-4; 1. 2. 80-2)

---

[128] Hinman, *Printing and Proof-Reading*, I, 334-65. In fact, one would expect Jaggard to have procured the copy for most of the plays before printing began, and since *Measure* is the fourth play in the volume it had almost certainly been transcribed before printing started. Such considerations would push the *terminus a quo* back to Feb. 1622. Howard-Hill suggests that *Measure* may have been the first of the 5 Crane texts in the Folio to be tran-scribed (*Ralph Crane*, 137-8), and although we must regard the conclusion—as he does—with some caution, it would be safest to assume that the MS of *Measure* was probably available by 1 Jan. 1622.

All editors since Capell (1780) have cited Overdone's sentence as part of the evidence for dating *Measure* in 1603–4.[129] Lever conveniently summarizes this line of argument (p. xxxii): 'Overdone's complaint links a number of factors operative in the winter of 1603–4: the continuance of the war with Spain; the plague in London; the treason trials and executions at Winchester in connection with the plots of Raleigh and others; the slackness of trade in the deserted capital.' Only one of the links has any basis in fact: in December 1603 ten convicted conspirators were hanged.[130] The outbreak of plague which began shortly after Queen Elizabeth's death was, indeed, the most spectacular event of 1603–4; but no one has ever provided parallels for the assertion that 'sweat' could mean 'plague'.[131] Shakespeare certainly never used it in that sense elsewhere, nor does *OED* recognize such a sense. Instead, as Dr Johnson observed, 'the sweat' was current slang for the medical treatment for the variety of disease most often contracted in an establishment like Mistress Overdone's: syphilis. For that disease 1603 was no worse than any other year. Nor was 1603 particularly conspicuous for 'poverty'. It sat in the middle of a six-year run of good harvests, and the woollen trade was at the peak of its prosperity.[132] The new King had, in one of his first proclamations, abolished oppressive monopolies (7 May 1603), and was busy dishing out honours and offices; he brought with him flocks of Scots hangers-on, and a new atmosphere of extravagence; several observers contrasted this, favourably, with the parsimony of the dead queen.[133] Dekker's famous pamphlet described 1603 as *The Wonderful Year*: the Citizen 'seeing the golden age returned . . . resolves to worship no Saint but money' (C2); tailors, merchants, mechanicals, players, tobacconists,

[129] Although E. Capell's *Notes* (1779–83) was published posthumously, it could easily have been influenced by Tyrwhitt's 1766 argument for dating *Measure* after James I's accession. Without Tyrwhitt's evidence, and that independently adduced by Malone in support of it (1778), Capell's argument would probably have been treated more sceptically; as it is, Malone rather unkindly describes Capell's contribution here as 'the only' passage in his *Notes* 'that I met with, which in the smallest degree could throw any light on the present inquiry into the dates of our authour's plays' (1790: i. 347). Peter Cunningham's discovery, in 1842, of the reference in the Revels accounts appeared to provide clear documentary proof that Capell had been right; but he may nevertheless have been right for the wrong reasons.

[130] Ten conspirators were 'dragged to the gallows, hung, and quartered'. See *State Papers Venetian, 1603–7*, 120, 124 (dispatches from London on 9 and 15 Dec. 1603).

[131] Eccles cites Capell as simply glossing 'the sweat' as 'The plague' (p. 28), but in fact Capell's full note is much more revealing: '"*the sweat*;" which if we may construe—the plague, (and what should hinder us doing so?) we have in these circumstances a picture of the situation of England . . . in the latter end of 1603' (*Notes*, ii. 34).

[132] W. G. Hoskins, 'Harvest Fluctuations and English Economic History, 1480–1619', *Agricultural History Review*, 12 (1964), 28–46; Godfrey Davies, *The Early Stuarts, 1603–1660*, rev. edn. (Oxford, 1959), 261.

[133] Comments on James's extravagance from the beginning of his reign can be sampled in Ashton, *James I* (see n. 115), 14; McElwee, *Wisest Fool* (see n. 116), 107–16, and D. Harris Willson, *King James VI and I* (London, 1956), 159–66.

taverns, vintners, all saw a revival of trade; 'London was never in the highway to preferment till now' (C2ᵛ). In June 1603 James called off hostilities with Spain, and during the winter of 1603–4 negotiations were conducted in preparation for the successful peace conference of 1604.[134] But even in 1602 levies for overseas service had been the lowest in seven years.[135] As Dekker said, as soon as James was proclaimed Elizabeth's successor, 'the Souldier now hangs vp his armor and is glad that he shall feede vpon the blessed fruits of peace' (C2).

Syphilis would naturally be bad for any bawd's business, and the gallows could be expected to take its toll of her more disreputable clients. Probably 20–30 per cent of all convicted felons were hanged, in this period;[136] a man could be hanged for stealing 13½d.[137] These items in Overdone's catalogue need have no specific topical interest. Only 'the war' must refer to something specific, current, and intelligible to the play's audience; 'poverty' probably also does. If this passage were our only evidence for dating *Measure*, it seems to us unlikely that it would offer much encouragement for 1603–4: business was booming, the war over, and the year's most momentous event (the plague) is not, despite Capell and his followers, mentioned at all. The plague would not only have decimated Overdone's customers; many more of them would have fled from London in order to avoid it. Both Dekker and Middleton, in pamphlets written early in 1604, remarked upon the mass exodus from the capital.[138] Overdone doesn't.

The years 1619–24 saw the worst depression of James's reign—indeed Charles Wilson describes it as 'the worst economic depression' in England's history, to that date.[139] Those years also saw England's first military engagement since the peace declared upon James's accession in the spring of 1603. In 1602 England had levied 3,300 troops for the Netherlands; in 1621 it was promising to levy 24,000 for the defence of the Palatinate.[140] In the summer of 1620, Sir Horace Vere led an army of 4,000 volunteers to the Palatinate;[141] in February 1621 the report of the Council of War to the House of Commons recommended raising a force of 30,000 men to intervene in the war in Europe.[142] In April 1621 the

---

[134] *Stuart Royal Proclamations*, i, no. 15.

[135] See C. G. Cruickshank, *Elizabeth's Army*, rev. edn. (Oxford, 1966), 290. (There are no satisfactory figures for levies in 1603 itself.)

[136] Penry Williams, *The Tudor Regime* (Oxford, 1979), 232.

[137] See Middleton's *No Wit, No Help like a Woman's* (1611), 5. 1. 395–7, and *Tell-trothes New-yeares Gift* (1593), New Shakespere Society, 6 (London, 1876), pt. 1, p. 43.

[138] *The Wonderful Year*, D1ᵛ; *The Black Book* (quoted below, p. 202).

[139] *England's Apprenticeship, 1603–1763* (London, 1965), 47, and see pp. 53–5; also Davies, *Early Stuarts* (see n. 132), 23.

[140] *State Papers Venetian, 1621–3*, 228.

[141] J. W. Fortescue, *A History of the British Army*, 13 vols. (London), i (1910), 168. On the same page Fortescue gives the figure we quote for English forces in the Netherlands.

[142] *State Papers Domestic, 1619–23*, cxix. 93.

twelve-year truce between the Spanish and the Dutch came to an end; 'a large contingent of English' volunteers (perhaps as many as 6,000 men) fought on the Dutch side. England was at war, effectively if not officially; Austria was at war both effectively and officially. In 1621 'the war' would have been as real for the fictive Viennese bawd as for her actual London audience. (In August 1621 the enemy was raiding just outside Vienna.)[143] The years 1619–22 saw a much heavier depletion of England's resources of able-bodied men than any in the period 1601–4; moreover, in 1619–22 the war was new and expanding, while in 1603–4 it was an unexceptional and diminishing problem. Economic depression and war were the most urgent problems of England in 1620–2; Overdone mentions both. Neither was particularly remarkable in 1603–4; what was remarkable (the plague) Overdone does not mention.

Another alleged topical allusion comes at the very beginning of the suspected passage:

> *Luc.* If the *Duke*, with the other Dukes, come not to composition with the King of *Hungary*, why then all the Dukes fall vpon the King.
> *1. Gent.* Heauen grant vs its peace, but not the King of *Hungaries*.

(TLN 97–101; I. 2. 1–5)

As Wilson noted, there is a 'King of *Hungary*' in Shakespeare's source, George Whetstone's *Promos and Cassandra*. In Whetstone's plot this King occupies the position of Shakespeare's Duke; here in 1. 2, the Duke and the King are clearly differentiated. Shakespeare's play never again alludes to this King. Wilson is too confident in asserting that the reference to the King of Hungary here 'cannot be explained as a relic of the old play' (p. 104); but if it is such a relic, it has left no other trace on Shakespeare's plot. Moreover, the very gratuitousness of the reference makes a topical allusion likely enough.

Wilson himself took this passage as direct evidence that the beginning of 1. 2 was a late interpolation.

After a war of thirteen years, the Empire concluded peace with the Turks at Zsitva-Torok, on Nov. 11, 1606. This peace was signed, against the Emperor's will, by his brother Archduke Matthias, King of Hungary; it was a disgraceful peace, by which 700 villages were said to have passed under Turkish dominion, together with certain fortified towns; it was a peace which was likely to be long remembered against its author, the King of Hungary, by an indignant Christendom. 'Heaven grant us its peace, but not the King of Hungary's.'—the words, at once so pointed and so irrelevant, must be a topical allusion; and there can be little hesitation in attaching them to the peace signed at Zsitva-Torok in November, 1606 (pp. 104–5).

This alleged topical allusion is of course incompatible with the evidence that *Measure* had been performed at Court as early as 26 December

[143] *State Papers Venetian, 1621–3*, 138 (28 Aug. 1621).

1604: if the lines do refer to actual continental events, they must have been added later. Editors have tried hard to wriggle out of this dilemma. E. K. Chambers suggested that the Gentleman was alluding to 'the peace made and treacherously broken by Sigismund of Hungary in *2 Tamburlaine*'—but it is not clear why these Gentlemen should allude to *Tamburlaine*, or why they should deplore a fellow Christian's treachery against the Turks.[144] Lever, more plausibly, thought it likely 'that the dialogue here turned upon King James's negotiations for a settlement with Spain' (p. xxxi). The peace James negotiated was proclaimed on 19 August 1604, and if the play were written earlier in 1604 some such allusion might, indeed, be natural. Both Wilson and Lever agree that the passage refers to events outside the theatre.[145] As with Mistress Overdone's speech, the question is thus, does the apparent allusion better fit 1603–4, or 1617–22?

What exactly does the Gentleman *mean* by 'Heauen grant vs its peace, but not the King of *Hungaries*'? He draws a distinction between religious salvation and temporal peace: as a soldier, he does not want the latter at all. This would have been a highly censorable statement in a play submitted to the Master of the Revels at the very time when—according to Lever's own dating of the play—a draft treaty was being prepared by an international conference at Hampton Court. Lever's interpretation thus forces us to suppose: (1) that Shakespeare deliberately inserted a topical reference, favouring continued war with Spain, and (2) that the censor let this pass. Neither of these assumptions seems to us very attractive. King James was the moving spirit behind the negotations with Spain, and was proud of his role as peace-maker; King James was also the new patron of Shakespeare's company. Almost all modern scholars accept that Shakespeare went out of his dramatic way to flatter James in various passages of *Macbeth*, *King Lear*, and *Measure* itself. Yet here, in what may

---

[144] *William Shakespeare*, i. 454.

[145] Blakemore Evans, in his introductory remarks on 'Chronology and Sources', notes that 'The Duke referred to in connection with the King of Hungary's peace . . . has recently been identified with the Duke of Holstein, Queen Anne's brother, who was in England in 1604 to raise men in the Protestant cause against Rudolph II of Hungary' (*Riverside Shakespeare*, 54). Eccles does not record Evans's comment, either in his discussion of dating or in the commentary to I. 2; nor can we trace who proposed the identification which Evans reports. The Duke of Holstein did not arrive in England until early in Nov. 1604 (*State Papers Venetian, 1603–7*, 193); acceptance of this identification therefore entails composition after *Othello*, very late in 1604. The identification seems, however, intrinsically unlikely. The Duke of Holstein was not even attempting to 'come ... to composition' with the King of Hungary, nor were any other dukes accompanying him; while a certain level of popular interest in peace negotiations with Spain in 1603–4, or in continental manœuvres involving the Palatinate, could be expected, the Duke's arrival seems to have generated little or no public enthusiasm. Finally, acceptance of such a late date for *Measure* would remove any topical significance in Overdone's reference to 'the gallows', since the Winchester executions would have occurred almost a full year before: improving one topical allusion to 1603–4 would only weaken the other.

well have been the first play Shakespeare wrote in the reign of his company's new patron, he has allegedly laid on with a trowel an allusion casting aspersions on James's attempt to 'come . . . to composition with the King of' Spain. Even if Shakespeare were so unwise, the Master of the Revels should have been more careful—especially when the play was performed at Court. In short, the alleged applicability of these lines to the most cherished ambitions of Shakespeare's new monarch and patron argue not for but against their composition in 1603–4.

Wilson, however, cannot be right about the Hungarian treaty of 1606; Lever shows that it was not such 'a disgraceful peace' as Wilson claimed.[146] But 'the King of *Hungaries* [peace]' does sound to us (as to Lever and Wilson) like an epithet of some topical significance. Regardless of the merits of the 1606 settlement, the general plight of the Hungarians was well understood: as Blundeville said in 1594, 'the better part of them have bene subdued in our time, and are made most miserable slaues to the Turkes'.[147] To compare James's planned peace for England with the condition of Hungary would hardly have pleased him.

In short, even without the other evidence that this passage is a late, unauthoritative interpolation, one would be justified in seeking some other referent for the lines about peace and war and Hungary. On the evidence of state papers, Hungary did not much obtrude upon the English consciousness during the years from 1597 to Shakespeare's death, and the few dramatic references all allude to its unfortunate position as a battleground between Christians and Turks.[148] But in August 1619 James I's son-in-law Frederick, the Elector Palatine, accepted the crown of Bohemia, thus entangling England in the beginnings of the Thirty Years War. Over the next two years the English public quickly developed a fervid interest in continental politics;[149] war-fever ran increasingly high, and Bethlehem Gabor, elected King of Hungary in October 1619, was on Frederick's, and hence England's, side.

During this period the English public became engrossed with the war in Central Europe, in which Hungary was a key participant, vital to Frederick's cause. Yet Hungary was also unpredictable. At the crucial

---

[146] Lever, p. xxxi. Wilson's hypothesis in any case presupposes an early date for the interpolation: we have found no evidence, in the English drama or state papers, that the treaty of 1606 was 'long remembered by an indignant Christendom', and consequently one would (if Wilson were right) be forced to date the interpolation in the years immediately following 1606.

[147] Thomas Blundeville, *Blundeville his Exercises* (1594), fo. 252.

[148] For the drama, see Edward H. Sugden, *A Topographical Dictionary to the Works of Shakespeare and his Fellow Dramatists* (Manchester, 1925), 257–8. The relevant vols. of *The Calendar of State Papers, Domestic* contain only a handful of passing references to Hungary between 1596 and 1619.

[149] Davies, *Early Stuarts* (see n. 132), 23. See also Roger Lockyer, *Buckingham: The Life and Political Career of George Villiers, First Duke of Buckingham, 1592–1628* (London, 1981), 79, 82.

battle of Prague, in November 1620, the collapse of Frederick's forces had been begun by the flight of the Hungarians.[150] In July 1621, the Venetian ambassador in London reported to his superiors that England's representative at the German Diet would not consider Hungary's interests, because Prince Gabor had 'some months ago approached the emperor for peace separately from the Palatine'. In February 1621/2, he reported that, according to the Spanish ambassador, Gondomar, 'all the affairs of Hungary are settled'.[151] These diplomatic reports are confirmed by the testimony of more ordinary mortals. John Chamberlain, in a letter written on 18 April 1621, told his friend Dudley Carleton, among other 'yll newes', that 'the Hungarians have submitted themselves'.[152] In short, from spring 1621 to spring 1622 it appeared in England that the Hungarians had disgracefully abandoned their (and England's) ally. Public feeling against Spain and its allies ran high.[153] Moreover, King James was trying hard to avoid war with Spain;[154] his pacific inclinations and Spanish sympathies were well known; Buckingham, the King's favourite, had married a Roman Catholic in May 1620, and in September 1621 was privately assuring the Spanish ambassador that not a penny of English money should be spent in the Palatinate.[155] For all these reasons the possibility that England might go the way of Hungary, and disgracefully abandon Frederick by concluding peace with Spain, seemed real enough in 1621–2. In particular, on 23 May 1621 James had dispatched Lord Digby *to Vienna* to try to negotiate a solution to the Palatinate problem; Digby arrived there on 4 July. Digby's efforts eventually failed, and by August the fragile truce on the Continent had been broken, and fighting resumed.[156] But throughout the spring and summer, James was actively pursuing a negotiated settlement, one which some of his subjects might very well regard as a sell-out. Nevertheless, though this possibility clearly existed, officially England was still committed to the restoration of Frederick. English troops were fighting on the Continent; Parliament had been summoned partly in order to raise money for the defence of English interests in Europe; at one point James himself had threatened to go in

---

[150] S. R. Gardiner, *History of England from the Accession of James I to the Outbreak of the Civil War, 1603–42*, 10 vols. (London), iii (1890), 383.

[151] *State Papers Venetian, 1621–3*, 95, 233; see also p. 177, for Gabor's surrender in Bohemia (13 Dec. 1621).

[152] *Letters of John Chamberlain*, ed. N. E. McClure, 2 vols. (Philadelphia, 1939), ii. 365.

[153] *State Papers Venetian, 1619–21*, 92. More generally, of course, events like the parliamentary resistance to the Spanish marriage, and the instant popularity of Middleton's *Game at Chess*, provide striking instances of this antipathy.

[154] In his speech at the opening of Parliament in Jan. 1621, James had said 'I will leave no travail untried to obtain a happy peace': Gardiner, *History* (see n. 150), iv (1890), 26.

[155] *The Compact Edition of the Dictionary of National Biography*, 2 vols. (Oxford, 1975), 2159 (George Villiers, Duke of Buckingham). See also Lockyer, *Buckingham* (see n. 149), 85, and Gardiner, *History* (see n. 150), iii. 353–4.

[156] Gardiner, *History*, iv, 200–31.

person to fight the Turks, who were menacing Hungary. In 1620–2, therefore, topical allusions supporting the war would not only be popular; they also ran little risk of censorship.[157]

In 1603–4, the reference to the King of Hungary's peace would have been, as a topical allusion, potentially censorable; as an insult to James, it would have been not only impolitic but uncharacteristic of Shakespeare; moreover, such an interpretation requires us to suppose that 'Hungary' is a euphemism for something else. In 1620–2, by contrast, the allusion would have been politically acceptable, theatrically popular, and 'Hungary' could have meant Hungary. In particular, continental events in 1621, in which the English public took an exceptional interest, fit perfectly the allusion to Hungary at the beginning of 1. 2. Overdone's reference to 'war', at the end of the suspected interpolation, could very naturally refer to the same events alluded to here, at its beginning. Both these passages, long regarded as allusions to events outside the theatre, independently and in conjuction fit the events of 1621 far better than those of 1603–4. Since England was at peace from April 1603 to 1619, between the earliest possible date for *Measure*'s composition (1603) and the date when the extant text was set into type (1622), only 1620–1 combines all the elements apparently alluded to in these two passages.

Another detail of the dialogue in the suspect passage may also point to this period. Lucio's reference to 'the sanctimonious Pirat' (TLN 103; 1. 2. 7) need not be a topical allusion at all. But from 1609 onwards, partly as a result of deterioration of the English Navy under James's administration, pirates became a serious and increasing menace to English shipping.[158] In 1603–4, pirates figured in the public consciousness only because of the new king's efforts to recall English privateers, who had been allowed and encouraged to harass Spanish shipping during the war with Spain.[159] An allusion to pirates in 1603–4 would have had some topical significance, but in those years the pirates in the news were not harassing English shipping: they were themselves Englishmen harassing England's traditional enemy, and the weight of public sympathy would probably have favoured the pirates rather than King James's new policy. Between 1609 and 1616 no less than 416 British ships were taken by pirates; by early 1619 English losses to piracy had become so severe that a decision was

---

[157] Massinger's *The Maid of Honour*, probably performed in 1621, has been interpreted as a criticism of James's policy of restraint in Europe: see Margot Heinemann, *Puritanism and Theatre: Thomas Middleton and Opposition Drama under the Early Stuarts* (Cambridge, 1980), 217.

[158] C. D. Penn, *The Navy under the Early Stuarts* (London, 1913), 82.

[159] See *Stuart Royal Proclamations*, no. 15 (23 June 1603; also footnote 1 to this proclamation, which refers to a declaration to mariners of a month earlier, cancelling their letters of reprisal from Elizabeth), no. 28 (30 Sept. 1603), no. 46 (12 Nov. 1604); *State Papers Venetian, 1603–7*, 43 (4 June 1603), 100 (5 Oct. 1603), 125 (22 Dec. 1603). *State Papers Domestic, 1603–10*, aside from the proclamations already mentioned, in 1603–4, record only three pardons for English pirates and two orders for the arrest of others.

taken to prepare a major expedition against them—the first serious
employment of the Navy, in hostile action, since the death of
Elizabeth.[160] This fleet finally set sail on 12 October 1620; after a series of
delays it began serious offensive operations in May 1621; in July 1621
reports started reaching London of a major battle with the pirates; the
English fleet returned on 22 September 1621, after some success against
pirate strongholds in the Mediterranean; on 20 October 1621
Chamberlain wrote of the news that the pirates had captured a fleet of
fifty-seven British merchant ships.[161] At any time in 1621 (but particularly
from May to December) any allusion to pirates would have been topical.
Lucio's speech about the pirate would be especially pertinent from the
late spring to the winter of 1621—the months when the immediately preceding allusion to Hungary would have been most intelligible.

The allusion to Hungary's peace, at the very beginning of 1. 2, in itself
suggests that some lines have been interpolated here, probably in 1621.
That allusion leads directly, in form and content, to the conversation
about the sanctimonious pirate, and hence to the rest of the dialogue: it
would be difficult to remove it, without removing most if not all of the
opening section of the scene. At the other end of that conversation
between Lucio and the two Gentlemen, we have the well-known duplication of the report of Claudio's arrest; this, too, could not be removed
without displacing the entire first section of the scene. Then comes
Mistress Overdone's bridging soliloquy, which may also allude to events
of 1620–2; this soliloquy presupposes the existence of the preceding passage. In the space of eighty lines, we encounter three (and possibly four)
independent pieces of evidence suggestive of composition later than the
rest of the play: the Hungary allusion, the pirate allusion, the duplicate
revelation, and Overdone's soliloquy. None of these passages can be dislodged from its context without removing the entire opening of the scene;
yet if that opening were removed, the resulting scene would begin in a
demonstrably Shakespearian manner, clearly based on Shakespeare's
source, and the play would proceed smoothly, wholly unaffected by the
loss of the suspect material.

It remains possible that none of these passages are topical allusions.
The alleged allusion to pirates is particularly uncertain, because topicality
has not been suspected by previous investigators. But in the other cases
topicality has, in the past, been widely assumed. We have not seized upon
hitherto unsuspected lines because they can be so easily invested with a
significance which suits our own purposes; instead, we have simply re-
examined the meaning of passages long thought to be topical, by scholars

---

[160] Penn, *Navy* (see n. 158), 87, 89.
[161] Ibid. 99; *State Papers Domestic, 1619–23*, cxxii. 8 and cxxiii. 46; *State Papers Venetian, 1621–3*, 93, 155. On the expedition as a whole see also *Naval Tracts of Sir William Monson*, ed. M. Oppenheim, 6 vols. (Navy Rec. Soc.), iii (1913), 98–118.

with no textual axe to grind. *If* these passages are topical, then they point clearly to a late date. *If* they are not intentionally topical, then they still all accord surprisingly well with events of a later date. And *if* scholars who have previously accepted the topical impact of these speeches now deny it, one may reasonably ask whether that sudden shift of opinion results from an objective assessment of the nature of the passages, or from a desire to avoid at all costs a conclusion which would force them to admit that Shakespeare did not write this episode.

Being natural sceptics, we cannot accept that such a proliferation of coincidences is the mere idle fruit of accident. In particular, since the entirely independent evidence of the date of the suspected interpolation in 4. 1 agrees so perfectly with the evidence of the three separate topical allusions in the suspect passage in 1. 2, we find it impossible to avoid the conclusion that *Measure for Measure* suffered major theatrical adaptation in 1621—at least seventeen years after the play was written, and five years after William Shakespeare was buried.

VII

You may know that a crime has taken place, without being able to name whodunit. No one has ever plausibly identified the author of the additions to *Mucedorus*, for instance; but the title-page of the 1610 edition claims that the text has been padded out, and collation proves it. Nevertheless, in most cases we must do without a title-page confession, or any earlier text to collate against the late one. All studies of authorship are, in one sense, attempts to identify whodunit, and in that sense the identification of an interpolation is simply the identification of a second hand at work in a play. Interpolation is, after all, merely a sub-species of collaboration, in which the junior partner makes his contribution belatedly, ususally after the senior partner has retired or died. Ideally, therefore, as well as proving that a suspected interpolation was written later than the rest of the play, a critic should also be able to establish who did write it.

Such ideals can seldom be satisfied. It is often difficult enough to date whole plays, let alone parts of them; likewise, when the authorship of whole plays remains a matter of passionate dispute, no one will expect universal assent to a proposed attribution for two short passages. Any such attribution must rest upon internal evidence, which some modern scholars continue to regard with a fastidious and superior scepticism, despite the increasingly sophisticated accumulation of data about the distinguishing stylistic characteristics of Shakespeare and his contemporaries. Moreover, even an extensive interpolation provides much less verbal evidence for analysis than we would expect in even the most lopsided genuine collaboration. Anyone unwilling to make allowances for these special circumstances virtually vetoes, in advance, any possibility of persuasion. On the other hand, no on who suspects an interpolation can avoid the responsibility to search for a plausible candidate for its authorship. Nicholas Brooke based his 1964 Revels edition of Chapman's *Bussy D'Ambois* on the assumption that most of the additions and variants in the 1641 edition were written by Nathan Field, despite the explicit external evidence that these changes resulted from revision '*by the Author*'; yet the most extensive and authoritative study of Field's work had already, in 1928, declared that the variants showed none of the recurring characteristics of Field's other plays;[162] moreover, Cyrus Hoy's studies of the Beaumont and Fletcher canon had, in 1959, provided new linguistic evidence which, if applied to *Bussy*, would make Field's authorship of the additions even less plausible.[163] P. W. K. Stone, even more recently, dismissed many of the Folio variants in *King Lear* as unShakespearian, without providing any evidence for an alternative author;[164] linguistic and stylistic evidence in fact rules out all the plausible candidates, and points strongly to the variants having been written by Shakespeare, or someone indistinguishable from him.[165] Such precedents illustrate how heavily arguments for adaptation may depend upon an acceptable identification of the adapter. Given the insurmountable limitations of the evidence, we cannot expect to convince everyone that a particular playwright wrote the suspect passages in *Measure*; but the existence of plausible candidates would strengthen the probability that Shakespeare himself did not do so.

John Fletcher—apparently the author of the song borrowed from *Rollo*, and apparently Shakespeare's successor as chief dramatist for the King's Men—is a doubly obvious candidate. In fact, neither qualification is as genuine as it might appear. Though Fletcher probably did write the song, this gave him no proprietary rights over its transfer to another play: once the company had paid for *Rollo*, anything in it belonged to them. Fletcher may or may not have been consulted about its use elsewhere, and even if he were consulted he need not have supervised the transfer. Moreover, Fletcher's special position with the King's Men has been assumed, not proven. Critics have sometimes spoken as though Shakespeare's collaboration with Fletcher (in *Two Noble Kinsmen*,

---

[162] Roberta Florence Brinkley, *Nathan Field. The Actor-Playwright*, Yale Studies in English, 77 (New Haven, Conn., 1928), 145.

[163] 'The Shares of Fletcher and his Collaborators in the Beaumont and Fletcher Canon', *SB* 12 (1959), 91–116. Brooke's hypothesis depends on the belief that Field copied out the entire play (p. lxxii); hence we should expect linguistic evidence for Field throughout the play, as well as in the major passages added to Q2. Hoy's discussion of Chapman's linguistic traits appeared in *SB* 14 (1961); see n. 175. Like Q1, Q2 overwhelmingly prefers Chapman's 'o' to Field's almost-invariable 'oh': see App. II.

[164] Stone, *The Textual History of 'King Lear'* (London, 1980).

[165] Taylor, 'Date and Authorship', 395–401. (The summary there of Field's and Fletcher's relations with the King's Men should be modified by the discussion below, n. 167; the conclusion would, however, not be affected.)

Cardenio, and *All is True*) demonstrated that he was being groomed as Shakespeare's successor,[166] but in the years after Shakespeare's retirement, 1614–16, Fletcher was writing for Henslowe, not the King's Men.[167] When Shakespeare died, the man who succeeded to his share in the company was not Fletcher but, like Shakespeare, an actor-dramatist, Nathan Field.[168] Even after Field's death, the company never relied on Fletcher as it had on Shakespeare. Shakespeare wrote most of his plays single-handed; Fletcher was primarily a collaborator. A collaborator of genius, no doubt; but as a collaborator, someone who fitted into a play-factory like Henslowe's, or the post-Shakespearian King's Men, easily enough. For all we know his apparently constant association with one company after 1616 may have been based on debt, or habit, or personal choice, rather than a contract. Certainly, it seems odd that Shakespeare's alleged successor did not even contribute a commendatory poem to the First Folio.

Even if, as may well be true, Fletcher had contracted to write only for the King's Men, this need not have entailed a monopoly on play-

---

[166] See for instance Richard Proudfoot, 'Shakespeare and the New Dramatists of the King's Men, 1606–1613', in John Russell Brown and Bernard Harris, (eds.), *Later Shakespeare*, Stratford-upon-Avon Studies, 8 (London, 1966), 235–61. See also Bentley, *Jacobean and Caroline Stage*, iii. 308.

[167] A letter to Henslowe from Massinger, Field, and Daborne refers to 'the play of m^r ffletcher & owrs': see *Henslowe Papers*, ed. W. W. Greg (London, 1907), 65–6, 90. This play was delivered on 5 Aug. 1613. The MS of *The Honest Man's Fortune*, in which Fletcher had a hand, tells us it was first 'Plaide in the yeare 1613'. However, that does not seem to be the play referred to in the letter: Daborne had no hand in it, and Tourneur did. (See Jackson, *Attribution*, 216–20.) Fletcher thus apparently collaborated on two plays for Henslowe in 1613. One of these was clearly delivered (5 Aug. 1613) after Fletcher's collaboration for the King's Men on *Cardenio* (played at Court in the Revels of 1612/13) and *All is True* (played at the Globe in June 1613). *Four Plays in One*, a Field/Fletcher collaboration for Henslowe, apparently dates from 1613–16 (see Ch. 1 above, p. 35). Hans Walter Gabler attributes Fletcher's *Monsieur Thomas* to the same period and theatrical provenance: *Beaumont and Fletcher Canon*, iv (1979), 417–20. *Wit without Women*, which must have been written in 1614 or after, also apparently belonged to Lady Elizabeth's Men. Of plays probably written after *All is True* but before Shakespeare's death, only one (*The Two Noble Kinsmen*) belonged to the King's Men. Richard Proudfoot gives 'the late summer of 1613' as the earliest likely date of performance in his edn. of *Kinsmen* (Regents Renaissance Drama Ser. (1970), p. xii); but the detachable business of the morris dance could have been added, or substituted, at a very late stage in the play's composition (or even after its completion), in which case the play might have been finished in the spring of 1613. Since *Cardenio* dates from 1612, and *All is True* from summer 1613, this would place *Kinsmen* in the middle, and provide a neater picture of Fletcher's movements in 1613. In any case, it seems clear that Fletcher had more to do with Henslowe than the King's Men in the period 1613–15. Not until 1616–17, with *The Mad Lover*, *The Jeweller of Amsterdam*, and *The Queen of Corinth* (the last two in collaboration with Field) does Fletcher's association with the King's Men become permanent.

[168] Bentley, *Jacobean and Caroline Stage*, ii. 435. Field is listed third in the cast-list for *The Mad Lover*, performed at Court on 5 Jan. 1616/17 (ibid. iii. 373): this play, written by Fletcher and acted by Field, is the first clear evidence of either's association with the King's Men after Shakespeare's retirement. William Peery, in his edn. of *The Plays of Nathan Field* (Austin, Tex., 1950), dates Field's change of company 'Sometime in 1617' (p. 21), rather than in 1616: if so, it must have been very early indeed in 1617.

botching. Richard Brome, in the late 1630s, had such a contract with the Salisbury Court theatre, and G. E. Bentley extrapolates the conditions of this contract backward in time and radially in space, presuming they applied to the relations between other companies and other play-wrights.[169] But during Shakespeare's own tenure as leading dramatist and sharer with the King's Men, we know of only two plays adapted for revival, *Mucedorus* and *The Malcontent*; Shakespeare wrote the additions to neither. Between Shakespeare's retirement and the publication of the First Folio, we know of only one other play which suffered such interpo-lation: *Macbeth*. Neither Field nor Fletcher had a hand in adapting *Macbeth*; the job apparently went instead to Thomas Middleton, who never let himself to tied to any particular company.[170]

Fletcher, then, can have had no special claims to the job of adapting *Measure* for a late revival, and the linguistic evidence decisively rules out his presence. In the added dialogue which accompanies the interpolated song in 4. 1, *hath* occurs three times, *has* never; Fletcher overwhelmingly preferred the latter, and never used *hath* more than six times in any com-plete play. Fletcher preferred *ye* just as strongly—yet in the eighteen added lines *you* occurs seven times, *ye* never.[171] Linguistic evidence deci-sively rules out Fletcher in the scene where we might most expect him. This fact in itself makes it unlikely that he contributed to the adaptation at all. The presence of another example of *you*, and none of *ye*, in the suspect passage in 1. 2 only strengthens this conviction.

Fletcher, whose song was interpolated in 4. 1, apparently did not write the added dialogue which accompanied it there; we may therefore doubt whether he wrote anything in 1. 2, either. But, Fletcher excepted, we can-not assume that a single author wrote both interpolations. The most famous 'additions' in a Jacobethan play are those written for *Doctor Faustus* by two playwrights, Birde and Rowley; Henslowe on another occasion records payments to *four* playwrights for additions to *2 The Black Dog*; four playwrights also contributed revisions to the theatrical manuscript of *The Soddered Citizen*.[172] Such precedents forbid the easy or

[169] *Profession of Dramatist*, 257.

[170] Middleton's authorship of the interpolations has been challenged by J. M. Nosworthy, in *Shakespeare's Occasional Plays: Their Origin and Transmission* (London, 1965), 8–53. His only direct evidence against Middleton, however, is the fact that Hecate is differently portrayed in *The Witch* and *Macbeth* (p. 25). But the Hecate of *The Witch* would have been even less appropriate to Shakespeare's play than the Hecate of the Folio text, and Nosworthy's argument seems to assume that Middleton was incapable of changing his tune. Nor are we persuaded by Nosworthy's overall hypothesis, that Shakespeare himself wrote the additions, for a revival of 1612. For new evidence of Middleton's presence, see Holdsworth, 'Middleton and Shakespeare' (see n. 32).

[171] See Cyrus Hoy, 'The Shares of Fletcher and his Collaborators in the Beaumont and Fletcher Canon (VII)', *SB* 15 (1962), 71–90. Crane was reliable in transmitting *ye* and *you*: see Hoy, 'The Shares . . . (I)', *SB* 8 (1956), 129–46, 139.

[172] For *Doctor Faustus* and *The Black Dog* see *Henslowe's Diary*, ed. R. A. Foakes and R. T. Rickert (Cambridge, 1961), 206, 224; for *The Soddered Citizen*, the Mal. Soc. Repr.,

automatic assumption that one man wrote both additions to *Measure*. In 4. 1, someone inserted a ready-made song from another play, and transposed two ready-made soliloquies; he wrote a minimum of new dialogue, chiefly characterized by its blandness, its random mixture of prose and blank verse and rhyming couplets, and its consistent preference for *hath* (three times); in 1. 2, someone wrote an extended invented passage, amounting to a whole new sub-scene, chiefly characterized by its accomplished repartee, its uninterrupted prose, and its consistent use of *has* (twice). Nothing guarantees that one hand supplied such divergent materials. Moreover, the change in 4. 1 might easily have been the work—as Alice Walker suggested (p. 3)—of a bookkeeper, or some other theatrical anonymity. It certainly required no extraordinary dramatic talent, and its management of the consequent transition evinces none. By contrast, whoever wrote the beginning of 1. 2 was no dabbling amateur: he could write convincing, articulate, ironic dialogue.

Since this latter interpolation is also the longest, any search for the interpolator must begin there. Fletcher seems ruled out; Field was dead; Chapman is unlikely to have been writing for the King's Men after Field's death;[173] the style seems wholly uncharacteristic of Jonson. This leaves three historically plausible candidates: Massinger, Webster, and Middleton. All three were at this period often working for the King's Men.[174]

These general considerations may be supplemented by an examination of linguistic evidence. Cyrus Hoy, in a series of articles which have come to be regarded as a classic contribution to the study of dramatic authorship, demonstrated that most seventeenth-century playwrights could be convincingly identified by their use of certain linguistic forms (*has* instead of *hath*, *ye* instead of *you*, etc.). Hoy's work has since been extended and confirmed by many scholars, most notably David Lake and MacDonald P. Jackson.[175] Exploiting this profitable seam of modern scholarship, we can quickly narrow the range of plausible candidates for authorship of the interpolations in *Measure*. Massinger almost never used *has* (twice here), and also avoided *whil(e)st* (once here); Webster, like Massinger and Fletcher, strongly preferred *yes* (only once here) to *ay* (three times). Middleton, on the other hand, strongly preferred *has* (twice here); he

ed. J. H. P. Pafford (1936), p. ix. The exact status of the *More* MS remains disputed; but it is at least clear that four playwrights contributed additions to a theatrical transcript originally prepared by a fifth. See the Mal. Soc. Repr., ed. Greg, rev. Harold Jenkins (1961).

[173] On Field and Chapman, see App. III.

[174] We have excluded Dekker because he never, to our knowledge, worked for the King's Men; nor does the dialogue sound like Dekker's work. Linguistic evidence confirms this impression: Dekker prefers *hath*, and also (usually) *yes*. See Jackson, *Attribution*, 94–118, and Lake, *Canon*, table 1.1, band 1 (*d*).

[175] C. Hoy, 'The Shares of Fletcher and his Collaborators in the Beaumont and Fletcher Canon', *SB* 8 (1956), 129–46; 9 (1957), 143–62; 11 (1958), 85–106; 12 (1959), 91–116; 13 (1960), 77–108; 14 (1961), 45–68; 15 (1962), 71–90; Lake, *Canon*; Jackson, *Attribution*.

favoured *ay* (three times here) but also used *yes* (once here); he made regular use of both *between* (twice here) and *whil(e)st*. Though the passage
lacks any of Middleton's most characteristic contractions, its brevity
makes this fact dubious evidence against his authorship, and in any case
Crane expanded many of these contractions when preparing transcripts of
Middleton's *A Game at Chess*.[176] Linguistically, the suspect passage looks
more like Middleton than any other candidate.

Middleton probably wrote the interpolations in the only other Folio text
in which posthumous adaptation has been widely suspected (*Macbeth*);
throughout his career—but particularly from 1613 on—he spent much of
his time doing theatrical piece-work, involving sometimes the composition
of as little as a single long speech. R. C. Bald, among many modern
scholars and critics, has noticed 'how often the mind automatically turns
to Shakespeare rather than to any of his contemporaries to interpret what
Middleton was trying to do in his latest, and greatest, works';[177] David
Holmes and Edward Bond have described him as the greatest of
Shakespeare's contemporaries, outranking even Jonson.[178] Middleton
could write masterfully ironic comic dialogue, specializing in what
Christopher Ricks has called 'urbane obscenity', or what R. B. Parker
describes as a 'mixture of realism and exaggeration, exuberance and dis-
gust [which] creates a mood of soiled saturnalia'.[179] Above all, Middleton
was obsessed with the conjuction of sex and sin, and his plays, poems,
pageants, and pamphlets teem with satiric juxtaposings of Christian allusion and ungodly action. Of all Shakespeare's comedies, *Measure for
Measure* is the one we might have expected to interest Middleton most,
and the one which (just as pertinently) would most bring Middleton to
mind, were a revival being contemplated. Neither Middleton's contribution to such an adaptation of *Measure*, nor his authorship of the particular addition in 1. 2, need occasion any surprise.

Linguistically, the suspect passage fits Middleton as well as
Shakespeare, and the same may be said of many individual words and
phrases. Unfortunately, because there are no concordances to

[176] See *A Game at Chess*, ed. R. C. Bald (Cambridge, 1929), 34, 171–2; Howard-Hill,
Ralph Crane, 47–51. Lake denies that Crane interfered with Middleton's *'em* (*Canon*, 284),
but there are three examples in the Lansdowne and Malone transcripts of *Game at Chess*
(Induction 74, 80).

[177] In his edn. of *Hengist* (New York, 1938), p. xliii.

[178] See the dust-jacket of Holmes's *The Art of Thomas Middleton* (Oxford, 1970); Bond,
'The Greatest Hack', *The Guardian* (13 Jan. 1960), 6. R. H. Barker's *Thomas Middleton*
(New York, 1958) concluded with the sentence 'He is the third greatest dramatist of the
Jacobean stage' (p. 153); S. Schoenbaum's *Middleton's Tragedies* (New York, 1955), gave
Middleton 'the foremost place after Shakespeare in the hierarchy of Jacobean writers of
tragedy' (p. 150).

[179] C. Ricks, 'Word-Play in *Women Beware Women*', *RES* 12 (1961), 238–50; *A Chaste
Maid in Cheapside*, ed. R. B. Parker, Revels Plays (London, 1969), p. lix.

Middleton's work, reliable comprehensive checks of his vocabulary are much harder to come by. Furthermore, the exact definition of the Middleton canon has been hotly contested, and it has always been known to include a high proportion of collaborative plays. In these circumstances, to restrict ourselves to texts universally agreed to have been written entirely by Middleton would have seriously misrepresented his work. Nevertheless, we believe that some attempt must be made to examine the suspect passages in *Measure* against the evidence of the Middleton canon, as modern scholarship has defined it.[180] The list of parallels which follows was turned up by our own unassisted reading; it is therefore almost certainly incomplete, and the availability of Shakespeare concordances automatically weights any such search for parallels in Shakespeare's favour. So does the fact that Middleton's canon is only about half the size of Shakepeare's—even if we include parallels from collaborative plays, and those of contested authorship.[181] We have included parallels from collaborative plays, but only from those passages and scenes which the most recent scholarship attributes to Middleton,[182] All collaborative plays and plays of contested authorship are preceded by an asterisk; where uncertainty exists about Middleton's authorship of the particular passage cited, the reference is followed by a query. (We have, for the benefit of scepticism, attached asterisks to *The Revenger's Tragedy* and *The Second Maiden's Tragedy*, though the evidence for Middleton's authorship of both plays is now so overwhelming that continued scepticism is rather more embarrassing than commitment.)

The verbal parallels with Middleton's works are of two kinds. Some simply establish that Middleton was as capable as Shakespeare of writing this passage. Middleton's work, like Shakespeare's, contains many of the words and phrases which appear in the suspect lines in 1. 2. These parallels—which can be called 'neutral' or 'neutralizing', in that they are

---

[180] The decision to accept the results of recent scholarship is not merely a matter of adding to the size of the Middleton corpus. Among the major revaluations of the canon has been the exclusion from it of *Blurt, Master Constable* (1602), the denial of Middleton's hand in large parts of *The Family of Love* (c.1602–5), recognition of the presence of Webster as a collaborator in *Anything for a Quiet Life* (c.1621), and the demotion of *The Spanish Gypsy* (1623) to a status of deep uncertainty. Thomas L. Berger, the most recent editor of *Blurt* (Salzburg, 1979), unhesitatingly identifies it on the title-page as 'Thomas Dekker's', and his thorough survey of the authorship question concludes that it is 'impossible' to attribute the play to Thomas Middleton, 'and extremely difficult not to assign the play to Thomas Dekker' (p. 30). Berger reached this conclusion even before the publication of Jackson's monograph, containing more evidence of the same conclusion. Dekker's authorship of *Blurt* (and Middleton's of *Revenger's Tragedy*) is also supported by Norman A. Brittin, 'Middleton's Style and Other Jacobean Styles: Adjective and Authorship', in Kenneth Friedenreich (ed.), *'Accompaninge the Players': Essays Celebrating Thomas Middleton, 1580–1980* (New York, 1983), 52–4.
[181] Holdsworth, p. 28 (based on word counts of all the works defined by Jackson and Lake as Middleton's).
[182] For our definition of the Middleton canon, and our references to his works, see App. V.

equally compatible with composition by either author—are tabulated and discussed in Appendix V. In terms of the bulk of its imagery and vocabulary, the beginning of 1. 2 could have been written by Middleton *as easily* as by Shakespeare.

The remaining parallels, by contrast, favour one candidate or the other. For convenience, we may begin with the features of the passage which favour Shakespeare. In our survey of the Middleton canon we have not noted any examples of the words 'raz'd' (TLN 107), 'meeter' (117), '*Mitigation*' (138), or 'healthy' (148).[183] Even if we could be sure that our search was comprehensively accurate, we would expect the larger vocabulary of the larger Shakespeare canon to contain some words not elsewhere paralleled in Middleton. Of course, even if all these caveats did not apply, unmemorable individual words hardly constitute 'evidence' of authorship.

Potentially more significant than any of these Shakespearian parallels is the pun on 'Dollours' (143). A pun on the same word also occurs in the Folio version of *King Lear* (*c*.1610)[184] and in *The Tempest* (1611):

> Fortune that arrant whore, nere turns the key toth' poore.
> But for all this thou shalt haue as many Dolors for thy
> Daughters, as thou canst tell in a yeare.
>
> (TLN 1324–6; 2. 2. 227–30)

> *Gon.* When euery greefe is entertaind͜
> That's offer'd[,] comes to th'entertainer[—]
> *Seb.* A dollor.
> *Gon.* Dolour comes to him indeed, you haue spoken
> truer then you purpos'd.
>
> (TLN 691–5; 2. 1. 17–21)

The Tempest has the pun, but no other connection with this passage; whereas Folio *Lear* specifies 'as many' Dolors 'in a yeare', and juxtaposes this pun with a reference to a 'whore'. Some recent scholars have questioned Shakespeare's authorship of the Folio additons to *King Lear*;[185] but we regard them as Shakespearian. However, the link between *Lear* and *Measure* may appear more striking than it is. The same pun found in Folio *Lear* and *The Tempest* also occurs in Henry Chettle's *Tragedy of Hoffman* (1602–3):[186]

---

[183] Middleton does use the verb 'mitigated' at *Game at Chess* 4. 2. 107 (immediately followed by 'sums' and 'sodomy').

[184] For the date, see Taylor, 'Date and Authorship' (see n. 165).

[185] See Stone, *Textual History* (see n. 164). Peter W. M. Blayney is known to share this view, which will be argued in vol. ii of *The Texts of 'King Lear' and their Origins* (Cambridge, forthcoming). For a defence of the authenticity of the Folio additions, see *Division*.

[186] Mal. Soc. Repr., ed. Harold Jenkins (1950), ll. 370–1. For further discussion of the problem of dating, see John Jowett's edn. (unpubl. Ph.D. thesis, Univ. of Liverpool, 1983).

> And his reward, be thirteene hundred dollers,
> For he hath driven dolour from our heart.

Obviously, Shakespeare was not the only playwright who could pun on 'Dollours'. Moreover, the pun in *Measure* clearly differs from the pun in *Hoffman, Lear,* and *The Tempest.* In Chettle and Shakespeare, *dollar* suggests *dolour,* in the sense 'sorrow, grief'. *Measure* makes a different point:

> I haue purchas'd as many diseases under her Roofe,
> as come to
>> *2. Gent.* To what, I pray?
>> *Luc.* Iudge.
>> *2. Gent.* To three thousand Dollours a yeare.
>> *1. Gent.* I, and more.
>> *Luc.* A French crowne more.
>
>   (TLN 139–44)

None of these three cynics is talking about sorrow, grief, or mental anguish. Though no editor of *Measure* notices the fact, until the eighteenth century 'dolour' had a physical as well as a mental sense: 'Physical suffering, pain . . . a painful affliction, a disease' (*OED* dolour *sb.* 1). Those who frequented prostitutes thus paid 'dollars' (money) to acquire 'dolours' (diseases): given the homophonic similarity and the Jacobean obsession with venereal disease, the pun becomes irresistible. The obsolete physical sense of *Dollours* must be the one intended here. Editors of Shakespeare have overlooked this fact not only because the sense is obsolete, but more particularly because Shakespeare never elsewhere uses it: all ten occurrences of the word elsewhere in his canon clearly require the sense 'sorrow, grief' (*OED* dolour *sb.* 2). Middleton, however, does use the word in its physical sense: **Fair Quarrel* (1615–17) 4. 2. 12, 4. 2. 14 (G4ᵛ). A surgeon is speaking of the condition of the Colonel, wounded in a duel: 'then straight I feared *Syncop*; the flankes retyring towards the backe, the Urine bloody, the Excrements purulent . . . and the *Dolour* pricking or pungent . . . his principle *Dolour* lies i'th region of the Liuer, and theres both inflamation and *Turmafaction* feard'. Every modern investigator agrees on Middleton's authorship of this particular scene; it therefore seems reasonable to regard this usage as Middleton's, not Rowley's. Middleton therefore apparently uses the word in the sense required in *Measure*; Shakespeare does not. In fact, Middleton never uses the word *except* in this sense.[187] Middleton also uses the word *dollar(s)*,

---

[187] For Middleton's authorship of 4. 2, see *A Fair Quarrel,* ed. R. V. Holdsworth, New Mermaids (London, 1974), pp. xix–xxii, and George R. Price's Regents Renaissance Drama edn. (Lincoln, Nebr., 1976), pp. xvi–xvii, as well as Lake (*Canon,* 200–2) and Jackson (*Attribution,* 120–4). Middleton also uses 'dolour' in **Nice Valour* (3. 1; 3U2ᵛb); there the sense may be both 'pain' and 'grief' (used in similar construction in adjacent speeches). What causes this 'dolour' is being thrown down stairs. In *Wisdom of Solomon* 17. 6. 12, the word is also ambiguous.

which is punned on here: in particular, the collocation 'thousand dollars' occurs five times in *The Widow* (*c*.1616), 4. 1. 88, 98, 99; 5. 1. 173, 233 (F4^v, G1, I1, I2), while the phrase 'three thousand a year' occurs twice in *Anything for a Quiet Life* (1620–1), 2. 2. 159, 190 (C4^v, D1). Middleton used, late in his career, all three elements which are fused here in *Measure*; Shakespeare never used one of these elements, and only punned on dollars/dollours several years after the original composition of *Measure*. If we accept the pun as evidence favouring Shakespeare, then we must also accept the special sense of *Dollours* as evidence favouring Middleton. Since the same word yeilds contradictory conclusions, it must be discounted in our assessment of the two dramatists' claims. Shakespeare's claim therefore rests on his use of four common words not found in Middleton.

The features of this passage which specifically favour attribution to Middleton are much more impressive, in both quantity and quality. For instance, we have already noted the unusual absence of Shakespearian verbal doublings from the suspect passage; we may now add that Middleton's work contains few such doublings. The use of *has* is another anomaly which points to Middleton. Like Fletcher, Middleton consistently prefers *has* to *hath*, and in this he differs not only from Shakespeare, but also from Armin, Barnes, Barry, Beaumont, Brewer, Chapman, Chettle, Cooke, Daborne, Davenport, Day, Dekker, Drue, Field, Ford, Goffe, Greville, Haughton, Heywood, Jonson, Marston, Mason, Massinger, Munday, Rowley, Sharpham, Shirley, Tomkis, Tourneur, Wilkins, and Webster.[188] The Folio text of *Measure for Measure* contains only seven examples of *has*, in contrast to seventy-one occurrences of *hath*. If we exclude the suspect passages in 1. 2 and 4. 1, the ratio for what we regard as Shakespeare's original play would be five *has* to sixty-eight *hath*; as would be expected from this proportion, each example of *has* is isolated from its fellows by runs of *hath*. The two cases of *has* in 1. 2 are therefore, in themselves, unusual:

Impiety *has* made a feast of thee.
   1. *Gent.* How now, which of your hips *has* the most profound Ciatica?
                   (TLN 150–2; our italics)

No parallelism of structure or grammar requires the echo of *has* here: two different speakers are addressing two different listeners, on different subjects, in a different mode. By contrast, in Shakespeare's uncontested parts of the play a speaker can switch from *has* to the preferred *hath* in mid-sentence:

---

[188] Holdsworth, pp. 389–90 (on doublings); ibid. 158 (on 'has'), drawing upon Hoy, 'Shares' (see n. 175), *passim*; Lake, *Canon*, table 1.1; Jackson, *Attribution*, 30–1.

> *Luc. Has* censur'd him already,
> And as I heare, the Prouost *hath* a warrant
> For's execution.
>   (TLN 426–8; 1. 5. 71–3; our italics)

Two successive examples of *has* in one doubtful passage at least increases suspicions, especially when the passage lacks any examples of *hath*. But because one of the original play's few examples of *has* also falls in 1. 2 (at TLN 177; Add. A 1. 2. 3), the Folio text in fact clusters three examples of *has*—almost half its total for the play—within the first half of that scene. Of course, this may be another one of the unfortunate coincidences which so beleaguer this hapless passage, and no one would claim that two successive examples of *has* constitute sufficient evidence on which to base an attribution to Middleton. But within the terms of the Folio text itself, the suspect passage is anomalous in its treatment of *has*, and the anomaly reflects Middleton's established preference rather than Shakespeare's.

The possessive *its* occurs only eleven times elsewhere in the Shakespeare canon; with the exception of a single anomalous appearance in the Folio text of *Contention* (TLN 2110; 3. 2. 397), all the other occurrences are in plays written in 1609 or later (*Winter's Tale, Tempest, All is True, Two Noble Kinsmen*). Moreover, in *Contention* the Quarto text (1594) reads instead 'his', and the 1623 reading 'its' must therefore be treated with considerable caution as a reflection of Shakespeare's early practice. With that one uncertain exception, before the late plays Shakespeare preferred the older possessives *his* or *it*.

The Folio occurrences of 'its' cannot be attributed to Crane: he did not prepare copy for *All is True*, and the three pre-1609 plays set from Crane transcripts have no inconsistency apart from this one in *Measure*. In his list of variants introduced by Crane in those of his extant manuscripts where another text may be compared, T. H. Howard-Hill gives no instance of Crane introducing *its* (*Ralph Crane*, 161–6). In the Shakespeare canon, *its* can hardly be due to compositors, since at least four different ones set *its*; two different printers are responsible; it would be extraordinary if sophistication had limited itself to Shakespeare's late plays.[189] The use of the more modern *its* in the suspect passage in 1. 2 is thus anomalously early; this might, as with *Contention*, be a coincidence.[190] But the spelling is also anomalous: except once in *Kinsmen* (1. 2. 65; C1ᵛ),

---

[189] Eccles (p. 20) quotes *OED*, which casts doubt on the authenticity of the Folio readings (Its, *poss. pron.*); *OED* does not mention *Kinsmen*, or draw attention to the dates of the relevant Shakespeare plays, and of course it could not have known about compositors. *OED* does, however, give good reason for regarding the single occurrence in *2 Henry VI* as anomalous, since otherwise the first recorded occurrence of the form is in 1598. It is also noted in *OED* that early uses of the word strongly favour the apostrophe.

[190] Middleton in 1621 would not have written 'God' where F has 'Heaven'. If Shakespeare wrote the scene, 'Heaven' (and hence 'its') might have been introduced by the

TABLE 9. *Middleton's use of* its/it's

Date	Work	Reference	Spelling
1614–17?	*Witch*	5. 3. 28 (2061)	its
1618	*Peacemaker*	p. 325 (A4)	its
		p. 334 (C3)	it's
1619	*Inner Temple*	'The Parts' (A2ᵛ)	it's
		l. 112 (B2)	it's
1619	*Love & Antiquity*	p. 323 (B4ᵛ)	its
1620	*Hon. Entertainments*	iv. 68	its
		ix. 44	it's
		ix. 66	its
1620	*World Tossed	l. 810. 1 (F1ᵛ)	*it's*
1621	*Sun in Aries*	p. 341 (B1)	It's
		p. 346 (B2ᵛ)	it's
c. 1621	*Quiet Life	5. 1. 164 (G1ᵛ)	its
		5. 1. 217 (G2)	its
1622	*Changeling	3. 4. 162 (F1ᵛ)	its
		5. 1. 54 (H1ᵛ)	it's
1622	*Honour & Virtue*	p. 365 (C1ᵛ)	Its
1623	*Integrity*	p. 385 (A3)	it's
		p. 393 (B4)	it's
1624	*Game* (Malone MS)	Dedication	it's
	(Trinity MS)	2. 1. 27	it's
		2. 2. 187	its
		3. 1. 169	its
		4. 1. 46	its
		4. 1. 71	its
1626	*Health & Prosperity*	p. 408 (B2ᵛ)	it's
		p. 410 (B3)	its

the word everywhere else in Shakespeare employs an apostrophe. The usage in *Measure* is thus doubly anomalous, in terms of both date and spelling. This, too, might be a coincidence, but Middleton did use *its* at the time we conjecture *Measure* was adapted, and texts of his works spell without the apostrophe at least fourteen times (see Table 9).[191]

bookkeeper, or whoever else expurgated Shakespeare's profanity. But 'its' is nowhere else introduced in F as a consequence of emending 'God' to 'Heaven'. Indeed there was no reason to do so: 'his' remained in common use as a neuter genitive. Shakespeare himself wrote 'heaven keepes his part in eternall life' (*Romeo* Q2, 4. 5. 70; TLN 2650). The practice in expurgated Folio texts is usually to retain 'his' with 'Heaven', as in *Richard II* 1. 2. 37–8 (TLN 254–5), 2. 2. 98 (TLN 1053), 3. 2. 56 (TLN 1415), 5. 2. 75 (TLN 2446), *1 Henry IV* 3. 2. 4–6 (TLN 1821–3); in *2 Henry IV* 4. 1. 254 (TLN 2128), 'his' is changed to 'Heavens'.

[191] We have not included a possible example in *Hengist* (1616–20): the 1661 Quarto reads 'its', but both MSS have 'it' (5. 2. 109). The MSS are not only generally more authoritative,

Middleton started to use *its* late, but the word would be as unexceptionable for Middleton in 1621 as it is suspect for Shakespeare in 1603–4. It was rather more usual to retain the apostrophe in early usage, as did Shakespeare.[192] Though Middleton spells both with and without the apostrophe, his preference is to omit it, a preference found in the printed texts and also—more particularly and more markedly—in the autograph manuscript of *Game at Chess*.[193]

Its occurs in the line about 'the King of *Hungaries*' peace. Shakespeare elsewhere makes no reference to Hungary other than Pistol's 'base hungarian [Q gongarian] wight' in *Merry Wives* 1. 3. 19 (TLN 319); this adjective is facetious and punning, and scarcely refers to Hungary as a geographical and historical reality. Middleton specifically mentions its king, in the context of *other* rulers, in *Sir Robert Sherley* (1609: p. 397, B3), a tract lauding a knight for his achievements as a diplomat and soldier in Eastern Europe and the Near East.[194] He also explicitly refers to the 'most glorious' war for the Palatinate in both *World Tossed at Tennis* (1620: F2ᵛ, l. 876) and *Anything for a Quiet Life* (1621: G1, 5. 1. 110). Some scholars also detect allusions to the Palatinate in *A Game at Chess* (1624).[195] Furthermore, the politics of the allusion to the Hungarian peace are unmistakably close to those of Middleton in the early 1620s. In *A Game at Chess* Middleton explicitly allies himself with popular Protestant opinion in its hostility to the King's foiled plans for a marriage alliance with Spain; the play's political satire is harshly anti-Catholic and anti-Spanish. King James, pacifically but naïvely, hoped that by pursuing the Spanish match he could dissuade the Spanish Habsburgs from supporting the Habsburg Emperor Ferdinand in Germany. The equivalent Spanish objective was to prevent England from intervening in the affairs of mainland Europe. As a cessation of hostilities

but probably at least two decades earlier than the Quarto; the Quarto variant may represent an accidental or deliberate modernization. Bald believes that the play probably belongs to the latter end of its chronological range; Harbage and Schoenbaum place it in 1618; its inclusion would therefore merely reinforce the existing pattern.

[192] The presence of *its* in *The Witch* must, on the basis of the pattern of distribution elsewhere in Middleton's work, be taken as further evidence for a relatively late date for *The Witch*. Middleton's prefatory reference to the play's having lain 'so-long in . . . Obscuritie' is taken by Bentley as evidence for a date no later than 1616, but we can hardly demand that 'long' means a decade, and a date as late as 1618 cannot be ruled out. See also n. 196 on the play's relation to the Essex divorce scandal and n. 52 on John Wilson's composition of the music.

[193] We have examined the Trinity MS of *Game at Chess* ourselves, since Bald removes 'redundant apostrophes' in his edn. (He does, however, retain that in the Dedication, in autograph in the Malone MS.) In *Barnavelt* Crane uses the apostrophied form (l. 1255), and Crane provided Folio copy for *Winter's Tale* and *Tempest* too, so the anomalous spelling in *Measure* seems unlikely to derive from Crane's influence.

[194] *Roaring Girl* alludes to the earlier wars in Hungary, but the passage in question was almost certainly written by Dekker (5. 1. 86–93).

[195] See Edgar C. Morris, 'The Allegory in Middleton's *A Game at Chess*', *Englische Studien*, 38 (1907), 39–52, and J. W. Harper's New Mermaids edn. (1966), 15, 29, 36, 54.

which let down the Protestant cause in central Europe, the King of Hungary's peace was, from the anti-Catholic viewpoint, a betrayal similar to the threatened Spanish marriage alliance. Even if it was misguided to extrapolate an authorial point of view from Lucio's comments, the arena of political interest and the appeal (ironic, or otherwise) to a specific popular sentiment are both clear.

As we have suggested, Hungary was more topical in 1621 than 1603–4, as was an unfavourable attitude to pirates. Middleton mentions pirates in *Second Maiden's Tragedy* (1611) 3. 3. 69–71, *Anything for a Quiet Life* (1621) 1. 1. 204, B3, *No Wit, No Help* (1611) 4. 2. 151, F8ᵛ, *Hengist* (1619–20) 4. 2. 28, *Women Beware Women* (1621) 3. 1. 153, K6, *Game at Chess* (1624) 3. 1. 86–8 ('the Infidell pyrate'). The last passage—and probably that in *Women Beware Women*—alludes to the 1621 expedition in particular, as may that in *Measure*. In *Women Beware Women*, the allusion is laid on with a trowel: Bianca, out of the blue, asks, 'What news now of the Pirats, any stirring?'. In general, Middleton was much more prone than Shakespeare to exploit topical material. All his masques and pageants, beginning with his contribution to *Magnificent Entertainment* in 1604, turn civic ephemera into drama; pamphlets like *Sir Robert Sherley's Entertainment in Cracovia* (1609) and *The Peacemaker* (1618) exploit an interest in current political events; *Roaring Girl* (1611) brings on to the stage a notorious contemporary Londoner; in *Yorkshire Tragedy* (1605) he dramatizes a notorious recent murder; in *No Wit, No Help* (1611–12) and *The Inner Temple Masque* (1619) he satirizes the latest almanac; in *Chaste Maid* (1613) he brings superfluous watermen on stage, taking sides in a current dispute; *The Witch* (1612–17?) has been plausibly interpreted as, in part, a comment on the Essex divorce scandal;[196] *Game at Chess* (1624) is the most famous political allegory in the history of English drama. The presence, in a brief passage, of probable topical allusions to 'the King of *Hungary*', the expedition against the pirates, 'the war' in Europe, and the current depression would be as typical of Middleton as it would be uncharacteristic of Shakespeare.

Shakespeare only once refers to the 'ten Commandements', and on that occasion the phrase is a facetious metaphor for 'ten fingers' (*Contention* 1. 3. 145; TLN 534). Middleton, by contrast, several times writes of them, once in a manner strikingly reminiscent of the joke in *Measure for Measure* about the 'Sanctimonious Pirat'.

Luc. Thou conclud'st like the Sanctimonious Pirat, that went to sea with the ten Commandements, but scrap'd one out of the Table.

---

[196] See A. A. Bromham, 'The Date of *The Witch* and the Essex Divorce Case', *N. & Q.* 225 (1980), 149–52; Heinemann, *Puritanism and Theatre* (see n. 157), 107–14; Anne Lancashire, '*The Witch*: Stage Flop or Political Mistake?', in Friedenreich (ed.), '*Accompaninge the Players*' (see n. 180), 161–81.

> *2. Gent.* Thou shalt not Steale?
> *Luc.* I, that he raz'd.

In *Your Five Gallants* (1604–7), Pursnet—a thief and highwayman—is speaking of his boy:

> . . . he has his Creed by heart, reads me his chapter duly euery night; hee will not misse you one title in the nine commandments.
> *Bungl.* Thers ten of em.
> *Purs.* I feare he skips ore one; thou shalt not steale.
>
>   (3. 5. 103–7; F1)

The same idea crops up in *Trick to Catch the Old One* (1606).[197] 'He lookt as if hee would obay the commandment[s] well, when he began first with stealing' (1. 1. 17–18; B3). Likewise, in *Game at Chess* (1624), the White Queen's Pawn speaks of 'the 3 Vowde people | For povertie, obedience, Chastitie, | The last the most forgot' (2. 1. 88–90). Middleton also satirizes people who sanctimoniously keep only the commandments which suit them in *The Puritan* (1604–6):

> *Nich.* Why Couzen? you know tis written, thou shalt not steale?
> *Cap.* Why, and foole, thou shalt loue thy Neighbour, and helpe him in extremities?
> *Nich.* Masse. I thinke it bee, indeed, in what Chapter's that Couzen?
> *Cap.* Why in the first of Charity, the 2. verse.
> *Nich.* The first of Charity, quatha, that's a good iest; there's no such Chapter in my booke!
> *Cap.* No, I knew twas torne out of thy Booke, & that makes so little in thy heart.
>
>   (1. 4. 143–55; C1–1ᵛ)

In *The Ant and the Nightingale* (1604) Middleton writes of one 'protesting he would keepe all those [admonitions to vice], better then the ten Commandments' (D2ᵛ, p. 78); in *Mad World, My Masters* (1604–6), he writes of 'the honestest theeues' who will 'rob a man with conscience' (2. 5. 6–8; C2ᵛ); in *Revenger's Tragedy* the Bastard was 'Begot against the seuenth commandment' (1. 2. 162; B2). All these passages manifest a recurrent idea, also present here in *Measure*. Moreover, Shakespeare's only other use of the word *sanctimonious* (*Tempest* 4. 1. 16) is approving rather than ironic; Middleton uses the word ironically in *Game at Chess* (1624: 1. 1. 31, perhaps also 4. 2. 141, 5. 1. 22); he similarly uses *sanctify* in *Hengist* (1619–20; 4. 2. 210); he uses *sanctity* ironically in *World Tossed at Tennis* (1620: l. 390, D2ᵛ, 'A white-fac't hyppocrite, Lady Sanctity'). Shakespeare never elsewhere quotes the phrase 'Thou shalt not Steale' (TLN 106); Middleton does in both *Your Five Gallants* and *The*

---

[197] For the date, see *A Trick to Catch the Old One*, ed. G. J. Watson, New Mermaids (London, 1968), pp. xii–xiv.

Puritan (already quoted). This single four-line passage thus contains four elements which point to Middleton rather than Shakespeare: the exact parallel with a passage in *Your Five Gallants*, the general topic of violations of the ten commandments, the phrase 'Thou shalt not Steale', and the ironic use of *sanctimonious*.

Lucio says that he will 'learne to begin thy health' (TLN 133), and Lever notes the apparently innovative idiom *begin thy health*.[198] Certainly, the Shakespeare canon provides no parallels for this locution. But in Middleton's *Honourable Entertainments* (1620) a whole passage rings repetitions of this idiom: 'a Gentleman' tell us that 'heere the noble Health begins to All' (1. 93; B3); the stage direction informs us, 'hee beginning the Health' (1. 95–6; B3^v); a song declares *'The Health's begun'* (1. 99; B3^v), and *'The Ceremonies [i.e. healths] . . . were begun to you'* (1. 104–5; B3^v). Moreover, just as Lucio says he will *learne* to begin the health, but *forget* to drink after the First Gentleman, so in Middleton's entertainment the assembled dignitaries are entreated to *'Forget not'* the healths that *'were begun to'* them (1. 104; B3^v), and told that the Health *'taught'* the next pledger to honour their pledge (1. 110–11; B4).[199] The peculiarity of the idiom *Measure* shares with Middleton's pageant, its insistent repetition in the pageant, the presence of the 'Gentlemen', and the collocation of this phrase with *'Forget'* and *'taught'*, all make a connection between the two works probable. The same idiom, or a variant of it, also occurs in three other Middleton plays: *No Wit No Help* (1611–12), 4. 2. 201, G1^v ('begin a health') and, less significantly, **Yorkshire Tragedy* (1605), 4. 52, l. 446 ('begin to you'), and **1 Honest Whore* (1604), 1. 5. 37–8, ('begin you to the Gentleman . . . I begin to him?').[200] In none of these earlier plays does the context bear any other resemblance to that in *Measure*, nor is the phrase given the emphasis so noticeable in *Honourable Entertainments*.[201]

---

[198] 'A new idiom' (Lever, p. 11). Eccles (p. 25) does not note this, instead recording Schmidt's cross-reference to Sonnet 114. But in fact this sonnet nowhere includes the word 'health', or any reference to the practice, though it does build throughout on the imagery of drinking, and 'drink . . . up' occurs twice. The final line—'mine eye . . . doth first begin'— can therefore hardly be glossed as even an implied example of 'begin [thy health]'; the natural interpretation would be 'begin [to drink]'. The edns. of W. G. Ingram and Theodore Redpath (London 1964, rev. 1978), Stephen Booth (New Haven, Conn., 1977), and Hyder Rollins (Philadelphia, 1944) all agree—as have all editors since Steevens—that the image is of a 'taster' to the King; none interprets it as in any way referring to the pledging of healths.

[199] See also *Michaelmas Term* 2. 1. 25–8, where 'your health' is juxtaposed with 'remembrance', 'remembrance', and 'remember'd' (B4^v–C1).

[200] Another example may occur in **Second Maiden's Tragedy* (1611): 'ther ar many knaves will begin first | And bringe their lordes the bottome' (2. 3. 122–3; ll. 1165–6). It is not absolutely clear, however, that this refers to a health.

[201] A tantalizing (though inconclusive) link between this passage in *Measure* and Middleton may be provided by the anonymous *Solemne Joviall Disputation Theoreticke and Practicke; briefly Shadowing The Law of Drinking* (attributed to Richard Brathwaite, 1617). This mock-dissertation may have influenced *Women Beware Women* (see J. R. Mulryne edn.

At the end of the suspected interpolation, a bawd complains, directly to the audience, about how bad business has been lately (TLN 172–5).[202] In Middleton's *The Black Book* (1604), the Devil visits a whorehouse, in disguise; after he reveals himself, the pander begins 'complaining to me of their bad takings all the last plaguy Somer, that there was no stirrings, and [they were] therefore vndone for want of doings: whereupon, after many such inductions to bring the scene of his pouerty vpon the stage, he desired, in cool terms, to borrow some forty pence of me' (p. 16; C1). The devil is outraged ('Why, for shame! a bawd and poor?'), and launches into a long tirade in which he claims that anyone but a pander might be afflicted with 'pouerty', and that it is 'most impossible' to be 'a right bawd and poor'. The Devil concludes with a joking allusion to syphilis ('monsieur Drybone, the Frenchman'). Nevertheless, the pander persists: '*what with this long Vacation, and the fidging of Gallants to* Norfolke *and vp and down countries*', the 'poor' pimp cannot earn a decent living (p. 23: C4ᵛ; our italics). This passage bears, we believe, a remarkable resemblance to that in *Measure*. The bawd's ironic complaint, the reference to the pox, the repetition of 'pouerty' (and 'poor'), even the syntax ('what with . . .'), all point to some direct connection between the two passages. A third passage similar to these occurs in *The Widow* (*c*.1616), where a thief addresses the audience, in a mid-scene interval between the exit of one character and the entrance of others,

> When the high-ways grow thin with Travellers,
> And few Portmantues stirring, as all trades
> Have their dead time wee see; Theevery, poor takings,
> And Lecherie cold doings . . .
>
>   (4. 2. 21–4; G2)

Like the speech in *Measure*, this soliloquy repeats much of the imagery of the passage in *Black Book*: 'bad takings'/'poor takings', 'no stirrings'/'few . . . stirring', 'want of doings'/'cold doings'; 'dead time' might also be thought to echo 'the last plaguy Somer', while the thief's complaint about the dearth of travelling corresponds to the pimp's complaint about the excess of it. This passage in *The Widow* amply confirms that the passage

---

(Manchester, 1975), 94). Potentially pertinent passages include: 'who knowes not how many there be, who in these HEALTH-cups, intending the health of another, impaire ther owne?' (p. 10), and 'anyone may civilly refuse such . . . healths, though another begins them . . . For such things as prejudice piety, our healths safety . . . wee are not to imagine them to be done by us' (p. 22). Eccles (p. 25) cites a good parallel from Montaigne, whom Shakespeare certainly read; so the possible sources for the passage—if any, beyond common observation—demonstrate nothing about authorship.

[202] It may be pertinent to note that Middleton probably makes more use of direct address to the audience than any dramatist of the period: see Bruno Nauer, *Thomas Middleton: A Study of the Narrative Structures* (Zurich, 1977), 149, 188.

in *The Black Book* was—like so many of Middleton's striking effects—recycled in his later work.[203]

Lucio says that he has 'purchas'd . . . many diseases' (TLN 139) under Overdone's roof. A very close verbal parallel for this phrase can be found in 3. 3 of *1 Honest Whore* (1604), one of the few scenes in that play attributed to Middleton:

> What shallow sonne and heire then, foolish gallant,
> Would waste all his inheritance, to purchase
> A filthy loathd disease?

> (3. 3. 60–2)

A reformed prostitute speaks these lines: the disease in question is the pox, purchased from prostitutes. She goes on to say that such diseases will 'eate out' his body (with which compare 'Impiety has made a feast of thee'). Shakespeare's canon contains nothing so close to *Measure* as this passage.[204]

As well as these extended parallels, we may cite a number of lesser links. Shakespeare never uses the phrase 'come . . . to composition' (TLN 97–8); Middleton does, in *Wisdom of Solomon* (1597), 1. 7. 8.[205] Shakespeare never elsewhere has 'speake feelingly' (TLN 130), which occurs in *More Dissemblers* (1619), 5. 2. 87, F7. Shakespeare never repeats 'Behold, behold', as at TLN 138; in both *The Inner Temple Masque* (1619), l. 256 (C2), and *Revenger's Tragedy* (1606), 5. 1. 106 (I1), Middleton does.[206] Middleton also uses 'Behold' twice in quick succession elsewhere: for example, in *Wisdom of Solomon* (1597), he four times repeats the imperative at the beginning of adjacent verse lines (6. 17. 8–9, 9. 4. 1–2, 14. 10. 5–6, 11–12), and once uses it three times in two lines (18. 11. 3–4). The Shakespeare canon provides no examples of

---

[203] See also *Wit at Several Weapons* (c.1613), where a thief excuses his poor takings to an accomplice: ''Tis but young Tearm, Atturnies ha small doings yet, | Then High-way Lawyers, they must needs ha little' (2. 1. 39–40; 6K1ᵛa). Hoy, Lake, and Jackson all agree on Middleton's authorship of the scene.

[204] Sir John says 'I will turn diseases to commodity' (2 *Henry IV* 1. 2. 249–50); he is not talking specifically about veneral infection, but simply making a joke about the abundance of diseases his body suffers, a superfluity that encourages him to try marketing his surplus. Closer to *Measure* is a speech in *Pericles*: 'diseases have been sold dearer than physics' (19. 123). Mariana here clearly refers to the pox, sold in the whorehouse in which she is now herself a prisoner. But unique parallels from *Pericles* are perilous evidence of Shakespeare's practice, and in any case this passage does not use the specific verb 'purchase', or refer to 'young gallants' or to the pox 'eating' its victims.

[205] This stanza and the following are devoted to the subject of 'grace' and God's 'peace'. The phrase also occurs twice in scenes of *Wit at Several Weapons* (c.1613) usually assigned to Rowley (2. 4. 79, 5. 2. 279). Jackson notes that Middleton may well have written parts of Act 5 (*Attribution*, 127).

[206] The preceding words in *Revenger's Tragedy* are 'Over what roof hangs this prodigious comet | In deadly fire', which have been glossed as 'Under what roof lies the evidence of this reported disaster?' (ed. Lawrence J. Ross, Regents Renaissance Drama Ser. (Lincoln, Nebr., 1966), 107). In *Measure*, of course, 'vnder her Roofe' occurs in the line after 'Behold, behold'.

such repetition. Shakespeare never elsewhere uses *controversy* of religious or theological disputes; Middleton does (*World Tossed at Tennis*, 1620: 453, 722; D3ᵛ, E4). The first of these is almost immediately followed by 'religions', as 'religion' immediately precedes the word in *Measure*. Shakespeare never elsewhere uses the phrase 'as for example'. Middleton does at least five times: *Meeting of Gallants at an Ordinary* (1604), p. 132 (D2ᵛ), *No Wit, No Help* (1611), 1. 3. 195 (B7ᵛ), *Wit at Several Weapons* (1613), 4. 1. 222 (6l2ᵛ), *World Tossed at Tennis* (1620), l. 479 (B4), *Women Beware Women* (c. 1621) 1. 1. 81 (G5ᵛ).[207] Shakespeare's works contain no other example of the phrase 'I belieue thee' (TLN 114), which occurs in *Wit at Several Weapons* 2. 2. 219 (6k2ᵛa) and *Roaring Girl* 4. 1. 202 (H4ᵛ).[208] In fact, Shakespeare's works contain only one dubious example of the parallel reply 'I believe you': *Pericles* 13. 25. In Middleton's works, by contrast, the phrase occurs in *No Wit No Help* 1. 3. 134, *Chaste Maid* 5. 3. 29, and *Wit at Several Weapons* 4. 1. 285.

The preceding examples are, we believe, straightforward enough. Two other sets of parallels may be more disputable. Shakespeare never elsewhere uses 'Madam' as a facetious title; *OED* does not otherwise record the usage before the early 1620s. Middleton probably uses the word facetiously in *Micro-cynicon* (1599), p. 126 (B8), 'Fine Madam *Tiptoes* in her veluet gowne'; *The Puritan* (1606), 1. 2. 92–3 (B2), 'Peace is a good Madam to all other professions, and an arrant Drabbe to vs'; *Revenger's Tragedy* (1606), 1. 1. 55 (A2ᵛ), 'bald Madam, Opportunity'; and 2. 2. 58 (D3) 'the good antient Madam', of Castiza's mother, prepared to act as bawd for her own daughter. Certainly, such ironic titles are in Middleton's mode: we have already noticed 'Lady Sanctity' in *World Tossed at Tennis* (1620), and many similar collocations could be cited— including 'Mistress wimble-chin' as the name of an old bawd (*Black Book*, p. 12, B3ᵛ).

Middleton also uses the collocation 'any language' (TLN 119) at least twice, in *Game at Chess* (1624), 1. 1. 146, and *Women Beware Women* (c.1621) 3. 2. 136, L4; it occurs nowhere else in the Shakespeare canon. This may seem, in itself, fairly unremarkable, but the unique verbal parallel co-exists with a preoccupation of Middleton's thought. Shakespeare may or may not have been 'a papist', as Richard Davies declared, but he seems at least to have been a High Church Anglican, whose works are correspondingly free of any abuse of the Latin liturgy.[209] In *Measure*, the

---

[207] The phrase 'as for example' also occurs at p. 109 of *World Tossed* (assigned to Rowley). The instance in *No Wit* occurs in a speech contrasting one 'language' with another. Another interesting collocation occurs at 4. 1. 116–17, F2; 'You shall ne'r finde me a knave in mine own tongue; | I have more grace in me'.

[208] On Middleton's authorship of 4. 1 of *Roaring Girl*, see—in addition to Lake and Jackson—Hoy's commentary (which cites several striking parallels with Middleton's work) and Paul Mulholland's Revels edn. (Manchester, 1987), 9–11.

[209] See. S. Schoenbaum, *William Shakespeare: A Compact Documentary Life* (Oxford,

conjunction of 'any language' with 'any Religion' make it fairly clear (as Lever observes) that an allusion to 'Latin graces and hence Roman Catholic practice' is intended. Whether or not Middleton belonged by temperament to the Puritan opposition, he certainly showed little sympathy or patience with the Catholic use of Latin. In *Game at Chess* the beginning of 5. 1 not only ridicules the practice but associates it firmly with the machinations of the Black House. In *The Witch* (1614–17?) Hecate 'spitts Latten' (5. 2. 32; TLN 1968). In *Chaste Maid* (1613), Latin is associated with 'papistry' (1. 1. 93–5), and contrasted with 'the Protestant tongue', English (4. 1. 149–51); the play's penultimate speech declares that 'a woman may be honest | According to the English part, when she is | A whore in the Latin' (5. 4. 107–9). In *Revenger's Tragedy* Vindice refers to old men so steeped in the Latin of the law that they 'cannot so much as pray but in' Latin (4. 2. 60). In *Second Maiden's Tragedy* (1611) a soldier complains that 'I could never knowe the meaninge yet of all my latin prayers' (5. 2. 22–3; TLN 2239–40), and in *The Puritan* a Puritan widow complains that to remarry would be equivalent to speaking 'false Lattin' (1. 1. 134). Middleton often made satiric capital out of the Catholic practice of praying in Latin—as does this passage in *Measure*.

Alongside such verbal parallels can be set a number of features of dramatic technique which seem more characteristic of Middleton than of Shakespeare. We have already noticed that the Folio calls for an idiosyncratic entrance first for Mistress Overdone, and then for Juliet, of a kind apparently unexampled in the Shakespeare canon. But Middleton's plays provide several parallels. In 3. 1 of *More Dissemblers Besides Women* (c.1619),[210] 'Lords' enter during a conversation between the Cardinal and Lactantio; the Cardinal sees and refers to them ('Here come the Lords'), but then continues his speech to Lactantio; Lactantio exits, after a short speech of his own (aside); only then do the Lords participate in the dialogue. In the first scene of *Women Beware Women* (c.1621), Bianca enters with Leantio and his mother; they discuss her for 110 lines before she is addressed; she remains silent all the while. Later, in 1. 3, Bianca and the mother enter during the course of one of Leantio's soliloquies; he soliloquizes about Bianca for another twenty-three lines before they speak to one another.[211] In *Game at Chess* (1624) the Black Bishop's Pawn enters at 1. 1. 34, is seen and talked about, but does not enter the dialogue until l. 70; at 2. 2. 44, the Black Knight and Black Bishop enter, are seen and

1977), 55–62. Shakespeare got into trouble for satirizing a Protestant martyr (Oldcastle); Middleton, for satirizing Catholic contemporaries (*Game at Chess*).

[210] See D. J. Lake, 'The Date of *More Dissemblers Besides Women*', *N. & Q.* 221 (1976), 219–21, and A. A. Bromham, 'Middleton's *Cardinal of Milan*', *N. & Q.* 225 (1980), 155–7.

[211] G. B. Shand, 'The Stagecraft of *Women Beware Women*', *RORD* 28 (1985), 29–36.

referred to (abusively), for eight lines before either speaks.[212] For Overdone, Juliet, Bianca, and the Black Bishop's Pawn alike, the character's first appearance in the play is marked by her or his silence.

Further examples of a similar technique probably occur in *A Trick to Catch the Old One* (*c*.1606) and *Women Beware Women* (*c*.1621). In *Trick*, the Quarto does not provide any entrance for Dampit and Gulph in 1. 4; the play's most recent editor argues convincingly that the two men enter twenty-seven lines before they are addressed—during which time Witgood and the Host paint a derogatory portrait of Dampit.[213] In *Women Beware Women* Bianca exits at 3. 1. 60 (K4ᵛ); the earliest text does not provide her with a re-entrance, but she speaks at 3. 1. 109 (K5ᵛ).[214] The Revels edition places this re-entrance just before Bianca speaks, but it seems to us likely that Bianca should enter some lines earlier, when Leantio abruptly changes the subject to declare:

> Now for a welcome
> Alike to draw mens envies upon man;
> A kiss now that will hang upon my lip . . .
>   (3. 1. 102–4)

The change of subject, and his strong expectation of a welcome and a kiss 'Now . . . now', suggest that he has seen Bianca. Likewise in **Revenger's Tragedy* (1606), the Quarto provides no direction for Spurio's late entrance in 1. 2; editors usually place it just before the Duchess says 'here comes he' (1. 2. 109; B1ᵛ). Spurio does not speak, and is not addressed, until the end of her speech, eight lines later. If, as the dialogue suggests, both Bianca and Spurio enter early, then these two scenes provide further Middletonian examples of the dramatic technique of the suspect passage in *Measure*. In particular, they provide further parallels for the entrance of Overdone.[215]

Another intriguing parallel for the staging of *Measure* 1. 2 may be present in *Michaelmas Term* (1604–6). In 5. 1 the Quarto of Middleton's play omits any entrance direction for the officers who come to arrest Shortyard; when these officers next appear (5. 3), they have with them

---

[212] After the entrance of Black Knight and Black Bishop in 2. 2 of *Game at Chess*, the actual silence is realistically excused by the pretence of an unheard conversation. It therefore resembles Juliet's entrance more closely than Overdone's.

[213] *Trick* (see n. 197, ed. Watson), 17.

[214] The 1657 octavo, which does mark scene directions elsewhere, does not call for a division here, and Mulryne is almost certainly wrong to follow Oliphant in supplying an exit for the Mother and so breaking 3. 1 into two scenes. As noted above, Middleton frequently calls for separated stage groupings, and in the light of this habit it seems probable that the Mother never leaves the stage.

[215] Another parallel in **The Old Law* (*c*.1618) is less distinctive. In 3. 2 Lysander enters alone 12 lines before he speaks, while Eugenia and her suitors ridicule him; however, they are concealed, and so the staging resembles the conventional eavesdropping scene (of which there are numerous examples in Shakespeare). However, it remains typical of Middleton that for 12 lines of this 'eavesdropping' scene the victim in silent.

both Shortyard and his partner Falselight. At 5. 1. 41, Easy tells the officers, 'This is the other, bind him fast', and on the basis of this line Dyce and subsequent editors called for the officers to enter *with* Falselight, already under arrest. This is certainly an attractive reconstruction of the staging. Richard Levin, in his Regents Renaissance Drama edition (London, 1966), nevertheless rejected it, arguing that 'it is not likely that Shortyard would completely ignore his partner here' (p. 114). But such silences are common in Middleton, and if Dyce was right then the appearance of Falselight in 5. 1—under arrest but silent, and not addressed by his 'partner' in sin—provides a striking parallel for the entrance of Juliet in 1. 2.

In *Game at Chess* (1. 1) and at least once in *Women Beware Women* (1. 1; probably 3. 2) the person who enters long before being addressed is alone, as is Overdone; in the other examples more than one such person enters, creating the possibility of a mimed dialogue 'apart', as with Juliet. The character who enters without directly joining the stage conversation proves to be one manifestation of a staging technique highly characteristic of Middleton: separated stage groupings. These occur throughout the Middleton canon, with great frequency, and in many forms. The prevalence of such groupings may be illustrated by taking as examples the two late plays with unequivocal examples of what we might call 'emphatic silent entries', *Game at Chess* and *Women Beware Women*.

Game at Chess opens (after the Induction) with two pawns arriving on stage from different directions and soliloquizing separately. Later, at 1. 1. 204, the Black Knight's Pawn enters; his company is at first rejected by the White Queen's Pawn ('There's my grief, my hate'), and the Black Knight's Pawn then speaks aside for eleven lines before addressing the white pawn. Later again in the scene, the Black Knight enters (l. 241) and makes a solo speech of some twenty-seven lines; the Black Bishop's Pawn only then speaks to him. After his entry at 2. 1. 8, this same pawn observes the White Queen's Pawn, then becomes preoccupied with a sealed note to him; the White Queen's Pawn, until she speaks to him at l. 32, in the mean time silently studies a book. When the White and Black Houses appear together on stage at 2. 2. 85, some sixty lines of ensuing dialogue concern the affairs of the White House only; the black pieces who speak aside early in the episode were on stage before the Houses made their mass entry. Like Act 1, Act 4 opens with two pawns who delay direct contact with each other: for twelve lines the Black Knight's Pawn satirically comments on the Jesuit Black Bishop's Pawn. The latter assumes a mantle of silent preoccupation later when the White and Black Queens' Pawns enter; the Black Queen's Pawn first speaks to him at l. 67.

These separated groupings following entrances in *Game at Chess* certainly contribute to the play's evocation of the machinations of the chess-game. But they are far from unique to the play: Middleton here adapted an established technique to a unique purpose. In *Women Beware Women* separated groupings occur with even greater frequency.

To the rest of the action, the Ward and Sordido are tangential in their folly. They are incapable of sustaining conversation with other characters, and nearly all their speeches are to each other. Their dialogue comes in isolated blocks, though they are never on stage without other characters present. Fabritio persistently attempts and more or less fails to draw the Ward out of his lavatory-closet world, and no communication is possible between the Ward and his bride-to-be Isabella. By corollary, other characters fall silent when the Ward and Sordido speak. The pair form a quarantined grouping almost whenever they enter.

Isabella herself, like Bianca, uses silence to conceal her thoughts. Though addressed at 4. 2. 73–5, she remains speechless from her entry at l. 47 to l. 130, by which time all other characters but Hippolito have parted; she then speaks aside for seven lines before addressing her lover. This behaviour is striking because in the episode before her speech her incestuous affair with Hippolito has been exposed. One must infer that she stands apart in silent dismay. Earlier, Hippolito enters at 2. 1. 179 and both Isabella and Hippolito meditate separately (like the Pawns in 1. 1 of *Game at Chess*) before Isabella speaks to Hippolito at 2. 1. 195. Livia likewise uses silence to distance herself from the action. Like Isabella, she can refuse participation by declining to reply when addressed, as she does after 1. 2. 20. In 3. 2. 29–37 Leantio enters, he is briefly discussed by Bianca and the Duke and then himself speaks apart before the Duke gives his complimentary welcome. Leantio gives the Duke a single line of thanks for his new office at l. 44, but remains a grumbling and jealous observer of the Duke's entertainment: he goes on to make a fourteen-line speech, spoken apart, and the painful aside remains his characteristic utterance though the scene. Before 4. 2. 157 Hippolito and Isabella are on stage; when Guardiano and Livia enter, their first thirteen lines are spoken aside to each other.

Middleton's most visually emphatic separate stage groupings are achieved through the use of the upper acting area. This is where the Mother and Bianca appear when Leantio departs on the main stage in 1. 3. Here there is dialogue between the two levels; not so immediately after, when the Mother and Bianca see citizens appear below and then the Duke and his retinue process across the stage. The chess-scene of 2. 2 most fully exploits the separate acting areas. The dialogue below freezes as Bianca is brought to the upper acting area to see the 'monument'. This scene achieves complete split-staging: the characters below have no cognizance of the seduction being enacted above. The isolated areas of contrasted consciousness continue when Guardiano, then Bianca, appear below. From Guardiano's entrance below (at l. 398. 1) to l. 414 he speaks apart from Livia and the Mother. These two continue their chess-dialogue from l. 415 to l. 424. Bianca enters after l. 424, speaks apart to l. 431, then turns to Guardiano; Guardiano then speaks aside (ll. 449–52), and only then does Bianca address the Mother, so breaking a separate grouping that has been sustained for almost 140 lines.

The masque-scene, 5. 1, is equally sophisticated in its use of the upper area to separate stage groups. The groups have now become, overtly and literally, action and audience. Middleton crams the upper acting space, usually confined to a few characters, with '*Duke*, B[i]ancha, *L. Cardinal*, Fabritio, *and other Cardinals, Lords, and Ladies in State*'. The main action of the masque proceeds below, and is, naturally, a discrete and self-contained action. But it is itself full of internal fractures as the various groups of characters perform their particular variants, their respective revenges. The masque itself operates on three distinct physical levels, the main stage, Livia's free flight in the air above, and the Ward and Sordido's subterranean machination with the trap-door. *Women Beware Women* ends in a state of co-ordinated fragmentation leading to complete chaos.

Every one of Middleton's plays, without exception, makes use—prolonged and repeated use—of the same theatrical technique. One might notice in 3. 2 of *The Widow* (*c*.1616), the remarkable encounters of Francisco and Martia who are on stage together—and see each other—for most of the scene, but never address each other; or the first entrance of De Flores in *The Changeling* (1622), which begins with a twenty-five-line soliloquy about the onstage Beatrice, followed by eight lines of 'dialogue' in which both speak, but only eight words are actually addressed to the other onstage character; or Savorwit's entrance '*aloof off*' from the others, where he remains for over 100 lines of 4. 1 of *No Wit No Help* (1611–12).[216] A thorough survey of Middleton's varied but persistent use of this technique would require a long essay in itself; but any reader who dips into the Middleton canon will see the pattern quickly enough. Of course, Shakespeare's own plays contain some examples of the same technique, and consequently the mere fact of separated stage groupings does not in itself support Middleton's claim rather than Shakespeare's. What these examples do demonstrate, however, is that the very particular form of silent entrance common to *Game at Chess*, *Women Beware Women*, and 1. 2 of *Measure* is itself merely an extreme example of a relatively unusual dramatic technique which Middleton used almost obsessively.

Juliet's entrance in 1. 2 is itself suggestive of Middleton's stagecraft; so too is the emphasis that entrance gives to the theatrical display of a pregnant woman. When the Duke interviews Juliet in 2. 3 her pregnancy is a

---

[216] 'Aloof off' also occurs twice in dialogue in *Michaelmas Term* 1. 1. 231, 3. 1. 241, and also in another stage direction at *Roaring Girl* 4. 2. 236, though in a scene probably written by Decker.

source of pathos: she is about to lose the father of her child; she is herself imprisoned; she repents her deed of love, but affirms the love that led to it. This is probably the first time Shakespeare put a pregnant woman on the stage.[217] Later, Hermione and Thaisa would evoke a stronger poignancy: the pregnancy of these women is central to the themes of death, separation, and restoration in *Winter's Tale* and *Pericles*.[218]

Middleton uses the spectacle of a pregnant woman more frequently than Shakespeare and in ways that more closely resemble Juliet's presence in 1. 2 and 5. 1. In every case the child is conceived out of wedlock; in no instance is the pregnancy treated with reverence or as a source of pathos. Maria in *Family of Love* (1602–4?), Grace in *No Wit, No Help* (1611), Francisca in *The Witch* (1614–17), Jane in *Fair Quarrel* (1615–17), the 'Cupid' in *Nice Valour* (c.1616), and the 'Page' in *More Dissemblers Besides Women* (1619) are all victims of love affairs who are displayed pregnant on stage before the common resolution, marriage. In the scene where she is exhibited out of her male disguise (5. 2), the 'Page', like Juliet and Francisca, remains speechless. Likewise, Maria's appearance, in the final scene of her play, visibly pregnant, is completely silent—as is the Cupid's and Francisca's and Grace's. By denying these women any dramatic role as characters, such silences emphasize the emblematic fact of their pregnancy. Allwit's wife is a slightly different case: though married to Allwit, she conceives by Whorehound in a spirit of unrestrained free enterprize. But she too is comically displayed to the audience; as with Juliet, this scene (1. 2) is the first in which she appears.

In the broadest terms Shakespeare takes a poetic attitude to pregnancy on the stage; he juxtaposes the woman's vulnerability with the positively valued mystery of procreation. This attitude is developed furthest in the late plays but clearly present in the tender, and almost romantic, characterization of Juliet in 2. 3. Juliet suffers under the law, not her physical burden. To Middleton pregnancy is an inevitable constituent of his satiric social realism, and is something to be presented on stage as a self-evident seriocomic comment on sexual indulgence. This interest, where pregnancy is the determined consequence of sin, is practically non-existent in Shakespeare, but expresses itself repeatedly in Middleton's works.[219]

---

[217] Tamora, whose sexual liaison with Aaron in *Titus* is condemned, and who has a child outside wedlock in the course of the play, is not shown pregnant on stage.

[218] In *Measure* too Juliet's pregnancy initiates similar developments through Claudio's supposed death to his restoration, but there is little emphasis on this as a poetical idea: Juliet is marginal and never actually gives birth.

[219] It has been suggested above that Claudio and Juliet enter in penitential garb, probably white sheets, and that the addition of Juliet to the scene would heighten the emphasis on this spectacle (p. 167 and n. 110). Against the Shakespearian example cited there we may set a number of Middleton allusions: 'his name stands in a white sheete heere, and does penance for him' (*Michaelmas Term* 3. 5. 3–4, G2); 'The generation of a hundred such | Cannot make a man stand in a white sheet' (*Wit at Several Weapons* 4. 1; 6l2ᵛb; pp. 117–18); how often a man may lye with another mans wife, before a come to the white

Juliet supplies silent comment; Overdone first enters to be noisily commented upon. Both, before speaking a word, colour the scene they appear in. The local effect of these characters within the scene is essentially static; so, in a wider sense, is the whole suspected sub-scene. As we have already observed, it could be omitted without loss to the plot, and this superfluousness itself suggests that the passage may be a later addition. But the suspected addition does serve one dramatic function—a function also served by scenes in other Middleton plays. It simply (but crucially) contributes to the tone of the play as a whole, and to our sense of its social context.

In *Women Beware Women* (*c.*1621) Bianca carries on a bawdy conversation with two ladies (4. 1. 1–22). These ladies do not appear elsewhere in the play. As the Revels editor, J. R. Mulryne, comments, 'The little scene leads nowhere, in terms of the play's action; its sole function is that of dramatic symbol or summary'. The disreputable tone, and the distribution of dialogue between a named character and two nameless 'gentle' but scurrilous supporters, similarly recall the dramatic technique of the dialogue between Lucio and the two Gentlemen. And when Leantio enters after the episode with the two ladies, he is flamboyantly dressed—as, we assume, are the *'fantastique'* Lucio and the *'Other like Gentlemen'*.

In *Hengist* (*c.*1619–20) the same scene-type is presented for the opposite purpose: so that the main character can affirm her virtue by rejecting the company of anonymous ladies. The entry for 3. 2 reads *'Enter Castiza A Booke: two Ladyes'*. The ladies represent the flippant and worldly sexuality of court life; Castiza prefers the company of her book. The sub-scene is necessarily short, for Castiza turns her back to bawdy repartee. Earlier in *Hengist* (1. 2), a bawdy conversation between the Felmonger, Buttonmonger, Brazier, and Grazier likewise serves no direct function in the plot, but precedes the entrance of the virtuous Constantius with '2 Gent⟨lemen⟩'; Constantius proceeds to rid himself of his gentlemen hangers-on, before the others offer their petitions. Both the gentlemen and the petitioners exemplify the social values which Constantius rejects.

In *Game at Chess* (1624) almost every detail of the action contributes directly to the development of the allegorical chess-game; but even here one scene serves no direct function in the plot. The Black Jesting Pawn at the end of 3. 1 appears again at the end of the play, but the two other (jesting) pawns in this episode do not reappear, and the whole scene seems to exist solely for the sake of its picture of a lower social class otherwise notably absent from the action: the true 'pawns' in the great battle between the Black and White Houses. Again, the scene is not only structurally superfluous, but is also almost entirely devoted to social comedy.

sheet, (*Family of Love 4. 4. 86–8, G1ᵛ); 'pennaunce in a Sheete' (*Family of Love 5. 1. 44–5, G3ᵛ). Though the original staging was Shakespeare's, Middleton's interest in such penances makes it plausible that he should wish to make more of the spectacle.

R. B. Parker, the Revels editor of *Chaste Maid in Cheapside* (1613) defines 'four main actions' (p. xliii)); but despite the complexity of the plot, some scenes have virtually nothing to do with it: 'the scenes with the promoters, the gossips, the tutor (and, to a lesser extent, the watermen) are treated at a length out of all proportion to their function in the intrigue' (p. xlii). These too are 'tone' scenes. Like the two Gentlemen in *Measure*, the two Promoters at 2. 2, the two men and the Country Wench of the same scene, the two Puritans of 2. 3 and 3. 2, the two Gossips of 2. 3, the five Gossips of 2. 4 and 3. 2, the two Servants of 1. 2, the four Servants of 5. 3, and the Watermen of 4. 3 are all anonymous representatives of the city they inhabit. The more they dominate the dialogue, the more the drama moves from action to tone. As Mistress Overdone suffers the sneers of Lucio and the Gentlemen, so the two Promoters in 2. 2 enter to stand apart and be verbally abused by Allwit (in soliloquy) before they enter the dialogue. The episode that follows, in which the Promoters are seen at work detecting fast-breakers, bears only a thematic relationship to the rest of the plot. The very stasis of the Promoters' episode and the christening scene, as with the dialogue between Lucio and the Gentlemen, contributes to the atmosphere of seediness. And all three share an ambivalence towards physical existence which Parker describes as 'Swiftian' (p. liv).

Every scene in *A Yorkshire Tragedy* (1605) forwards the drama between the husband and the wife except the first one, in which, uniquely, neither appears. A comic scene quite different in tone from the rest of the play, it consists of a conversation between Oliver and Ralph, two serving-men, who are joined by Sam. Sam is *'Furnisht with things from London'*, and also bears gossip from the city. The episode sets the scene, providing a social context for the action that follows, but is almost superfluous to the play's plot.

The Puritan (1606) begins its second scene with a conversation between two more or less disreputable characters, one of whom is an old soldier. As in the second scene of Folio *Measure*, the first topic discussed is war and peace. In *Measure* the First Gentleman quibbles on the divine and secular senses of 'peace'; in *The Puritan* they quibble on the domestic and international senses ('Warr sitts now like a Iustice of peace'). In *The Puritan* they go on to refer to peace as 'a good Madam to all other professions' (1. 2. 92–3), a passage we have already quoted for its use of 'Madam'. Like the addition to *Measure* 1. 2, the beginning of 1. 2 of *The Puritan* is a sustained piece of prose which gratuitously entertains with a series of jokes, often on topical subjects, before making its very modest contribution to the action. After a hundred lines or so of such jesting, the two men agree to deceive the Widow. What makes the resemblance between 1. 2 in *The Puritan* and *Measure* particularly striking is that in both plays the opening dialogue is followed by the spectacle of a guarded prisoner passing over the stage on his way to prison; this event is witnessed by the earlier conversants, who are on friendly terms with the victim, and by implication might possibly become subject to the same misfortunes themselves. Unlike Claudio, but like Juliet, Captain Idle is shown to the world without himself speaking. And as Lucio earlier leads the Gentlemen offstage, saying 'Away: let's goe learne the truth of it', Pyeboard, one of the conversants in 1. 2 of *The Puritan, says 'but come, letts follow after to the Prison, and know the Nature of his offence'. The similarities of organization, structure, tone, and verbal detail in the second scenes of the two plays suggest that for these scenes one of the plays had a particularly direct influence on the other.

A scene only slightly more closely related to the action, and again remarkable for its structural similarities to the addition in *Measure*, occurs in *The Phoenix* (1603–4). Once again the scene is the play's second. The conversation is between the Captain and 'soldiering fellows'; they specifically debate the wisdom of the Captain's recent marriage, but in broad terms the passage is concerned with both the disjunction and the parallels between the soldiering, seafaring life and the urban preoccupation with the commodity of sex. Like Lucio, the Captain goes on to appear elsewhere in the play. Like the two Gentlemen, the unnamed soldiering fellows appear in no other scene: apart from supplying humour they serve merely to place the Captain in a context and identify him as a character-type. The opening dialogue leads outwards into the plot for which it has set the tone and scene: the soldiering fellows depart and the Captain's wife Castiza enters, and so the Captain's mistrust of women is transferred from the realm of discussion to the realm of dramatic conflict.

In an earlier enumeration of the 'unShakespearian' features of the suspected passage in 1. 2, we noticed that its use of the two anonymous Gentlemen was uncharacteristic; *Women Beware Women* 4. 1 provides an exact Middleton parallel, written at about the same time that *Measure* was apparently adapted. The presence of structurally similar scenes in *Hengist*, *A Game at Chess*, *A Chaste Maid at Cheapside*, and *A Yorkshire Tragedy* simply confirms Middleton's interest in and employment of such techniques, while both *The Puritan and *The Phoenix* supply apparent models for the structure of the adapted scene. For the second scene of the play as (we conjecture) Shakespeare wrote it, a very close structural parallel can be found in *Contention* 2. 4 (Eleanor being led to prison), and the transition between the Pompey–Overdone dialogue and the entrance of Claudio closely resembles a similar transition in *Cymbeline* 1. 1. For the structure of the Folio scene we have found no Shakespearian parallels.[220]

---

[220] In *All is True* 2. 1 Buckingham's entrance on his way to execution is preceded by a dialogue of two Gentlemen; but their conversation is entirely devoted to a report of

Finally, we may note an important parallel in *Timon of Athens*. Lake, Jackson, and Holdsworth have recently provided compelling new evidence that, as earlier scholars had conjectured, about a third of the Folio text was written by Middleton.[221] Naturally, of all the collaborative plays in the Middleton canon *Timon of Athens* must, in an investigation like our own, be treated with most caution, because the two hands identified there are the two at issue in I. 2 of *Measure for Measure*. Nevertheless, all these investigators have assigned I. 2 of *Timon* to Middleton, and have done so without any notion that *Measure for Measure* might also contain a small amount of Middleton's work. We therefore find it more than a little suspicious that, alone in the First Folio, I. 2 of *Measure* and I. 2 of *Timon* contain a reference to or example of a metrical grace:

> . . . I thinke thou neuer was't where Grace was said.
> 2. *Gent.*   No? a dozen times at least.
> I. *Gent.* What? In meeter?
>
> (*Measure* TLN 114–17)

> Apermantus Grace.
> Immortall Gods, I craue no pelfe,
> I pray for no man but my selfe,
> Graunt I may neuer proue so fond,
> To trust man on his Oath or Bond.
> Or a Harlot for her weeping,
> Or a Dogge that seemes asleeping,
> Or a keeper with my freedome,
> Or my friends if I should need 'em.
> Amen. So fall too't:
> Richmen sin, and I eat root.
>
> (*Timon* TLN 404–14; I. 2. 61–70)

In *Timon* this grace is spoken during a 'great Banquet'; immediately afterwards Timon turns to address the soldier Alcibiades, referring to his preference for 'a breakefast of Enemies' rather than 'a dinner of Friends'; the grace itself is spoken by 'an *Athenian*' giving thanks 'to the Gods'. Before and after the grace Apemantes mentions the 'meale'; immediately before it comes an ironic allusion to the pledging of healths. (Shakespeare elsewhere only employs this motif twice, in *2 Henry IV* and *Hamlet*; Middleton, in a much smaller dramatic canon, uses it at least nine times.) In *Measure* both speeches are spoken by soldiers, who have just been declaring their preference for war rather than peace, talking about a soldier's 'thanksgiuing before meate'; immediately afterwards they refer to graces 'in any language' or 'in any Religion'; within twenty lines Lucio

---

Buckingham's offstage trial. (The scene is almost certainly Fletcher's, in any case.) Likewise in *Contention* the dialogue before Eleanor's entrance looks forward to the entrance—as does Pompey's and Overdone's in the conjectural original of I. 2.

[221] See n. 32.

ironically alludes to the pledging of healths. The links between these two passages—several of them apparently fortuitous—seem to us quite remarkable. If we accept the verdict of recent scholarship, this parallel links the suspected passage in *Measure* to the work of Middleton, not Shakespeare. Anyone who wants to deny the value of this parallel as evidence of Middleton's authorship of the interpolation must challenge all the evidence which identifies Middleton as the author of 1. 2 of *Timon*.

From this welter of parallels, what conclusions can be safely drawn? For most features of the passage, parallels can be found in the works of both Shakespeare and Middleton. (See Appendix V.) These parallels make attribution to either dramatist equally possible. They do not rule out composition by some third figure, because we have not exhaustively checked all surviving plays of the period: some, or even many, writers might share these words, phrases, images, and dramatic techniques. But we have thoroughly checked all the plays of Nathan Field, and half those of Fletcher; in neither group, nor in the unMiddletonian parts of Middleton's collaborative works, did we find many parallels—or any striking parallels—for the suspect passage in 1. 2. Therefore, in so far as these other works provide a minimal 'control' for this vocabulary evidence, that control suggests that the presence of so many parallels from Middleton and Shakespeare may be significant: like the linguistic evidence, the shared vocabulary evidence (less securely) indicates that Middleton is the most plausible alternative to Shakespeare.

Far more important are the cases where parallels can be found either in Shakespeare or in Middleton, but not in both. Only four words favour Shakespeare: 'raz'd', 'meeter', 'Mitigation', and 'healthy'. Individually, none is remarkable. Collectively, there are fewer features of the passage which specifically favour Shakespeare's claims than there are features which—if accepted as uncritically as these Shakespeare parallels—would appear to rule out both playwrights.

By contrast, parallels can be found in Middleton but not Shakespeare for:

1. the probable use of *Madam* as a facetious title
2. the phrase *any language*, and satire on the Roman Catholic use of Latin
3. *controuersie*, used of religious or theological disputes
4. the ironic use of *Sanctimonious*
5. a grace *in meeter*
6. allusions to Hungary (combined with a fondness for topical material, and an interest in Balkan politics)
7. *come . . . to composition*
8. *Thou shalt not Steale*
9. *I belieue thee*

10. *Behold, behold*
11. *purchas'd . . . diseases*
12. *as for example*
13. *speake feelingly*
14. references to neglect of one or all of the *ten Commandements*

In addition, and more important, Middleton's work but not Shakespeare's contains:

15. a striking parallel for *begin thy health* (itself a phrase which Shakespeare never uses elsewhere, but Middleton does)
16. a striking parallel for Lucio's joke about keeping all of the ten commandments, except the one most pertinent
17. two parallels, one striking, for Overdone's complaint about the obstacles to profitable pimping
18. numerous examples, from Middleton's late work, of a form and spelling of the neuter possessive pronoun (*its*) identical to that in 1. 2, which would be demonstrably anomalous for Shakespeare in 1603–4
19. exact parallels, in Middleton's late work, for the unusual mode of entrance adopted here for Overdone and Juliet
20. good parallels for the structure and dramatic function of the suspected episode
21. several parallels (three striking) for the emblematic presentation of a pregnant young woman

Obviously, the beginning of 1. 2 shares more discriminating features with the Middleton than the Shakespeare canon. Moreover, the number of parallels unique to Shakespeare may well be exaggerated, for the perception of Middleton parallels has depended on fallible human sifting, whereas the Shakespearian parallels have been mechanically harvested. It would not surprise us to learn that we have overlooked an example of *raz'd* or *meeter*. Even assuming that no Middleton parallels have gone unnoticed, and that the results are consequently *not* for this reason slightly biased in Shakespeare's favour, the bulk of these parallels clearly points to Middleton rather than Shakespeare. Since Middleton's canon is only about half the size of Shakespeare's, this result is itself surprising.

All parallels are not created equal. As important as the difference in quantity is the noticeable difference in quality. All of the last seven Middleton parallels are better evidence than any of the Shakespeare parallels. The Shakespeare parallels consist of four words. The Middleton parallels—even if we momentarily disregard the last seven—include eight phrases ('any language', 'come to composition', 'thou shalt not steal', 'I believe thee', 'as for example', 'speak feelingly', 'Behold, behold', and 'purchased diseases'), three specific senses ('sanctimonious', 'controversy', 'Madam'), and three topics (graces in metre, Hungary, and the ten commandments). The Middleton parallels are not only more numerous; they

also include larger units of material (phrases and topics). Middleton parallels 15, 16, and 17 belong to what Schoenbaum identifies as the most
reliable category of verbal evidence, 'parallels of thought coupled with
some verbal parallelism';[222] 19, 20, and 21 embrace the most distinctive
features of the dramatic technique of the suspected passage.

Could any of these parallels be due to Middleton imitating
Shakespeare, or Shakespeare imitating Middleton? For the moment let us
continue to pretend that we have no other reason to suspect the authenticity of the opening of 1. 2 of Folio *Measure*; we may then evaluate the
possibility of plagiarism independently of all the other evidence. In this
situation, the bawd's complaint might be due to literary influence.
Middleton's *Black Book* was entered in the Stationers' Register on 22
March 1604, and Shakespeare's *Measure for Measure* was written either
before or after 27 March 1604 (the day when Armin's *Time Triumphant*
was itself entered in the Stationers' Register). If we were to assume
Middleton's influence on Shakespeare, we would have to adopt the later
dating of *Measure* (April–December 1604), which seems to us unlikely,
though possible. No one will want to contend that between 22 and 27
March *The Black Book* was printed, that Shakespeare read it and wrote
Overdone's speech under its influence, that Armin then read or performed
in the finished play, and that Armin then completed *Time Triumphant*
under the influence of Shakespeare's play. Nor does it seem likely that
Shakespeare read in manuscript a minor pamphlet by Middleton (a
young dramatist for a rival company) or that the said young rival was
allowed to read *Measure for Measure* in manuscript. Hence, if *Measure
for Measure* was written before 27 March 1604 (as seems to us likely),
and if Middleton's pamphlet echoes Shakespeare's play in the bawd's
compaint, then Middleton must have seen an early performance of
Measure. But the London theatres were apparently closed without respite
from 19 May 1603 to 9 April 1604: Middleton therefore could hardly
have seen a public performance in London. In short, it seems most
unlikely that the parallel between *Measure for Measure* and *The Black
Book* results from the influence of *Measure for Measure* (as represented
by the full Folio text) upon Middleton; nor does an examination of the
two contexts encourage such an hypothesis, for the bawd's complaint is a
major episode in the pamphlet, and only a brief, structurally unimportant
aside in the play. Moreover, Middleton clearly echoes this passage in *The
Black Book* in *The Widow* (*c.*1616) and—less clearly—in **Nice Valour*
(*c.*1616). If the parallel results from one writer's influence on the other, it
apparently must have been Middleton's influence on Shakespeare—and
Measure must have been written in the latter part of 1604. Quite apart
from the relative improbability of this dating, such a reconstruction

---

[222] S. Schoenbaum, *Internal Evidence and Elizabethan Dramatic Authorship: An Essay in
Literary History and Method* (London, 1966), 191, 194.

accepts that the passage in 1. 2 is 'Middletonian' in origin. Given the other evidence for Middleton's presence, authorship rather than influence seems the most economical explanation.

The joke about a rogue's scrupulous observance of nine of the ten commandments might also be a case of literary imitation. *Your Five Gallants* might have been written at any time between 1604 and 1607, though most authorities incline to place it later than 1604. If imitation were the explanation for the parallel between *Your Five Gallants* and *Measure*, then Shakespeare probably influenced Middleton. But while Middleton 'is without doubt the most self-repetitive of Elizabethan and Jacobean dramatists', he 'echoes other writers scarcely at all. Every one of his plays, masques, and poems is an intricate web of verbal reminiscences and anticipations [of his *own* work]'.[223] In terms of the general shape of Middleton's *œuvre*, verbal imitation of Shakespeare seems intrinsically unlikely. In terms of this specific parallel it seems even less probable. Middleton often alluded to violation of the ten commandments, from the beginning to the end of his career, whereas Shakespeare never did. We can hardly attribute all of these Middleton allusions to the influence of one joke in a rather inconspicuous dialogue in *Measure for Measure*, and consequently there seems little reason to attribute the one parallel in *Your Five Gallants* to such influence. Moreover, in *Your Five Gallants* theft is an essential element of the plot, and both the boy and Pursenet are important characters: in *Measure for Measure* theft is not important, dramatically or theatrically, and the person so described has no role in the play. What is intrinsic to *Your Five Gallants* is extraneous to Folio *Measure for Measure*.

Measure for Measure 1. 2 (1603–4) can hardly have influenced Middleton's *Honourable Entertainments* (1620). Shakespeare's play was not in print; its influence could only have been exerted through performance. Even if the play had been recently revived, it seems unlikely that the casual phrase 'begin thy health'—unexampled elsewhere in Shakespeare, but used by Middleton—should have been made the basis for the entire climactic sequence in a civic entertainment.

Nor can imitation explain the structural parallel between Folio 1. 2 and the 'tone' scenes in *Women Beware Women, A Game at Chess, Hengist, Chaste Maid, *Yorkshire Tragedy, *The Puritan,* and *The Phoenix.* With the uncertain exception of *The Phoenix,* all these plays postdate the composition of *Measure,* so any influence must have been Shakespeare's on Middleton. Yet Shakespeare's other works provide no other examples of the structure of 1. 2; it occurs in at least seven of Middleton's plays; it is endemic in one of them (*Chaste Maid*); the closest parallels come from two early plays (*The Phoenix,* *The Puritan*) and one very late one

---

[223] Holdsworth, 268.

(*Women Beware Women*). Middleton's influence on the Folio text of *Measure* seems more probable than Shakespeare's influence, through one unremarkable scene, on so much of the Middleton canon.

Dekker and Middleton received a payment from Henslowe in earnest of *1 Honest Whore* at some time between 1 January and 14 March 1604; it may not have been finished until September.[224] The parallel phrase 'purchase . . . disease' in one of Middleton's scenes of that text might therefore result from the influence of Shakespeare's play. But no one will seriously conjecture that Middleton's use elsewhere of 'come to composition' (in 1597), or 'thou shalt not steale' (in 1605–7), or 'I believe thee' (in 1611), or 'Behold, behold' (in 1606 and 1619), or his five uses of 'as for example' (from 1604 to *c*.1621) or his one use of 'speak feelingly' (*c*.1619) influenced or were influenced by this passage in *Measure for Measure*; nor can any of the other parallels of wording or subject matter be plausibly attributed to such imitation. Middleton had not begun using 'its' until long after *Measure* was written, and long after Shakespeare himself did so. Middleton's career-long penchant for bringing emblematically pregnant women on to the stage can hardly have been encouraged by the two awkward silent appearances of Juliet in 1. 2 and 5. 1; nor could the unusual form of silent entrance evident in Middleton's late work result from imitation of one such entrance by a minor character in a relatively unpopular, unprinted play written at least fifteen years before the earliest clear Middleton parallel—especially when that form of entrance is a natural development of Middleton's own technique of separated stage groupings.

Muriel St. Clare Byrne, in 1932, proposed a set of five 'Golden Rules' for the evaluation of parallels. The first was that 'Parallels can be susceptible of at least three explanations: (*a*) unsuspected identity of authorship, (*b*) plagiarism, either deliberate or unconscious, (*c*) coincidence'.[225] Only one of the parallels between the Middleton canon and the suspect portion of 1. 2 can reasonably be attributed to plagiarism. But the first thirteen 'unique' Middleton parallels could be due to coincidence. Coincidence might also explain *all* the parallels which link this passage to Shakespeare rather than Middleton—especially as these parallels are fewer in number, and less impressive as evidence, than the first thirteen in Middleton's list. Either some of the Middleton parallels *or* some of the Shakespeare ones must be coincidental; equally clearly, in both number and nature the Shakespeare parallels are much more vulnerable to this explanation than the Middleton ones. The argument for coincidence weakens Shakespeare's claims much more seriously than it weakens Middleton's.

[224] Cyrus Henry Hoy, *Introductions, Notes, and Commentaries to Texts in 'The Dramatic Works of Thomas Dekker', Edited by Fredson Bowers*, 4 vols. (Cambridge, 1980).
[225] Muriel St. Clare Byrne, 'Bibliographical Clues in Collaborative Plays', *The Library*, 4/13 (1932), 24.

Coincidence might explain the anomalous appearance of 'its' in i. 2, though the distribution of this word in the rest of the Shakespeare and Middleton canons cannot be fortuitous. And the appeal to coincidence becomes more and more implausible if we must invoke it to explain in turn the striking parallels for the bawd's complaint, the sanctimonious pirate, the beginning of a health, the theatrical emphasis on a young silent pregnant woman, the peculiar entrances of Overdone and Juliet, and the function and structure of the episode as a whole. Either the suspect passage in i. 2 is by Middleton, or it has anticipated by coincidence an extraordinary accumulation of 'Middleton' features.

Finally, in evaluating the probabilities of coincidence one must distinguish our investigation of *Measure for Measure* from the use of verbal parallels by earlier students of authorship. The very brevity of the passage, which reduces the usefulness of so many authorship tests, actually increases the praticability of an examination of verbal parallels. Early investigators like Oliphant, Sykes, and Wells offered only a haphazard selection of parallels in support of their attribution of whole plays, or halves of plays, to one author or another; such claims may reasonably be criticized simply because they are selective and because the selection of evidence may be unrepresentative, or even deliberately prejudicial. In the context of such an investigation, parallels like 'come to composition' or 'as for example' could legitimately be dismissed as unreliable evidence. But the brevity of the suspect passage in *Measure*—or any text in which interpolation of this kind is suspected—makes it possible to conduct a comprehensive comparison of verbal links with the work of the two dramatists under consideration. Moreover, large amounts of the writing of both candidates survive.

If anything, such a comprehensive survey should favour Shakespeare, whether or not he wrote the passage. Shakespeare's extant canon is not only about twice the length of Middleton's (and has been mechanically and systematically concorded); it also almost certainly represents a much larger proportion of his total output. Shakespeare's plays were collected, shortly after his death, by his professional colleagues, and we know of only two lost plays which can be attributed to him: *Love's Labour's Won*, an early play, and *Cardenio*, a very late collaboration with Fletcher. Neither of these would be very close, in date of composition, to *Measure for Measure*. Middleton's work, by contrast, was never collected, and we know of at least ten lost works: an unnamed lost play for Henslowe (1602), a collaborative play called *Caesar's Fall* (1602), *The Chester Tragedy* (1602), a new prologue and epilogue for *Friar Bacon and Friar Bungay* (1602), *The Viper and Her Brood* (1606), *The Masque of Cupid* (1614), an unnamed and unacted pageant for the entry of the King and Queen (1626), *The Puritain Maid, Modest Wife, and Wanton Widow* (of unknown date), *The Conqueror's Custom or The Fair Prisoner* (of unknown date), and all of Middleton's *Annals*, written in his role as City Chronicler from 1620 to his death in 1627. Many more of Middleton's works have probably perished without trace. For instance, for the years between 1607 (*Your Five Gallants?*, **Revenger's Tragedy?*) and early 1611 (*Roaring Girl), we possess from Middleton's hand only two small pamphlets. More generally, Shakespeare was an actor and sharer in a very successful theatrical company from at least 1594 on; the resulting financial security made it possible for him to produce plays at what was, for a commercial dramatist, a rather leisurely rate. He seems to have retired altogether in 1613; in the years 1607 to 1613 he seems to have written only seven plays, of which four were certainly or probably collaborations (*Pericles, *All is True, **Two Noble Kinsmen*, *Cardenio). Even if we push the beginning of Shakespeare's career as a writer back to 1589, it did not last as long as Middleton's (1597–1627). Middleton, moreover, did not acquire financial security or independence until at least 1620, if then. Simply in order to feed himself and his family, he must have turned out much more writing than Shakespeare. Middleton's prose pamphlets, his civic entertainments, his collaboration with men like Dekker and Rowley, the anonymous publication of so much of his work, Jonson's description of him as a 'base fellow', all fit the pattern of an indigent theatrical workhorse. We probably possess 95 per cent of Shakespeare's work, from at least 1589 on; the extant Middleton canon probably represents less than 50 per cent of his output. If the extant texts represented all Middleton ever wrote, we could identify the full range of his vocabulary on the basis of the texts we have examined; as only a proportion survives, we can claim no such certainty. Any comprehensive search for verbal parallels in the work of Middleton and Shakespeare will therefore, inevitably, be heavily biased in favour of Shakespeare.

To the extent that the investigation of verbal features is systematic, it cannot be accused of random or prejudicial selectivity; instead, it should constitute an accurate account of the totality of verbal correspondences between this passage and the work of two candidates for its authorship. In the context of such an investigation, phrases like 'come to composition' and 'as for example' do become valid evidence, favouring one candidate or the other. Collectively, as part of a systematic account of verbal features, such parallels seem to us to constitute clear and reliable evidence that the passage is, in its verbal texture, more Middletonian than Shakespearian. This conclusion can be reached even on the basis of the first fourteen least reliable items in the pro-Middleton list; the other, stronger parallels of thought, imagery, and dramatic technique confirm it in the strongest possible way.

Byrne also insisted that, in accumulating parallels, 'we may logically proceed from the known to the collaborate . . . but not from the collaborate to the anonymous'; to this Schoenbaum adds the caveat that 'parallels from plays of uncertain or contested authorship prove nothing'.[226] These rules are perhaps unnecessarily rigid: after all, Rowley's shares of *A Fair Quarrel* and *World Tossed at Tennis* have been agreed, on the basis of a whole range of tests, for a very long time, and it seems somewhat pedantic to decree that parallels drawn from the agreed shares of 'Middleton' in those two plays 'prove nothing'. Rigidly applied, such principles would, for instance, force us to exclude the pun on 'Dollours' in Folio *Lear*. However, even if we exclude all plays of contested or divided authorship, our list of Middleton parallels would be little affected. Only 'controversy' (from *World Tossed at Tennis*), 'I believe thee' (from *Roaring Girl* and *Wit at Several Weapons*), 'purchase . . . disease' (from *1 Honest Whore*), and the metrical grace (from *Timon of Athens*) would need to be discounted. All the remaining parallels are drawn entirely or in part from works of Middleton's sole and uncontested authorship.

Some measure of the validity of such verbal evidence may be gleaned by a simple negative test. Concordances are available for the complete works of Herbert, Kyd, Marlowe, and Webster, the poems of Donne, Jonson, Marvell, Milton, Spenser, and Sidney, the sonnet sequences of Daniel and Drayton, and the anonymous plays *Arden of Faversham*, *The Troublesome Reign of King John*, and *The Taming of a Shrew*. These sixteenth- and seventeenth-century works collectively provide a considerable word-hoard, and should give us at least a rough notion of how common or rare certain words and phrases were in this period. For instance, these works contain parallels for all but one of the four features of this passage which pointed towards Shakespeare rather than Middleton. Herbert uses 'healthy' three times; Webster uses 'metre'; 'raze' appears forty-two times in the work of these twelve authors, and we have noticed it another twenty times in the plays of Day, Dekker, and Massinger. Only 'mitigation' lacks a parallel in these concordances. But 'mitigation' does occur in, for instance, Nashe's *Lenten Stuff* (III. 211. 5). In our reading of Fletcher we also noticed 'healthy' (*Loyal Subject* 2. 1. 166) and 'metre' (*Humourous Lieutenant* 4. 4. 159). The latter—'Turnes all his Proclamations into meeter'—is particularly interesting, since 'metre' clearly seems to make the proclamations ridiculous, as it does the graces in *Measure*. Massinger's *Duke of Milan* also includes 'meeters' (3. 2. 18). As might have been expected, this negative check confirms that the features of this passage linking it to Shakespeare do not deserve our trust.

By contrast, the evidence for Middleton emerges largely unscathed. These concordances provide no parallels for iteration of 'behold', for the the idea or the phrase 'purchas'd diseases', for the ironic use of

---

[226] Schoenbaum, *Internal Evidence* (see n. 222), 192.

'Sanctimonious', for the idiom 'begin thy health', or for the phrases 'I believe thee' (or 'I believe you'), 'come to composition', 'any language', 'Thou shalt not steal', and 'speak feelingly'. Only Herbert uses 'as for example' (twice); only Jonson uses 'Madam' as an ironic title (twice); only Webster jokes about the Roman Catholic use of Latin (twice). Unsurprisingly, Marlowe's *Tamburlaine* plays refer to Hungary eight times; it crops up once in *The White Devil*; Jonson once refers to it, in an epigram 'To Captain Hungry'. Herbert ('Church-Militant', 'Priest 12'), Sidney (Psalm 19), Marvell ('Instructions'), Milton (*Paradise Regained*), and Kyd (*Householder's Philosophy*) allude to the ten commandments, but no one jokes about them, and only Marvell refers to their number; Herbert and Spenser use 'controversy' in its theological sense. The concordances of Donne and Marvell do not distinguish 'its', but of the remainder only Webster, Jonson, Herbert, and Milton use the word, with or without the apostrophe; the earliest of these parallels is in Webster's *White Devil* (1612).

One would like concordances to all the major and many of the minor playwrights of the period, and the absence of such materials for the plays of Chapman, Dekker, Fletcher, Heywood, Jonson, and Massinger is particularly unfortunate. For allusions to Hungary a comprehensive catalogue is provided by Sugden's *Topographical Dictionary*. If we exclude allusions which are mere puns on 'hungry', the only additional parallels come from the anonymous *Selimus* (1592?) and *Alphonsus* (1594?), Jonson's *Every Man in his Humour* (1598), Dekker's *Match Me* (1611; 'Hungarian velvet'), a portion of **Roaring Girl* usually assigned to Dekker (5. 1. 73–9), Massinger's *Picture* (1629), and Glapthorne's *Wallenstein* (1634). What makes the 'Hungary' allusion suggestive of Middleton is not simply the topographical reference, but its occurrence in conjunction with a tendency to exploit topical allusion and a particular interest in the Palatinate *c*.1620–2; nevertheless, these parallels from other dramatists do diminish the force of the 'Hungary' parallel.

For the other features of the passage no comprehensive data base to the works of other dramatists is readily accessible. In an attempt to remedy this deficiency, at least in part, Gary Taylor has read the dramatic works of Day (five plays), Dekker (twenty-six plays), and the complete works of Massinger (thirty-four plays, eight poems), specifically looking for parallels to the items which link the passage to Middleton. A single fallible human reading can hardly be compared to a computerized concordance, but it does at least provide a further check on the verbal evidence. These sixty-five plays provide three further ironic uses of 'Madam'; a single parallel for 'any language' (*Renegado*, 1. 3. 149); two Dekker references to Catholic Latin (*Patient Grissil* 5. 1. 1–2, *Westward Ho* 2. 1. 24–7); four parallels for 'I believe thee' (*Satiromastix* 1. 2. 272, *Duke of Milan* 4. 3. 303, *Very Woman* 4. 3. 39, *Renegado* 1. 1. 63); a single parallel for the idea, though not the phrase, 'purchas'd . . . diseases' (*Roman Actor* 1. 1. 17, 'To buy Diseases from a glorious strumpet'); two more examples of 'as for example' (*Patient Grissil* 4. 3. 197, *City Madam* 2. 1. 68); a single parallel for 'speak feelingly' (*A Very Woman* 4. 3. 139, 'How feelingly he speaks'—a passage attributed to Fletcher); four examples of the idiom 'begin thy health'. Taylor also found twenty-seven examples of possessive 'its', including five with an apostrophe; none is earlier than *c*.1613. In Massinger's *City Madam* (1632), a prostitute and a bawd lament the slackness of their trade (3. 1. 1–29). However, the independence of this parallel may be doubted: Massinger is notorious for his plagiarism of Shakespeare and other writers, and *City Madam* might here have been influenced by the printed text of *Measure* itself.

To our knowledge, this is the most extensive negative check ever undertaken for verbal parallels as evidence of authorship. Even after this search, of the eighteen 'unique' verbal links pointing to Middleton rather than Shakespeare, seven remain (4, 5, 7, 8, 10, 14, 16). In the case of another (15), examples have been found of the phrase 'begin thy health', but none offers any parallelism of context; for yet another (18), the existence of further parallels after 1612 in no way diminishes the anomaly of the appearance of 'its' in a text composed *c*.1603; for a third (17), the single Massinger parallel is not as good as the two Middleton parallels, and in any case may be due to influence through a printed text (as they cannot be). The most important verbal and dramatic parallels (15 to 21) have thus hardly been scratched.

If we looked in more works we would no doubt find further parallels for the 'unique' words and phrases, and perhaps even a few parallels for the more striking links. But such evidence would not materially diminish the case for Middleton's authorship. For instance, Middleton still uses 'its' more often than any other writer examined; in all of the works examined 'as for example' occurs fewer times than it does in Middleton alone.

On the basis of this extensive sample, manually and mechanically collected, it seems to us unlikely that any author of the period will be found who shares with Middleton all the verbal and dramatic features we have checked in this way; even if one did, in order to compete with Middleton's claim that author would also have to fit the linguistic profile of the passage as well as Middleton; his work would have to provide comparable parallels for all the other aspects of the passage which we have treated as 'neutral', because present in both Middleton and Shakespeare. The alternative candidate would also, of course, have to be a dramatist of some standing, alive *c*.1621, who on occasion worked for the King's Men. Even if—as seems to us virtually impossible—an author could be found who satisfied all these requirements, his claim would only be as good as Middleton's, no better. This negative test suggests that the verbal evidence here accumulated not only confirms Middleton's claim relative to Shakespeare's, but Middleton's claim absolutely, against all comers.

To our knowledge nothing about the passage contradicts Middleton's known habits. But in a whole variety of ways the passage fits uneasily into the Shakespeare canon: its dramatic technique is unparalleled in Shakespeare's work, it contains no examples (or, in other cases, uncharacteristically few) of a whole range of verbal idiosyncrasies which consistently differentiate Shakespeare's work from that of other writers, and there is less than one chance in ten thousand of its vocabulary having been written at the same time as the rest of the play. Even if the passage did not fit Middleton so perfectly, even if we had no reason to suspect it as a late interpolation, it should be clear that the passage does not belong among the works of Shakespeare's uncontested authorship. The internal evidence points away from Shakespeare as decisively as it points towards Middleton.

Against the testimony of the internal evidence we must set the testimony of the First Folio. Inclusion of a play in the First Folio constitutes irrefutable external evidence that Shakespeare had 'an entire hand, or at the least a maine finger' in its composition. But we have no external evidence, and no valid reason to infer, that Heminges and Condell would have excluded any collaborative or adapted play, so long as Shakespeare wrote the lion's share. Collaboration and adaptation were a normal part of the theatrical world to which Condell, Heminges, and Shakespeare devoted their professional lives, and they can hardly have regarded it with the fastidious distaste of some modern critics. Like most others who have studied the evidence carefully, we believe that at least four Folio texts—*1 Henry VI*, *Timon of Athens*, *Macbeth*, and *All is True*—contain passages which Shakespeare did not write. *Measure for Measure* itself, if we are right about the song in 4.1, and the dialogue which follows it, also contains material which Shakespeare did not write. The testimony of the First Folio therefore cannot be said to contradict the ascription to Middleton of eighty lines from 1.2 of *Measure for Measure*. No pertinent external testimony exists. In order to identify the author of the suspect passage, we must rely entirely on internal evidence.

The foregoing analysis of that internal evidence demonstrates that the whole structure and content of the suspect passage is typical of Middleton, and that the Middletonian features are scattered throughout it. With the exception of four individual words, every idiom and image in the passage can be paralleled in Middleton's canon. The passage lacks the verbal idiosyncrasies which characterize and distinguish Shakespeare's work throughout his career; a reliable vocabulary test for the chronology of Shakespeare's writing indicates that it was not written at the same time

as the rest of the play. All of this in a mere eighty-four lines of prose—
which virtually all scholars agree impossibly duplicates a genuine
Shakespearian passage later in the same scene. Either the historical
Thomas Middleton wrote this passage, or Shakespeare in 1603–4 did a
brief but perfect imitation of how Thomas Middleton would be writing in
1621, and designed this imitation so that it would bear all the hallmarks
of a late theatrical interpolation. By chance, Shakespeare happened to
perform this act of anticipatory plagiarism in a play which would be
printed from a late transcript of a late prompt-book, and which includes
one other passage which seems to have been interpolated for a theatrical
revival in or after 1619. If *Measure for Measure* were a play by anyone
but Shakespeare, would you doubt that the beginning of 1. 2 is the work
of a second hand?

Barring the discovery of some more plausible candidate, Middleton must
be regarded as the probable author of the interpolation in 1. 2. We are
not so sure of Middleton's responsibility for the changes in 4. 1.
However, none of its vocabulary seems demonstrably un-Middletonian,
and many parallels could be cited for its unusual mixture of blank verse,
prose, and rhyme. Shakespeare never used the expression '[noun] of com-
forts' (4. 1. 8; TLN 1778); by contrast, Middleton's work contains at least
twenty-one examples.[227] Moreover, as the Friar is described in 4. 1 as a
'man of comfort', so Middleton describes a doctor as a 'man of art'
(*Widow* 4. 2. 117, 5. 1. 67, 439; G3ᵛ, H3ᵛ, K1), and 'men of art' occurs at
Changeling 2. 2. 46 (D1ᵛ). Shakespeare never uses the two separate words
'well come' as a greeting, as at 4. 1. 26 (TLN 1797). Middleton does:
'Now y'ar well com Sir, yf you'll'd come alwaies thus' (*Witch* 2. 2. 122–3;
ll. 853–4). Crane might be responsible for the word division in both
Witch and *Measure*, but Middleton does frequently play upon 'well' or
'come' in conjunction with 'welcome', in ways which suggest a sharp
awareness of the word as a compound of two elements.[228] No Folio text,

---

[227] *Solomon* 1. 7. 5, 1. 7. 8, 2. 9. 15, 3. 9. 2, *Hubburd*, p. 95 (F2), **Revenger's Tragedy*
3. 4. 61 (E4), **Second Maiden's Tragedy* 1. 2. 189, 208 (ll. 472, 492), *No Wit* 1. 2. 154,
4. 2. 79, 5. 1. 241 (B3ᵛ, F7ᵛ, G6ᵛ), *Witch* 5. 3. 88, 116 (ll. 2132, 2163), *Widow* 4. 1. 11, 5. 1.
91 (F3ᵛ, H3ᵛ), **Fair Quarrel* 4. 2. 96, 4. 3. 3 (H1ᵛ, H2), *Aries*, p. 347 (B3ᵛ), *Women Beware
Women* 4. 2. 142 (N3).

[228] *Trick to Catch the Old One* 3. 3. 66, E2ᵛ ('Oh you come well'), *Women Beware
Women*, 4. 1. 142, M6 ('He comes, *Hippolito* welcome') and 1. 1. 138, G6ᵛ ('welcome, and
us'd well'), *More Dissemblers Besides Women* 2. 3. 16–17, C6 ('welcome | . . . come') and
5. 1. 130, F3ᵛ ('If you come, y'are welcome'), *Mad World* 5. 1. 28–9, G4ᵛ ('they are welcome; they'le grace my entertainment well'), **Wit at Several Weapons* 1. 1, 6l3ᵛ ('Hee's
come; Sir *Gregory*, welcome'), **Revenger's Tragedy* 3. 5. 109, F2 ('now come and welcome'),
Michaelmas Term 2. 1. 47, C1 ('well, come'), **Family of Love* 5. 3. 55–6, H2ᵛ ('they come,
they come? welcome'), *No Wit* 5. 1. 135–6, G4ᵛ ('come . . . welcome'), *Triumphs of Truth*, p.
241, B2 ('Art come? O welcome'), *Witch* 2. 1. 94–5, ll. 550–2 ('come . . . wellcom'),
2. 1. 137, l. 600 ('if more come, 'tis wellcom'), and 5. 1. 1–2, ll. 1768–70 ('*You* are Wellcom
Sir' answered by 'I thinck I'am worthie on't | for looke you (Sir,) I come un-trust'), *Phoenix*

and no quarto believed to have been set from Shakespeare's own papers, treats 'alittle' as one word (4. 1. 22; TLN 1793);[229] Middleton does three times, once in an autograph manuscript.[230] Middleton similarly compounds 'alate' and 'apurpose'.[231] The expression 'but pleas'd my woe' (4. 1. 13; TLN 1783) resembles, in thought as well as meaning, Middleton's 'to please my feare', also at the end of a line in a couplet, in *The Widow* 3. 2. 120–1 (F1).

We have noticed that the Duke's allusion to the harmful effects of music (4. 1. 14–15; TLN 1784–5) is atypical of Shakespeare; it is typical of Middleton. In *Your Five Gallants* a brothel is disguised as a music school for young ladies; in *Game at Chess* music is associated with devilish Catholic idolatry (5. 1) and with a deceitful false 'apparition' (3. 3). In *Micro-cynicon* Middleton writes of 'The musick sweet, which al that while did sound, | Rauish the hearers, and their sence confound' (p. 125; B7ᵛ). In **Revenger's Tragedy*, a rape is committed 'in the height of all the reuels, | When the music was heard loudest' (1. 4. 37–8; Clᵛ–C2); later there are references to 'villanous music' (4. 1. 28; Glᵛ), and music is part of a lustful Court entertainment at 2. 1. 199, 3. 5. 88, 3. 5. 185–220 (D1ᵛ, F2, F3ᵛ). In *The Witch* the witches sing, and we are told 'ther's no Villany but is a Tune methinckes . . . A Tune: 'tis to the Tune of dampnation then' (5. 2. 81–3; ll. 2017–19). In *The Black Book* Middleton writes of the 'rauishing music' of the Devil (p. 8; B1ᵛ); in *Ghost of Lucrece* music is 'The very Synode-house of Venerie' (p. 292; B6); in *Mad World*, a devil appears to Penitent Brothel, dancing and singing (4. 1).

Just as the scene's attitude to music can be found in Middleton's work, so can its staging of a musical episode. In **Anything for a Quiet Life*, 2. 2 opens with the discovery of three characters, one of whom sings for the first ten lines of the scene, until the entrance of another character. In *A Trick to Catch the Old One*, 4. 5 begins with the discovery of '*Dampit, the usurer, in his bed; Audrey spinning by*', and then a song: the song in question was in fact written by Thomas Ravenscroft, not Middleton; Ravenscroft's published version is longer, and it seems likely that Middleton shortened it in order to remove elements not appropriate to

1. 1. 30, A2ᵛ ('you come well'), etc. For the possibility of Crane influence on this compound's form in *Witch* and *Measure*, compare Middleton's 'A Song in Several Parts' (1622): 'Bountie wel come all your Guests' (Public Record Office MS, *State Papers Domestic*, v. 129, Doc. 53), where Crane's division on the page cannot reflect an authorial intention to convey two distinct words.

[229] The only three examples elsewhere in the Shakespeare canon all occur in Quarto *Othello* (1622), apparently set from scribal copy by a single compositor.

[230] **1 Honest Whore* 1. 5. 14, **Revenger's Tragedy* 2. 1. 21 (C3), the Trinity MS of *Game at Chess* 3. 3. 57. Crane is unlikely to be responsible for the form in *Measure*: in *Witch*, at least, he always treated 'a little' as two words. Bald transcribes the example in *Game* as two words, but in the MS the *a* and *l* are clearly linked (as they are in no other example of the words in that play).

[231] For 'alate' and 'apurpose' see Jackson, *Attribution*, 16.

the dramatic situation in *A Trick*.[232] Act 1 of *More Dissemblers* begins with a song, about a woman who 'singing weeps, and sighing plays', having kept herself in isolation since the death of her husband. And in **Second Maiden's Tragedy*, Govianus '*in black, a booke in his hand*' enters with '*his page*' to mourn at the tomb of his dead betrothed (4. 4); after a short speech, '*Govianus kneeles at the Toomb w[o]ndrus passionatly, His Page singes*' (ll. 1891–4); after the song, Govianus tells the boy, 'prythee wth drawe a litle and attend me | at Cloyster doore' (ll. 1916–17). As in *Measure*, the boy is brought on to sing, and then dismissed. Such parallels make it evident that the basic dramatic technique of Folio 4. 1 could easily be Middleton's. So also is the technique of song-abridgement, as the example of *A Trick* shows. Furthermore, if we accept the usual dating for the plays, Middleton took the first stanza of his own three-stanza song 'CUPID *is* VENVS *onely Joy*' from *Chaste Maid* (1613) and inserted it, with an added couplet, in 1. 4 of *More Dissemblers* (*c*.1619).

Such parallels make Middleton a much more attractive candidate than Shakespeare for the authorship of the suspect passage in 4. 1, but they depress Shakespeare's claim more effectively than they exalt Middleton's. An equally good case might possibly be made, on this basis, for other dramatists, and of course we have no way of testing the preferences of an unknown actor or bookkeeper for the King's Men, *c*.1621. For instance, in our incomplete survey of Fletcher's canon we have noticed 'I constantly beleeve ye' (*Valentinian* 1. 3. 66), 'As you do constantly beleeve' (*Woman's Prize* 2. 2. 55), 'alittle' (*Captain* 3. 6. 16), and 'a word of comfort' (*Captain* 2. 3. 34). It seems, for reasons we have already elaborated, extremely unlikely that Fletcher was responsible for the interpolation, but on such a basis his claim is as good as Middleton's. The passage gives us, by its blandness, little to go on, and though it would be simplest to assume that one man was responsible for all the alterations to *Measure*, that assumption can by no means be taken for granted. The triple use of *hath*, the metrical regularity of the verse, and the very blandness of the writing, all point away from Middleton.[233]

At the beginning of our investigation of the authorship of the suspect passage in 1. 2, we pointed out that historical and stylistic considerations effectively limited the choice of candidates to three playwrights:

---

[232] See *Trick*, ed. Watson (see n. 197), 4. 1. 1–4 (p. 82). Watson suggests that the Quarto's omission of Ravenscroft's first two lines is 'probably . . . the result of a compositor's blunder'; but there is no hint in the play that Dampit is a wittol (or even married), so the missing lines would be inappropriate. Since Dampit is an usurer, the remaining lines are relevant.

[233] Crane might be responsible for the uncharacteristic predominance of *hath*: see *Game at Chess*, ed. Bald, 34, 171–2. Crane's transcript of *Witch* contains more examples of *hath* than any other Middleton play: see Lake, *Canon*, table 1.1, band 2(3). The verse in Middleton's pageants could be consistently regular, but 4. 1 seems uncharacteristic of the verse in his plays.

Massinger, Middleton, and Webster. The same considerations apply to
4. 1, and just as the linguistic evidence makes Middleton the most plausible candidate for authorship of the interpolation in 1. 2, so it makes him
an implausible candidate for authorship of the interpolation in 4. 1. On
the other hand, the suspected passage's preference for *hath* would fit
Webster's work very well, just as it fits Middleton or Fletcher badly.
Moreover, unlike Fletcher—and like the suspect passage—Webster made
relatively little use of *ye*. Webster collaborated with Middleton as early as
1602 (on the lost *Caesar's Fall*); Middleton wrote commendatory verses
for the 1623 edition of *The Duchess of Malfi*; in 1624, when Middleton
went into hiding, as a result of the *Game at Chess* affair, Webster apparently stood in for him, writing the only civic pageant of his career. Most
important, Middleton and Webster collaborated on *Anything for a Quiet
Life* in 1621 or shortly after, the very period when *Measure* is most likely
to have been adapted. Given the abundant contemporary evidence for
multiple authorship of 'new additions', a Middleton–Webster collaboration on the 1621 revamping of *Measure* makes sense.[234] Moreover,
Webster was clearly capable of using songs he did not himself write: the
1623 Quarto of *The Duchess of Malfi* pointedly specifies that 'The Author
disclaimes this Ditty to be his' (3. 4. 11–14). For the adapter's use of
Fletcher's song in 4. 1 Webster's work thus provides a plausible parallel.
Moreover, the presence of Webster might also explain the undistinguished
style of the added dialogue. After the twin peaks of *The White Devil* and
The Duchess of Malfi Webster's work subsides into a long and permanent
decline. Middleton, by contrast, was in 1621 entering the most brilliant
period of his career. We hesitate to attribute the opening of 4. 1 to him
any more than to Shakespeare. But the lines are not self-evidently
beneath the capacities of Webster in 1621.

Webster is therefore an attractive candidate for the authorship of the
suspected interpolation in 4. 1. Fortunately, Webster's extant work has
recently been concorded. In *The Devil's Law Case*, Webster wrote 'here's
a man of comfort' (4. 1. 121)—which comes closer to *Measure*'s 'Here
comes a man of comfort' than anything in either the Shakespeare or the
Middleton canon. *Fair Maid of the Inn* also contains 'the man of art'
(3. 1. 59, 4. 1. 15) and 'a messenger of comfort' (3. 2. 229). Webster's
work also provides verbal parallels for another passage:

> I shall craue your forbearance alittle, may be
> I will call vpon you anone for some aduantage to your
> selfe.
>   *Mar.* I am alwayes bound to you.
>
>   (TLN 1793–6)

---

[234] Heinemann, *Puritanism and Theatre* (see n. 157), 130–1.

> I pray forbear a little
> >   (*Appius and Virginia* 1. 1. 39)
>
> the rest forbear vs till we call
> >   (*Appius and Virginia* 3. 1. 24)

The two lines in *Appius and Virginia*, both followed by an exit, come closer to the lines in *Measure* than anything in the Shakespeare canon, and Webster elsewhere treats 'alittle' as one word (*Westward Ho* 3. 4. 33). Neither Webster nor Shakespeare provides an exact parallel for Maria's answer, but Webster does use 'I am euer bound to you' twice (*Devil's Law Case* 1. 1. 141, *White Devil* 1. 1. 59). The closest Shakespeare comes is 'I am bound to thee for euer' (*Othello* 3. 3. 213)—which is admittedly close, but changes the order, changes the pronoun, and adds 'for'; moreover, in *Othello* the declaration constitutes a powerful dramatic moment, whereas in Webster and *Measure* it simply contributes to the small change of polite conversation. Webster also, like Middleton, associates music with lust and evil (*White Devil* 3. 2. 79, 4. 2. 91).

One must concede that these parallels are pitiably little evidence on which to attribute the passage to Webster. In 1. 2, the evidence for Middleton's hand is so strong that it would be hard to dismiss even if there were no other reason to doubt the passage; but if we had no other reason to doubt Shakespeare's authorship of the opening of 4. 1, such Webster parallels would be dismissed. Of course we do have other reason to deny Shakespeare's responsibility for these lines, and if Shakespeare did not write them then Webster may well have done so. Linguistically and historically Webster is an attractive candidate, and his extant work provides parallels for virtually everything in this passage. The only words he does not elsewhere use are 'quick' adverbially (1773), the verb 'still'd' (1779), and the word 'brawl' (1779); he does not use the phrases 'break off' (1777) or 'haste . . . away' (1777). Given the size of the extant Webster corpus—only about 13 per cent of Shakespeare's—such lacunae should not surprise us.[235] Moreover, the brief blandness of the writing forestalls many striking verbal parallels. Such restrictions render confidence unattainable. But Webster's work does provide interesting parallels for 'forbearance alittle, may be I will call vpon you', 'I am alwayes bound to you', and (especially) 'Here comes a man of comfort'. In conjunction with the linguistic evidence, such parallels make him as likely as Shakespeare to have written this passage.

Massinger, too, is theoretically an attractive candidate for the authorship of the beginning of 4. 1. He had strong connections with the King's

---

[235] See Charles R. Forker, 'Webster or Shakespeare? Style, Idiom, Vocabulary, and Spelling in the Additions to *Sir Thomas More*', in T. H. Howard-Hill (ed.), *Shakespeare and Sir Thomas More* (Cambridge, 1989), 169; Forker draws upon Richard Corballis and J. M. Harding, *A Concordance to the Works of John Webster*, 12 vols. (Salzburg, 1978–81).

Men; he did a lot of play-botching; he preferred *hath* but avoided *ye*. Massinger's work has never been concorded, and so in evaluating his claim we have had to rely upon our own unassisted reading of his eight extant poems and of the thirty-four extant plays of which he was sole or part author. This survey has convinced us, however, that Massinger cannot have written the additional dialogue for 4. 1. We have failed to find, in a canon substantially larger than Webster's, anything comparable to the Webster parallels already noted, or any other striking parallels between the suspect passage and Massinger's extant work. More important than this negative result—which might be attributed to our negligence—is a 'positive' one: Massinger hardly ever wrote prose. In the plays of Massinger's sole authorship we have found prose only in *The Duke of Milan* 2. 1. 372–6 (a letter), *The Emperor of the East* 4. 3 (the speeches of a quack chirurgeon), and *The City Madam* 2. 2 (the speeches of a quack astrologer); in the collaborative plays prose never occurs in passages assigned to Massinger, except in *Love's Cure* 1. 2 and 2. 2. 158–64, where Massinger may have touched up scenes originally written by someone else. Massinger's consistent avoidance of prose in all but clearly defined eccentric circumstances (a letter, speeches full of technical jargon) make it completely unacceptable to attribute to him the interpolation in 4. 1—or, of course, that in 1. 2.

Although the undistinguished style of the passage in 4. 1 is an obstacle to positive attribution, it argues, like much else, against attribution to Shakespeare. The passage might have been written by an actor or bookkeeper (whose claims are permanently imponderable), or by Middleton (whose claim is certainly better than Shakespeare's, and strengthened by his presence in 1. 2), or by Webster. At the very least, any of these candidates is more likely than Shakespeare to have written the dialogue between the end of (Fletcher's) song and the entrance of (Shakespeare's) Isabella.

VIII

Acceptance of the evidence for posthumous adaptation in *Measure for Measure* entails only five emendations of the Folio text: omission of TLN 1169–96 (4. 1. 0–24), transposition of the Duke's two soliloquies (TLN 1746–67 and 1834–9), omission of TLN 96–174 (1. 2. 0–116), alteration of the entrance direction and adjacent dialogue at TLN 205 and 207, and omission of '*Julietta*' from the direction at TLN 2875. These are, of course, major emendations, and we do not advocate them lightly. In each case we merely propose to solve a substantial problem which has troubled previous scholars, scholars who never dreamt that Thomas Middleton might in 1621 have adapted Shakespeare's play. Editors have left these problems unsolved because no obvious or satisfactory solutions presented themselves; each problem was faced in isolation from the others and as a consequence appeared insoluble. The hypothesis of adaptation provides a single explanation for all these difficulties. That hypothesis may sound implausible simply because it sounds new;[236] but many editors have been dissatisfied with the individual details which we suspect, and only the suggestion that those individual difficulties have a single common cause is new. In some sense, our entire investigation amounts to no more than an attempt to demonstrate that editors should indeed do what many of them have always wanted to.

But doubt, once awakened, is not easily sedated, or easily leashed. If two passages were added to *Measure for Measure*, why not three? or six? or ten? How much has been omitted, how much drastically refashioned? How can we trust the text at all? By such a progress of rhetorical questions reasonable men like Dover Wilson have rapidly found themselves contending that the plays of the Shakespeare canon bear little relation to the plays Shakespeare originally wrote.

In fact, little else in *Measure* can be seriously suspected. The play may have been shortened; but this is true of other plays, too. Shakespeare may, indeed, have cut it himself before it ever saw the light of first performance. The extant play, though short, is not suspiciously so, and shows no scars of inept amputation which might betray missing limbs. The original's very compactness may have been one motive for commissioning additions, just as the complete absence of songs from both *Macbeth* and *Measure* may have been one motive for adding songs to both. After all, what stage-manager in his right mind would commission additions to *Hamlet*? Shorter plays, like *Measure* and *Macbeth*, would be particularly attractive candidates for interpolation. As for wholesale refashioning, the essential fabric of the play, its characterization, the conduct of its plot, its themes, its verbal detail, are undoubtedly Shakespeare's. We have ourselves worried over the text of *Measure* from end to end; these inconsequent anxieties are presented in Appendix VI, but in this place it will be enough to say that we have found little else in the text which justifies suspicion, and nothing which could justify editorial intervention.

In a famous British Academy lecture, E. K. Chambers attacked what he called 'The Disintegration of Shakespeare'. The metaphor of his title has had far more influence than any of the arguments in the lecture itself. Like Lucio, the epithet 'disintegrator' is like a burr, and will stick: disintegrators destroy, in particular they shatter into disparate atoms the

---

[236] For a specimen of this kind of instant rejection, see the review by Brian Vickers of the Oxford *Complete Works* (*RES*, NS 40 (1989), 407), where—without having even seen our reasons for suspecting interpolation in *Measure*, which are being published in the present vol. for the first time—Vickers attacks what he imagines our reasons must have been ('Neoclassical pedantry'). Vickers's entire review is of this calibre.

wholeness which is Shakespeare. Upon reflection we must realize that this metaphor emotionally maligns a legitimate and indeed necessary activity. Disintegrators do not disintegrate Shakespeare, but the accepted Shakespeare canon; they do so not in order to evaporate a solid presence, but to dislodge in particular cases the foreign accretions which encrust an ancient original. Properly and cautiously conducted, the disintegration of the Shakespeare canon permits and contributes to the reintegration of Shakespeare.

Without the passages which we suspect as interpolations, *Measure for Measure* emerges as a marginally different play: still a problem play, still straddling genres and yoking disparate moods, but doing so in a less familiar fashion. Without the seamy conversation between Lucio, his two companions, and Overdone, the play gets off to a rather lighter, more clearly comic start. Instead of three gaudy gallants, with their talk of war, their cynicism about religion, their smutty jokes; without Mistress Overdone's introduction as 'Madam *Mittigation*', and the immediately ensuing 'fooling' about venereal disease; without Overdone's own complaint to the audience about the decline in her business, because of war and poverty and hanging and (again) syphilis; without Juliet's grossly pregnant presence, grouped in the background with those two disreputable 'Gentlemen'—without all this, Vienna might strike us as a less obviously seedy place. It only gradually dawns on us that Overdone is a bawd; our recognition is, moreover, a comic dawning which winks over the horizon with her horrified question, 'what shall become of me?' (TLN 194; I. 2. 97).

The interpolated passage implies that Claudio is himself one of Overdone's customers; moreover, it specifies that he has already been sentenced to death, 'within these three daies his head to be chop'd off' (TLN 159–60; I. 2. 67). Without this information, our initial responses to Claudio's predicament may be rather different. When Claudio himself appears, in the authoritative part of the scene, he is simply being led 'to prison', and shown 'to th' world' (TLN 207–8; I. 2. 107–8). He never tells Lucio that he has already been sentenced to die within three days—surely a point of rather urgent importance. Lucio, when he has been told of Claudio's predicament, does comment that 'thy head stands so tickle on thy shoulders, that a milke-maid, if she be in love, may sigh it off' (TLN 265–7; I. 2. 160–2), but this only gives a flippant intimation that Claudio may be in some danger of more than imprisonment. Not until I. 4 do we hear that Claudio's 'life' has fallen 'into forfeit': Isabella is incredulous, and only then does Lucio confirm that Angelo 'Has censur'd him already, | And as I heare, the Prouost hath a warrant | For's execution' (TLN 426–28; I. 4. 71–3). Still we do not know when the sentence will be carried out: only later, in 2. 1, does Angelo tell the Provost to 'See that *Claudio* | Be executed by nine to morrow morning, | Bring him his

Confessor' (TLN 487–9; 2. 1. 33–5). By this time, we already know that Isabella is on her way (1. 4) and that the Duke has disguised himself as a friar (1. 3). If we remove the interpolated beginning of 1. 2, then Claudio's mortal danger does not dominate our awareness until near the end of Act 1, and by the time that danger becomes imminent we are already aware of two obstacles to the implementation of Angelo's sentence.

The alterations to 1. 2 influence our sense of the play's, and Vienna's, tone; more specifically, they prejudice our attitude towards Overdone and Lucio. The addition to 1. 2 becomes our introduction to both characters, and makes their moral corruption unmistakably obvious. Without that interpolation, Lucio first appears on the scene as a somewhat bawdy but genial character, concerned for his friend Claudio; in Isabella's company he quickly snaps out of his irreverence and into gentlemanly verse. That change is less abrupt without the interpolated episode in 1. 2. Only in 3. 1 does Lucio's real turpiturde reveal itself (especially if we replace his expurgated oaths). Lucio falls, as it were, after Angelo.

All this does not mean that the play loses its sting, or that we are any less conscious of the moral importance of its fable. The great central scenes between Isabella and Angelo, the Duke and Claudio, Claudio and Isabella, lose none of their immediate urgency and passion; indeed, if we restore their profanity, they become even more powerfully Christian. But the turn from the brink of tragedy back towards comedy will come as less of a jolt. Without the act-break interpolated by a Jacobean adapter, without the scene-break interpolated by an eighteenth-century editor, the play bridges the chasm between its two genres in a single, uninterrupted, finely articulated scene, over 600 lines long, which reaches from the Duke's peroration on the misery and folly of human life to his exit with Mariana and Isabella, having secured their assent to the moral trick which assures us of a 'happy' ending. We do not pause to linger, dolefully, over the sadness of Mariana in her moated grange; the Duke does not pause, *in media res*, to reflect upon Angelo's hypocrisy. Instead, we sweep straight on, past Pompey, past Lucio, past Overdone and the Provost and Escalus, absorbing all these morsels of comic mortality, on our way from Isabella's exit to Isabella's re-entrance; then, as the culmination of this sequence of arrivals, comes Mariana. So the scene that began with Isabella's cruel anguish concludes with an agreement which will solve the unsolvable by sleight by body. As the Duke ends his onstage journey it seems, at last, that all may be well. By the time the Duke speaks his chorus-like soliloquy Mariana, whose role has so far been confined to the functional solving of Isabella's problems, has nevertheless actually been seen on stage; the bed-trick is becoming a reality. The Duke declares 'With *Angelo* to night shall lye | His old betroathed (but despised:)', and we accept his prediction. The play will eventually face both the practical and ethical efficaciousness of the bed-trick, but the Duke has, at the moment of his soliloquy, just made the first and decisive move in a plot that promises to save Angelo's soul, save Claudio's life, save Isabella's chastity, and right the wrong done Mariana. And his confidence is endorsed as soon as Isabella and Mariana re-enter: 'Shee'll take the enterprize vpon her father, | If you aduise it'.

The Folio adaptation produces a different (though more familiar) play. The alteration of 4. 1 gives an added prominence to the role chiefly expanded by the adaptation of 1. 2; the addition of the singing boy in 4. 1 and the mute Juliet in 5. 1 both assume the availability of a third boy actor, not required by the original text; Juliet's interpolated mute entrance in 5. 1 repeats her interpolated mute entrance in 1. 2. Both the boy's song and Juliet's final appearance pluck at our heart-strings, stopping the play for an indulgence in static sentiment. As the second half of the play is made more sentimental, so the first half has been shrouded with a complementary darkness. Knowledge of the full horror and urgency of Claudio's predicament is thrust upon us almost immediately; the two guilty lovers both appear on stage, together but apart, so that our consciousness of Claudio's extreme danger is reinforced by an emblematic image of the fruits of sin.

Middleton may have been commissioned to do no more than 'give Lucio an extended new introduction'. But the 'new addition' he supplied had the effect of alchemizing the moral context: presenting us with a memorable dramatic cameo of a depraved society, a tripartite alliance of sex and disease and godlessness, exuding a moral smudge which clings to our impressions of Lucio, Overdone, Claudio, Juliet, Vienna in general. The influence of his interpolation on our view of the whole play testifies to the brilliance of his writing and the craft of his remodelling—and to the intensity of his own commitment to the issues the play raises. But like the other interpolations and alterations, Middleton's refashioning of 1. 2 arguably confuses the development of the play, by trying to alter its course. Both the addition to 1. 2 and the adaptation of 4. 1 disrupt Shakespeare's transition from one tone to the other. The changes in 1. 2 darken the play's first half, and the changes in 4. 1 interfere with the transition from something like darkness into something like light.

We did not set out to make critical sense of *Measure for Measure*; we set out to solve certain textual problems related to the kind of manuscript from which the Folio text derived. If we had begun with strong critical views, or if we wanted to make our textual argument appealing to purely literary critics, then we should hardly have wished or chosen to conclude that Shakespeare's original was a lighter, more confident play than the adapted Folio version. In the current hermeneutical climate, bitter is beautiful; a difficult darkness is the most admired of styles. But the cynicism and bleakness of a passage hardly constitute reliable evidence that

Shakespeare wrote it. *Measure for Measure* is complex enough, without the artificial complexity created by the imposition on it of another playwright's rather different view of its story.

On the basis of a series of independent lines of argument and evidence, two passages should be stigmatized as unShakespearian interpolations, added to *Measure for Measure* on the occasion of a revival *c.* 1621, and written at least in part by Thomas Middleton. Some literary critics might prefer Middleton's adaptation to Shakespeare's original; that would be their privilege; Middleton is a playwright easy to admire. But such a critical preference would in no way invalidate the evidence that the play has been adapted. In retrospect it seems to us that the interpolations weaken Shakespeare's play, confuse its structure, and contribute in some small measure to the dissatisfaction many critics have felt with its mixture of genres. In *Measure*, less really may be more.

Post-Script

by GARY TAYLOR

THE preceding essays attempt to isolate certain kinds of alteration made to Shakespeare's plays in the Jacobean theatre, changes of which he might not have approved. The postulated adaptation of *Measure for Measure* took place after his death; about the expurgation of profanity, the law left him little choice; for the interpolation of act-intervals, he may or may not have been consulted, depending upon the date of revival of any given play. This book thus tells a story of the betrayal of Shakespeare's own textual intentions by functionaries in the theatre of his time. That has been a popular story in the history of the editing of Shakespeare, from Alexander Pope (1725) to David Bevington (1988). But it is not a story much associated with the 1986-7 Oxford edition of Shakespeare's *Complete Works*, an edition conspicuously committed to the textual and critical implications of the recognition that Shakespeare was a theatre poet, whose work found its intended fruition only in the collaborative theatrical enterprise for which he wrote.

On the one hand, Shakespeare's plays *were* written for performance, and an edition of the plays should remain loyal (as Shakespeare was) to the theatre; on the other hand, Shakespeare's plays *were* betrayed in the theatre, and an edition of the plays should not perpetuate those betrayals. There is no real contradiction between these two propositions. The difficulty—as with all textual criticism—is to identify the specific places in any given text where someone entrusted with the transmission of a play corrupted it instead. Texts can, of course, be corrupted in the theatre, just as they can be corrupted in the printing-house, or the scriptorium; the editors of the Oxford Shakespeare (including the two authors of this book) always appreciated that fact. But other editors have tended to believe, or to act as though they believed, that *anything* which happened to Shakespeare's texts in the theatre constituted, by definition, corruption. That assumption makes life easier for the editor, but it constitutes a betrayal of the dramatist's purposes. We have therefore operated on the principle that it is our duty as editors to recognize Shakespeare's commitment to collaborative performance, while at the same time trying to identify and correct theatrical corruption of his texts.

In distinguishing collaboration from corruption we have drawn a line, in some ways arbitrary, after the first performance of a play. We have regarded as authoritative virtually everything which happens to the text of a play in its evolution from initial idea to first performance: whether a change was suggested by the author or an actor, whether the author's enthusiasm endorsed it or his indifference acquiesced in it, the result has been treated as part of a natural social process, culminating in a collaborative public performance. The script of that first performance is, for us, the first complete text of the play.

After that first performance, history begins to create a succession of post-scripts, in which the author may or may not be involved. In the case of Shakespeare and many other professional dramatists, the author is routinely engaged and respected in the collaborative process that leads to the first script; but authorial participation in the collaborative evolution of the post-scripts is much more haphazard, much less predictable. The author may later revise the text (as we believe happened with *King Lear*), or someone else may later revise the text (as we believe happened with *Measure for Measure*). The difference between these two situations has nothing to do with the theatre, *per se*; both the postulated revision of *King Lear* and the postulated adaptation of *Measure for Measure* were made for, and presumably acted in, the Jacobean theatre. The difference between the revision of *King Lear* and the adaptation of *Measure for Measure* is thus not a difference in place (the theatre) or in action (textual revision); it is not even a difference in quality (for it is possible to regard the changes to *King Lear* as unfortunate, and the changes to *Measure* as inspired); the difference is a difference in agent. Shakespeare seems to us to have been the author of the changes in *King Lear*, but not of the changes in *Measure*. In both cases, in all such cases, editorial practice must be based upon an attribution, and editors cannot avoid making an attribution, one way or the other. Our own practice, in preparing the Oxford edition, was to assume (conservatively) that Shakespeare was responsible for a reading, unless strong evidence contradicted that assumption.

One kind of evidence for such attributions is chronological. Scripts and post-scripts are created by agents who act temporally, and whose actions are therefore always, theoretically, datable. Practically, we often cannot date particular textual actions (an addition, a deletion, a change in staging); but sometimes we can. This book has been concerned with three kinds of textual action which are, we believe, datable: the expurgation of profanity (after 1606), the interpolation of act intervals (after 1608), and the adaptation of *Measure for Measure* (*c.* 1621). The chronological evidence, if accepted, establishes that these variants belong to the post-scripts of the relevant plays. It does not establish, in itself, who was responsible for the changes; but it makes it possible for editors to distinguish these theatrical changes (which may well betray the author's purposes) from other theatrical changes (which belong to the initial collaborative process). Of course, it is always possible that other changes, which cannot now be identified, also belonged to the post-script, and not the initial script; but we have assumed (conservatively) that readings belong to the initial script, unless strong evidence contradicts that assumption.

Textual scholars continue to disagree over the existence or character of 'foul papers' and 'bad quartos', but there can be no doubt about the existence of manuscripts licensed by the Master of the Revels for use in the theatre: what we call the 'prompt-book', what Shakespeare and his contemporaries would have called the 'book'. Such texts were and are material objects; they are not figments of the editorial imagination. As material objects, they are also, necessarily, historical objects: they are the result of the temporal actions of particular agents. A material object may be acted upon by different agents and at different times; the 'book' as a whole is the site and the sum total of the actions of all those agents over time. Consequently, the script of a play (as I have defined it) is not necessarily identical to the 'book' of that play. The 'book' includes the script, but may overlay that script with many post-scripts. The script which an editor seeks to recover is therefore a specific temporal slice of a specific material object. The script is a place (the 'book') at a time ('the first performance').

The printed texts of Shakespeare's plays are at various removes from such a script. They may derive from a pre-script (a manuscript written down before completion of the script) or a post-script (a manuscript written down after completion of the script). The same manuscript might, at different times, be both a pre-script and a post-script: the 'book' would be (1) a pre-script before rehearsals began, then evolve into (2) a completed script, then further evolve into (3) a post-script. Copies might theoretically be made of this document at any of these three stages in its evolution. For editors of Shakespeare, attempting to understand and reflect the textual process which produced his plays, it is important to be able to distinguish pre-scripts from post-scripts.

This is not the place to attempt a thorough reconsideration of the evidence that may enable us to distinguish pre-scripts from post-scripts. However, the evidentiary value of one feature of the texts of the period has in the past been overlooked or misunderstood. Textual critics often speak of 'act- and scene-divisions' as though the two were intrinsically related, but the two kinds of division have different purposes and different sources. If I am correct in my analysis of act-intervals in the London theatres, then act-divisions in the texts of Shakespeare's plays published after 1609 may reflect theatrical practice; they need not be interpreted as a symptom of 'literary' or editorial tampering with the text. On the other hand, although it is quite clear that Shakespeare, throughout his career, regarded the scene as the basic unit of dramatic construction, scene-divisions are not marked in any of the plays published before 1623; moreover, although the clearing of the stage between scenes was an organizing principle of Renaissance performance, and although scene-breaks were usually indicated in theatrical plats, scene-divisions were not usually indicated in prompt-books, and scene numbers seem never to have been added by theatrical annotators. A prompt-book would tolerate scene-divisions which had been indicated by an author or scribe, but bookkeepers did not add or emphasize such divisions. This conclusion has certain implications for deductions about the underlying manuscript copy for a number of texts in the First Folio. If—as the quartos give us good reason to believe—Shakespeare himself did not mark or number scene-divisions in his manuscripts, and if theatrical functionaries were not interested in adding such divisions, then the presence of scene-divisions in a Folio text is excellent evidence of a scribal transcript. Scene-divisions are found in the Folio texts listed in Table 10.

TABLE 10. *Folio texts containing scene-divisions*

Play	Copy
Tempest	Crane transcript
Two Gentlemen	Crane transcript
Merry Wives	Crane transcript
Measure	Crane transcript
As You Like It	'Prompt-book or a literary transcript'
Twelfth Night	Scribal transcript
Winter's Tale	Crane transcript
King John	Scribal transcript
Richard II	Q3, annotated by reference 'probably, to a promptbook'
1 Henry IV	Q6, 'annotated, perhaps from a transcript of a prompt-book'
2 Henry IV	Scribal transcript
1 Henry VI (mixed)	Collaborative foul papers
Richard III	Q3 and Q6, annotated by reference to 'a transcript, presumably though not certainly scribal'
All is True	Scribal transcript
Macbeth	Scribal transcript
Hamlet (mixed)	Scribal transcript
King Lear	'Q2, annotated from either holograph or scribal transcript of holograph'
Othello	Scribal transcript
Cymbeline	Crane transcript
Kinsmen (1634)	'Probably holograph . . . but possibly a scribal transcript'

The conclusions about printer's copy cited above are taken from the *Textual Companion*; they are not dependent upon the argument made in the preceding paragraph about the source of scene-divisions (an argument which occurred to me only after the *Companion* was published). In almost every text which contains scene-divisions, we concluded, on the basis of other evidence, that the printer's copy was a scribal transcript. The argument that scene-divisions *should* be scribal in origin is thus reinforced by the evidence that the overwhelming majority of them occur in texts which we have other reasons to believe were set from scribal copy. Of the exceptions, one is *1 Henry VI*, where the scene-divisions only occur in Act 3 and part of Act 5, where they coincide with much other evidence of non-Shakespearian authorship: since some authors clearly did mark scene-divisions in their manuscripts, their presence in parts of *1 Henry VI* reinforces the evidence of multiple authorship, and does nothing to undermine the normal association of scene-divisions with scribal copy in Shakespeare's own work. This explanation cannot apply, however, to *Kinsmen*, where the scene-divisions occur in the shares of both Shakespeare and Fletcher; the scene-divisions are accordingly difficult to explain, unless the 1634 quarto was set from scribal copy (as Fredson Bowers and Paul Werstine have argued).[1] Likewise, in both *Richard III* and *King Lear* the presence of scene-divisions tilts the evidence in favour of scribal rather than holograph copy.

Finally, this evidence draws attention to an important aspect of the Folio collection: its extensive use of scribal copy. Paul Werstine has exposed the theoretical bias which encouraged modernist editors to believe that most early printed texts of Shakespeare's plays were printed from the author's own foul papers.[2] On purely pragmatic grounds, the *Textual Companion* had already argued that two of the 'good' quartos (*1 Henry IV* and *Othello*) were set from scribal copy, with scribal copy also possible for *Merchant*; *Kinsmen* may now be added to the scribal list. Likewise, the *Textual Companion* had concluded that thirteen plays (*Tempest, Two Gentlemen, Merry Wives, Measure, Twelfth Night, Winter's Tale, King John, 2 Henry IV, All is True, Coriolanus, Hamlet, Othello,* and *Cymbeline*) were set directly from literary transcripts, and that the same sort of manuscript might have been used as copy for another five (*As You Like It, Taming, Caesar, Macbeth,* and *Antony*). The evidence of

---

[1] *The Two Noble Kinsmen*, ed. Fredson Bowers, in *The Dramatic Works in the Beaumont and Fletcher Canon*, vii (1989), 147–68; Paul Werstine, 'On the Compositors of *The Two Noble Kinsmen*', in *Shakespeare, Fletcher, and 'The Two Noble Kinsmen'*, ed. Charles H. Frey (Columbia, 1989), 6–30.

[2] Paul Werstine, 'Narratives about Printed Shakespearean Texts: "Foul Papers" and "Bad Quartos"', *SQ* 41 (1990), 65–86; see also G. Taylor, *Reinventing Shakespeare* (1989), 278–83. Werstine's description of the Oxford edn. is inaccurate in certain respects: it is, for instance, simply wrong to say that in the Oxford edn. 'all the "good" quartos of Shakespeare's plays are said to have been printed *directly* from his "foul papers"' (p. 75 and n. 35), and it is at least misleading to associate my conclusions about the reporter of Q1 *Hamlet* with the inane speculations of Nosworthy (pp. 80–1), or to imply that the Oxford Shakespeare is programatically committed to Greg's account of a single actor's memory behind every 'bad' quarto.

scene-divisions puts *As You Like It* and *Macbeth* firmly in the 'literary transcript' category. In contrast to these fifteen to eighteen plays which were surely or possibly set from literary transcripts, only seven (*Comedy, All's Well, Henry V, Contention, Richard Duke of York, 1 Henry VI,* and *Timon*) appear to have been set from holograph copy, probably pre-scripts; to these might be added another two (*Taming* and *Antony,* if they were not set from transcripts). Moreover—although, in cases where the Folio text was set from an earlier quarto annotated by reference to a manuscript, it is more difficult to be sure of the nature of the manu-script—for *Richard II, 1 Henry IV, Richard III,* and *Lear* those manu-scripts, too, seem to have been literary transcripts. Holograph pre-script manuscripts, by contrast, were apparently never used for annotating early quartos. Thus, in collecting copy for the Folio collection literary tran-scripts were favoured over holograph pre-scripts by a margin of (at least) nineteen to nine, or (at most) twenty-two to seven.

Noticeably, there is not a single clear instance in the Folio of the direct use of a prompt-book as printer's copy. Prompt-books were certainly used as the source of variants for two texts set from annotated quartos (*Much Ado, Dream*), and almost certainly for another four such texts (*Love's Labour's Lost, Merchant, Titus,* and *Romeo*). But the collation of a prompt-book for occasional variants, mostly in stage directions, could of course be done by someone other than the printer, and it clearly differs from the direct use of a prompt-book by compositors. We might therefore draw two tentative conclusions. First, when we are faced with a choice between a literary transcript and a prompt-book as copy for a Folio text—as we are with *Caesar*—then it would be prudent to opt for a liter-ary transcript. Second, it appears that prompt-books were preferred when a quarto was to be lightly annotated (as in the six cases listed above), but literary transcripts were preferred when a quarto was to be heavily anno-tated (as in *Richard II, Richard III,* and *Lear*).

This pattern would suggest that the manuscript consulted in preparing copy for Folio *Troilus* might have been a literary transcript, rather than a prompt-book (as I had earlier suggested).[3] All the features which I had cited as evidence the manuscript was a prompt-book could be explained equally well by a literary transcript of the prompt-book; moreover, assuming that the manuscript was a literary transcript would remove the need to postulate an 'intermediate transcript' between the foul papers and the prompt-book. Since I doubt the existence of such intermediate tran-scripts,[4] and since *Troilus* was the only play in the canon in which we had

[3] G. Taylor, '*Troilus and Cressida*: Bibliography, Performance, and Interpretation', *SS* 15 (1982), 99–136.
[4] See my 'General Introduction' in *Textual Companion*, 12–14. I would now qualify my statement that, 'for most plays, probably only two manuscripts ever existed'; in the Shakespeare canon, certainly, a third MS of many plays—the 'literary transcript' from which most of the Folio texts were printed—clearly did exist. However, this fact does not

been forced to postulate one, it would obviously be more elegant and economical to get rid of the exception. Hence, I am now inclined to believe that the manuscript behind Folio *Troilus* was a non-authorial literary transcript of the prompt-book.

If both these deductions are correct, then the Folio editors used at least twenty-one, and possibly twenty-four, literary transcripts. When we add to these totals the three to four play quartos (and the *Sonnets*) set from such transcripts, it becomes clear that the bulk of Shakespeare's œuvre comes down to us in editions which reflect non-authorial literary transcripts. We thus find ourselves, *after* almost a century of the New Bibliography, in approximately the same position we were in *before* the New Bibliography, when Sir Sidney Lee argued that most of the First Folio was set from literary transcripts.[5] The long detour has been informative; thanks to Greg and his disciples, we know much more than Lee about the transmission of Shakespeare's texts, before and after their initial publication. But the New Bibliography's distrust of scripts, its search for the uncontaminated authorial pre-script, has in the end been defeated by the very evidence it taught us to look for.

weaken the argument against 'intermediate transcripts'. The later preparation of a special literary transcript, for a patron or for the publisher of the Folio, is quite different from the routine production of intermediate transcripts antecedent to the promptbook. There would, for instance, be no reason to supply scene-divisions in an intermediate transcript—and every reason *not* to do so.

[5] Sir Sidney Lee, *A Life of William Shakespeare* (London, 1916), 558–9 and n. 1.

APPENDIX I

The Printer's Copy for Folio *2 Henry IV*

The printer's copy for the Folio texts of *2 Henry IV, Hamlet*, and *Othello* has been a matter of acrimonious scholarly dispute for decades. In each case the Folio was either set from a manuscript or from a heavily annotated exemplar of a 'good' quarto text (Q *2 Henry IV*, Q2 or Q3 *Hamlet*, Q1 *Othello*); in each case the use of quarto copy has been defended primarily on the basis of certain positive links between the Quarto and Folio texts, and the acceptability of that hypothesis has depended upon a personal judgement about the degree of credence which should be afforded to such coincidences. But the extensive work of Charlton Hinman, T. H. Howard-Hill, and others in identifying the stints of Folio compositors has now made it possible to test such hypotheses in a more objective, quantifiable, reliable manner, which should resolve the dispute once and for all. Certainly, in the case of *Hamlet* and *Othello* the weight of bibliographical evidence for manuscript copy is now overwhelming. In itself this new evidence casts considerable doubt on the use of printed copy for Folio *2 Henry IV*: all three texts have, in the past, inevitably been lumped together, because the argument for quarto copy in each is almost identical. If such evidence has proven untrustworthy in the two other plays, few people should be inclined to trust it in this one—especially as *2 Henry IV* has always been the member of the triumvirate about which most doubt was expressed. Nevertheless, each text must be considered on its own merits, and the hypothesis of quarto copy in *2 Henry IV* must be objectively tested before it can be affirmed or rejected.

Folio *2 Henry IV* was set by two compositors: Compositor B at case y, and a second compositor at case x. This second workman was, when Alice Walker wrote, confidently identified as Compositor A; Charlton Hinman cast doubt upon this identification, and more recently I have suggested that a new compositor, 'J', was B's partner for both *Henry IV* texts. (See *Textual Companion*, 148.) However, the identification of the case x compositor in *Henry IV* may continue to be disputed, and for safety's sake it seems wisest not to commit ourselves yet to one identification or the other. We may, however, take it for granted that B's partner was *either* A or 'J'. Both of these figures (if they are distinct) set plays from known printed copy, and that other work from printed copy can be compared with their work on *2 Henry IV*.

B's partner in *2 Henry IV* set 136 pairs of round brackets; only 20 of these coincide with brackets in Q. If B's partner were setting from quarto copy, he must therefore have added 116 pairs of brackets, in setting a mere 11½ Folio pages. But in *1 Henry IV*, B's partner set only 11 brackets, of which 7 simply reproduce brackets already present in his printed copy: he therefore added only 4 pairs, in setting 11 Folio pages. Everyone agrees that the same man worked alongside B in both *Henry IV* plays; whether we identify this figure as 'J' or A, the discrepancy between the two plays could hardly be more remarkable:

1 Henry IV 4:11pp.   *2 Henry IV* 116:11½pp.

The same discrepancy exists between *2 Henry IV* and the universally acknowledged work of Compositor A. In *The Winter's Tale* A set 242 pairs of brackets in
16 pages; but the exceptional frequency of brackets in *The Winter's Tale*, in the
stints of both Folio compositors, almost certainly results from the fact that their
copy was a transcript by Ralph Crane, who strongly fancies this species of punctuation. The number of brackets in A's stints of *The Winter's Tale* thus apparently reflects the influence of manuscript copy, rather than a compositorial
preference. In all of A's other Folio work, he set only 112 pairs of brackets:

   Winter's Tale 242:16pp.   Nine Other Plays 112:104pp.

The discrepancy between *Winter's Tale* and the nine other plays on which
Compositor A worked makes it reasonably clear that the brackets in *Winter's
Tale* derive from his copy. Therefore, if Compositor A were B's partner in *2
Henry IV*, then the brackets in his stints must largely derive from his copy:

   2 Henry IV 136:11½pp.   Nine Other Plays 112:104pp.

The frequency of round brackets in Folio *2 Henry IV* constitutes exceptionally
strong evidence against the use of printed copy, whether B's partner was 'J' or A.
   The evidence of exclamations and hyphens in the case x pages amply reinforces
this conclusion. First, exclamations:

   2 Henry IV 7:11½pp.   *1 Henry IV* ('J') 1:11pp.   Comp. A 9:120pp.

The single exclamation in *1 Henry IV* has been reproduced from the compositor's
printed copy; in contrast, none of the seven in *2 Henry IV* can derive from the
Quarto. Compositor A actually omitted all six of the exclamations which he
encountered in his printed copy for *Richard II*. Neither 'J' nor A (if different) is
likely to have added the seven exclamations in the case x pages of *2 Henry IV*. As
for hyphens, in *1 Henry IV* B's partner added them to his copy at a rate of one
for every 172 words; in *Richard II* Compositor A added them to his copy at a
rate of one for every 213 words; in *2 Henry IV* B's partner, by contrast, added
them to Q at the rate of one for every 100 words. This evidence is more important than that of the added exclamations, for one might always argue that the use
of exclamations was based on contextual factors, especially as it only affects seven
individual pieces of punctuation in Folio *2 Henry IV*; but it would be hard to
argue that *2 Henry IV*'s language called for twice as many hyphens as *Richard II*
and *1 Henry IV*.
   Exceptional numbers of brackets and hyphens also occur in Compositor B's
stints of Folio *2 Henry IV*. Since Compositor B set pages in thirty-five of the
thirty-six Folio plays, we can be even more confident in comparing his practice in
2 Henry IV with his practice elsewhere. Again, only in *The Winter's Tale*, apparently set from a Crane transcript, does the frequency of hyphens exceed that in *2
Henry IV*:

   Winter's Tale 126:11pp.   *2 Henry IV* 127:16½pp.

B set 86 pages in eleven plays apparently set from printed copy (*Much Ado,
Love's Labour's Lost, Dream, Merchant, Richard II, 1 Henry IV, Richard III,
Titus, Romeo, Lear*, and *Troilus*); these eleven plays contrast strikingly with *2
Henry IV*:

   2 Henry IV 127:16½pp.   Eleven Other Plays 218:86pp.

In the plays from known printed copy B averages 2.6 brackets per page; in *2 Henry IV* he averages 7.7 per page. Nor can this discrepancy be due to differences in the quartos B was working from, as can be seen by a check of the number B added to the relevant quartos:

2 Henry IV 110:16½pp.   Eleven Other Plays 133:86pp.

No more than his partner at case x can Compositor B at case y be held responsible for the exceptional numbers of brackets in Folio *2 Henry IV*. They must derive from the copy; hence, that copy cannot have been the Quarto.

Hyphens in B's stints also tell against the use of printed copy, as may be seen by a comparison of the numbers he added to his quarto copy in *1 Henry IV* with the numbers he would have had to add to his alleged quarto copy in *2 Henry IV*:

1 Henry IV 46:12½pp.   *2 Henry IV* 98:16½pp.

The rate at which hyphens are added is almost doubled between the two plays, just as the rate at which brackets are added more than quadruples. Therefore Folio *2 Henry IV* cannot have been set from annotated quarto copy—unless *both* compositors drastically departed from their habits everywhere else, or unless *both* compositors are hitherto-unidentified workmen who worked on no other Folio play and who shared an exceptional affection for both brackets and hyphens. The first alternative can be confidently dismissed; the second is always theoretically possible, but in practice extraordinarily improbable. We can therefore be honourably confident that Folio *2 Henry IV* was set from manuscript copy.

APPENDIX II

'O' and 'Oh' in English Renaissance Dramatists

The purpose of this appendix is to provide documentation for two claims: that Shakespeare strongly preferred the spelling 'o' without 'h', and that Ralph Crane reproduced whichever spelling he found in his copy. Since we are interested only in the spelling variant, we have not indicated whether or not the word is capitalized.

Shakespeare

For most of the Shakespeare texts the figures for each spelling differentiate any instances of the word which occur in crowded lines, where justification may have affected the spelling; figures for these spellings are placed after the main count, in round brackets. It will be seen that the justification in fact makes no difference to the pattern, and for this reason we have not differentiated these examples in *Richard III*, *King Lear*, *Sonnets*, Quarto *Othello*, *Timon of Athens*, or Folio *Hamlet*; our figures for these texts are drawn from published sources which did not distinguish justified from 'unjustified' lines.[1] Identification of printers and compositors is based on the most recent investigations (as recorded in *Textual Companion*). Texts or parts of texts which depart from the author's apparent preference are marked by an asterisk. Texts are bracketed in Table II.1 when they appear to have been set from memorially reconstructed copy, and thus offer dubious evidence for Shakespeare's own spelling preferences (*Richard III*, *Pericles*), or because the attribution to Shakespeare is disputed (*More*).

Of certainly or potentially 'good' quartos printed in Shakespeare's lifetime, only two—*Titus* and *Richard II*—prefer 'oh'. *Richard II* may have been set from a transcript; certainly the copy for Q1 was very tidy. Jackson notes that 'The complete authenticity of *Titus* has been doubted' (*Attribution*, 215 n. 5), but this cannot explain the anomaly, since the Shakespearian 'O' spellings predominate in the very parts of the play most often questioned (1. 1 and 4. 1). However, since John Danter set no other substantive Shakespearian text, the anomaly might in this instance be compositorial. (Certainly, Jackson himself demonstrates that George Eld's 'Compositor A' preferred 'oh', a discovery which explains the distribution of the exceptionally high number of such spellings in the *Troilus* and *Sonnets* quartos—though in each Shakespeare's 'o' predominates overall.)[2] We will return to these two quartos below. In the mean time it should be noted that neither is necessarily good evidence of Shakespeare's practice as each could have been distorted either by scribe (*Richard II*) or compositor (*Titus*).

The anomaly in Quarto *Richard III* is also probably compositorial. The striking disparity between the two halves of the book makes it clear either that the two

---

[1] MacD. P. Jackson, 'Two Shakespeare Quartos: *Richard III* (1597) and *1 Henry IV* (1598)', *SB* 36 (1983), 176; id., 'Punctuation and the Compositors of Shakespeare's Sonnets, 1609', *The Library*, 5/30 (1975), 2–24; id., *Attribution*, 214–15; Taylor, 'Folio Compositors and Folio Copy: *King Lear* and Its Context', *PBSA* 79 (1985), 45–6.

[2] 'Punctuation' (see n. 1) *passim*.

TABLE II.1. *Shakespeare good quartos*

Shakespeare good quartos	O	Oh	Printer	Compositors
Venus (1593)	15	10	Field	?
Lucrece (1594)	41(+2)	2	Field	?
*Titus (1594)	19(+1)	39(+5)	Danter	?
*Richard II (1597)	8	26(+2)	Simmes	A, S
[*Richard III* (1597)]			Simmes/Short	A, N, O
*Sheets A–G	26	29	Simmes	A
Sheets H–M	31	0	Short	N, O
LLL (1598)	60(+18)	2	White	(3)
1 Henry IV (1598)	27(+20)	5	Short	X, Y
Romeo (1599)	122(+13)	13(+3)	Creede	A, B
Dream (1600)	52(+8)	1(+2)	Bradock	(1)
Merchant (1600)	29(+4)	0	Roberts	X, Y
2 Henry IV (1600)	28(+16)	1	Simmes	A
Ado (1600)	24(+22)	0	Simmes	A
Hamlet (1604)	89(+11)	3(+2)	Roberts	X, Y
Lear (1608)	74	3	Okes	B, C
[*Pericles* (1609)]	21(+16)	5(+4)	Creede/White	x, y, z
Troilus (1609)	57(+8)	17(+6)	Eld	A, B
Eld A	36	17(+6)		
Eld B	29	0		
Sonnets (1609)	43	22	Eld	A, B
*Eld A	1	19		
Eld B	42	3		
Othello (1622)	133	6	Okes	(1)
Kinsmen (1634)	50(+3)	12(+1)	Cotes	(1)
[*More*, Hand D]	1	0	[MS]	

printers were working from different kinds of copy, or that one shop altered the preference of its copy. The character of the substantive readings in the two sections of the book does not suggest a change in the nature of printer's copy. It thus seems likely that the disparity in the spellings results from compositorial interference in one shop or the other. Three possibilities exist: (1) Short's compositors preferred 'o'; or (2) Simmes's Compositor A changed his preference between 'oh' in *Richard III* and *Richard II* (both 1597) and 'o' in *Much Ado* and *2 Henry IV* (both 1600); or (3) more than one compositor set Simmes's share of *Richard III*. If we accept the first of these explanations, the preference for 'o' in Short's quarto of *1 Henry IV* might be compositorial rather than authorial; but it is by no means clear that the same compositors worked on both quartos. If we accept the second explanation, the disparity in *Richard II* might be compositorial; but that disparity affects the stints of both Simmes's compositors. The third explanation is undoubtedly the simplest, particularly because the incidence of 'o' and 'oh' spellings in Simmes's portion of the book clearly falls into an alternating pattern; Jackson demonstrates that 'the probability is less than one in a thousand of such clustering occurring purely by chance'.[3] Jackson himself suggests that the fluctuation derives from the copy; but this would imply either a change in the nature of the copy for Short's compositors, or that at least *two* (and perhaps *four*)

[3] 'Two Shakespeare Quartos' (see n. 1), 176.

different compositors in Short's shop had an overwhelming preference for 'o'. A confident resolution of this problem must await further study of Simmes's share of *Richard III*, though we incline to the belief that two compositors were involved, one with a strong preference for 'oh'. In any case, most scholars believe (as do we) that the 1597 quarto derives from memorial reconstruction, and hence provides dubious evidence of Shakespeare's own spelling preferences.

Making appropriate allowances for compositorial interference, Shakespeare's good quartos show an overwhelming preference for the spelling 'o'. If we exclude the portions of *Troilus* and the *Sonnets* set by Eld's Compositor A, that preference is manifest in sixteen of the eighteen good quartos; these sixteen were produced by ten different printers, set by at least nineteen different compositors, over a period of forty-one years. The consistency of this pattern can hardly be disputed, or dismissed as a coincidence. Nevertheless, two troubling exceptions remain: *Richard II* and *Titus*. An explanation may be provided by an examination of First Folio texts apparently set from manuscript copy (see Table II.2).

Clearly, the Folio contains more anomalies than the good quartos—just as it

TABLE II. 2. *First Folio texts apparently set from manuscript copy*

Shakespeare Folio	O	Oh	Compositors	Copy
Tempest	35(+9)	8(+1)	B, C, F	Crane
*Two Gentlemen	9(+3)	22(+11)	C, F	Crane
Wives	13(+11)	5(+4)	B, C, F	Crane
*Measure	3(+4)	47(+9)	B, C, D, F	Crane
Winter's Tale	31(+1)	20(+7)	A, B	Crane
All's Well	17(+14)	4(+2)	B, C, D	foul papers
Henry V	33(+15)	2	A, B	foul papers
Timon				foul papers
Shakespeare	10	0	B, E	
*Middleton	10	13	B, E	
*Comedy	(4)	18(+7)	B, C, D	foul papers
*Shrew	3(+10)	27(+20)	B, C, D	scribal(?)
Twelfth Night	32(+11)	6(+3)	B	scribal
As You Like It	16(+23)	10(+2)	B, C, D	scribal
John				(?)
1–1893	40(+2)	7	B, C	
*1941–2729	3	17(+2)	B, C	
2 Henry IV	24(+11)	6(+4)	B, J	scribal
*1 Henry VI	18(+2)	18(+1)	A, B	scribal (?)
*2 Henry VI	17(+9)	16(+2)	A, B	fair copy
*3 Henry VI	19	22(+2)	A, B	scribal
All is True	25(+3)	5	B, I	scribal
*Coriolanus	8(+4)	32(+8)	A, B	fair copy
Caesar	67(+2)	1	A, B	scribal
Macbeth	16(+1)	6(+1)	A, B	scribal
*Hamlet	39	69	B, E, I	scribal
*Othello	32(+20)	90(+27)	B, E	scribal
*Antony	12(+1)	76(+7)	B, E	fair copy
Cymbeline			B, E	(Crane?)
1. 1–2. 4	15(+2)	(1)		
*2. 5–end	4(+1)	55(+4)		

clearly contains fewer texts set from authorial copy. For convenience, we have divided the plays into those set from Crane transcripts, those set from foul papers, and others. Excluding *Measure for Measure*, only one Crane transcript (*Two Gentlemen*) prefers 'oh'; what Crane was copying in that instance cannot be determined. Of the foul-paper texts, 'o' is strongly preferred in *All's Well, Henry V*, and the portion of *Timon* assigned to Shakespeare by recent scholarship: taken together, these two-and-a-half plays contain 89 examples of 'o' to only 8 of 'oh'.[4] Even if we include the other Folio text probably set from foul papers, *Comedy*, the proportion would be 93 to 33. However, *Comedy* does appear to represent an exception, like the quartos of *Titus* and *Richard II*; moreover, since it was set by the same three compositors who set *All's Well*, and who in Folio reprints almost invariably reproduced copy, the discrepancy cannot be the result of compositorial interference.[5]

The simplest explanation for all or at least all but one of these discrepancies, in quartos and Folio alike, is chronological. Most scholars agree that Shakespeare's first eight plays were *Titus*, the three parts of *Henry VI, Richard III, Taming, Comedy*, and *Two Gentlemen*. For *Richard III* no reliable evidence exists: the Quarto appears to be memorial in origin, and the Folio was printed from annotated quarto copy. Every one of the remaining seven prefers 'oh', or uses both spellings indifferently: for the seven as a whole the figures are 85 'o', 162 'oh'. These seven plays include one printed by Danter in 1594, six set in Jaggard's shop in 1622–3 by five different compositors, one set from a Crane transcript, two set from foul papers, and four thought to have been set from different kinds of copy (*Shrew, Henry VI*). The similarity of these seven texts in their unusual treatment of 'o' and 'oh' cannot result from any accident of transmission: the only thing the plays have in common is their date of composition. *Venus and Adonis*, which probably follows, tolerates 'oh' (10 of 25 occurrences); but *The Rape of Lucrece* firmly comes down on the side of 'o' (43 of 45 occurrences). We find it difficult to avoid the conclusion that Shakespeare's habitual spelling of this word changed, perhaps consciously, *c*.1593. And this conclusion may in turn explain the only remaining anomaly in the quarto evidence, *Richard II*. Although most scholars now date *Richard II c*.1595, Eliot Slater's vocabulary evidence links it very firmly to the first tetralogy, rather than the second. Its preference for 'oh' might therefore be due to early composition, or to the use of scribal copy by the printers, or to compositorial preference (if there was a change in the preference of Simmes's

---

[4] Harold Oliver, in the new Arden edn. (London, 1959), claimed that *Timon* was set in part from a Crane transcript (pp. xvi–xxii). For a refutation of this hypothesis, see T. H. Howard-Hill, 'Ralph Crane's Parentheses', *N. & Q.* 210 (1965), 339, and Holdsworth, 176–8. One might add that the single page set by Compositor E (gg3ᵛ), though in one of Oliver's 'Crane' sections, in fact contains only two commonplace hyphenations, and all its apostrophes might be E's own. E was the most conservative of Folio compositors, and reproduced copy punctuation with unusual fidelity. Oliver claimed that Crane's 'fondness for hyphens' could be found in *Timon*, but we count only 19 hyphens in Oliver's 'Crane' sections (1300 Folio ll.), as against 23 in the rest of the text (1307 Folio ll.): i.e. the 'Crane' sections have less than the rest, and the play as a whole only 1 for every 457 words. The lowest frequency of hyphenation in any known or suspected Crane text is 1 for every 243 words—almost double what it is in *Timon*. We can be confident that the copy for *Timon* bore no resemblance to a Crane transcript, and was either foul pages or the work of an unidentified scribe.

[5] On compositorial fidelity to copy spelling, see Ch. 3, p. 117, and n. 33.

Appendix II

Compositor A between 1597 and 1600). Whichever explanation we accept, *Richard II* hardly constitutes good evidence of Shakespeare's spelling preference at any time after *c.*1593.

If we exclude Shakespeare's eight earliest plays (and *Measure*), the Folio contains only six anomalies: *Hamlet, Othello, Coriolanus, Antony*, the last half of *King John*, and *Cymbeline*. Since *Othello, Antony*, and *Cymbeline* are the last three plays in the Folio, all set by Compositors B and E, compositorial interference cannot be ruled out; but it would require us to assume that both compositors simultaneously developed a very sudden preference for 'oh', which one of them then abandoned when he set *Troilus*. Such a scenario is implausible. In any case, scholars have widely recognized that the manuscripts consulted for Folio *Othello* and *Cymbeline* (and *Hamlet*) were scribal; the influence of an unknown scribe's spelling preference thus provides an obvious and acceptable explanation of the predominance of 'oh' in these texts.

In *King John*, the discrepancy between the beginning of the play and the last third can hardly be a coincidence. Alice Walker once conjectured that the copy for *King John* may have been composite, a conjecture given some further support by Greg;[6] Philip Williams, in 1956, pointed to the variant 'oh' spellings as 'rather convincing' evidence for that hypothesis.[7] But all three scholars divided the play at the end of Act 3, whereas in fact the change of spelling comes near the end of 4. 2. The shift cannot be compositorial, since both B and C set pages in both parts of the text, and both routinely followed copy elsewhere; nor can one easily believe that Shakespeare himself drastically revised his preference in the middle of a scene. All of the confusions pointing to foul papers occur in the earlier 'O' section of the play. The two sections are also differentiated by many other spelling variants, as Table II.3 makes clear.

In all the examples listed, a single compositor spelt the same word differently in the two parts of the text. Though such words must constitute the primary evidence for a change in copy, a number of other words reinforce that conclusion. Both compositors prefer *againe*, setting it 29 times in *King John* alone; but both use *again* once, each in the earlier section (1206, 1720). Both prefer *all* (90 occurrences); but Compositor C in the early section twice used *al* (1095, 1379)—the only occasions in the Folio when he set it in unjustified lines. C set *Ayery* at 1286, in his only encounter with the word; B set *Ayerie* at 2405, although elsewhere he preferred the -*y* form of the suffix generally and the spelling *Ayery* in particular. Both compositors prefer *eye(s)* (44 occurrences); all seven uses of *eie(s)*, set by both compositors, come in the first section (29, 471, 521, 812, 819, 821, 943). Both prefer *keepe* (16 times); each uses *keep* once, both in the later section (2006, 2172), but both lines are justified. In the first section B spells *pittie* (794, 824) and *warme* (1517); in the second section C spells *pitty* (2275) and *warm* (2310). Correspondingly, C has *nought* (1496) and *strait* (449) in the first section where B in the second sets *naught* (2728) and *straight* (2020, 2456, 2650, 2689). Both com-

---

[6] W. W. Greg, *The Editorial Problem in Shakespeare* (Oxford, 1942; rev. 1951), 143 n. 1: he here records Alice Walker's suggestion and comments on it, concluding 'But I find it difficult to envisage a composite manuscript actually made up partly of foul papers and partly of a section of the prompt-book'. Greg does not even mention the conjecture in his later discussion of *John*, in *First Folio*, 248–55.

[7] 'New Approaches to Textual Problems in Shakespeare', *SB* 8 (1956), 6.

TABLE II.3. *Spelling variants in* King John

1–1893	1941–2729	Compositor responsible in both sections
affraid (1594)	afraide (2001)	B
allegeance (1102)	allegiance (2177)	C
alreadie (1548)	already (2495, 2699)	B
amitie (857)	amity (2481)	B
confirm (673)	confirme (2072)	B
contrarie (931)	contrary (1923)	B
controle (22)	controll (2333)	C
cosen (1858, 1880)	cozen (2661)	B
den (195)	denne (2225)	C
diuel (888)	diuell (2097, 2463)	B
fairer (742)	fayrer (1983)	B
flye (1897)	fly (2471); flie (2563)	B
furie (278)	fury (2381)	C
ilanders (318)	islanders (2356); isle (2276)	C
line (666)	lyne (2022)	B
neither (645)	neyther (2419)	B
ready (517)	readie (2425)	B
saide (541)	said (2542)	B
souldier(s) (667, 887, 1051)	soldier (2568)	B
spread (301)	spred (2241)	C
steppes (1774)	steps (2513)	B
turne (704, 717)	turn (2413)	B

positors strongly prefer *it* (170 occurences); Compositor C twice in the early section—and nowhere else in his work—sets *yt* (461, 463).

It seems reasonably clear, therefore, that *King John* was set either from a scribal transcript, in which a second scribe took over towards the end of 4. 2, or from a composite manuscript, with foul papers at the beginning of the play and a transcript at the end. (The first hypothesis seems to us intrinsically likelier.) In any case, no one will want to attribute the disparity in 'oh' spellings here to Shakespeare; nor, even if one did so, would *King John* constitute a serious anomaly, for taken as a whole the play prefers 'o' (45:26).

The resemblance between *King John* and *Cymbeline* is striking. E. A. J. Honigmann first noticed the pattern of spellings in the latter, attributing it—reasonably enough—to the presence of two different scribes.[8] In 1967, when Honigmann wrote, Compositor E's participation in the setting of *Cymbeline* had not been discovered;[9] that discovery makes Honigmann's conclusion all the more certain, for both compositors set text in both parts of the play. Moreover, the 'oh' section of *Cymbeline* resembles the 'oh' section in *King John* in at least one striking respect: aside from the five Comedies apparently set from Crane transcripts, these are the only Folio texts which contain round brackets in stage direc-

---

[8] E. A. J. Honigmann, 'On the Indifferent and One-Way Variants in Shakespeare', *The Library*, 5/30 (1967), 189–204.

[9] E's presence in *Cymbeline* was first established by T. H. Howard-Hill in two privately circulated monographs (1976, 1977), summarized in 'New Light on Compositor E of the Shakespeare First Folio', *The Library*, 6/2 (1980), 156–78.

tions: at *King John* 2250 (set by Compositor C) and *Cymbeline* 3065, 3067, 3069 (set by Compositor B). Few of the words which most clearly differentiate the two sections of *King John* appear more than once in the stints of one compositor in *Cymbeline*, and of those that do most are mixed in their spellings and so dubious evidence of copy influence rather than compositorial preference. However, the later half of *Cymbeline* does contain, all in Compositor B's stints, *fayrer* (2949), *fury* (1446, 3258), *isle* (1397), *keep* (2528, in a tightly justified line), and *steps* (2523). For none of these words does the alternative spelling occur in the play at all, but it may nevertheless be significant that all five characterize the second half of *King John*.

For the two sections of *Cymbeline* we have found less corroborative evidence of a division in the copy. To begin with, Compositor E set only 633 lines in *Cymbeline*, of which only 123 occur in the second section; not surprisingly, E's work contains no clear examples of words (except 'o'/'oh') which occur in both sections with consistently different spellings. As a result, all our corroborative evidence of a division in the copy comes from the stints of one compositor (B), and although *Cymbeline* is almost 1100 lines longer than *King John*, it yields a much smaller crop of reliable data (see Table II.4; lines where justification might have affected the spelling are marked with an asterisk). Of these discriminants, some are more problematic than they appear. B overwhelmingly prefers *Britaine* and *do*; the variants in this list represent his only uses of an alternative. The apparent discrepancy between spellings of *brief* and *courtesy* is weakened by contrasting spellings for related words: *briefely* (3374) and *discourtesie* (1070). If we removed these words, only thirteen spellings would remain (beyond 'o'/'oh' itself). In part, this may be due to the fact that *Cymbeline*, unlike *King John*, contains a significant amount of prose: our lists for both plays exclude all cases where the apparent difference between the two parts of the text might be the result of compositorial justification in a crowded line of type.

TABLE II.4. *Spelling variants in* Cymbeline

1–1336	1337–3819
breast (1311)	brest (3145, 3253*)
Breedes (51)	breeds (2102, 2288)
briefe (120)	breefe (1856, 3444, 3480)
Brittaine (726)	Britain (1380)
Charitie (1084)	charity (2462, 3205*)
Curtesie (100)	courtesie (2825)
dogs (535)	dogges (3505, 3542)
doe (1243)	doo (2991)
embrace (471*);	imbrace (1868)
embracements (137)	
intreat (801)	entreate (3348); entreats (1770)
failing (28)	fayling (3317)
iniury (1243)	iniurie (1804)
lippes (717, 758)	lips (3301, 3586)
Prime-Roses (585)	Primrose (2531)
Trunke (819, 836)	truncke (2680)
Tyrant (100)	Tirants (2584)
weigh'd (329*)	waigh (3059); waight (2265); waights (1997)

As in *King John*, a number of other words may also, less certainly, suggest a division of copy. Compositor E spells *aloud* (621), *memorie* (951), *walls* (899), and *wrack* (692); B *alowd* (3406), *memory* (1768, 1952), *walles* (1723), and *wracke* (2694). In Act 1 B consistently prefers the speech prefix *Cor.*; in Act 5, he sets *Corn.* six times and *Cor.* only twice (3288, 3295). In the first section B and E both spell *Clotten* (226, 839, 961); in the second B prefers *Cloten*, setting it twenty-four times, to only three of *Clotten*. Before 1336, the prefix *Pis.* occurs only once, set by Compositor E; *Pisa.* occurs thirteen times, set by both compositors. After 1336, *Pis.* strongly predominates (32:11).

Although the corroborative evidence for mixed copy in *Cymbeline* is less compelling than in *King John*, it seems clear that the abrupt change of preference to the spelling 'oh' cannot be compositorial.[10] The first section of *Cymbeline* runs from zz3 to near the end of aaa2. Compositors B and E finished work on the zz quire before beginning the aaa quire; but in the latter they set pages aaa3^v, aaa4, aaa3, aaa4^v, aaa2^v, and aaa5 *before* B set aaa2; and thereafter they alternated between pages before the apparent division of copy (aaa2, 1^v, and 1) and pages after it (aaa5^v, 6, and 6^v). Both compositors therefore began consistently setting 'o', then switched to 'oh', back to 'o', for half a quire alternated between 'o' and 'oh', then consistently set 'oh'. The change of spellings in *King John* straddles a similar pattern of composition, for the break occurs in the middle of b2^v: compositors B and C set some late 'oh' pages before and some early 'o' pages after B set this pivotal scene. Even without the clear evidence that the three compositors who set these two plays almost invariably reproduced the copy spelling of this word, the sequence of setting in both plays would make it undeniably apparent that the change in spelling reflects a change somewhere in the middle of a manuscript rather than midway in a sequence of compositorial setting. In *King John* the half of that manuscript which *might* have been set from authorial copy (1–1893) constantly prefers the 'o' spelling. In *Cymbeline*, no one has ever doubted that the entirety of the text was set from scribal copy: the remarkable number of round brackets and apostrophes would, in itself, make that reasonably clear. *Cymbeline* was therefore set from a scribal manuscript prepared by two different scribes, or prepared by one scribe who abruptly changed his spelling from *o* to *oh* half-way through, or by one scribe faithfully copying a manuscript which itself abruptly changed its spelling half-way through. Only the third of these explanations would cast any tiny doubt on Shakespeare's personal preference for 'o'—*if* we could be sure that the scribe was copying Shakespeare's own papers. Therefore, although the nature of the Folio copy for *Cymbeline* remains rather more problematic than that for *King John*, the problems do not affect the apparent reliability of the spelling 'oh' as a symptom of scribal rather than authorial copy.

Philip Williams also believed that *Coriolanus* and *Antony* were set from transcripts; unfortunately, he never published the evidence for this conclusion.[11] Given his use of the 'oh' spellings in his analysis of *King John*, we suspect he may

---

[10] For the sequence of printing described here, see Charlton Hinman, *The Printing and Proof-Reading of the First Folio of Shakespeare*, 2 vols. (Oxford, 1963), II, 514–18; an updated version of the same table is in *Textual Companion*, 148–52.

[11] For Williams's conclusions, see Fredson Bowers, *On Editing Shakespeare* (Charlottesville, 1966), p. 193.

have made use of the very evidence we are considering here. A detailed consideration of the copy for *Antony* and *Coriolanus* would be inappropriate here, but two
facts may be pertinent. *Coriolanus* begins the Tragedies section—a position of
prominence, which we might expect Jaggard to fill with a text set from a manuscript of unusual cleanness and literary polish (like *The Tempest*) rather than one
set from messy authorial papers. Secondly, both *Coriolanus* and *Antony* have been
widely recognized as texts which share a number of unique features, the most
remarkable being the literary character of their stage directions; both contain an
exceptional amount of mislineation, which can hardly be compositorial in origin.[12] Such considerations cannot, in themselves, prove that *Coriolanus* and
Antony were set from scribal copy; but one may at least claim that nothing in
either text rules that hypothesis out, while a number of features (discussed in
greater detail in *Textual Companion*) would appear to support it.

In short, if we exclude Shakespeare's earliest plays, and plays which must
(*Hamlet*, *Othello*, the last half of *Cymbeline*, the last third of *King John*) or very
plausibly may (*Coriolanus*, *Antony*) have been set from transcripts prepared by
unknown scribes who preferred 'oh', then all Shakespeare's works—except
Measure for Measure—prefer 'o'. If we take all of these texts as a group (discounting Compositor A's share of *Troilus* and the *Sonnets*, and Middleton's share
of *Timon*), the preference for 'o' is over 7:1. Ralph Crane demonstrably followed
copy in spelling this word; so did the Folio compositors who set *Measure*. Yet
Measure contains a greater preponderance of 'oh' spellings than any other substantive text in the Shakespeare canon. On the basis of the evidence here assembled, it seems reasonably clear that the discrepancy can only be accounted for by
assuming that Crane's own copy was either a play of Shakespeare's written in or
before 1593–4, or a scribal transcript. Every species of internal evidence invalidates the first of these propositions; only the second can be seriously entertained.

This conclusion—that Crane was copying a copy—could only be weakened by
demonstrating (*a*) that *Richard II*, *Coriolanus*, and *Antony* could not have been
set from transcripts, (*b*) that the accepted compositor attributions in *Troilus* and
Sonnets are incorrect, (*c*) that Middleton had no hand in the writing of *Timon*, (*d*)
that the preferences of Simmes A did not change between 1597 and 1600, and (*e*)
that *Richard II* could not have been written as early as 1594. But even if all of
this could be done, the fact would still remain that all but two of Shakespeare's
works written after 1595, and printed from what may have been authorial copy,
prefer 'o'; the two exceptions (*Coriolanus* and *Antony*) are both later than
Measure, strikingly different from *Measure* in the character of the text they reproduce, and much more tolerant than *Measure* of 'o' spellings. Any attempt to
claim that the preponderance of 'oh' spellings in *Measure* reflects Shakespeare's
foul papers must therefore hypothesize that *Measure* is, in its treatment of this
exclamation, unique.

Other Dramatists and Ralph Crane

Most of the figures in Table II.5 create no difficulties of interpretation.
Middleton's autograph *Game at Chess* provides strong evidence of his own prefer-

---

[12] Paul Werstine, 'Line Division in Shakespeare's Dramatic Verse: An Editorial Problem',
Analytical and Enumerative Bibliography 8 (1984), 73–125.

TABLE II.5. *Use of 'Oh' and 'O' by other dramatists and Crane*

	Play	Text	O	Oh
Middleton	Game at Chess	autograph	1	36
	Game at Chess	Crane (3 mss.)	2	96
	Witch	Crane	3	39
	Nice Valour	1647	1	59
	*Second Maiden's Tragedy	scribe	54	5
Massinger	Believe As You List	autograph	18	0
Fletcher	Mad Lover	1647	57	2
	Loyal Subject	1647	25	4
	Women Pleased	1647	46	1
	Humorous Lieutenant	1647	45	9
	*Demetrius and Enanthe	Crane	21	34
	Faithful Shepherdess	Q (1609?)	28	10
	*Island Princess	1647	10	20
	Bonduca	Knight	57	5
Field	Weathercock	1612	0	68
		1647	55	14
	Amends	1618	0	59
Tourneur	Atheist's Tragedy	1611	61	1
Fletcher/Massinger	Barnavelt	Crane	37	6
⎰ Massinger	Fatal Dowry	1632	10	5
⎱ Field	Fatal Dowry	1632	4	15
⎰ Fletcher, Massinger	Queen of Corinth	1647	17	1
⎱ Field	Queen of Corinth	1647	1	20
⎰ *Fletcher, Massinger	Knight of Malta	1647	13	20
⎱ Field	Knight of Malta	1647	1	15
⎧ Fletcher, Massinger, Tourneur	Honest Man's Fortune	Knight	9	0
⎨ Field	Honest Man's Fortune	Knight	1	18
⎩ 4. 2	Honest Man's Fortune	Knight	13	0
⎰ Fletcher	Four Plays	1647	42	15
⎱ *Field	Four Plays	1647	53	8

ence; Crane's transcripts reproduce this. Hoy, Lake, and Jackson all agree that the extant text of *The Nice Valour* must be all, or virtually all, Middleton's work; the consistent preponderance of 'oh' tends to confirm this. In the case of *The Second Maiden's Tragedy*, the spelling may be interpreted as evidence against Middleton's authorship, or as evidence that the unknown scribe there employed by the King's Men strongly preferred 'o'. In terms of the Middleton preference established here, the division in spelling in the two parts of *Timon* does (as Jackson pointed out) reinforce Middleton's claim to a share of that play.

Massinger's preference for 'o' seems equally clear. For Fletcher we are dependent upon printed or scribal texts, but only two anomalies disturb the pattern of 'o' preferences. The preponderance of 'oh' in *Demetrius and Enanthe* almost certainly does not reflect Fletcher's own preference, as the distribution of the spellings makes clear. In 3. 5 and 4. 2–end the 'oh':'o' ratio is 29:0, whilst in 1. 1–3. 4 and 4. 1 the ratio is 5:21. This pattern strongly suggests that two hands (scribal or authorial) contributed to the manuscript from which Crane was copying. Likewise, though George Walton Williams expresses no opinion about the printer's copy for *The Island Princess*, nothing in the text itself would contradict the hypothesis of scribal copy.

These conclusions are borne out by an examination of several collaborative plays. Fletcher and Massinger's shares of *The Fatal Dowry*, *Barnavelt*, *The Queen of Corinth*, *The Honest Man's Fortune*, and *Four Plays in One* all show the expected preference for 'o'.[13] The distribution of spellings in *The Knight of Malta* suggests that some modification of the accepted division of authorship may be necessary. Acts 1 and 5, usually attributed to Field, reflect his preferences clearly enough; in Acts 2, 3, and 4, by contrast—if we except two scenes (2. 2, 4. 2), where the 'oh':'o' ratio is 15:3—that ratio is 5:12. However, no change of attribution may be necessary: 14 of the occurrences of 'oh' outside Field's acknowledged scenes occur in doublets ('Oh, oh'), and it seems possible that a scribe or author may have spelt the word differently in these circumstances. (None of Field's examples here is in doublets.) If we disregard these doublets, the proportion of 'oh':'o' in the middle acts is 6:12. The proportion of 'oh' is still rather high for Fletcher and Massinger, and scribal interference must be suspected. Likewise, if Field was Fletcher's collaborator in *Four Plays in One* (as linguistic, metrical, and stylistic evidence all suggest), then the Folio must have been set from scribal copy.

Although the evidence in Table II.5 suggests that the spelling of the exclamation 'o' or 'oh' may be of further value in determining the authorship of certain plays, or the nature of an underlying manuscript, our primary purpose in collecting it has been to establish the practice of Ralph Crane. Crane's transcripts of Middleton and Massinger reproduce the preference already demonstrated by the autograph and printed texts of both dramatists. In Fletcher's case, the absence of any extensive autograph material forces us to rely upon secondary evidence, but 'o' is clearly preferred in the bulk of the plays (and parts of plays) examined. Only *The Island Princess* and *The Knight of Malta* are potential exceptions; and even if we attribute these exceptions to Fletcher rather than a scribe, we would still be forced to conclude that Fletcher *usually* preferred 'o'. In this context, Crane's practice in *Barnavelt* and the first half of *Demetrius and Enanthe* accords with the known or probable preferences of the authors; only in the second half of *Demetrius* does Crane apparently depart from that pattern of passivity, and in the light of his other work (and of the distribution of spellings in *Demetrius* itself) it seems most probable that the discrepancy originates in Crane's source, rather than Crane himself.

John Webster's preferred spelling is difficult to determine. As with Fletcher, we must rely entirely on printed texts; in Webster's case few such texts are available for analysis. The 'oh':'o' ratio is 10:113 for *White Devil* (1612), 72:13 for *Duchess of Malfi* (1623), 47:26 for *Devil's Law Case* (1623), and 40:14 for *Anything for a Quiet Life* (1662). *White Devil* looks like the odd man out; but it was apparently printed by two different compositors from papers which 'might well have been in [Webster's] handwriting'.[14] *Devil's Law Case* may also have been set from an authorial fair copy. *Anything* is attributed on its title-page entirely to Middleton, but most scholars since 1921 have accepted Sykes's suggestion that Webster had a major hand in the play; Jackson and Lake strongly confirm this conjecture,

---

[13] We have accepted Jackson's division of stints in *The Honest Man's Fortune*: see *Studies in Attribution: Middleton and Shakespeare* (Salzburg, 1989), pp. 216–20.

[14] John Webster, *The White Devil*, ed. John Russell Brown (Manchester, 1966), pp. lxvii–lxviii.

though there are areas of the play where confidence of attribution is impossible. Both assign 1. 1, 2. 1, and 4. 1 to Webster; for these scenes the 'oh':'o' figures are 14:8, which is close to the pattern in *Duchess*. For the first two acts (mostly by Webster) the figures are 9:11; by contrast, for the last three (mostly by Middleton), they are 31:3. Divided or undivided, *Anything* provides further confirmation of Middleton's preference for 'oh'; the distribution of spellings also provides some slight confirmation of another hand in the play.

On the basis of *Devil's Law Case* and *Anything* we might conjecture that Webster preferred 'oh', or at least was indifferent; *White Devil* might be anomalous because of compositorial interference, or because the printer's fair copy was not in Webster's hand, or because Webster's preference changed. *Duchess of Malfi* apparently confirms the preference for 'oh'. But the copy for *Duchess* was probably prepared by Crane; hence it could be argued that Crane imposed his own 'oh' preference on the text. Because two compositors set the quarto, compositorial interference seems relatively unlikely (as in *White Devil*); hence the preference for 'oh' probably reflects Crane's manuscript, and we can only conjecture whether Crane's manuscript itself reflected its copy. *Devil's Law Case* and—to a much less reliable extent—*Anything for a Quiet Life* would suggest that Webster's own manuscript preferred 'oh'; *White Devil* would suggest otherwise. But even if we could be sure that *White Devil* reflected Webster's consistent practice better than the other quartos, the 'oh' preference in *Malfi* might still derive from Crane's copy rather than Crane himself, for Crane may well have been copying a prompt-book. John Russell Brown's thorough consideration of the evidence leaves the matter unresolved. Only by assuming both that Crane's copy was autograph, and that *White Devil* presents the most accurate picture of Webster's own preference, could we take *Malfi* as evidence for Crane's imposition of a personal preference for 'oh'. Neither assumption is, in the present state of our ignorance, warranted; nor, to us, does either seem the most probable explanation of the relevant facts. But even if we make these assumptions, Crane's alleged interference in *Malfi* (47 'oh': 26 'o') comes nowhere near the degree of interference which would need to be conjectured in *Measure* (56:7).

APPENDIX III

The Date and Authorship of *Rollo, Duke of Normandy*

Massinger's most recent editors have described *Rollo* as an 'impossible problem'.[1] Difficult it may be, but the impression of insurmountable perplexity has been largely created by the fragmentation of recent scholarship. Since the Second World War there have been four major investigations of the play: John D. Jump's critical edition (Liverpool, 1948), which in its conclusions about authorship drew heavily upon material in his unpublished MA thesis (Liverpool, 1936); another unpublished dissertation, Bertha Hensman's 'John Fletcher's *The Bloody Brother; or Rollo, Duke of Normandy*' (Chicago, 1947); G. E. Bentley's account in *The Jacobean and Caroline Stage* (Oxford), iii (1956), 401–7; and Cyrus Hoy's 'The Shares of Fletcher and his Collaborators in the Beaumont and Fletcher Canon (VI)', *Studies in Bibliography*, 14 (1961), 45–67. Jump mentions in his Preface that, after his edition had gone to press, he received a 'long letter' from Hensman, and as a result he has inserted a few references to her conclusions in his Introduction; yet he had clearly not seen the thesis itself, and makes no attempt to assimilate or refute its evidence. Hensman, likewise, makes no reference to Jump's thesis (or, of course, his edition). Bentley, who had supervised Hensman's thesis, endorses its conclusions without reservation, yet gives only the skimpiest account of her evidence; nor had he seen Jump's unpublished thesis. None of these scholars, naturally, could have taken account of Hoy's article; Hoy himself takes no account of Hensman or Bentley. Hensman published in 1974 a two-volume study of *The Shares of Fletcher, Field and Massinger in Twelve Plays of the Beaumont and Fletcher Canon* (Salzburg); one chapter of this monograph summarizes the argument of her 1947 thesis, with only minor modifications to her conclusions about the authorship of parts of three scenes (ii. 239–79). But although she there makes offhanded reference to Hoy, she makes no attempt to deal with the implications of his evidence. The Oxford Massinger (1976) refers only to Hoy and Bentley. In short, no modern scholar seems to have collected or assessed all the evidence accumulated in these separate investigations.

For convenience one may distinguish three distinct problems (though in fact they are interrelated). When was the play originally written? Was it revised? Who wrote it?

Three very different dates of composition have, at various times, been proposed. The earliest of these, 1613–15, was never based on any evidence, beyond the supposition that *Rollo* might be the play on which Fletcher, Massinger, Daborne, and Field were collaborating at about that time, according to a letter to Henslowe.[2] If one could establish, on other grounds, that the play dates from these years, and that these authors all had a hand in it, then a tentative identification of *Rollo* with the anonymous play might be hazarded; but one cannot begin with such an identification, and then make it the basis for asser-

---

[1] *The Plays and Poems of Philip Massinger*, ed. Philip Edwards and Colin Gibson, 5 vols. (Oxford, 1976), i, p. xx n. 5.
[2] *Henslowe Papers*, ed. W. W. Greg (London, 1907), 65–6.

tions about date and authorship. No modern scholar takes this early date seriously.

Jump accepts an alternative tradition, dating the play *c*.1625, and conjecturing that Fletcher left it unfinished at the time of his death (pp. xxx–xxxi). Three pieces of 'evidence' have been advanced for this date; of these, the most important is a parallel between a passage in *Rollo* and one in Jonson's *Neptune's Triumph* (1624). But Jump himself elsewhere (pp. xxv, 84) disparages the significance of this parallel, and Bentley seems entirely justified in objecting that 'Other plays had such passages, and apparently many court cooks aspired to such elaborate creations . . . One is, in fact, constantly amazed at the repeated assumptions by scholars that men who had enough originality to write successful plays could not observe the ordinary types about them with their own eyes but had to resort to another writer's observation of a given phenomenon' (iii. 404). Hensman in 1974 strengthened this argument with the observation that 'I have found no parallel instance of Jonson rehashing his own lines in a later work; neither was it Fletcher's habit to borrow other men's lines' (ii. 270). The parallel with *Neptune's Triumph* thus constitutes dubious evidence for either the date or the authorship of 2. 2 or *Rollo*. A second fact cited in support of a late date is the possible influence of a Latin play, *Querolus*, on 4. 2 of *Rollo*; an edition of *Querolus* was printed in 1619. But even if *Querolus* did influence *Rollo*—and Hensman shows that other sources could have contributed the same ideas—several earlier editions of the play had already appeared (Hensman thesis, 118–28). The parallels with *Querolus* are thus as worthless as that with *Neptune's Triumph* in dating *Rollo*. This leaves Jump's late date entirely dependent on his assertion that Fletcher's parts of the play are 'in his latest style' (p. xxx). No evidence for this assertion is forthcoming, in Jump's edition or his thesis. Nor are we aware of any reliable internal evidence which could distinguish Fletcher's work in 1617–20 from his work in 1623–6. Jump's own selection of the 'more striking' verbal parallels points to an earlier date: thirteen come from plays dated 1617–20, but only eight from plays of 1621–6.[3] *The Mad Lover* (January 1617) and *The Loyal Subject* (November 1618) have three parallels each, more than any other play in the Fletcher canon. What evidence there is points to Fletcher's contribution having been written earlier than Jump imagines.

Hensman argues persuasively that the play was originally composed in or not long after the summer of 1617. She points out that the play's allusions to and attitude towards duelling almost certainly date from 1616 or after (thesis, 106–8), that the allusion to Charlemagne making 'Three thousand Knights' (1. 1. 94–5) looks like a dig at James I's mass-dubbing in June 1617 (pp. 109–10), that the poisoning scene (2. 2) and its aftermath (3. 2) draw upon a whole series of details from the notorious Overbury murder trial, which continued from 19 October 1615 to 25 May 1616 (pp. 114–18), and that the astrologers satirized in 4. 2 all had connections with that trial (pp. 126–8). She also suggests that there may have been some personal satire of Lord Haye (pp. 110–14); this is very conjectural, though given the prominence of other topical allusions from 1616–17 it can hardly be dismissed outright. Hensman might also have mentioned the metaphorical description of

---

[3] We have checked Jump's parallels against recent scholarship on the authorship of the plays in the Fletcher canon, and only included plays or parts of plays currently attributed to Fletcher himself.

'this nights Freedome' as 'a short Parliament' (1. 1. 408): Parliament was dissolved after short sittings in 1614, 1621, and 1626. Which of these dates pertains can hardly be demonstrated, but the 1614 Parliament was the shortest of the three: it lasted only two months.

Cumulatively, Hensman's evidence points very strongly to composition in or not long after mid-1617. Though some of this material could have been exploited for some time afterwards, it would be most attractive when most topical. Nothing in Hoy's or Jump's investigations in any way imperils this conclusion. No topical references to events later than June 1617 have been identified. Moreover, the absence of any reference to the play among Sir Henry Herbert's surviving memoranda supports—albeit tenuously—this early dating.

But Hensman also contends that the extant texts of *Rollo* derive from a substantial revision of the play, by Massinger, between 1627 and 1630. Despite Bentley's endorsement, Hensman's case for this revision is feeble. It depends upon the argument that Massinger wrote all the parts of the play which make use of Gentillet's *Discours sur les moyens de bien gouverner* (thesis, 74–101); in her view Massinger substantially rewrote the play under the influence of this source. This hypothesis requires Massinger to have written 4. 3, a scene with a large number of heroic couplets, which previous investigators have assigned to Field or Chapman. No one has ever assigned 4. 3 to Massinger. Moreover, Hensman admits that neither Fletcher nor Massinger can be responsible for the bulk of 3. 1 precisely *because* of the number of heroic couplets in that scene (p. 167); she never mentions that 4. 3, on the same evidence, cannot have been written by Massinger either. If it was not, her whole hypothesis collapses. Likewise, in 3. 1 she originally offered Jonson as Fletcher's collaborator on the original play; Jonson's hand has otherwise never been detected in that scene, and Hensman supplied no evidence of his presence beyond the statement that he used heroic couplets in his Roman tragedies (though not at all in this fashion). On its own terms, then—and even before Hoy's linguistic evidence has been examined—Hensman's identification of the shares of original author(s) and reviser is self-contradictory and implausible. Moreover, attribution to Massinger of all the material inspired by Gentillet, or which involves the characters Aubrey and Latorch, produces an unwieldy, unnecessary, and bewilderingly implausible pattern of revision.[4]

Hensman's case for revision is, even within the terms of *Rollo* alone, implausible; more generally, we have little faith in the intellectual procedures which produce this hypothesis. She begins with the postulate, most succinctly articulated in 1974, that 'whenever a play is supposed to be a collaboration . . . when stylistic differences are commingled within speeches and episodes, the passages in which such commingling occurs may reasonably be supposed to have undergone subsequent revision' (i. 4–5). Collaborators presumably did not sit down together taking turns writing every other speech, and the mixing of authorial characteristics in one passage or episode does suggest that one writer has gone over another's

---

[4] Massinger seems to have undertaken a revision of *Love's Cure* similar to that which Hensman conjectures for *Rollo*: see George Walton Williams's introduction, in *Beaumont and Fletcher Canon*, iii. 4–7. However, in this case Massinger's Spanish source was not published until 1625, so its influence palpably derives from late adaptation of Beaumont and Fletcher's original play. Moreover, in *Love's Cure* Hoy's linguistic evidence clearly links Massinger with the material influenced by this source.

work. But by 'subsequent revision' Hensman does not mean the reshaping and tidying which occur between the authors' first separate drafts and the first performance; instead, she believes that such a mingling of authorial characteristics proves that a play has been substantially revised, years later, by one of those authors. Hensman thus rules out any possibility of one collaborator modifying his colleague's first draft, in the effort to pull their separate labours together into a coherent whole. As collaborators ourselves, we find this assumption incredible. Moreover, as John Kerrigan has elsewhere demonstrated, later adaptation for theatrical revivals generally confined itself to relatively self-contained interpolations and alterations.[5] If anything, logic and the evidence would suggest that a tangled interweaving of the traits of two authors in one passage proves that the intervention of the second hand came very soon after the original composition, rather than later. Hensman's postulate seems unwarranted, and the evidence she uses in applying that postulate is equally unreliable. Hensman bases her claim for the presence of Massinger or Fletcher entirely on her account of their respective 'verse styles'. The verse of each of these playwrights does exhibit tendencies relatively rare in the other's, but such criteria are of dubious value in determining their share of a particular collaborative play, particularly when the argument concerns Massinger's responsibility for a single speech, or a few lines, embedded in a scene written by Fletcher.

To such unreliable evidence of authorship Hensman adds, finally, the evidence of source material. Hensman deserves considerable credit for identifying the sources which contributed to *Rollo*, but she conspicuously fails to prove a direct relationship between authorship and sources. Gentillet was available when *Rollo* was originally written; Massinger was at that time already collaborating with Fletcher; consequently, even if Gentillet's influence were only discernible in passages clearly written by Massinger, such an association could not establish that Massinger's contribution was written after Fletcher's death. Nor does the use of Gentillet in certain passages written by Massinger create a presumption in favour of his authorship of other passages influenced by Gentillet: after all, Fletcher and Shakespeare both drew upon Chaucer's 'Knight's Tale' in writing their respective shares of *The Two Noble Kinsmen*, and an examination of Cyrus Hoy's introductions to the plays of the Dekker canon confirms the normality of such overlapping. By assuming a constant correlation between the use of certain sources and the presence of Massinger, Hensman is forced to construct similarly elaborate hypotheses for Massinger's revision of many other plays (*The Queen of Corinth*, *Thierry and Theodoret*, *The Laws of Candy*, *A Very Woman*, etc.). One's confidence in Hensman's conclusions about *Rollo* diminishes with every additional play forced into the same Procrustean mould.

Hoy's linguistic evidence gives this whole scenario the scholarly kiss of death. Hensman must assign 4. 1 to Massinger, since it contains some of the most striking parallels with Gentillet; yet it contains one *o'th'* and one *o'the*, forms which Massinger never uses in any of his acknowledged work. She must also, for similar reasons, assign 3. 1. 388–420 to Massinger; yet it contains two examples of *ye*, which Massinger likewise never uses. Hensman must also assign to Fletcher certain passages in Act 1, which all previous investigators have given, in its entirety,

[5] See Ch. 3 n. 90

to Massinger. But there is nothing to suggest Fletcher in any of these passages; the total absence of *ye* argues against him, as does the presence of the contraction *t'* (I. I. 54), a form which occurs only once elsewhere in Fletcher's acknowledged work. The same contraction occurs three times in 4. 2, which Hensman would assign to Fletcher; *hath* also occurs three times in that scene, though Fletcher elsewhere never used it more than six times in any single play. Hoy's linguistic evidence, in all of these scenes, merely confirms standard attributions based on parallel passages, metrical practice, and stylistic mannerisms. Hensman's account of the text's evolution must be rejected, as much for its own weakness as for the strength of the authorship evidence arrayed against it.

Of course it remains possible that the extant text has suffered some degree of revision or adaptation, even if not in the drastic form conjectured by Hensman. But Hensman offers no evidence for such a redaction. The play was certainly performed at Court in 1630, and this performance must surely have been prompted by a public revival; thereafter the play was extremely popular. However, records of performance survive only by chance. A play with such provocative allusions to the Overbury murder trial may well have been kept out of the royal repertoire for a decade or more, even if it were popular in the London theatres.[6] No prologue advertises that the play has been in any way recast; as Jump notes, this suggests (though it cannot prove) that no substantial revision has taken place (p. xxix). Hensman's conjectural dating of the revision (1627–35) depends upon the twin assumptions that Aubrey's part was played by and written for John Lowin, and that Lowin must have been the same age as Aubrey when he first played it (pp. 20–1). Neither contention seems reliable evidence for the date of a revision, even if we could be sure that one took place.

Moreover, even if the extant texts do represent a Caroline redaction, we have no particular reason to suspect that any of the songs have been interpolated. Like most other investigators, Hensman assigns to Fletcher—and hence to the original period of composition—all three songs; she also includes 4. 3, which prepares for the seduction in the final scene, among the unrevised material. Everyone assigns to Fletcher the central portion of 3. 1, which initiates the Edith plot. Therefore, beyond the presence of a similar stanza in 5. 2 of *Rollo* and 4. 1 of *Measure*, we have no extrinsic or intrinsic reason to suspect that the song in *Rollo* was interpolated at a date later than the original composition of the play, *c.*1617–20. Whatever our view of the textual situation in either play, no one doubts that the original composition of *Measure* preceded the original composition of *Rollo*; therefore, anyone who wants to defend the integrity of the song in *Measure* can always claim that it was lifted from Shakespeare's play *c.*1617–20. Speculations about a late revision of *Rollo* do little to strengthen that defence.

Who wrote the play?[7] That Fletcher and Massinger were the main contributors

[6] For an exact parallel see *The Chances*: Bentley plausibly dates this *c.*1617 (iii. 318–23), but the first recorded performance was on 30 Dec. 1630. As Walton Williams remarks, 'Though there are no records of performances of the play during Fletcher's lifetime, it is probable that a play that was to become most popular on the stage would have been so from the first' (*Beaumont and Fletcher Canon*, iv. 543).

[7] The Stationers' Register entry (4 Oct. 1639) assigns the play to 'J:B', and Q1 (1639) to '*B.J.F.*'. These initials have been interpreted as a reference to Fletcher and/or Beaumont and Jonson; no one has ever suspected Beaumont's hand (he was almost certainly dead before the play was written), and although Jonson has been suspected the initials are poor external

has never been seriously doubted; nor (with the exception of Hensman's Byzantine theory of revision) has there been much dispute about their shares of the play: Massinger wrote Act 1 and 5. 1. 1–89; Fletcher Act 2, 3. 1. 263–330, 3. 2, the closing soliloquy in 5. 1, and most if not all of 5. 2. Hoy's linguistic evidence amply confirms these attributions. But these tests also confirm that the rest of the play—Act 4, and all but 67 lines of 3. 1—cannot have been written by either Massinger or Fletcher; moreover, as previous investigators have almost universally agreed, the linguistic evidence suggests that two different authors may have contributed to this central section of the play. The probable date of composition almost certainly rules out Daborne and Wilkins; the linguistic evidence argues against ascription to Middleton, Rowley, or Daborne, and does little to encourage Wilkins's candidacy.[8] Only three plausible candidates remain among those often identified in this portion of the play: Chapman, Field, and Jonson.

Hoy demonstrates that Jonson could, on the linguistic evidence, have written 4. 1 and 4. 2, the scenes assigned to him by Jump; Chapman, likewise, could well have written 4. 3 and the bulk of 3. 1—which Jump, following William Wells, assigned to him. Field's linguistic pattern could in fact fit either set of passages; in some ways it fits them better than Chapman's or Jonson's do. However, the total absence of prose, or of rhyming couplets, from 4. 2 makes Field's presence unlikely, as does the learnedly arcane vocabulary, and no one has ever been tempted to see Field's hand there. Herford and Simpson concede that there are some striking parallels between 4. 1 and Jonson's work, particularly in *Discoveries*, and their only argument against his authorship is the assertion that 'The verse is too fluid for Jonson'.[9]

Hensman demonstrates that most of the political theory in 4. 1 derives from Gentillet, a major source for the play's plot; Jonson's expression of similar sentiments in *Discoveries* thus constitutes the weakest of evidence on which to attribute to him the authorship of this scene. Likewise, no significant verbal parallels between 4. 2 and the Jonson canon have ever been offered. The mockery of astrological jargon *might* be Jonson's; but Hensman shows that such satire was frequent enough in the early seventeenth century, and by no means a Jonsonian monopoly. As for metrical statistics, Jump in his own thesis was forced to admit that they 'not only fail to give striking confirmation of the presence of Chapman and Jonson . . . in *Rollo* but even fail to bring out at all clearly the quite unmistakable fact that the author of IV.iii and the riming parts of III.i did not write IV.i and ii' (p. 54). Metrical evidence does not rule out Jonson; but nor does it compel us to rule him in. As for the linguistic evidence, Hoy himself conceded that, in itself, it hardly constitutes convincing proof of Jonson's presence: it merely 'confirmed' an attribution made primarily upon other evidence. Such

evidence. As Jump concludes, after a droll summary of the various interpretations of the crytogram, 'It seems that a study of these initials will not solve the authorship problem' (p. xxvi). The more reliable, independent Q2 (1640) identifies only 'JOHN FLETCHER' as the author.

[8] Compare Hoy's tables with Lake's (bands 1 and 4). Middleton, Rowley, and Daborne all prefer *has* and *does*; only Rowley and Wilkins offer any parallels for *i'the* and *o'the* (one each). The date of Wilkin's death is not known, but his last known writing dates from 1608.

[9] Ben Jonson, *Works*, ed. C. H. Herford and Percy and Evelyn Simpson, 11 vols. (Oxford 1925–5), x (1950), 295.

'other evidence' turns out, upon closer examination, to be illusory. Hoy might, indeed, have turned the linguistic evidence against Jonson's authorship: 4. 1 contains one example of *w'yee*, a form which appears nowhere else in the Jonson canon, but which does occur four times in Field's two unaided plays. The most probable date for *Rollo*'s composition also tells against Jonson's participation. Jonson's last known collaborations were *Sejanus* (1603) and *Eastward Ho* (1605)—both, for different reasons, disastrous. *Rollo* would not only constitute a puzzling exception to the artistic independence of Jonson's subsequent career; it would also interrupt his period of silence, from 1616 to 1624, when he appears to have written nothing else for the public stage. Such considerations cannot be regarded as decisive: if Jonson did contribute to *Rollo* then we would have to revise our picture of his career, and that picture cannot itself be allowed to arbitrate on his presence in *Rollo*. However, the oddity of Jonson's participation, in terms of his personal circumstances, does cast further doubt upon an attribution based on such flimsy internal evidence. Moreover, the very same considerations make Field an attractive candidate. Field was, in 1617–20, at the height of his career; all of his known work from 1611 on was written in collaboration; in particular, he collaborated with Massinger in *The Fatal Dowry* (1616–19), with Fletcher in *Four Plays in One* (1614–16?), and with both in *The Honest Man's Fortune* (1613), *The Jeweller of Amsterdam* (1616), *The Queen of Corinth* (1617), and *The Knight of Malta* (1618). No other playwright is known to have collaborated with both men between 1616 and 1626; only Middleton, Rowley, and Dekker collaborated with either, and all three seem ruled out of *Rollo* on other grounds. Field may not have contributed to *Rollo*, but on present evidence he seems likelier than Jonson to have done so.

The fourth playwright is also difficult to identify. Chapman in his other tragedies never uses *'em*; it occurs twice in the first part of 3. 1.[10] He only uses *i'th'* four times, over the course of four entire plays; it, too, occurs twice in the first part of 3. 1. On this basis one can hardly be confident about assigning that scene to Chapman; yet both anomalies, along with the liberal sprinkling of couplets and the rest of the linguistic pattern, would be acceptable in Field. Likewise, the value of the verbal parallels with Chapman's work is perhaps somewhat diminished by the fact that Field, whom Chapman called his 'son', was especially prone to imitate Chapman in scenes of high tragedy, like 3. 1 and 4. 3 of *Rollo*.[11] A. R. Braunmuller raises a number of plausible objections to the attribution to Chapman: '(*a*) little of *Rollo* is dense enough to be unrevised Chapman and (*b*) there's rarely the wealth of (often obscure) classical allusion one would expect and (*c*) it's surprising to find Chapman writing a scene with all female characters (4. 3).'[12] Moreover, the concentration of couplets, which so remarkably distinguishes 4. 3 and most of 3. 1 from the rest of the play, if anything tells against the attribution to Chapman. Braunmuller, like Jump in his thesis, compares *Rollo* to *Caesar and Pompey*, which many scholars regard as Chapman's last play; but

---

[10] We have here been able to supplement Hoy by means of Jackson, *Attribution*, 13.

[11] For Chapman parallels elsewhere in Field see *The Plays of Nathan Field*, ed. William Perry (Austin, Tex., 1950), 30; on Field's straining after high style, see Hoy.

[12] Private communication, 10 Nov. 1983. (Braunmuller kindly commented for us on the plausibility of attributing anything in *Rollo* to Chapman; he did not discuss the merits or demerits of Field's claim.)

Braunmuller analyzes the distribution of couplets, where Jump merely counts them:

Excluding pairs of lines that end (or happen to end?) on the same word, often a proper noun, I would judge that Chapman uses couplets for the same purposes most of the older Elizabethan survivors did: as scene endings, to mark *sententiae*, and (less frequently) to close a speech, especially a *Nuntius* or semi-narrative speech. With those exclusions, I see only eight, widely dispersed, couplets in *Caesar*, and nothing to match the stretch at *Rollo*, 3. 1. 22–29, or even the four lines at 4. 3. 54–57. In *Rollo*, the same exclusions leave (in addition to the long passage): 3. 1. 35–6, 84–85, 149–50, 341–42 (?), 346–47, 379–80 (?), 4. 3. 13–14, 34–35 (? a flabby sentence), 59–60, 74–75. Moreover, the proportion of speech-ending couplets is much higher than in any comparable stretch of lines in *Caesar*.

Field, by contrast, used couplets much more generously, in the manner of *Rollo* 4. 3 and 3. 1. His share of *The Fatal Dowry* (three-and-a-half scenes) contains fifteen examples, to *Caesar*'s eight; they are extraordinarily frequent in his two early unassisted plays. Finally, Braunmuller notes that there is little real evidence for attributing to Chapman the end of 3. 1, after Fletcher's episode; we may add that there is no real evidence for attributing 4. 3 to him. This leaves us with only a handful of Chapman parallels, in the first section of 3. 1, which could claim to be of any positive value in identifying Chapman rather than Chapman's 'son' Field.

All in all, Chapman's claim cannot be considered at all secure. Like Jonson, Chapman had a markedly idiosyncratic style, particularly in his tragedies, and although certain scenes of *Rollo* gesture in the direction of that style, none actually achieves it. Imitation is, in the circumstances, a strong possibility, and Field's candidacy is if anything buttressed by the sense that we are dealing with writing 'like but not by' Chapman. On the other hand neither scene contains the exclamation 'Pish', or a speech spoken by '*Omnes*'—mannerisms of which Field was fond.[13] The slight discrepancy between *Rollo* and Chapman's linguistic pattern in his earlier tragedies could be explained by the fact that we have no certain examples of his unadapted late dramatic work. Furthermore, Brinkley's rejection of Field's claim to a part of this play carries some weight: it depends, not on any subjective judgement that the scenes in question fall below Field's standard, but on the alleged absence—not only from these scenes but from the whole play—of certain mannerisms present elsewhere in Field's work.[14] However, her statement that metrical tests 'preclude the possibility of his collaboration' should be treated with some scepticism. The most important of such tests involves Field's consistent preference for 'strong stops' (full stop, exclamation, query, dash, colon, semi-colon) at line-ends rather than in mid-line. For 4. 3 and non-Fletcherian 3. 1 the totals are, by our count, 15 line-end: 7 medial. Such a distribution contrasts

---

[13] Field overwhelmingly preferred 'oh' (see App. II, above), and Chapman, in *Bussy D'Ambois* at least, preferred 'o'; 4. 3 lacks the exclamation altogether, but in the non-Fletcherian lines of 3. 1 it occurs 10 times, always as 'o'. While the presence of 'oh' would argue strongly for Field, the use of 'o' (also overwhelmingly preferred elsewhere in Q2) is of little value, since it may merely represent the preference of the scribe who prepared the printer's copy.

[14] R. F. Brinkley, *Nathan Field: The Actor-Playwright*, Yale Studies in English, 77 (New Haven, Conn., 1928), 141. The % of feminine endings in the unFletcherian part of 3. 1 is 34, in 4. 3 34.5; Field's highest % elsewhere is 19 (*Fatal Dowry*). However, Field's % rises from his early to his late work, and *Rollo* might be his last play.

strongly with 4. 1 and 4. 2 (24 line-end: 64 medial), and could actually be Field's. Since this metrical test is crucial to Brinkley's rejection of Field, her argument can hardly be considered compelling. In fact, the two scenes do contain some of Field's favourite tricks, such as the tree image at 3. 1. 15–16 or the classical allusion at 3. 1. 353. The use of *præter* in the stage direction (3. 1. 387) would also be characteristic of Field (or Chapman, Massinger, or Jonson). In the absence of a more detailed investigation of the differences between Field's work and Chapman's, we can hardly rule out either; but one or the other probably contributed to the play, and at the moment Field looks more attractive than Chapman.

We had reached this conclusion even before seeing Hensman's 1974 book, where she abandons Jonson and instead advocates Field's authorship of the non-Fletcherian parts of 3. 1. She does not mention the linguistic evidence, but does draw attention to the 'invariable regularity of iambic pentameter rhythm', the 'inverted and awkward grammatical structure' of several lines (e.g. 3. 1. 8–9, 15–16, 26), and 'numerous examples of Field's characteristic use of words in their archaic or root sense' (ii. 273–4). Elsewhere she mentions Field's fondness for metaphors based on minerals or precious stones, his (sometimes incongruous) appeals to the five senses, and his frequent use of mild oaths and Anglo-Saxon verbs (i. 57–60)—all applicable to the language of 3. 1 and 4. 3. Despite the vagueness of some of these criteria, they do usefully demonstrate that the writing of 3. 1 and 4. 3 is within the range of Field's habitual manner, and that Brinkley's rejection of his claims cannot be given any credence. Unfortunately, though, Hensman makes no attempt to distinguish Field's manner from Chapman's, and bases her rejection of the Wells/Jump/Hoy attribution entirely on what she herself called an '*ad hominem*' argument (ii. 274 n. 38). She alleges that Chapman had given up playwriting by this time, and last collaborated in 1605— two false statements, which therefore hardly constitute convincing arguments against Chapman's participation.

What conclusions can we draw from all of this? Most of *Rollo* was undoubtedly written by Fletcher and Massinger; just as clearly, the linguistic, stylistic, and metrical evidence all testify that one or more other hands was involved. Though they radically disagree on what he may have written, Jump, Hensman (originally), Bentley, and Hoy all identify Jonson's hand in the play; but of the three candidates usually advanced, Jonson's claim is far and away the weakest. Certainly, the Hensman–Bentley attribution to him of most of 3. 1 has no discernible basis in either logic or evidence, and the detectable signs of his presence in Act 4 are manifestly unreliable.

We are disposed to regard Jonson's participation as unproven and relatively unlikely. By contrast, the presence of either Field or Chapman, or both, is highly probable, but intrinsically difficult to prove. *Rollo* might well have been Field's last play, and for almost a decade before its most probable date of composition, he had been working only in collaboration. These two facts in concert make it difficult to evaluate apparent discrepancies between *Rollo* and Field's other work. Likewise, *Rollo* would have been Chapman's first play for many years; only one Chapman play undoubtedly later than *Rollo* survives (*Chabot, Admiral of France*), and its extant text has suffered an indeterminable amount of posthumous revision. These circumstances render the evaluation of internal evidence more than usually hazardous. The personal and artistic relationship between the two men does not make it any easier, particularly since (for reasons explained below) Chapman's influence on Field may have been forcefully renewed in 1619. Chapman clearly prefers 'while' and Field clearly prefers 'whil(e)st', but the word does not appear at all in the relevant parts of *Rollo*. Field's claims to 4. 3 and most of 3. 1 seem to us, on present evidence, better than Chapman's. But one or the other almost certainly contributed to the play, possibly in collaboration with a fourth unidentified figure.

Chapman's presence, or Field's, would reinforce the evidence for dating the play *c.*1617–20. If Field contributed to the play, it must have been written between his move to the King's Men and his death in early 1620.[15] Chapman's complete translation of Homer was published in 1616; his translation of Hesiod appeared in 1618, prefixed with a commendatory poem by Jonson. After the Hesiod, Chapman's next known work was *Chabot, Admiral of France*, which Bentley assigns to 1621 or January 1622; his lost collaboration with Brome, *Christianetta*, may well date from the following years, and in any case can hardly be much earlier, since Brome first surfaces as a dramatist, in another collaborative play, in October 1623. So far as the fragmentary record allows us to judge, after completing his translations of Homer and Hesiod, Chapman again, after a long absence, turned to writing plays—in the same period that *Rollo* must have been written.

There is thus nothing intrinsically implausible about Chapman collaborating in a play written for the King's Men *c.*1617–20. However, neither *Christianetta* nor *Chabot* was written for the King's Men; nor, for that matter, were any of Chapman's other plays. Chapman only ever had one connection with the King's Men: Nathan Field. Early in his career Field had performed—certainly or probably—in Chapman's *Gentlemen Usher*, *May Day*, *Sir Giles Goosecap*, *All Fools*, *Bussy D'Ambois*, *Monsieur D'Olive*, *The Widow's Tears*, *Eastward Ho*, *1* and *2 Byron*, and *The Revenge of Bussy*; the only commendatory verses attached to Field's first play were written by Chapman, and addressed 'To his Loved Sonne, Nat. Field'; Field's most recent editor regards Chapman as the major influence on his work.[16] Moreover, although *Bussy D'Ambois* originally belonged to a children's company, Field obviously took it with him when he joined the King's Men; it is the only one of Chapman's plays which ever formed part of their repertoire. Some of Chapman's editors go so far as to claim that Field had a main hand in the much-altered redaction of *Bussy*, published in 1641; whether or not this is true, there can be little doubt that Field, in some sense, 'took Chapman with him' when he joined the King's Men. Field's brief tenure with that company therefore provides the only obvious opportunity for Chapman's collaboration on a Fletcher/Massinger play for the King's Men.

Since Wells first proposed him, in 1928, every investigation but Hensman's has accepted Chapman's presence in the play; Hensman completely ignored Wells, and made no attempt to contest his conclusions. If, notwithstanding Braunmuller's doubts, Chapman did contribute to *Rollo*, then his personal

[15] On the date of Field's death, between May 1619 and Aug. 1620, see Bentley, *Jacobean and Caroline Stage*, ii. 435 and iii. 301.
[16] Perry edn. (see n. 10), 14, 29–32.

circumstances would allow us to date the play with greater precision than Hensman attempted. A series of documents from a lawsuit, discovered by C. J. Sisson and Robert Butman, make it clear that, for several years after 1612, Chapman was in financial straits, living in obscurity in Hinckley; he returned to London in the autumn of 1619, but before that he seems clearly to have stayed out of the capital, except for an appearance in June 1617, of indeterminate but probably brief duration.[17] Chapman's participation would therefore limit composition of *Rollo* to either the summer of 1617, or to some time in or after autumn 1619. Field's death, some time in 1619 or early 1620, provides a probable terminus for any association Chapman may have had with the King's Men; a date later than 1620 would also presuppose the use of 'topical' material the topicality of which had already waned. In terms of Chapman's own circumstances, the later of these two dates—1619/20—seems the more probable; but the topical allusions would favour mid-1617.

The later date might also explain an anomaly in the sources which Hensman left unresolved. The plot of *Rollo* is clearly based on Roman, not French, history, and the change of date and locale has never been satisfactorily explained; yet all but one of Chapman's tragedies have French settings. More specifically, Hensman pointed out that the portrayal of Rollo as a tyrant was highly unusual, and that this treatment would seem to derive from Duchesne's *Gesta Normannorum in Franciae Ante Rollorem Ducem* (1619); the authors 'either drew upon Duchesne's volumes, or upon early Norman chronicles similar to them' (Hensman thesis, 136). Her own extensive survey uncovered no such 'similar' chronicles, and in terms of the historical literature—and popular consciousness—Duchesne's volumes represent a clear departure, the first polemical representation of Rollo as a tyrant. Until some other source for this point of view can be found, *Rollo* must be dated in 1619–20 rather than 1617.

Two other facts might also lend support to this date. One is the already-mentioned publication of a reprint of *Querolus* in 1619. The other is Jonson's reference, in January 1618/19, to a number of contemporary playwrights, in his private conversations with Drummond (Fletcher, Chapman, Field, Day, Middleton, Shakespeare). Massinger is not mentioned at all, which would perhaps be rather surprising if Jonson had collaborated with him during the last eighteen months. But neither of these considerations carries much force: earlier editions of *Querolus* were available, and Jonson probably didn't contribute to *Rollo* at all. The extant source materials favour 1619–20, the topical allusions favour late 1617 or 1618, and for our purposes no decision need be taken about which of these dates should be favoured.

The perceptive reader will perhaps have noticed that we have as yet said nothing about the authorship of the beginning of 5. 2, in which the song 'Take oh take' occurs. Jump, like virtually every earlier investigator, assigns the entirety of 5. 2 to Fletcher, yet in the first 134 lines he cites only two verbal parallels: 'spring of beauty' at 5. 2. 35 (which occurs in *The Elder Brother* and *The Prophetess*) and 'Angell eyes' at 5. 2. 87 (which also occurs in *The Humorous Lieutenant*, *Monsieur Thomas*, and *Women Pleased*). Yet these 134 lines contain eighteen examples of

---

[17] 'George Chapman, 1612–22: Some New Facts', *Modern Language Review*, 46 (1951), 185–90.

you, and not a single *ye*; Hoy on this basis concludes that they can hardly be Fletcher's, and he assigns them to Massinger. Hoy cites Massinger parallels for two phrases in this section of the scene. For Massinger's 'my sacrifice | Of love, and service' (*Roman Actor* 3. 2. 174–5) *Rollo* has 'The gentle sacrifice of love and service' (5. 2. 26), and we have noticed no parallels for this phrase in Fletcher's undoubted work. Hoy also attributes to Massinger references to the 'wind' in '*Arabia*', associated with 'perfumes or . . . spices' (*Duke of Florence* 2. 3. 62–4, *New Way to Pay Old Debts* 3. 1. 73–4, *Bashful Lover* 1. 1. 234; *Rollo* 5. 2. 39–41). But Fletcher also refers to the 'sweet . . . Arabian gums' (*Noble Gentleman* 1. 4. 12–13). The evidence of verbal parallels in the first ninety lines of 5. 2 strongly suggests either that Fletcher and Massinger both worked on this passage, or that verbal parallels are of little use here in distinguishing Fletcher from Massinger. Given the close working relationship of the two playwrights and Massinger's tendency to echo other men's plays, it would be unwise to be dogmatic about their shares here; but shared composition is obviously possible. Hoy assumes instead that Massinger later revised something of Fletcher's, but it is difficult to see why or how this should have happened. The play must always have included something like this scene, with the death of Rollo and the culmination of the Edith subplot; anyone wanting to interpolate the song could have done so without altering much of the preceding or following dialogue. The first part of the scene (ll. 1–92) in fact uses *you* only twice, and contains one *Has* (for 'He has'), a form Massinger only uses once elsewhere. This section of the scene also contains both of the striking verbal parallels with Fletcher's work (Jump, p. 106), and many of Fletcher's stylistic mannerisms (Hensman thesis, 187). Fletcher, moreover, had been given the 'Edith' section of 3. 1, and the dramatic material at the beginning of 5. 2 seems entirely to his taste. By contrast, the middle of the scene, 5. 2. 93–134, contains sixteen examples of *you*, no examples of *ye*, no clear parallels of style or vocabulary with Fletcher's work, and nothing which would contradict ascription to Massinger. Massinger, by universal agreement, wrote the beginning of 5. 1, which prepares for Hammon's attack on Rollo, and this section of 5. 2 begins with Hammon's entrance and ends just after he has killed Rollo and been fatally wounded himself; Fletcher, likewise by consent, wrote most or all of Aubrey's long closing soliloquy in 5. 1, and Fletcher's hand clearly resumes with Aubrey's entrance at 5. 2. 136 ('I charge yee let us passe'). Assuming that Massinger wrote 5. 2. 93–134 will thus account for all the available evidence, and produce a pattern of collaboration no more implausible than Fletcher's intervention to write sixty-two lines in the middle of 3. 1 (which everyone acknowledges).

Rollo thus appears to have been written in mid-1617 or between autumn 1619 and summer 1620; the extant text shows no signs of later revision or adaptation. Massinger wrote Act 1; Fletcher Act 2, 3. 1. 263–330, and 3. 2; both contributed to both scenes in Act 5. The authorship of Act 4, and of the remainder of 3. 1, remains uncertain, but Jonson's participation seems relatively unlikely. Either Field or Chapman very probably contributed to the play, and an unidentified fourth dramatist may also have been involved.

APPENDIX IV

The Text of 'Take oh take those lips away'

The proliferation of extant printed and manuscript versions of the song found in *Measure* and *Rollo* bears ample witness to its popularity in the seventeenth century. A number of manuscripts of the song survive, both with and without the musical setting by John Wilson, and a two-part arrangement of Wilson's setting was printed in a succession of song-books published by John Playford. The number of surviving manuscripts easily surpasses that for any other song in the Shakespeare canon; within the Beaumont and Fletcher canon it is exceeded in popularity only by 'Care-charming sleep' (Fletcher's *Valentinian*) and 'Hence, all you vain delights' (Middleton's *Nice Valour*). But neither of these songs exists in such a variety of independent printed texts.

This Appendix attempts to establish a reliable text for the song as it would have been performed by the King's Men, to explain the relationship between the various texts of the song, and so perhaps to shed some further light on the problem of the relationship between the two plays in which it appears. We have collated all the texts known to exist (including six not recorded in previous studies of Shakespeare and Fletcher).[1] Some gaps between extant texts can be made good with conjectural lost manuscripts; but even then the picture we have of the song's textual history will be in some areas unclear or ambiguous, in other areas incomplete. The words of a well-known song may be contaminated or sometimes actually restored through memorial transmission, which could affect the work of a scribe following copy as well as one depending upon memory. This could possibly explain why the text of the second stanza is less stable than that of the first: the memory is usually more accurate at learning the earlier part of a given text. Aural transmission also may have corrupted the text: individuals may have learnt the song through hearing it performed. We cannot determine the extent to which indirect transmission has influenced the evolution of the text. As Harold Love put it, 'a significant percentage of anomalous agreements seems to be present in every "real life" textual situation'.[2] But despite these complications, the variants (whatever their cause) are sufficiently numerous and consistently grouped to make it possible to construct plausible stemmas. 'Editors have every right to feel that they *should* be able to make sense of the genealogical relationships—even when faced with groups of twenty or more manuscripts'.[3] The apparent textual history of the song is consistent with the most prob-

[1] There is a limited collation of variants in John P. Cutt's *La Musique de la troupe de Shakespeare: The King's Men sous le règne de Jacques Ier* (Paris, 1959), 114 and 172. Cutts prints the text of F and *Rollo* Q1 and collates, with some errors, MSS 1, 6, 8, and 11. E. H. Fellows, in *Songs and Lyrics from the Plays of Beaumont and Fletcher* (London, 1928), claims that 'the song-books read "bound in *iron* chains by thee" ', and later records 'in Ion' in the British Museum copy (pp. 47 and 68); we have found no such reading, though we have not traced a MS Fellowes mentions as then belonging to Col. W. G. Probert, FSA, of Beville, Bures, Suffolk. Finally, a partial collation was published, after our own investigation had been completed, by Donald W. Foster in ' "Shall I Die" Post Mortem: Defining Shakespeare', *SQ* 38 (1987), 58–60.

[2] Harold Love, 'The Ranking of Variants in the Analysis of Moderately Contaminated Manuscript Traditions', in *SB* 37 (1984), 39–57, 43.   [3] Ibid. 40.

able textual history of the two plays: although in themselves the textual variants cannot prove that the song originated in *Rollo*, they do nothing to contradict that hypothesis, and in some respects encourage it.

In Ex. 1 is an edited text of the words and music. The control text for both words and music is Wilson's song-book, listed in the collation as MS 6. The music notation varies from Wilson in the base stave for the word 'sweetly' (see Collation), and has been regularized to the usual modern conventions for printed music. This edited version of the song anticipates some of the conclusions reached through the following collation and textual analysis, but is required here as a base text for the collation itself.

Manuscripts

1. BL, Add. MS 11,608, fo. 56 (*c*.1656–9)
2. BL, Harley MS 3991, fo. 136ᵛ–137 (late 17th century)
3. BL, Harley MS 6057, fo. 36ᵛ (*c*.1630s)
4. Bodleian, Ashmole 47, fo. 130ᵛ (*c*.1630–40s)
5. Bodleian, MS Eng. poet. fo. 27, p. 66 (*c*.1638)
6. Bodleian, Mus. b. 1, fo. 19ᵛ (*c*.1656)
7. Bodleian, Rawl. poet. 65, fo. 26ᵛ (*c*.1680–90)
8. Christ Church, Oxford, MS 434, fo. 1 (before *c*.1650)
9. Folger, MS 452. 4, fo. 20 (Oxford, mid-17th century)
10. New York Public Library, MS Drexel 4041, no. 44 (*c*.1640)
11. New York Public Library, MS Drexel 4257, no. 16 (*c*.1659)
12. Rosenbach Museum and Library, Philadelphia, MS 239/27, p. 126 (*c*.1634)

Printed texts

F: *Measure for Measure*, in the Shakespeare Folios:
  F1, 1623 (G2)
  F4, 1685 (F4)
Q1: *The Bloody Brother* [*Rollo Duke of Normandy*] (1639), H4ᵛ:
  Q1a uncorrected state
  Q1b corrected state
Q2: *The Tragœdy of Rollo Duke of Normandy* (1640), I2–2ᵛ
Poems: *Poems Written by Wil. Shake-speare. Gent* (1640), K6
Play: books published by John Playford:
  Play 1 *Select Musicall Ayres, and Dialogues* (1652), B1ᵛ
  Play 2 *Select Musicall Ayres and Dialogues, In Three Books* (1653), G2ᵛ
  Play 3 *Select Ayres and Dialogues* (1659), B1
  Play 4 *Treasury of Musick*, by Henry Lawes (1669), I. 1
BF: Beaumont and Fletcher Folio of 1679, pp. 428–46

In collating and evaluating the variants in these twenty-three texts, only two of which are alike, we begin by considering the music. Substantive music variants are neither more nor less significant than substantive verbal variants. We begin with the former not only because the number of texts in which music appears is smaller, but also because the music texts must either form a distinct group or be more authoritative than their counterparts without music: a group of texts, as it evolves, can lose but cannot normally acquire music. In a situation of some complexity, the music allows us the opportunity to establish some first bearings.

Ex. 1.

Song

2 Hide o hide those hills of snow   [7]
    that thy froazen bosom beares   [8]
    on whose topps the Pinkes y^t grow   [9]
    are yet of those y^t Aprill weares   [10]
    But first sett my poore heart free   [11]
    bound in those Icye chaines by thee   [12]

Collation of Music Variants

MSS 1, 6, 8, 10, and 11 are music manuscripts. The collation of music variants in these texts and the Playford printed texts is—necessarily—somewhat simplified. Key signatures and barlines are treated separately from other notational variants. Transposition of key is regarded as a major but single variant, even though it affects every single note. In order to establish comparability between transposed and untransposed manuscripts for individual notational variants, in Exx. 2 and 3 the notes of the transposed manuscripts are reconverted to the original key. For the treble of *kisses*, for example, the Drexel manuscripts actually have crotchets on C and E♭. Similarly, key signatures and barlines are not recorded for individual notational variants.

Key signatures in the music texts are as follows:

> 1 flat: Play
> 2 flats: MSS 1, 6, 8, 11
> 3 flats: MS 10

The actual key of MSS 1, 6, and 8 is G minor and that of MSS 10 and 11 is F minor.

Notation variants for the treble are shown in Ex. 2*a–n*. Notation variants for the bass are shown in Ex. 3*a–q*. A slur before a word indicates that the note also accompanies the end of the previous word. A slur after a word indicates that the following note also partly accompanies that word.

The positions of barlines are as listed below. Notes tied across the bar are indicated by a slur; a bar in one clef (bass) only is indicated by parentheses.

MS 1   *after* Take, a-, so, sweetly, forsworne, yᵉ, day, mis-, morne (*repeat*), kisses, agayne, though, vaine.

MS 6   *after* Take, so, for-, those, of, that, the, morne (*repeat*), kisses, agayne, love, in, vaine.

MS 8   *after* Take, (lipps), away, forsworne, those, yᵉ, that, the, my, a-, -gayne, love, in, vaine.

MS 10 *after* Take, lipps⌣, away, sweetly, forsworne, yᵉ, day, mis-, morne, kisses, agayne, though, vaine.

MS 11 *As MS. 10, but* . . . agayne, love, vaine.

Play   *after* Take, lipps ⌣, a-, so, for-, -sworne, yᵉ, day, mis-, morne (*repeat*), kisses, agayne, though, vaine.

The music manuscripts provide an instructive glimpse of seventeenth-century music-making. Few of the recorded variants result from error: almost all represent deliberate alteration to the music. No two manuscripts share even the same positioning of barlines. MS 2 freely introduces ornamentation; all manuscripts have incidental variation such as dotted and half notes instead of equal notes, or crotchets split into quavers. In some versions the bass is simplified; in others a phrase in the bass will be raised or lowered by an octave. These last changes may be dictated by practical circumstance—the capacities of instrument or player. Two manuscripts transpose the entire song a tone lower, presumably to bring the song more comfortably within a singer's range. It seems that anyone who undertook to transcribe the music was competent and perhaps even expected to embellish, simplify, rearrange, or transpose it.

Ex. 2. *Notation Variants: Treble*

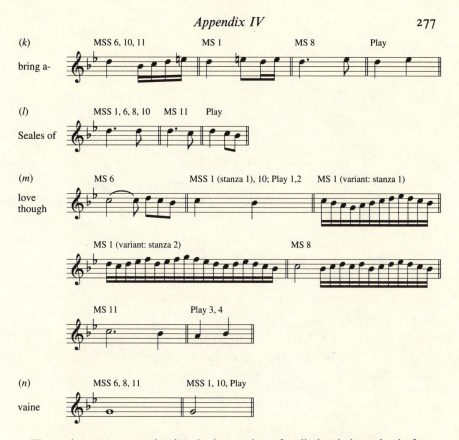

The variants consequently give the impression of radiating independently from an invisible source. Yet all is not chaotic. Wilson's song-book (MS 6) gives, as may be expected, a text evidently close to the point from which it and others diverge. This manuscript is a large and handsomely bound song-book which John Wilson had prepared in the 1650s. Antony Wood recorded that 'This book . . . he gave to the public library at Oxon before his majesty's restoration, but with this condition that no person should peruse it till after his death'.[4] If Wilson's wish was respected, his book cannot have supplied copy for any other text before 1674, the year of his death. Though Wilson was not himself the main scribe, he directed and supervised the scribe, sometimes correcting his or her work.[5] The song-book is an important and authoritative source for Wilson's music. But even this text has readings which are quite distinct from those of the other versions. These readings may be Wilson's revisions, though only the variant on the bass for 'sweetly' can be identified as such with any confidence. In our edited text, the reading of the other manuscripts is supplied, as this must reflect the music in Wilson's earlier manuscript, the one which the King's Men would have used when performing the song.

The Christ Church manuscript (MS 8) is fairly close to Wilson though it

Ex. 3. *Notation Variants: Bass*

introduces a little more diversity. MS 1 is more varied, and in different ways; in particular it adds ornamental runs and turns, both in the text itself and as appended variants for particular words in both stanzas. The two Drexel manuscripts, which share the transposed notation, also share many other distinctive traits; MS 11 is, however, clearly closer to other manuscripts. In particular, there are perhaps more similarities between MS 11 and the Playford texts than coincidence would permit, and Playford does not share readings with MS 6 against the Drexels. Direct line of succession is not possible, but the versions evidently belong to the same group. The texts printed by Playford, as would be expected, constitute a distinct group textually. Two variants within this group, taken in conjunction with the dates of printing, indicate that each Playford text was printed from its immediate predecessor. These variants are in the treble notes for 'lips a-', where Play 1 differs from Play 2–4, and 'love', where 1 and 2 share a C but 3 and 4 have A. Closer inspection shows that Play 3 and Play 4 were printed from the same engraved plate. Play 1 and Play 2, however, were set independently in movable type.

The music is sufficient to suggest the pattern shown in Fig. 1. These relationships are not necessarily direct; on the contrary, it is most probable that only a small proportion of all the original seventeenth-century manuscripts is now extant. Nevertheless, any of the proposed (and provisional) links *could* be direct.

The presence of music is itself, as mentioned above, a highly significant variant. Its loss is irreversible. Despite their variousness, the music manuscripts constitute a distinct group which cannot be penetrated by a text without the music.

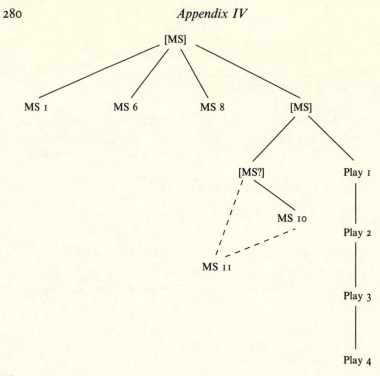

Fig. 1.

Collation of Verbal Variants

Substantive variants are recorded below. Texts are listed in the order of the manuscripts and printed texts given in the full listing above. The incidentals of the
lemma are those of the text given in Ex. 1; other incidentals follow the first
named text.

[*Heading*] Song] *Q1, BF*; 22th Song *MS 2*; A Sonnet *MS 3*; Loves ingratitude *Play
4*; The Song Q2; *not in MSS 1, 4–12; F, Poems, Play 1–3.*

2 that] *MSS 1–12; F, Q1, Play, BF*; which Q2
2 were] *MSS 1–6, 8, 10–12; F, Qq, Poems, Play, BF*; are *MSS 7, 9*

3 y[e] breake of] *MSS 1–7, 9, 10* (thee ~) *11, 12; F, Poems*; that breake the *MS 8*;
like breake of *Qq, BF*; that breake of *Play*

3–4 day, lights] *MSS 1–4, 6–12; F, Qq, Poems, BF*; day | Light *MS 5*; days, light
Play

4 that] *MSS 1–12; F, Qq, Play, BF*; which *Poems*
4 doe mislead] *MSS 1–4, 6–12; F, Qq, Poems, Play, BF*; doth misled *MS 5*

5 bring agayne] *MSS 1–12; Qq, Poems, Play, BF*; bring againe, bring againe *F*
5 bring] *MSS 1–12; F, Q1b, Q2, Poems, Play, BF*; being *Q1a*

6 though] *MSS 1, 3–12; Qq, Poems, Play, BF*; but *MS 2; F*

6 seald' in vaine] *MSS 1–12; F4, Qq, Poems, BF*; seal'd in vaine, seal'd in vaine *F1–3*; seals in vain *Play*

7–12 Hide . . . thee] *MSS 1, 3–12; Qq, Poems, Play, BF*; not in *MS 2, F*

7 those] *MSS 1, 3–6, 8–12; Qq, Poems, Play, BF*; these *MS 7*

8 that thy] *MSS 1, 3–6, 8, 9, 12; Q2, Play*; whom that *MS 7*; which thy *MSS 10, 11; Q1, Poems, BF*

8 bosom] *MSS 1, 3–6, 8–12, Q1b, Q2, Poems*; breast doth *MS 7*; blossome *Q1a, Play, BF*

8 beares] *MSS 1, 3, 4, 6–9, 10* (bares), *11, 12; Qq, Poems, Play, BF*; weares *MS 5*

9 on] *MSS 1, 3–9, 10* (one), *11* (And corrected On), *12; Qq, Poems, Playford, BF*

9 topps] *MSS 1, 3–10, 12; Qq, Poems, Play, BF*; topp *MS 11*

9 the Pinkes y^t] *MSS 1, 3–6, 8, 9, 10* (~ doe corrected to that), *11, 12; Qq, Poems, Play, BF*; their Pincks doe *MS 7*

9 grow] *MSS 1, 3–8, 10–12; Qq, Poems, Play, BF*; growes *MS 9*

10 are yet of those y^t] *MSS 6, 8, 12; Q2, Play*; Are of those that *MSS 1, 3, 4, 9–11; Q1, Poems, BF*; Sweeter are then *MS 5*; Like to those that *MS 7*

10 Aprill] *MSS 1, 3–9, 11, 12; Qq, Play, BF*; abriell *MS 10*; Aprils *Poems*

10 weares] *MSS 1, 2, 4, 6–12; Qq, Poems, Play, BF*; beares *MS 5*

11 But . . . free] *MSS 1, 3–9, 11, 12; Qq, Poems, Play, BF*; line written twice, with first line and but first se in second line deleted, *MS 10*

11 first sett my poore heart] *MSS 1, 3–12; Qq, Play, BF*; my poore heart first set *Poems*

11 sett] *MSS 1, 3, 4, 6–12; Qq, Poems, Play, BF*; Let *MS 5*

12 in those] *MSS 6, 8, 11, 12; Qq, Poems, Play, BF*; in *MSS 1, 3, 4, 5, 7, 9, 10*

12 Icye$_\wedge$] *MSS 1, 4–8, 10–12; Qq, Poems, Play*; Ivory$_\wedge$ *MS 3*; Ice, *MS 9*; Ioy *Q1a*; gay *Q1b*; Ivy *BF*

12 thee] *MSS 1, 3–9, 10* (the), *11, 12; Qq, Poems, Play, BF*

[*Attribution*] *None in MSS 2, 3, 5–7, 9, 12, Play 1–3*; Dr Wilson *after 1st stanza and music, MS 1*; W.S. *after second stanza, MS 3*; Jo: Wilson *after second stanza, MS 8*; *Title-page attributions to*: MR. WILLIAM SHAKESPEARE: *F, Poems*; B.J.F. *Q1*; JOHN FLETCHER Gent. *Q2*; FRANCIS BEAUMONT AND JOHN FLETCHER, GENTLEMEN *BF*.

No single text has readings which are preferred throughout by the majority of the others. However, three texts find themselves in the minority for only one reading: MS 1 (for 'in' at l. 12) and MSS 6 and 12 (for 'are yet of' in l. 10). The two variants concerned are the most widely contested; moreover both can be seen as deliberate changes designed to smooth the metre—if the longer reading is held to be the original in each case. MSS 6 and 12 have both ametrical longer readings. If indeed these two manuscript versions have priority over other texts, we can establish a working hypothesis that in general it will hold true that the minority reading will be a corruption (which is self-evidently true in many cases); but that the minority reading 'are yet of' is an exception that has greater authority than 'are of'. As with the music, though not so conclusively, the textual evidence

Appendix IV

supports the historical circumstances in suggesting that Wilson's song-book supplies an authoritative text. MS 12 agrees with it in every reading, but is clearly less authoritative in that it is not a music manuscript.

Most texts can be related to each other without too much difficulty, and with little consequence for the central textual problems. After establishing these relationships, the discussion below proceeds to consider a particular group of manuscripts and printed texts where the pattern of dependence, if there is one, is more complicated. Here the argument may necessarily be somewhat difficult to follow. The problems of this group, however, are connected with the larger question, the nature of the link between the song in *Rollo* and *Measure*. Our final approach to this question is made through a study of the relationship between the quartos of *Rollo*.

We may begin with versions which are manifestly terminals: individual texts, or groups of texts, which are distinguished by corrupt readings which are not further perpetuated and which do not undergo a further corruption or reversal. One probable such terminal is the last of the Playford texts, Play 4. As a group, the Playford texts share with *Rollo* Q1 the misreading 'blossome'; this must be a coincidence, as none of the other distinctive Q1 readings ('like', l. 3; 'which thy', l. 8; 'are of', l. 12) appears in Playford, and neither of the other distinctive Playford readings ('days light', ll. 3–4; 'seals', l. 6) appears in Q1. The error 'blossome' for 'bosom' is one of contextual association compounded with misreading: the following two lines refer to flowers, specifically to 'Pinkes'. This helps to explain the coincidence.

If, as the music suggested, the Playford texts are associated with the Drexel manuscripts, the words do little to confirm this; the groups have their own distinct variants, and have no corrupt readings in common. This does not mean that the original hypothesis was wrong, but only that a lost manuscript stemmatically quite close to Wilson's original may have introduced music variants whilst accurately reproducing Wilson's text. The words are no refutation of the suggested stemma arising from the music.

On the other hand, the fact that MS 8 does not share these music variants suggests that there can be no stemmatic connection between Playford's 'that breake of' in l. 3 and 'that breake the' in MS 8. 'That' cannot even be explained as a misreading of the same manuscript, as the earliest manuscript with 'that' on the Playford branch of the stemma would have the music variants not found in MS 8. That the variants 'the breake of' / 'that breake of' / 'that breake the' do not result from progressive corruption is less surprising than might appear. In MS 6 Wilson's scribe may have been reproducing a feature of his copy when he wrote 'ye breake of'. Such a form may also have been reproduced in a manuscript connecting the song-book text to the Playford and Drexel manuscripts.[6] Whether or not this was so, the locution obviously caused difficulty to its seventeenth-century transcribers. 'Y^t' or 'that' is the easiest of corruptions, one which may occur through misreading, substitution, or dittography (from l. 2 or l. 4); if the text is thought to be corrupt it is also the most obvious, if not the most satisfactory, of

---

[6] Wilson himself may have prepared the first or both of the conjectured manuscripts. 'The'/'that' would be the simplest of errors, one which he himself might have been responsible for, especially if he originally wrote 'y^e' (the form preserved in MS 6).

emendations. In any case, the textual development could not be viewed as a simple linear corruption, for Playford outbids MS 8's 'that break the' by continuing 'days' light': surely part of the same botched, bungled, or misunderstood attempt to make improved sense of the original as 'that breake of'. MS 8 adopts neither this nor Playford's 'seals' (l. 6) and 'Blossome' (l. 8).

As has already been intimated, the largest verbal divide amongst the manuscripts is between those that adopt one or both of the shorter readings for ll. 10 and 12 and those with the ametrical extra word. There is a large measure of overlap between the texts having both shorter forms; indeed, all the texts without 'those' in l. 12 also omit 'yet' in l. 8 (or, in the case of MS 5, reword to give the same metrical effect). This overlap indicates a connection between the two variants. If connected, they must be deliberate; if deliberate, they almost certainly must be metrical emendations; if metrical emendations, the lists with the shorter readings are the more derivative—but 'emended'—texts. By this logic, MS 6 emerges as more authoritative than MS 1.

It would be natural to contemplate these 'emended' texts—the ones omitting 'these' and 'yet'—as a single extended group. In fact there are probably two distinct groups. The smaller one, the texts with only one metrical variant, is characterized, together with MS 11, by the variant reading 'Which' in l. 8. This conclusion is not self-evident; indeed the situation is complicated enough for the whole matter to be reserved for more detailed treatment (pp. 285–6). It is a conclusion that we must in the mean time anticipate.

If therefore we disregard the Drexel manuscripts, *Rollo* Q1 and the 1640 *Poems*, the remaining texts with metrical variants can quite easily be accounted for. The group comprises MSS 1, 3, 4, 5, 7, and 9. Of these, MS 1 cannot derive from any of the others, for it alone has music. However, MS 1 must derive from a similar earlier manuscript, for it was evidently prepared later than some other members of the group. MSS 1 and 4 are textually identical (apart from incidentals of spelling and punctuation); MS 4's spelling 'sweetely' may derive directly from MS 1's 'sweetelye'. MSS 3 and 9 each have unique readings: MS 3's 'Ivory' (l. 12), and MS 9's 'growes' (l. 9) and 'Ice' (l. 12). MS 9 also reads 'are' in l. 2, which it shares with MS 7. The latter text has a whole series of unique readings in ll. 7–10 and retains 'grow' in l. 9. There may have been a manuscript originating 'are' from which MSS 7 and 9 spring independently. One further extant manuscript, as yet unmentioned, has two metrical variants; this is MS 5. At l. 12 it omits 'these'; at l. 10 it opts for rewording to 'Sweeter are then'. MS 5 could derive from the version of either MS 1 or MS 4. The incidentals do not decide the issue conclusively, but tend to favour MS 1. It is scarcely significant that MSS 4 and 5 agree in lowering some capitals and deleting terminal '-e' s. MS 5 fails to reproduce MS 4's introduction of 'y^t' in l. 4 and 'y^e' in l. 9, but again this is not remarkable. What does seem significant in the light of both texts' tendency to have lower-case initials is that, of MS 5's three mid-line capitals for common nouns, all three are found in MS 1 but only one in MS 4.

The arrangement in Fig. 2 is suggested for the group of manuscripts just surveyed. Most of the manuscripts in this group have a connection with Oxford (see list of manuscripts on p. 273), as do MSS 6, 8, and 12. It would therefore be useful to conjecture that the manuscript at the head of the above stemma was not the manuscript used in the playhouse, but Wilson's own copy which he later kept

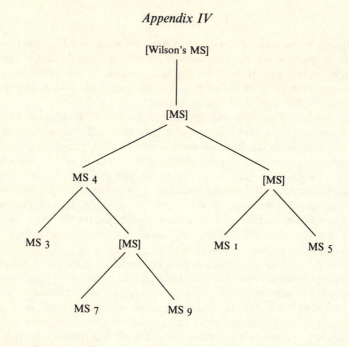

Fig. 2.

in Oxford. The single musical revision between Wilson's original and his song-book suggested above is consistent with this scenario.

We now turn to the group of texts characterized by reading 'Which' in l. 8, as defined in the collation above. In John Benson's notorious 1640 edition of (mostly) Shakespeare's *Poems*, 'Take, oh take' is ambiguously placed between a sequence of non-Shakespearian verse (G1-K5ᵛ) and Shakespeare's 'Phoenix and Turtle'. The text is particularly corrupt, perhaps deliberately so, but most closely resembles MS 11, a version from which it may be taken to derive.[7] In practice, it cannot have been this actual manuscript which Benson sent to the printers, for MS 11 was not prepared until almost twenty years later. The scribe was John Gamble, who was not only himself a musician and composer but, also, significantly, in view of the musical similarities between his copy and Playford's, a music publisher.

MS 11 looks (stemmatically) back to the Playford group and forward to the 1640 *Poems*; it also has marked affinities with *Rollo* Q2. But it most closely resembles MS 10, as the music variants first indicated. The links with Playford are purely musical; apart from their other affinities, MSS 10 and 11, *Poems*, and *Rollo* are the group distinguished by the variant 'Which'. We may now examine the complications of supposing this textual or genealogical group belongs to the same branch of the stemma as the other texts with the metrical emendations.

[7] In his New Variorum edn. of the *Sonnets* (Philadelphia, 1944), Hyder Edward Rollins states that ' "Take, oh take" in Q 1640 is from *The Bloody Brother* [*Rollo*]'. Josephine Waters Bennett noticed complications, and disagreed: 'collation shows that this is improbable' ('Benson's Alleged Piracy of *Shake-speares Sonnets* and Some of Jonson's Works', *SB* 21 (1968), 235–48, 246 n.).

One first notes that the 'Which' texts do not conveniently fit into the stemma for the other manuscripts, even if the latter is radically reorganized. Q1 cannot stand at the head of the enlarged group, for there is no reason why 'like' should be changed to 'the' in l. 2, bringing derivative texts into agreement with Wilson's song-book and Folio *Measure*. 'Like' cannot be described as an obtrusive or reversible error. Further down such a stemma, one would find a second reversion: abandonment of the corrupt 'Which' (a variant which may indeed be prone to reversal, but which is not self-evidently corrupt). Nor is it possible that the 'Which' texts stand at the end of the line of development, though at first sight this is the obvious place to locate them. One would have to assume that a metrical irregularity was reintroduced in three of these texts: that an ametrical word was inserted, that it was the same word as had been omitted, and that someone starting with the metrically regular version would create an irregularity in one line that was not matched in its rhyming partner. If one believes that one of the irregularities could have been restored as a memorial correction, another, more intransigent, problem emerges. Q1 was set from a play manuscript whose copy almost certainly had the song in it. It would be an argument of some desperation to conjecture that this manuscript initially omitted the song, but that it was reintroduced from a derivative song manuscript which had already— before 1639—all but exhausted the line of textual development.

It seems quite clear that at least Q1 must be broken away from the texts with the two metrical variants. We must therefore, without proceeding any further than this, postulate that metrical emendations took place quite independently. But in one instance only one ametrical word was omitted; in most of the remaining texts, both were.

Which side of this necessary divide do the Drexel manuscripts and the *Poems* lie? The disadvantages of leaving them hanging as derivative from the group of other manuscripts are threefold:

1. they share 'Which' with Q1;
2. two of them would have to make the awkward single ametrical restoration outlined above;
3. these texts share this single metrical emendation also with Q1.

Ametrical restoration would not only supply the right word, but also result in the same *combination* of metrical and ametrical lines as Q1.

These considerations not only weigh heavily against the texts in question belonging with the group of metrically regular manuscripts; they weigh almost equally in favour of a connection between Q1 and these texts. Admittedly individual readings are not conclusive evidence in a text so short and so widely dispersed. It would be easy enough to attribute the appearance of 'Which' in two separate groups as a coincidence: the substitution is easily made. What compels attention is the way this particular piece of evidence neatly coincides with the rest. The three texts with only one metrical variant not only share this distinctive and deliberate feature; they also share in reading 'Which'. The only other text to read 'Which', MS 10, is firmly linked to the group of three in any case, on account of other similarities with MS 11. On the basis of evidence presented so far, the connection between Q1 and the other three texts looks inevitable. Yet on the basis of other considerations it looks most implausible.

The first problem concerns the constitution of the group itself, but it is not, we believe, a fundamental problem. The case for the group reading 'Which' in l. 8 being independent of other texts with metrical variants would be more immediately convincing if all the texts in this group were also characterized by having just one metrical variant. As it is, MS 10 has both variants. The manuscript has, as it were, conflicting loyalties. As we have seen, its features cannot argue for a continuity between the two groups of texts: we can only ask which group the manuscript belongs to, and then attempt to account for the conflicting evidence.

In fact, the introduction of the second metrical emendation into a version having the first, which would be a procedure unique to MS 10, is, of all the textual variants, the most readily explained. In Wilson's song-book and similar versions, the two metrical irregularities lend credence to each other: the two lines are paired by rhyme, and parallel metre is to be expected. The single metrical variant results in a text more strikingly odd than the original. If scribes operated in a vacuum, this might never be noticed, or might be ignored, depending on the temperament of the scribe, though the ametrical line would always be vulnerable to alteration. As with a prompt-book, however, a song manuscript may be prepared with performance in mind, or annotated after such performance. MS 10 did not have 'those' written then deleted, but its scribe's copy may have done. Below we offer an illustration of how, in particular circumstances, a scribe could himself have noticed the irregularity (p. 287), but those circumstances are conjectural and we by no means depend on that conjecture for present purposes. The first metrical emendation creates an imbalance whereby it becomes extremely probable that at some point the second will be made. MS 10's agreement in this reading with a group of texts to which it does not belong simply illustrates the connection between textual development and practical music-making.

The 'Which' texts can therefore be seen as an independent and stable group, at least in terms of the verbal variants so far considered. Yet there is an unavoidable difficulty, only half iterated above, which confronts *any* attempt to link Q1 with music manuscripts. As already mentioned, the music manuscripts could only have supplied a fragment of copy for the entire play, and a fragment which would not be needed, in that the copy manuscript would itself supply the song's words. Equally, Q1 (or its copy) could not supply a scribe with copy for the song's music. If Q1 and the other 'Which' texts are linked, some sort of conflation must have taken place. We have just seen that it is difficult to imagine circumstances in which a manuscript would supply secondary copy for Q1. We must therefore consider whether the manuscript underlying both Drexel manuscripts could itself have mixed authority.

Such a manuscript is likely to have been influenced not by Q1 but by a play manuscript underlying it: Q1 has some readings not shared by the conjecturally related texts. Such a manuscript would, however, inevitably read 'like' in l. 2, which is not self-evidently corrupt in either sense or metre. The Drexel and *Poems* reading 'the' is therefore a significant detail pointing to the most likely circumstances in which a play manuscript and a music manuscript could share in influencing subsequent texts.

We conjecture, somewhat tentatively, that the copy for Q1 was consulted to provide a scribe with the text for the second stanza. Such a scribe would be copying or expanding an incomplete manuscript which had the music, with the first stanza interlined between the staves, but in which the second stanza was omitted.

There are indications that a scribe may in fact have added a second stanza to a pre-existing music manuscript. The scribe who prepared the derivative MS 10 had some difficulty in transcribing the second stanza. He or she first supplied 'doe' after 'pinks', then corrected it to 'that'. Evidently he or she could make no sense at all of 'Aprill' and transcribed it as 'abriell', presumably imagining an unknown or undecipherable common noun.[8] The scribe then wrote out the penultimate line of the song twice (miscorrecting by crossing out all the first transcription of the line and the first words of the second attempt as well). The scribe obviously showed some carelessness in preparing the manuscript, but the difficulties would have been worsened if the copy had the second stanza squeezed in as an afterthought. It may even have been fitted between the staves below the words of the first stanza. Such an assumption may help to explain why the second stanza in MS 10 is unique in having no initial capitals (with the possible exception of the first deleted 'But' in l. 11). And after reading 'pinks that grow' in his copy, the scribe's eye may have been momentarily caught by the words 'lights that doe' immediately following and more clearly written in the line above; this could lead to the scribe's temporary confusion of 'that' and 'doe'. Furthermore, it would be plain to the scribe, if the second stanza was fitted below the treble stave of the music, that there was no note available for 'those' in the final line.

In preparing MS 11 Gamble was not so beset by difficulties, and was no doubt more careful. One error potentially derives from a manuscript in which the second stanza was interlined below the first. When beginning l. 9, Gamble first wrote 'And', then overwrote 'on'. 'And', it is true, could be misreading of 'one' (MS 10's spelling). But it may not be a coincidence that 'And' is also the word which opens the equivalent line in the first stanza: the word would appear directly above 'On' if the second stanza was interlined, and would presumably be more prominent. However, as we have seen, Gamble was probably copying from a script prepared before 1640 which in turn derives from the conflated manuscript, in which case he should not have been confronted with late interlineation.

There are two prerequisites for the conflated manuscript. First, the second stanza is not initially present; second, someone expands the text by referring to a theatrical document. Given a two-stanza original the omission would be a relatively simple matter: whereas the first stanza would be interlined between the staves of the music and so inseparable from it in a given manuscript, the second would be separately appended. A transcriber may have been too uninterested in the words to reproduce the second stanza, or may have not left room to transcribe it at the foot of the manuscript. A manuscript could have been damaged at the bottom, or simply torn. Or the second stanza could have been written on a separate leaf that subsequently became detached from the first. Such causes are various and general. More particular circumstances must have brought a play manuscript to the holder of the incomplete song, or the individual to the playhouse.

We know that play manuscripts were sometimes prepared for particular patrons. It is conceivable that the documents were brought together under the roof of an individual who took a literary interest in plays and a musical interest

---

[8] The form *abriell* could perhaps be explained, not as a substantive variant, but as a variant spelling with a slip of the pen giving a literals error (*p/b*). But such an explanation may not have been evident to a 17th-cent. transcriber.

in the songs performed in them. It is rather more likely that the second stanza
was collated with the one-stanza manuscript in, or as a result of a visit to, the
theatre. The kind of person who would be interested in a music manuscript of a
song from a play would be likely to see the play itself. Noting that the song had a
second stanza, this playgoer may consequently have made arrangements to gain
access to a theatre manuscript with the text of that stanza. One cannot be too
confident that such an event occurred. But it is only necessary to establish that in
a variety of circumstances someone desirous to add the second stanza to a one-
stanza music manuscript could have found the opportunity to fulfil this desire.

The majority of manuscript versions of 'Take, oh take' belong to one of two
branches of the stemma. One of these branches is best explained as deriving from
a lost manuscript of mixed authority; as the circumstances are somewhat unusual,
however, one should recognize that the entire conjecture might be wrong, and
that what appears as a very odd coincidence in the variants may be no more than
that.

We may confirm that MS 6 occupies a central position of authority by noting
how, in the largest branch of the stemma, the text becomes increasingly close to
Wilson's as one traces back from some of the most idiosyncratic manuscripts
towards MS 1. This manuscript is itself similar to MS 6 apart from the latter's
metrical variants. Other texts, particularly *Rollo* Q2 and MSS 8 and 12, approach
MS 1 and 6 from quite independent directions, but agree with Wilson's song-
book in their irregular metre in ll. 10 and 12. The words confirm what the music
suggested: MS 1, MS 6, MS 8, and Playford all radiate from a central text which
MS 6 most closely resembles. The printed *Rollo* texts and F *Measure* diverge from
the same point. Whether this means that the text most faithfully rendered in MS
6 is also the origin of the *Rollo* quarto texts and F is a question to which we may
now turn.

It is natural enough to assume that Wilson's music was used for *Measure* as well
as for *Rollo*. There would seem little point in a reviser of *Measure* taking the
words but not the music from a popular song in a play belonging to the same
company, and equally little point in Fletcher taking the words but not the music
from *Measure* (and adding a second stanza) when writing *Rollo*. Whichever play
the song originally appeared in, the advantages of making use of an extant and
known song would be squandered if the company then had to commission a composer to provide new and unfamiliar music. Indeed the established music might
be expected to be a song's most valuable asset: if 'Take, oh take' was borrowed in
a second play its evocative qualities there might be thought to reside in the music
at least as much as in the words, and probably most of all in an indissoluble
union of the two. This would be most particularly so if Wilson's clearly successful
setting was the first to have been composed—in other words if the song was
transferred from *Rollo* to *Measure*.

There are no settings of 'Take, oh take' other than Wilson's music known to
survive or recorded as once existing. But, as shown above, this music is subtly
varied from text to text. The repeated phrases in the Folio text of *Measure* are
not remarkable given such practices; they would provide poor evidence indeed for
conjecturing a radically different setting. Unlike some of the notational variants,
which require both musical skill and scribal effort to introduce, variant repeat

marks (if indeed they needed to be formally indicated in the manuscript) could be supplied in a moment by someone with only the most basic musical knowledge. If the song was transferred from *Rollo* to *Measure*, it is not hard to think of reasons why these particular repeats may have been thought desirable. They lay stress on the words most poignantly appropriate to Mariana; it may also have been felt that they more convincingly rounded off a somewhat obviously curtailed song.

Of course if *Measure* had the song in 1603–4 there must have been another set-ting of it—which raises the question why Wilson was employed to replace it. But if the song was introduced into *Measure* around 1621, a new manuscript of Wilson's music would probably have been needed for the revival. The nature of this manuscript would determine that it was prepared independently of the prompt-book for *Measure*: the prompt-book would not supply the music, the very *raison d'être* of the manuscript. The manuscript's affinities would be with the song-book for *Rollo*, from which, with the simple omission of the second stanza, it would have been copied. Verbal variants between prompt-book and music man-uscript for *Measure* might have mattered no more than such minor inconsistencies in stage directions as are found in prompt-books. Such a consideration opens up the possibility that the one-stanza manuscript conjectured to underlie the Drexels was a copy of the song manuscript prepared for *Measure*—or even that manu-script itself. But this situation could only arise if *Measure* was supplied, probably after Shakespeare's death, with Wilson's music as also used in *Rollo*. For the first stanza, the Drexel manuscripts conform to the textual tradition of other *Rollo* texts ('though', not 'but', in l. 6, and no indication of F's repeated phrases). If these manuscripts partly derive from a song manuscript for *Measure*, the distinc-tive features of F are shown to be corruptions. Although there are no reasons for being committed to such a scenario, it will be noted that it allows the two conjec-tural sources for the Drexel manuscripts to have been located together: with the King's Men.

The 1623 Folio *Measure* has three variants which immediately identify it as a version which influences or is influenced by only one text other than the later Folios. These are the absence of the second stanza, the reading 'but' in l. 6, and the repetitions in ll. 5 and 6. The second of the repetitions was omitted in the derivative Fourth Folio; neither appears in MS 2, a text which in other respects shows every sign of deriving from one of the Folios. As F4's single repetition gives an awkward and implausible text, it is probable that MS 2 was transcribed from it and, in anticipation of Rowe, regularized—though if the manuscript actu-ally dated from the early eighteenth century Rowe could have supplied its copy. In either case, the regularization of metrical imbalance is analogous with MS 11's introduction of the second metrical variant.

These variants give no indication of whether the Folios and MS 2 together rep-resent a derivative terminal or whether the text that passed to F1 stands at the head of the entire stemma. But from 1623 to 1639 F1 was the song's only pub-lished and hence generally available text; if F1 is the original version, it is remark-able that no one drew upon it, apart from the author of the second stanza.

Rollo was printed in two independent Quartos of 1639 (Q1; entitled *The Bloody Brother*) and 1640 (Q2; probably actually printed and published in 1639).[9] In

[9] Greg noted that the Bodleian copy of Q2 'belonged to Robert Burton who died on 25 Jan. 1640' (*Bibliography*, ii. 565).

1676 *Rollo* was included in the enlarged Beaumont and Fletcher Folio. This text is advertised as offering independent authority; the Folio's title-page announces that the plays are 'Published by the Authors Original Copies, the Songs to each Play being added'. For *Rollo* at least this is not true: Q1 served as printer's copy and variants show that 'Take, oh take' was set from an uncorrected sheet.

The *Rollo* texts constitute a distinct group in that both Quartos and the Folio read 'like' in l. 3. Q2 is closer to the most similar non-*Rollo* version than either Q1a or Q1b; that version is MS 6. Hensman and Jump, the two scholars who have studied the *Rollo* texts in most detail, agree that Q2 is closer to authorial papers than Q1.[10] It therefore seems likely that the Q2 version of the song derives from MS 6 rather than the other way round. We may elaborate on this observation by looking more closely at the relationship between the *Rollo* quartos. In his edition, Jump observed that Q1 and Q2 must be printed from separate manuscripts. The copy for Q1, according to Jump, was probably a literary transcript, and that for Q2 the prompt-book or a transcript of it. A stemma based on Jump's hypothesis and linking the printed texts as closely as possible to authorial papers, would take the form shown in Fig. 3.

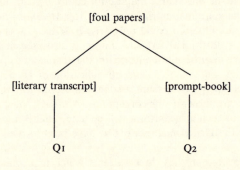

Fig. 3.

When Jump argues that a text printed from a prompt-book 'would normally be less distantly removed from the author's manuscript' than would one printed from 'a more "literary type"'' (p. xiii), he may be referring to the kinds of sophistication introduced into such 'literary' manuscripts, without necessarily suggesting that Q2 is fewer stages removed from the authorial manuscript. Jump finds no stage directions typical of a prompt-book in Q1, but as a 'literary' scribe may have eliminated such characteristics, Jump's thesis would also permit an arrangement in which Q1 *is* at a greater remove from foul papers than Q2, the copy for the literary transcript being the prompt-book, not the foul papers. Such a relationship

[10] *Rollo, Duke of Normandy*, ed. John D. Jump (Liverpool, 1948), pp. xiii–xiv. If the error were a simple misreading, it would be easier for the article 'the' to be the consequent error. The words are sufficiently graphically similar to allow a misreading, though it would not be a particularly probable one. Contextually, 'the' gives the harder reading, as it requires 'the break of day' to be a somewhat eliptical parenthesis or 'break of day' to be an adjectival phrase qualifying 'Lights' (though no editor of *Measure* has even conjectured that the line should be emended). 'Like' may be an attempt to smooth the sense, a deliberate sophistication.

between manuscripts would be similar to that Hensman suggests, but with the difference that she finds the copy for Q1 to have been prepared as a second prompt-book. Hensman also plausibly argued that Q1 and Q2 have a common origin in the original prompt-book.

But a further elaboration seems necessary, one that Jump recognised as a possibility: a manuscript intervening between the original prompt-book and Q2. In the 1630s *Rollo* was one of the most popular plays on the London stage. Q2 was printed in Oxford. The King's Men would surely not have allowed such a valuable asset as the prompt-book to be deposited in a printing house in Oxford. Q2's introduction of scene-divisions in Act 1 on the classical principle of beginning a new scene whenever a new character enters provides supporting evidence of non-theatrical copy.

Therefore the textual history of *Rollo* is unlikely to be simpler than that shown in Fig. 4. The authority for dubious readings common to Q1 and Q2 depends on the unresolved question as to whether their point of common origin—evidently the prompt-book—was a manuscript prepared by the author of the passage concerned.

As for *Measure*, the conclusion that Crane transcribed a prompt-book that was not prepared by Shakespeare himself (see pp. 109–19) is independent of considerations of the date of that prompt-book. Even if the original *Measure* prompt-book was based on an autograph fair copy, the song in *Measure* must stand a minimum of three removes from an autograph text of the song—whether that autograph was in Shakespeare's hand or Fletcher's (see Fig. 5).

The *Rollo* Quartos independently testify that the manuscript from which both derive read 'but' in l. 6; if this manuscript was not itself the prompt-book, Wilson's concurrence indicates that 'but' was nevertheless the reading the King's Men used in the song as it appeared in *Rollo*. Even if Shakespeare first wrote the song, the two-stanza texts here provide an independent source of authority. 'Though' and 'but' are common conjunctions and roughly equivalent words. One

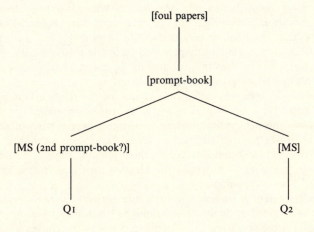

Fig. 4.

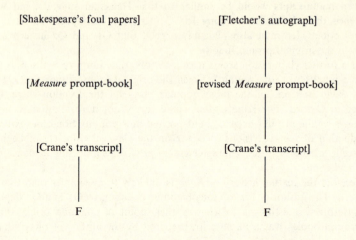

Fig. 5.

of the readings is almost certainly an unintended substitution. 'But' may perhaps make a subconscious appeal to a scribe on account of its relative shortness—half the number of letters. Furthermore, and more significant, 'But' is found beginning the previous line: the prominence of such a synonym could easily encourage substitution of 'but' for 'though'. No comparable explanation is available for the reverse error. Although an editor who rejects our case for revision of *Measure* may wish to follow F, 'though' is rather more likely than 'but' to be the correct reading, even if Shakespeare originally wrote the song. If the song is Fletcher's, the case for 'though' is stronger still.

The song in *Measure* might derive either from Wilson's manuscript or from the *Rollo* prompt-book. In the latter case, *Measure* and MS 6 are independent witnesses to a prompt-book reading 'the' in l. 3, and a manuscript between the prompt-book and the divergence of the Q1 and Q2 text becomes necessary to the stemma. If the song found its way into *Measure* via Wilson's setting, there is no independent verification, and either 'the' or 'like' may have been the original reading. Even in this situation, we believe that 'the' is probably the correct reading, and that Wilson's academic leanings would incline him to accuracy. 'The' is the commoner word, but, as the other variants to the line indicate, gives a contextually difficult reading which invites deliberate alteration.

It is not possible to offer any definitive stemma for the relationships between the *Rollo* play texts, the song, and *Measure*, as the various possibilities can only be narrowed down through textual analysis of variants on the basis of an arbitrary decision as to whether 'the' or 'like' is correct. If, as seems more likely, 'the' is the original reading, there remain at least three possible ways of relating the texts (see Figs. 6, 7, and 8). The stemma for *Measure* itself (continuous line) and the song (pecked line) is shown in Fig. 9.

We may finally present a stemma for the entire network of two-stanza texts. The possibility of reversed or duplicated corruptions which may be misinterpreted or undetected makes the result less than definitive. Some of the conjectural underlying manuscripts facilitate a logical stemmatic development, but would be unnec-

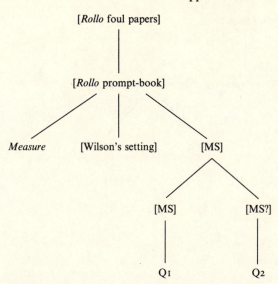

Fig. 6.

essary in such circumstances. In fact, the verbal variants often establish straight-forward textual relationships. They are supported by various considerations that are external to the song's texts: the hypothesis that *Measure* is a revised text, the factor of music, the bibliographical links between the Playford books, the general textual history of *Rollo*, and the historical circumstances of a group of manu-scripts being associated with Oxford. Though there remain some details about which one can be less certain, and places where the variants may be misleading, this stemma (Fig. 10) represents as plausible an overview of the relationship between the twenty-three collated texts of 'Take, oh take those lips away' as their relatively numerous but sometimes puzzling variants permit.

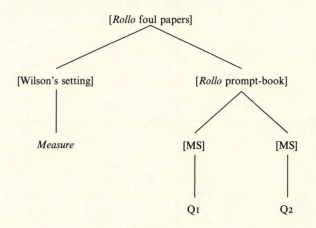

Fig. 7.

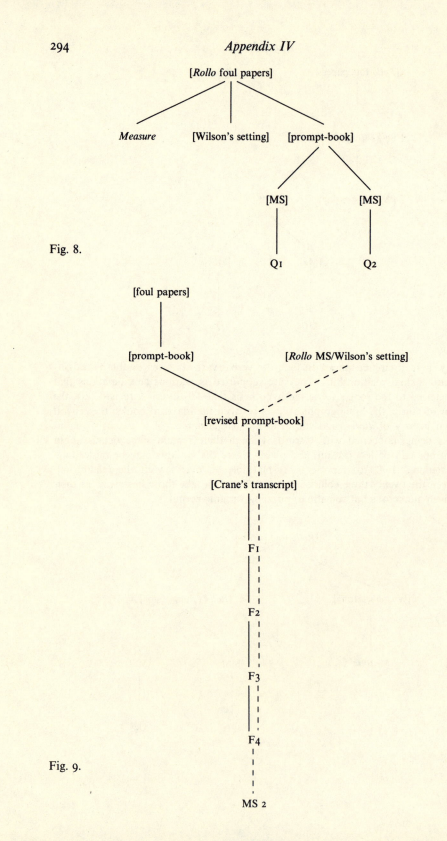

Fig. 8.

Fig. 9.

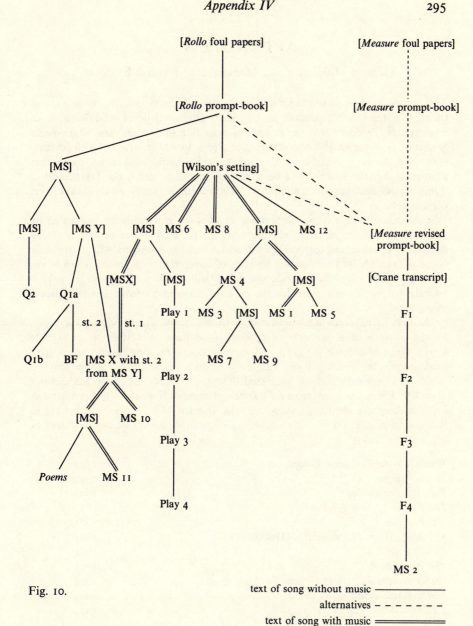

Fig. 10.

text of song without music ——————
alternatives – – – – – –
text of song with music ══════
text of *Measure* without song --------------

APPENDIX V

Thomas Middleton and *Measure* I. 2: Neutral Evidence

This appendix exists to substantiate that the bulk of the vocabulary, imagery, and thought of the suspect passage in I. 2 is *as* characteristic of Middleton as of Shakespeare. Evidence that the passage is *more* like Middleton than Shakespeare is contained in the main body of Chapter 3 (pp. 191–226); here we wish to illustrate only the many features of the passage which could have come from either dramatist, features which could be attributed to either, and hence are neutral in terms of the evidence for authorship. This appendix simply establishes a level playing field.

Shakespeare parallels for the features in question can easily be confirmed by reference to concordances or existing editions; we have therefore not provided detailed documentation for correspondences which most readers will in any case take for granted. By contrast, the absence of concordances to Middleton's work, and the unfamiliarity of our conjecture that Middleton wrote the passage, make it essential to provide references for the parallels between his work and the suspect passage.

The task of reference is complicated, here and in the main body of our essay, by the absence of a properly comprehensive edition of Middleton's complete works. Since Middleton is (to an undeserved extent) less familiar to readers than Shakespeare, the accompanying summary account of his extant canon may be useful. (These works will all be included in the Oxford edition of Middleton's *Complete Works*, now in progress.) Dates of composition are often conjectural. Collaborators are identified, where relevant; queries follow works which have in the past been ascribed to other authors (though in each case we are confident of Middleton's claim).

The Wisdom of Solomon Paraphrased	1597
Micro-cynicon	1599
The Ghost of Lucrece	1600
The Family of Love (Dekker)	1602–5
The Phoenix	1603
The Magnificent Entertainment (Dekker)	1603
Plato's Cap?	1604
The Black Book	1604
Father Hubburd's Tales (*Ant and the Nightingale*)	1604
Meeting of Gallants at an Ordinary?	1604
1 Honest Whore (Dekker)	1604
Michaelmas Term	1605–6
A Yorkshire Tragedy?	1605
Timon of Athens (Shakespeare)	1605
A Mad World, my Masters	1604–6
A Trick to Catch the Old One	1604–6
The Puritan?	1606
Your Five Gallants	1606–7

The Revenger's Tragedy?	1606–7
Sir Robert Sherley's Entertainment in Cracovia	1609
The Two Gates of Salvation	1609
The Roaring Girl (Dekker)	1611
The Second Maiden's Tragedy?	1611
No Wit, No Help like a Woman's	1611
A Chaste Maid in Cheapside	1613
Entertainment at the Opening of the New River	1613
Wit at Several Weapons (Rowley)	1613
The Triumphs of Truth	1613
The Witch	1614–16
A Fair Quarrel (Rowley)	1615–16
The Nice Valour?	1615–16
More Dissemblers Besides Women	1614–19
The Widow	1616
Civitatis Amor	1616
Hengist, King of Kent	1616–20
The Triumphs of Honour and Industry	1617
The Peacemaker	1618
The Old Law (Rowley)	1618
The Inner Temple Masque	1619
'On the Death of Richard Burbage'	1619
The World Tossed at Tennis (Rowley)	1619
The Triumphs of Love and Antiquity	1619
Honourable Entertainments	1620–1
The Sun in Aries (Munday)	1621
Women Beware Women	1621
Anything for a Quiet Life (Webster)	1621
An Invention for the Lord Mayor	1622
The Triumphs of Honour and Virtue	1622
The Changeling (Rowley)	1622
The Triumphs of Integrity	1623
'Upon this masterpiece of tragedy'	1623
A Game at Chess	1624
'A harmless game'	1624
The Triumphs of Health and Prosperity	1626

The largest readily available collection of Middleton's writing is the eight-volume edition by A. H. Bullen (1885–6), to which most of the following references are keyed. However, Bullen does not include a number of the works which most investigators now agree were written, in whole or part, by Middleton. For such works we have keyed our references (in this appendix, and throughout the book) to the following sources. Three works—*Plato's Cap*, *Two Gates*, and *An Invention*—have never been edited, and so are cited from the original documents. For *Meeting of Gallants*, see *The Plague Pamphlets of Thomas Dekker*, ed. F. P. Wilson (Oxford, 1925). For Middleton's contribution to *1 Honest Whore* and *Magnificent Entertainment*, see *The Dramatic Works of Thomas Dekker*, ed. Fredson Bowers, 4 vols. (Cambridge, 1956–61; rep. 1970); we have also used

Bowers's text of *Roaring Girl*, which is more reliable than Bullen's. References to
Wit at Several Weapons and *Nice Valour* are keyed to *The Dramatic Works in the
Beaumont and Fletcher Canon*, gen. ed. Fredson Bowers, vol. vii (Cambridge,
1989). References to *Timon of Athens* are keyed to the text in Shakespeare's
Complete Works (Oxford, 1986); references to *The Puritan* and *Yorkshire Tragedy*,
to *The Shakespeare Apocrypha*, ed. C. F. Tucker Brooke (Oxford, 1908). Our ref-
erences to *The Revenger's Tragedy* are keyed to *Thomas Middleton: Five Plays*,
ed. Bryan Loughrey and Neil Taylor (London, 1988). The following works are
keyed to individual editions: *Ghost* (J. Q. Adams, New York, 1937), *Second
Maiden's Tragedy* (Anne Lancashire, Manchester, 1978), *Hengist* (R. C. Bald,
New York, 1938), *Honourable Entertainments* (R. C. Bald, Mal. Soc. Repr.,
Oxford, 1954), and *Game at Chess* (R. C. Bald, Cambridge, 1929).

In the main body of the essay, we provide, in addition to such references to
modern editions, references to the first editions, or to diplomatic editions of the
manuscripts; quotations are in old-spelling. In this appendix, by contrast, we have
not provided references to the original texts, and our quotations follow the edited
texts. This change in the form of our citations is designed to cut down on the
documentation of material that is no more than ancillary. However, all these references were checked against the same early documents cited in the main body of
the essay; indeed, this appendix was originally included in the main body of the
essay, before a wise reader suggested its relocation.

Some of the parallels between Middleton's work and the suspect passage in
Measure 1. 2 can be provided in a tabular summary.

96	*and . . . other*	(*in stage directions*) **Changeling* 4. 1. O; *Women Beware Women* 4. 3. 0, 5. 2. 0; *Witch* 1. 2. 0; etc.
98	why then	*Women Beware Women* 2. 2. 58; *Chaste Maid* 2. 2. 129, 2. 2. 175, 5. 4. 102; etc.
99	fall upon	*Game at Chess* 2. 2. 215, 3. 1. 150; *Hengist* 5. 1. 124; **Changeling* 5. 1. 26; etc.
100	Heaven grant[1]	*Honourable Entertainments* 5. 36–7
102	Amen	*Peacemaker*, p. 346; *Black Book*, p. 33; **Family of Love* 1. 3. 127; *Father Hubburd's Tales*, p. 107
103	conclud'st	**World Tossed* 401, 779; *Honour and Virtue*, p. 362; *Health and Prosperity*, p. 403; etc.
105	scrap'd	*No Wit* 3. 1. 91 (scrape); **Family of Love* 4. 3. 72 (scraping); **Puritan* 2. 1. 223 (scrape)
105	Table	(*tabulated list*) **Nice Valour* 3. 2. 15, 4. 1. 220, 329, 5. 3. 9; **Old Law* 2. 1. 119; *Robert Sherley*, p. 306; etc.
108	command	*Honour and Virtue* pp. 359, 364; *Widow* 1. 2. 163; *More Dissemblers* 1. 1. 66, 1. 3. 87, 3. 1. 207, etc.
109	all the rest	*Witch* 5. 2. 50; *Michaelmas Term* 2. 3. 349; *New River*, p. 266; *Mad World* 1. 1. 97; *Father Hubburd's Tales*, p. 88; etc.

[1] Shakespeare in fact never uses this exact phrase, though he does have 'heavens grant'
(*Comedy* 1. 1. 66, *Duke of York* 3. 3. 112) and 'grant, heavens' (*Cymbeline* 3. 5. 52).

109	functions	*World Tossed* 787; *Family of Love* 3. 3. 25; *Mad World* 1. 2. 60; *Wisdom of Solomon* 2. 21. 2, 9. 11. 4, 14. 29. 6, 15. 17. 8, 16. 27. 4
110	put forth	*Game at Chess* 1. 1. 90; *1 Honest Whore* 5. 2. 372; *Anything for a Quiet Life* 5. 1. 192; etc.
110	of us all	*Chaste Maid* 4. 1. 32 (none of us all); *Michaelmas Term* 3. 4. 147
111	thanksgiving	*Game at Chess* 5. 2. 89; *More Dissemblers* 5. 2. 172; *Triumphs of Integrity*, p. 390
111	rallish	*Second Maiden's Tragedy* 1. 2. 229; *Black Book*, p. 15; *Game at Chess* 4. 1. 138, 5. 2. 50; etc.
113	I never heard	*Hengist* 3. 3. 288; *Chaste Maid* 2. 1. 111; *No Wit*, 5. 1. 464; *1 Honest Whore* 1. 5. 232; *Phoenix* 1. 4. 255; *Meeting of Gallants* p. 123 (I never heard of any); *Puritan* 5. 3. 2
113	dislike	*Anything for a Quiet Life* Epi. 4; *Women Beware Women* 3. 1. 120 (disliked)
114	thou never was't	*Revenger's Tragedy* 2. 2. 88 (thou wast never)
116	dozen	*Father Hubburd's Tales*, p. 73 (at least his dozen); *More Dissemblers* 1. 2. 225, 4. 1. 100; *No Wit* 3. 1. 179, Epi. 6; *Mad World* 1. 1. 172; etc.
118	proportion	*Game at Chess* 4. 1. 111; *More Dissemblers* 4. 2. 58; *No Wit* 1. 1. 119, 202; etc.
118	language	*Widow* 3. 3. 125; *More Dissemblers* 1. 2. 201, 1. 4. 80, 4. 1. 123, 126, 240, 4. 2. 194; *Wit at Several Weapons* 1. 2. 74 (in this Language)
119	Religion	*Honour and Industry*, pp. 304, 305; *World Tossed* 810; *More Dissemblers* 1. 2. 38, 2. 2. 27, 5. 2. 227; etc.
120	why not	*Michaelmas Term* 5. 3. 124. etc.
120, 122	despight of	*Puritan* 1. 2. 95; etc.
120	all controversie	*Widow* 4. 1. 117
121	wicked	*Widow* 4. 1. 107, 5. 1. 384; *Changeling* 3. 4. 121, 4. 2. 51, 54; *Puritan* 2. 1. 77; etc.
122	villaine	*Puritan* 3. 1. 52, 3. 4. 108; *Fair Quarrel* 2. 1. 59; *Women Beware Women* 2. 2. 442, 4. 2. 59; etc.
122	Grace	*Honour and Industry*, p. 299; *Health and Prosperity*, pp. 405, 408; *Puritan* 1. 3. 58; etc.
123	paire of	*No Wit* 2. 1. 39, 2. 3. 248; *Wit at Several Weapons* 1. 2. 140; etc.
125	I grant	*Women Beware Women* 4. 3. 38; *Wit at Several Weapons* 1. 2. 57
128	three pil'd	*Revenger's Tragedy* 1. 1. 46 (*of flesh*); *Mad World* 1. 2. 116 (third pile—*of wits*; spoken by a whore)

128	peece[2]	(*of cloth*) *Hengist* 3. 3. 77; *Anything for a Quiet Life* 2. 2. 83–4, 92, 97, 104, etc.; (*of a person*) *Witch* 5. 3. 89; *Chaste Maid* 1. 1. 6, 1. 2. 44, 2. 1. 105; etc.
128	I warrant thee	*No Wit* 2. 3. 18, 5. 1. 128; *Michaelmas Term* 4. 3. 67; *Puritan* 3. 4. 125, 3. 5. 114, 212
128	I had as liefe	*Wit at Several Weapons* 3. 1. 161 (I'd as lieve)
129	Kersey	*Michaelmas Term* 1. 1. 256, 2. 3. 12, 105, 3. 1. 256
130	French Velvet	*Widow* 1. 1. 168; (*velvet* very frequent)
131	painfull	*Women Beware Women* 4. 2. 231; *No Wit* 1. 1. 22; *Love and Antiquity*, p. 322; *More Dissemblers* 3. 1. 241; etc.
132	feeling	*Women Beware Women* 3. 1. 80, 4. 1. 188, 5. 1. 3; *Second Maiden's Tragedy* 2. 1. 124, 4. 3. 45; *Widow* 5. 1. 289; etc.
133	health	*Phoenix* 1. 4. 13, 2. 2. 269; etc.
133	whilst I live	*Hengist* 5. 2. 189; *Mad World* 4. 3. 110; (*also* while I live, while I lived, while you live, etc.)
136	tainted	*Game at Chess* 2. 2. 152, 280, 4. 2. 106; *No Wit* 4. 3. 83; *Black Book*, p. 6
137	free	*World Tossed* 737; *Witch* 5. 3. 59; etc.
139	purchas'd	*Fair Quarrel* 3. 3. 30 (pain purchas'd); *World Tossed* 666 (purchase), 844 (well-purchas'd); *Triumphs of Integrity* p. 386; *More Dissemblers* 4. 2. 85; etc.
139	diseases	(*often, but specifically of lust in:*) *Chaste Maid* 3. 1. 64; *Women Beware Women* 2. 2. 137–8 (diseas'd); *No Wit* 1. 1. 30
139	under her Roofe[3]	*Honourable Entertainments* 7. 184 (Under the Roofe of the chiefe *Magistrate*); *Michaelmas Term* 2. 2. 3 (under a poor thatch'd Roof)
142	Judge	*World Tossed* 792; *Widow* 1. 2. 226
143	three thousand	*Changeling* 3. 4. 62 (golden Florins)
145	French crowne	*Chaste Maid* 4. 3. 19
147	error	*Sun in Aries*, p. 348; *Game at Chess* Induction (*name of a character*); *More Dissemblers* 4. 2. 116, 5. 1. 4, 5. 2. 91, 238; etc.
147	sound	(= *healthy*) *World Tossed* 790; *Old Law* 3. 2. 145; etc.
149	thy bones are hollow	*Revenger's Tragedy* 1. 1. 6 (hollow bones)
150	Impiety	*Peacemaker*, pp. 345, 346; *Invention*, p. 375; etc.
151	How now	*Game at Chess* 2. 1. 265, 3. 1. 117. 4. 2. 9; *Women Beware Women* 2. 1. 57, 3. 3. 136, etc.

[2] Compare 'half-crowne-piece' (*Chaste Maid* 1. 1. 29), where the noun is similarly preceded by a compound qualifier, the first element of which quantifies the second.
[3] The closest Shakespearian parallel is in *Richard II* 4. 1. 282: 'under his household roof' (Folio only). In *Michaelmas Term* the roof in question is (as in *Measure*) that of a whorehouse.

152	profound	(*of wound*) *Old Law 3. 2. 316
152	Ciatica[4]	*Old Law 2. 1. 55, 3. 2. 137
154	five thousand	*Game at Chess* 4. 2. 118–19; *Witch* 3. 3. 3; *No Wit* 5. 1. 220; *Phoenix* 1. 6. 141; etc.
154	of you all	*Witch* 1. 2. 96; *Hengist* 5. 1. 195
155	pray'thee	*Anything for a Quiet Life* 5. 1. 166; *Chaste Maid* 2. 1. 90, 130, 151; *Family of Love* 1. 3. 60 (I pray thee); etc.
156	Marry	*Fair Quarrel* 2. 1. 58; *Witch* 4. 2. 36; *More Dissemblers* 4. 2. 100; *Anything for a Quiet Life* 2. 2. 102; etc.
156	Signior	*Widow* (repeatedly); *More Dissemblers* (repeatedly); *Changeling* 2. 1. 66; *Women Beware Women* 2. 2. 45, 3. 2. 201
158	arrested	*Widow* 3. 2. 66; *Puritan* 3. 4. 55, 3. 5. 11, 12, 13; etc.
158–9	Nay . . . which is more	*More Dissemblers* 5. 1. 69
159	carried away	*World Tossed* 556 (carry away); *No Wit* 2. 3. 54, 206; etc.
159	away: and which is	*More Dissemblers* 4. 1. 281–2 ('blew her away: And which is worse')
160	his head . . . chop'd off	*Sir Robert Sherley*, p. 316
161	fooling	*More Dissemblers* 3. 1. 33
163	too sure	*Nice Valour* 3. 3. 34; *Women Beware Women* 4. 2. 57
163–4	getting . . . with childe	*Women Beware Women* 3. 1. 30; *No Wit* 3. 1. 257; *Family of Love* 4. 4. 103, 171; etc.
165	Beleeve me	*More Dissemblers* 3. 1. 188; *Second Maiden's Tragedy* 2. 2. 159; *Chaste Maid* 3. 2. 15; etc.
165	promis'd	*Chaste Maid* 2. 2. 111; *Women Beware Women* 3. 1. 74; *More Dissemblers* 3. 1. 15, 21, 137

[4] Alexander Schmidt's *Shakespeare-Lexicon* (1886) glosses the word as 'a painful affliction of the hip; considered as a symptom of syphilis', citing not only this passage in *Measure* but both Shakespeare's other examples of the word. *OED* recognizes no such sense, but its existence is confirmed by Massinger's *Emperor of the East* (1631), 4. 3. 88–90: 'the pox Sir, | Though falsely nam'd the Sciatica, or goute, | Is the more Catholick sicknesse.' This example is, however, almost three decades later than the original composition of *Measure*, and we are aware of no earlier examples, other than this passage itself. Neither in *Timon* nor in *Troilus* does the context call for such a meaning: 'Thou cold sciatica, | Cripple our senators, that their limbs may halt | As lamely as their manners' (*Timon* 4. 1. 23–5), 'the rotten diseases of the south, the guts-griping, ruptures, loads o' gravel in the back, lethargies, cold palsies, raw eyes, dirt-rotten livers, wheezing lungs, bladders full of impostume, sciaticas lime-kilns i'th palm, incurable bone-ache, and the rivelled fee-simple of the tetter' (*Troilus* Add. A, 5. 1. 17–26). In *Troilus* Thersites is cursing Pandarus as a 'masculine whore', but even the most liberal interpretations have been unable to associate all of his catalogue of diseases with sexual infection. The *possibility* of a sexual reference in *Troilus* (which would support Shakespeare) must be balanced against the late date for any explicit parallel for the euphemism (which would support Middleton). Since both dramatists used the word, and since the pun would be particularly attractive (and might have been invented for) an old bawd, we have included it here, among neutral parallels.

166	precise	*Family of Love* 3. 6. 59, 4. 2. 35; *Nice Valour* 1. 1. 194, 2. 1. 69, 247, 4. 1. 149
168	Besides	*Witch* 3. 1. 32; *Chaste Maid* 1. 1. 116; *No Wit* 3. 1. 160; etc.
168	drawes . . . neere	*Sun in Aries*, p. 350; *Family of Love* 4. 4. 81 ('Draw somewhat near'); *Triumphs of Integrity* p. 387; *Honour and Virtue*, p. 358; etc.
168	something neere	*More Dissemblers* 4. 2. 106
169	purpose	*Women Beware Women* 1. 2. 4, 2. 1. 62 ('to great purpose'), 3. 3. 2, 297, 4. 2. 203 (a purpose); *More Dissemblers* 3. 1. 34, 35
170	proclamation	*Phoenix* 2. 3. 247; *Meeting of Gallants* B2; *Inner Temple Masque* 91
171	Away	(imperative) *Trick* 1. 1. 102; etc.
172	sweat	(as cure for VD) *Chaste Maid* 4. 1. 261; *Father Hubburd's Tales*, pp. 73–4; *Widow* 3. 1. 210–11; *Your Five Gallants* 1. 1. 324; *Michaelmas Term* 3. 1. 267; etc.
173	gallowes	*Chaste Maid* 5. 1. 62; *Roaring Girl* 5. 2. 213; *Plato's Cap* B2ᵛ; etc.
173	poverty	*Women Beware Women* 1. 1. 96; *Anything for a Quiet Life* 5. 2. 229; *No Wit* 1. 1. 30 (in conjunction with strumpet and diseases); etc.
174	Custom	*1 Honest Whore* 1. 5. 151; *Plato's Cap* D2
174	shrunke	*No Wit* 3. 1. 112

Many other similarities in thought and phrasing equally permit Middleton without excluding Shakespeare. As with the preceding tabulation, these may be considered in the order in which they appear in the scene.

Measure 1. 2 opens with a discussion of war and peace, temporal and spiritual; the speakers are soldiering gentlemen. The contrast between temporal war and spiritual peace is also found in the first speech of the first scene of *Witch*; again the speaker is an ex-soldier.[5] The second scene of *Puritan* opens with a debate on war and peace in which it is observed that 'War sitts now like a Justice of peace, and does nothing' (1. 2. 5–6), once again quibbling on 'peace' (cessation of war/rule of law). The Second Gentleman opposes divine and secular power ('Heaven grant us its peace, but not the King of *Hungaries*'); similarly in *Second Maiden's Tragedy* we read, 'Your king's poisoned!—The King of heav'n be praised for't' (5. 2. 167–8). Middleton's pamphlet *The Peacemaker* devotes itself entirely to this subject: 'Peace . . . hath her being in Heaven' (p. 325), 'peace of God' (pp. 325, 330), 'God of peace' (pp. 325, 334, 342).[6]

As in *Measure* 1. 2, Middleton associates baldness with pox (*Plato's Cap* A3, C4, *Roaring Girl* 2. 4. 282–4, *More Dissemblers* 1. 4. 80); he associates velvet

---

[5] 'My three years spent in war has now undone my peace for ever' (*Witch* 1. 1. 1–2). See also *Mad World* 2. 2. 28–9 ('Peace, lieutenant. | Maw [worm]. I had rather have war, captain'.)

[6] Middleton also clearly alludes to the peace of heaven in phrases like 'his last peace with his Maker' and 'his peace eternally', 'to grudge my soul her peace', 'my sacred peace', 'peace and mercy to one new departed' (*Fair Quarrel* 3. 1. 86–7, 4. 2. 90, 105, 4. 3. 31) etc.

with lust (**Plato's Cap* C4ᵛ, *Roaring Girl 3. 1. 14, **Revenger's Tragedy* 3. 5. 45, *Black Book*, pp. 16, 22, 35, 42, *Widow* 1. 1. 168, *More Dissemblers* 1. 4. 96–7, **Wit at Several Weapons* 1. 1. 52). Kersey is associated with plainness (*Michaelmas Term* 1. 1. 253–6). The pox has a debilitating effect on the bones (*Michaelmas Term* Ind. 20–1 and 2. 1. 163, *Phoenix* 2. 3. 184–6, *Black Book*, pp. 6 and 23, *Your Five Gallants* 3. 2. 74, *Women Beware Women* 3. 1. 78–9). The First Gentleman here complains that 'Thou art alwayes figuring disease in me'; Middleton writes of 'virtues figured . . . in you' (*Magnificent Entertainment* 1442).[7] Neither Middleton nor Shakespeare uses the compound 'promise keeping' (TLN 166–7); but (like Shakespeare) Middleton does write 'council-keeping' (**Wit at Several Weapons* 5. 2. 49) and 'housekeeping' (*Hubburd*, p. 75).[8] As the First Gentleman here says that 'there went but a paire of sheeres betweene us', so Vindice in **Revenger's Tragedy* speaks of his outward shape and inward heart being 'cut out of one piece' (3. 5. 10); the Devil in *Black Book* describes how 'when I cut out souls, I throw the shreds | And the white linings of a new-soiled spirit' (p. 7); Shrimp in *Family of Love says 'you are both cut out of a piece' (3. 2. 18–19), an image that recurs in 'out o' the same piece' (5. 1. 68).

As *Measure* contrasts 'English Kersey' and 'French Velvet', so Middleton contrasts 'a French lacquey . . . and an English page' (*Black Book*, p. 21), 'a French hood' and 'the English fashion' (**Anything for a Quiet Life* 4. 2. 134); he describes venereal disease as 'the common misery of an English strumpet, | In French and Dutch' (*Chaste Maid* 5. 1. 106–7), laments that 'so many of our English women should wear French bodies', and tells us that 'sin may be committed either in French, Dutch, Italian, or Spanish, and all after the English fashion' (*Black Book*, p. 22).[9]

Like Shakespeare, Middleton prefers the form '1. Gent.' for speech prefixes of the kind found here in *Measure*.[10] Many editors have felt that the logic of the dialogue in 1. 2 is confused by misattribution of numbered speech prefixes to the wrong gentleman; identical confusion seems to have affected a series of numbered prefixes in 5. 1 of *Your Five Gallants*. Lucio says 'thy bones are hollow; Impiety has made a feast of thee'; in *Mad World* Middleton wrote 'pox feast you' (2. 5. 50) and described a prostitute who 'consumes more than [his] sire could hoard' (4. 4. 70). In *Game* the nations of Europe are a 'large feast' for the 'vast ambition' of the Black House (5. 3. 92); in *Women Beware Women* Livia calls the incestuous Hippolito 'all a feast', comparing his blushes to 'saying grace before a feast' (1. 2. 151–2); in *Ghost* Iniquity has 'burnt out the honor of thy bones | And made them powders of impiety' (ll. 323–6); in *World Tossed recurs the image 'thy lust may feast' (l. 803), and *Mad World* expresses the same idea in the phrase 'We'll feast our lechery' (4. 3. 88). The image is implicit in *Chaste Maid* 2. 1. 50, 'The feast of marriage is not lust but love'. *Solomon* describes 'those whom death and sins devour' (18. 24. 6) and 'vice, which all thy body feeds' (14. 11. 12). The

---

[7] Though *The Magnificent Entertainment* is a collaborative work, we have not asterisked this item, since Dekker specifically attributes the speech to Middleton (ll. 1469–71).

[8] Brittin remarks on Middleton's use of 'original' and 'innovative' compounds ('Adjectives and Authorship', pp. 83–5).

[9] This sentence is offered as proof that there are 'knaves of all languages', and forms part of Lucifer's reply to the bawd's complaint about the decline in business; it therefore has an unusual number of links with the passage in *Measure*.

[10] See Lake, *Canon*, Band 2(g).

idea is present also in lines like 'the mouth of lust' (*Ghost*, l. 35), 'consumed by inchastity' (**Plato's Cap* D2), 'The sin of feasts, drunken adultery' (**Revenger's Tragedy* 1. 2. 188), and 'Diseases gnaw thy bones' (*Michaelmas Term* 2. 1. 163).

Lucio promises to 'learne to begin thy health; but, whilst I live forget to drinke after thee', which creates an ironic distinction between a health as an initiation to drinking and as an absence of disease. The same distinction is made in **World Tossed* 490: 'We drink no healths, but all for health' and **Wit at Several Weapons* 5. 1. 131–2, 'Ile pledge it | Were it against my health'. The traditional toast is repeatedly subject to Middleton's irony as he in turn associates drinking with lust (**Revenger's Tragedy* 1. 2. 180, 'deep healths went round ...'), sickness (*Witch* 2. 1. 200–1; 'we'll have one health . . . though I be sick at heart'), sin (*Solomon* 11. 7. 1–2, 'But let them surfeit on their bloody cup, | Carousing to their own destruction's health'), death (*Mad World* 1. 1. 48–9, 'when they're dead we may drink to their healths'; *Witch* 1. 1. 106, 'a health in a strange cup'—which is a skull), and deception (*Michaelmas Term* 2. 1. 27–8, 'your health shall likewise undoubtedly be remembered, and thereupon I pledge you', where the toast precedes a game of dice).[11] In *Ghost*, Lucrece's ghost offers Tarquin a cup of her blood, urging him to 'Drinke to my chastitie' (l. 68) and to 'Pledge thy desire, carowsing off my shame' (l. 73). All these connotations lie behind Lucio's proposed insincere toast whose real purpose is to prevent the pledger from suffering the fatal consequences of venereal disease.

Like Lucio, Middleton puns on 'sound' as a noise and as a state of being firm, reliable, or healthy (*Solomon* 10.17; *Michaelmas Term* 1. 1. 12; *Game at Chess* 4. 2. 7–9, 5. 3. 53–5; **Plato's Cap* D2). In *Michalemas Term* 1. 1. 10–13, a prostitute is compared to a 'lute that has all the strings broke', whom 'doctors enow in town' will make '*sound* as sweet as e'er she did'. The quibble here is surely unavoidable. Middleton also associates the verb 'sound' with things which are 'hollow' (*Solomon* 2. 10. 8). Like the First Gentleman, he quibbles on 'pil'd': compare 'thou Church-peeling, thou Holy-paring, religious outside, thou!' (**Puritan* 1. 3. 57–8). In **Puritan*, the word 'peeling' dazzlingly puns on 'pealing' (of church bells), 'pilling' (of hair), and 'peeling' (as in 'paring'); in *Measure* the same sound puns on 'pile' (layers), 'piles' (disease), and 'pill' (loss of hair). Middleton also puns on 'painful[ly]' as 'causing pain' and 'painstaking' (*No Wit* 2. 1. 384). The author of the suspect passage in 1. 2 puns on 'feeling[ly]', twisting it from the First Gentleman's positive 'appropriately' to Lucio's negative 'painfully'. In **Nice Valour*, an anonymous '*1 Gent.*' is struck, and comments 'I have took a villanous hard taske upon me; | Now I begin to have a feeling on't' (4. 1. 213–14). In *Hengist* Roxana asks 'Doost thinke Ile ever wrong thee' and Horsus replies 'Oh most feelingly' (2. 3. 260–1); since Roxana is at this moment stroking him, 'feelingly' can refer to her touch on him, to her faithlessly touching another, to the pain of the wrong she will do him, or to the acuteness of his own conviction that she will wrong him. The same pun crops up in **Old Law* 4. 2. 118–19, where parting kisses are described as 'a shower of graces upon my cheeks, | They take their leave feelingly', and possibly also **Family of Love* at 3. 3. 34–47, and more certainly at 5. 3. 288–96. When the Second Suitor in *Widow* says 'Everything now

[11] Middleton similarly quibbles on 'drink' meaning 'drinking someone's health' and 'consuming someone's means' in *Mad World* 3. 3. 102; *Michaelmas Term* 3. 1. 98–9; *No Wit* 4. 2. 167; and *More Dissemblers* 3. 2. 47–9; the joke is also in **Timon* 1. 2. 137–9.

must have a feeling first.— | Do I come near you, widow?' (5. 1. 288–9), a similar quibble on 'feeling' immediately precedes a paraphrase of 'Do I speake feelingly now?' (which itself sustains the joke). The 'fellow-feeling' of *Women Beware Women* 3. 1. 80 is one of pain as well as empathy. Middleton also shares with Lucio the pun on 'crown' as a head and a coin (*Father Hubburd's Tales*, p. 106; *Mad World* 1. 1. 72–5; **Plato's Cap* C3ᵛ).

In *Measure* Lucio alleges that the Second Gentleman 'never was't where Grace was said'. In *Phoenix*, Middleton writes 'We have no leisure to say prayers' (1. 4. 192) and 'You never say your prayers' (5. 1. 295), while in *Widow* 'one falls to meat and forgets grace' (5. 1. 152). In *World Tossed a sea captain claims 'I've seen no church these five-and-twenty years' (l. 687); in *No Wit* Savourwit admits 'I pray not often; the last prayer I made | Was nine-year old last Bartholomew-tide' (2. 2. 107–8); in **Revenger's Tragedy* Vindice says 'Save Grace the bawd, I seldom hear grace named' (1. 3. 16). The last example quibbles on 'grace' as Lucio does—and as Vindice himself does again (at 2. 2. 135 and 5. 1. 142–4), as Easy and Shortyard do in *Michaelmas Term* 2. 3. 451–4. In *Witch*, repentance after the event is metaphorically described as 'A sign you could say grace after a full meal' (3. 2. 97); in *Trick* Dampit tries to recall when he last said prayers (3. 4. 1–5). The imputation is that such behaviour is 'of no religion' (**Second Maiden's Tragedy* 5. 1. 64); in particular, 'a captain is . . . of no religion' (*Phoenix* 2. 2. 128–30). In *Measure* the Second Gentleman, a soldier, would say grace 'in any religion', an allusion to schisms found also in *Black Book* (p. 37, 'many of your religion'; p. 43, 'a breath of all religions save the true one') and in **Second Maiden's Tragedy* 4. 3. 47–8, where a soldier says 'turn me of some religion or other'.

The reflexive expression 'I have done my selfe wrong' resembles 'you do your-self wrong' (*Michaelmas Term* 2. 3. 366), 'you wrong yourself' (*Nice Valour 5. 3. 49), 'how much you wrong yourself' (*No Wit* 5. 1. 55), 'Your Grace much wrongs yourself' (**Revenger's Tragedy* 1. 2. 79), 'wrong done to yourself' (*Witch* 4. 1. 63), 'to wrong yourself' (*Roaring Girl 2. 2. 54), and 'you do yourselves . . . wrong' (*Solomon* 19. 14. 10).

Neither Shakespeare's canon nor Middleton's provides any parallels for 'dislike' meaning 'express aversion to' (TLN 113); *OED* cites no other examples before 1641 (*v*. 3b). Neither author uses 'proportion' in the specific sense required here, as an attribute of language (TLN 118). Neither uses the phrases 'wicked villain' (TLN 121–2), 'I, and more' (144), 'full of error' (147), 'as one would say' (148), 'and which is more' (159), 'to such a purpose' (169), or 'learne the truth of it' (171). Neither elsewhere uses 'profound' of a disease (152). The precise meanings of the interjection 'well' are in most cases difficult to discriminate, but it does seem likely that at TLN 123 it is 'used to show that note has been taken of an insult'. No other unequivocal parallel for this usage can be found in either Middleton or Shakespeare, though it had become proverbial by 1670, and is clearly used by Fletcher as early as 1612–14.[12]

Several of these images are similar to phrases found in Middleton's work, and Middleton sometimes comes closer than Shakespeare to using the same words.

---

[12] For the proverb see citations in Eccles, p. 123. For Fletcher see *Valentinian* 4. 1. 64 and (almost as certain) 1. 3. 208. Possible examples in Middleton occur in *No Wit* 3. 1. 131, *Michaelmas Term* 1. 1. 310, etc.

Though some special sense of 'proportion' seems required, it might also be taken literally, as an indication of the size or length of the unrehearsed graces; in *Family of Love*, a Puritan boasts 'I do use to say inspired graces, able to starve a wicked man with length' (3. 3. 74–5). The phrase 'wicked villain' is paraphrased when in *Wit at Several Weapons* 4. 1. 55–6 'the prime villaine' prompts the response 'A wicked prime'. Middleton comes close to 'I, and more' in both *Women Beware Women* 2. 2. 191 ('ay, or more') and *Michaelmas Term* 3. 5. 60 ('ay, and three more'); Shakespeare likewise has 'ay, and much more' (*Richard III* 1. 3. 262) and 'ay, more' (*Caesar* 4. 3. 42). Both Middleton and Shakespeare use the phrase 'full of fraud' (*Venus and Adonis* 1141; *1 Honest Whore* 3. 1. 147), and Middleton has the collocation 'Error, full of . . .' (*Triumphs of Truth*, p. 255). In *More Dissemblers* Middleton twice uses the parenthetical phrase 'as who should say' (3. 1. 66, 69), and in *Chaste Maid* employs the Latin 'ut ita dicam' (4. 1. 117); we have found nothing in Shakespeare so close to *Measure*'s 'as one would say'. Likewise, Middleton writes 'and which is worse' (*Mad World* 3. 1. 92; *Witch* 4. 1. 26; *More Dissemblers* 4. 1. 282), 'And which was worse' (*Revenger's Tragedy* 1. 2. 44), '& wch is worst' (*Hengist* 5. 1. 359), 'and which is heavier' (*Witch* 4. 3. 73), and 'nay, which is more lamentable' (*More Dissemblers* 5. 1. 69). The closest that either playwright comes to *Measure*'s 'to such a purpose' is Middleton's 'to such an end' (*Chaste Maid* 3. 1. 22). All the components of 'learne the truth of it' are present when Middleton writes 'A man is never too old to learn; your grace will say so when you hear the rest of it: the truth is . . .' (*Hengist* Quarto, in Bullen, 5. 1. 286–7). Middleton does use 'profound' of a wound (*Old Law* 3. 2. 316), if not a disease. In *No Wit* is a probable example of the 'menacing' use of 'Well'. Weatherwise, a fanatical believer in almanacs, is defending their veracity, when Sir Gilbert replies that they only seem to predict the truth 'because they're foolishly believed, sir' (3. 1. 29–30); since Weatherwise is the only party present who believes the predictions, Sir Gilbert's retort is clearly an insult, and Weatherwise replies 'Well, take your courses, gentlemen . . .' (3. 1. 131). This passage at the very least comes very close to the alleged use of the interjection in *Measure*.

Although we must concede that we have not found exact parallels for a few senses and phrases in either canon, the presence of such near-misses suggests, obviously enough, that these features were well within the range of either dramatist. In fact, as we have argued above, it seems to us extremely unlikely that any dramatist other than Shakespeare or Middleton wrote this passage. The elements of its language for which no reliable parallels can be found in either canon do not demonstrate that neither wrote it; rather, they indicate—as common sense should have told us anyway—that we should not expect to find parallels in one author for every feature of the passage. More specifically, they show the weakness of the evidence for Shakespeare: it is arguably less likely that *Shakespeare* wrote the passage, than that *neither* wrote it.

APPENDIX VI

Other Passages Potentially Suspect in *Measure*

Having raised questions about two passages in the Folio text, it seemed necessary to re-examine the entire text. This examination has persuaded us of the integrity of the text as a whole. This conclusion is suggested, first of all, by general considerations. Adapters usually interpolated or transposed blocks of material, or made major alterations of staging; they did not fidget with minutiae.[1] And if Middleton had contributed much more than the one passage in 1. 2, we should find more evidence than we do of his preferred oaths, phrases, and linguistic forms.[2] But only one of Middleton's most characteristic expletives is found in *Measure* ('a pox', also found in ten other Shakespeare plays), and of twenty-eight mostly commoner expletives which Middleton favours less distinctly, just seven occur in *Measure*.[3] Interference by Crane is unlikely to account for the 71 instances of *hath* to 5 of *has* outside the two major interpolations, nor for 24 *doth* to 9 *does*: both preferred forms are against Middleton's own preferences. Middleton frequently used the contraction *'em*; it does not appear anywhere in *Measure*. If Middleton had a hand outside the identified interpolations, the extent of his contribution must, to judge by the evidence, have been severely limited.

Only one other brief passage may warrant editorial anxiety. The stage direction at the beginning of 2. 1 reads in the Folio '*Enter Angelo, Escalus, and seruants, Iustice*' (TLN 450). As Dover Wilson suggested and W. W. Greg agreed, the last word 'seems to be a later addition':[4] the violation of decorum in the order of

---

[1] For a useful general distinction between authorial revision and theatrical adaptation see John Kerrigan, 'Revision, Adaptation, and the Fool in *King Lear*', in *Division*, 195–245.

[2] And, it may be added, his characteristic forms of stage direction. At 4. 2. 123 (TLN 1985) we find the direction '*The Letter*'. Immediately before, the Duke asks the Provost to read the letter, but the Provost is given no speech prefix when he does so. Lever (p. xxvii) compares the direction and omitted prefix with the Trinity autograph MS of *Game at Chess*, where the same features are found at 3. 1. 33. (There is no change of speaker in Eccles's further example at 2. 1. 15.) The direction itself is not unique to Middleton; we have already cited examples in *Edmund Ironside* and *Hamlet* (p. 111). There is also a missing prefix following a letter direction in Folio *Hamlet* 4. 6. 12 (TLN 2985), though it must be admitted that the omission could have arisen because the first word of the letter is the name of the reader (producing an apparent duplication). The combination of direction and missing prefix thus remains a peculiarity without convincing parallel in Shakespeare. The scribe or compositor may have omitted a prefix which only by chance followed the direction, or unthinkingly assumed that no change of speaker had taken place and that the prefix was redundant. We cannot rule out the possibility that Middleton transcribed this part of the text, though the present single doubtful piece of evidence hardly in itself warrants such a conjecture. [3] For Middleton's oaths, see Jackson, *Attribution*, 67–78.

[4] Wilson suggests that the *name* 'was added [to the stage direction] as an afterthought by someone who had not at first observed his presence in the scene'; he assumes that the Justice was always part of the scene, but conjectures that his original part may have been shortened (p. 124). Greg by contrast notes that the *character* 'seems to be a later addition' to the scene (*First Folio*, 355); he does not specifically remark on the form of the stage direction, though this must be a primary basis for his claim. Eccles (p. 57) rather misleadingly records: '*Iustice*] GREG (1955, p. 355): "seems to be a later addition", as suggested by WILSON (ed. 1922)'.

entry, and the violation of idiom in the placement of '*and*', both suggest as much. The said Justice plays no part in the next 250 lines of this long scene; he does not speak, he is not spoken to or of. Moreover, the Justice's presence seems, for the first part of that scene, awkwardly unwarranted. The '*seruants*' suggest, as editors have usually inferred, that the scene takes place in someone's house: the Justice implies a session in court. Whatever we make of the scene's location—and Shakespeare may not have cared much—the servants and the Justice do not obviously or easily coexist here. The Justice—like the two Gentlemen in 1. 2, and the boy in 4. 1—makes no other appearance in the play. He is also—with the exception of messengers and servants—the only speaking character in the play not included in the Folio's list of 'The names of all the Actors'.

The Justice exists solely for the sake of a brief conversation with Escalus, at the end of the scene:

> *Esc.* Looke you bring mee in the names of some sixe
> or seuen, the most sufficient of your parish.
> *Elb.* To your Worships house sir?
> *Esc.* To my house: fare you well: [*Exit Elbow*] what's a clocke,
> thinke you?
> *Iust.* Eleuen, Sir.
> *Esc.* I pray you home to dinner with me.
> *Iust.* I humbly thanke you.
> *Esc.* It grieues me for the death of *Claudio*
> But there's no remedie:
> *Iust.* Lord *Angelo* is seuere.
> *Esc.* It is but needfull.
> Mercy is not it selfe, that oft lookes so,
> Pardon is still the nurse of second woe:
> But yet, poore *Claudio*; there is no remedie.
> Come sir.   *Exeunt.*
>   (TLN 715–30; 2. 1. 260–75)

Presumably no one would want to include this passage in any anthology of Shakespeare's liveliest, or most characteristic, or most inventively dramatic, dialogue. Like the interpolation in 4. 1, it mixes prose, blank verse, and a rhyming couplet, to no particular purpose. Like the interpolation in 4. 1, it is much concerned with getting people off the stage: the question about the time, and the invitation to dinner, serve no other purpose. The whole thing could be omitted without loss to the plot, the characterization, or the theme.

Why then would anyone bother to add it? Presumably because it makes one point: it defends Angelo's severity. Escalus takes a very different attitude earlier in this scene, and again on his next appearance in 3. 1. Like the Provost, Escalus elsewhere serves as an unmistakably respectable choric figure, who casts doubt upon the wisdom of the excessive moral rigour of Angelo's punishment of Claudio. Yet here the same figure has been employed for the opposite function: to assure an audience that, however much one may pity Claudio, severity is morally justified. Of course, Shakespeare might himself have wished to balance our responses in this way. If Shakespeare decided that he needed such a comment, and needed another character who would prompt Escalus to make it, then he *could* have gone back over the whole scene, fitting in one or two earlier speeches for the Justice; these *could* easily have been added, or shifted from Escalus to his colleague, during the long interrogation of Pompey, Elbow, and Froth. An adapter, on the other hand, usually tried to interfere as little as possible with what had already been written, and in any case had much less concern for the coherence of the play in question, since his whole function was to append superfluities.

Nothing in this brief passage at the end of 2. 1 enables us to prove that it was composed after Shakespeare's death; its very brevity forbids any confident pronouncements about authorship; without the independent evidence of interpolation in 1. 2 and 4. 1, we could not claim that this passage in itself offered evidence of theatrical adaptation. But the Folio stage direction suggests that the Justice is an afterthought (whether Shakespeare's, or someone else's); his prolonged silent presence creates some dramatic awkwardness; he has no other function in the play; the dialogue for which he exists is extraneous and detachable, has been written in a pedestrian manner which betrays no evidence of Shakespeare's hand, and consists of a haphazard mixture of prose and blank verse and rhyme which occurs elsewhere in *Measure* only in an interpolated passage. That mixture, though rare in Shakespeare, can be found often in the work of the probable author of one of the identifiable interpolations in the play; the dialogue seems to exist solely for the purpose of expressing a sentiment not elsewhere endorsed by Escalus, but of which the Calvinistic Middleton would surely have approved—a sentiment common enough in Middleton, but which receives sustained expression only once elsewhere in the Shakespeare canon, in a scene (*Timon of Athens* 3. 5) which recent investigations have, on independent grounds, all attributed to Middleton.[5]

The only other extraneous passage of any length is Pompey's soliloquy at the beginning of 4. 3.

> *Clo.* I am as well acquainted heere, as I was in our
> house of profession: one would thinke it were Mistris
> *Ouer-dons* owne house, for heere be manie of her olde
> Customers. First, here's yong Mr *Rash*, hee's in for a
> commoditie of browne paper, and olde Ginger, nine
> score and seuenteene pounds, of which hee made fiue
> Markes readie money: marrie then, Ginger was not
> much in request, for the olde Women were all dead.
> Then is there heere one Mr *Caper*, at the suite of Master
> *Three-Pile* the Mercer, for some foure suites of Peach-
> colour'd Satten, which now peaches him a beggar.
> Then haue we heere, yong *Dizie*, and yong Mr *Deepe-*
> *vow*, and Mr *Copperspurre*, and Mr *Starue-Lackey* the Ra-
> pier and dagger man, and yong *Drop-heire* that kild lu-
> stie *Pudding*, and Mr *Forth[r]ight* the Tilter, and braue M^r
> *Shootie* the great Traueller, and wilde *Halfe-Canne* that
> stabb'd Pots, and I thinke fortie more, all great doers in
> our Trade, and are now for the Lords sake.
>
> (TLN 2078–95 4. 3. 1–18)

---

[5] 'Pardon is still the nurse of second woe' was proverbial (Tilley, P50), and has an obvious application in a play concerned with justice and mercy. It is not therefore surprising that Isabella should later express a similar thought, though more forcibly: 'Mercy to thee would prove it selfe a Bawd' (3. 1. 148; TLN 1372). There is nothing choric about Isabella's outcry.

This sort of comic set piece could easily have been interpolated, and the New Variorum edition itself contains more Middleton parallels for this passage than for any other in the play:[6] Middleton elsewhere writes of 'commodities in . . . brown paper' (*Michaelmas Term* 2. 3. 219–20), of cloth of a 'peach colour' (*Your Five Gallants* 3. 5. 160), and of 'rapier and dagger men' (*The Phoenix* 2. 3. 187); Lever said that Pompey's 'yong *Drop-heire*' (TLN 2091) 'suggests a figure like Middleton's "Bawd-gallant" ' in *Father Hubburd's Tales*, p. 78. The last of these parallels is rather dubious; in its place one might note Middleton's reference in *The Roaring Girl* to 'The book where all prisoners' names stand' (3. 3. 157), which perhaps suggests the property which lies beneath Pompey's repeated 'here's . . . heere . . . heere . . .'. However, all these parallels are with Middleton's early work: *The Phoenix* (1603), *Your Five Gallants* (1606–7), *Michaelmas Term* (1605–6), *Father Hubburd's Tales* (1604), and *The Roaring Girl* (1611). Such parallels do not point to composition by Middleton in 1621. Moreover, Shakespeare himself provides a more exact parallel for 'peach-colour'd' (2 *Henry IV* 2. 2. 19), and a parallel for 'rapier and dagger', though not qualifying 'men' (*Hamlet* 5. 2. 152). Short as the passage is, it contains, in its eighteen lines, many unusual verbal features characteristic of Shakespeare: unusual compounds (peach-colour'd, *Deepe-vow*, *Copperspurre*, *Starue-Lackey*, the Rapier and dagger man, *Drop-heire*, *Forth[r]ight*, *Shootie*, *Halfe-Canne*), and an agent noun in -er (doers). Though its rare vocabulary is too small for statistical analysis, it does contain slightly more than the expected number of links with plays of 1601–7.

Three other details also point to an early date. In the first place, rapier and dagger were a particularly topical lethal combination at the turn of the century; there would have been considerably less reason to specify them in 1621. Then, as we have already noted, Malone observed that four of the ten prisoners Pompey names are 'stabbers, or duellists', a fact which he related to disturbances in 1603–4, and the legislation they provoked; though shaky evidence for the play's date of composition, those disturbances give us little reason to doubt that Pompey's speech could have been, in its choice of inmates, apt enough in 1603–4. Thirdly, Pompey explains that 'then, Ginger was not much in request, for the

---

[6] There is another apparent cluster of Middleton parallels in 3. 1, again in a passage involving Pompey. But the actual evidence for his presence turns out to be insubstantial. (1) *bastard* (3. 1. 273; TLN 1493). The pun appears in *Fair Quarrel* 5. 1. 123 and *Mad World* 2. 1. 69–70, but not in Shakespeare. But the joke is shared by at least four dramatists: the scene in *Fair Quarrel* is always ascribed to Rowley, not Middleton, and the same pun (which is a particularly obvious one) occurs in Heywood's *1 Fair Maid of the West* and in *1 Honest Whore* 2. 1. 232 (Eccles, pp. 157–8). All investigators assign this last example to Dekker; they are divided about Dekker's or Middleton's responsibility for *Roaring Girl* 2. 1. 353–4, where the pun also occurs. (2) *what stuffe is heere* (3. 1. 274; TLN 1494). Equally well exampled in Shakespeare's *Tempest* 2. 1. 254 and Middleton's *Michaelmas Term* 3. 1. 205. (3) The usurer, 'furd with Foxe and Lamb-skins' (3. 1. 278; TLN 1498). The fox-furred usurer is common in Middleton, but as Lever pointed out, 'Elizabethan literature abounds in references to him'. (4) Pompey's 'strange Pick-lock' (3. 1. 285; TLN 1506). Chastity belts are alluded to in *Chaste Maid* 4. 4. 4–5, but also in *Cymbeline* 2. 2. 41–2. The passage contains city-comedy material, and, as with Pompey's speech at the beginning of 4. 3, Middleton's pre-eminence in this field accounts for the number of Middleton parallels. In tone the passage remains Shakespearian: ''Twas neuer merry world since of two vsuries the merriest was put downe' is exactly the kind of sentiment that distinguishes the work of Shakespeare from that of Middleton.

olde Women were all dead'. As we have already noted (p. 176), this is 'probably a reference to the plague in 1603'. Certainly, we know of nothing in 1619–22 which would explain such a claim. Cumulatively, these three allusions seem to us to argue decisively for the composition of Pompey's speech early in the seventeenth century, most probably in 1603–4.

Finally, another Shakespeare play provides a striking parallel for the form of this speech: *Macbeth*.[7] Like Pompey's soliloquy, the Porter's consists of a catalogue of contemporary vices. Of course, Middleton probably had a hand in the Folio text of *Macbeth*, and the parallel between *Measure* and *Macbeth* might be thought to make Pompey's speech more rather than less suspicious. But the Porter's speech can hardly be an interpolation. Its critical merits have been often and convincingly defended, and even Coleridge (who first cast doubts on its authenticity) admitted that its last lines must have been written by Shakespeare. The description of temptation as 'the primrose way to the everlasting bonfire' is strikingly, and idiosyncratically, Shakespearian.[8] Moreover, the Porter's reference to 'an equivocator . . . who committed treason' has usually been interpreted as an allusion to the Gunpowder plot; whether or not the passage will bear so much specific weight, there can be little doubt that the Porter's speech—like Pompey's—better fits the period when its play was written than it fits the years between Shakespeare's death and the publication of the First Folio.[9] The authenticity of the Porter's speech makes it even more difficult to doubt the authenticity of Pompey's, in a play written only two to three years earlier.

Beyond detachable passages such as the end of 2. 1 (plausibly) or the beginning of 4. 3 (implausibly), two other kinds of material come under the most suspicion. Because the interpolation at the beginning of 4. 1 creates an act-break, and because the original performances would presumably have been continuous, anything on either side of an act-break might have been tampered with; likewise, because the interpolation in 1. 2 (directly) and that in 4. 1 (indirectly) magnify Lucio's importance, anything in Lucio's role might be an addition. In fact, neither of these possibilities bears fruit.

Of the remaining act-divisions, only the break before Act 5 gives any cause for suspicion. At the end of Act 4 Isabella and Mariana are awaiting the Duke's entrance; Friar Peter comes in, and tells them he has found 'a stand most fit'; all three exit. The Duke and his train enter at the beginning of Act 5; Friar Peter and Isabella re-enter nineteen lines into the scene. The act-division might have been interpolated in order to provide a suspenseful pause at the end of Act 4, followed by a spectacular entrance at the beginning of Act 5; if so, Shakespeare might have intended 4. 6 and 5. 1 to run continuously, as one long scene, in which case Isabella and her companions need not have left the stage at all. But

---

[7] A. C. Bradley drew attention to this parallel, as evidence of the authenticity of the speech in *Macbeth in Shakespearean Tragedy* (London, 1904), 397.

[8] Compare *Hamlet* 1. 3. 50 ('the primrose path of dalience treads') and *All's Well* 4. 5. 54–5 ('the flowrie way that leads to the broad gate, and the great fire'). As G. K. Hunter notes, in his new Arden edn. of the latter (London, 1959), Shakespeare's description of the road to damnation as 'flowrie' does 'not find any warrant in Scripture' (p. 122); Harold Jenkins, in his new Arden *Hamlet* (London, 1982) calls this 'Shakespeare's own variation on the traditional metaphor' (p. 201).

[9] For a more extended defence of the authenticity of the Porter's speech, see Muir's edn., pp. xxiii–xxix.

the plausibility of this conjecture in the abstract is undermined by any attempt to apply it in detail. Mariana does not re-enter with Isabella and Peter; she does not, and cannot, re-enter until almost 180 lines later. In order to play 4. 6 and 5. 1 continuously we should have to provide an exit for Mariana, or remove her entirely from 4. 6. The latter course seems impossible; the former presupposes that something has been lost. But something must also have been added, for if the scene were originally played continuously then most or all of Friar Peter's speech must be an interpolation:

> *Peter.* Come I haue found you out a stand most fit,
> Where you may haue such vantage on the *Duke*
> He shall not passe you:
> Twice haue the Trumpets sounded.
> The generous, and grauest Citizens
> Haue hent the gates, and very neere vpon
> The *Duke* is entring:
> Therefore hence away.   *Exeunt.*
>   (TLN 2337–44; 4. 6. 11–16)

But Friar Peter must somehow have been introduced: he plays an important role in 5. 1, and apparently must enter (as in the Folio he does) with Isabella. If the exeunt and scene-break have been interpolated along with the act-break, then Friar Peter's extant speech must be largely an interpolation, which has displaced another speech, in which (perhaps) an exit for Mariana was both called for and motivated. If Shakespeare did intend a continuous scene, then the transition he wrote here has been irretrievably lost, and we have little choice but to accept the adapted text.

But we remain sceptical that any theatrical interference has taken place. Without Friar Peter's line about 'a stand most fit', no one would find anything odd about Isabella's entrance in 5. 1: she has just arrived. In fact, this explanation will serve anyway; but the alleged difficulty about Isabella's entering to, rather than waiting for, the Duke arises from the very lines allegedly interpolated in order to change the staging of her entrance. Moreover, Act 5 begins with the Duke meeting Angelo and his train; this would be clear from the dialogue, even without the Folio specification for entrance '*at seuerall doores*' (TLN 2347). It would be dramatic for Isabella and Friar Peter, like the Soothsayer and Artemidorus in 3. 1 of *Julius Caesar*, to stand on one part of the stage while a procession enters from one door and makes its way towards them; but Isabella and Friar Peter would instead have to stand aside while others entered from every direction. The form of the entrance, the dialogue, and the information imparted by previous scenes, all tell us that Act 5 begins at or near the gates of Vienna, and playing 4. 6 and 5. 1 as a continuous scene would require us to suppose that Isabella and Friar Peter stand alone at the gates until the moment when the Duke arrives, at which point the citizens and Lord Angelo's train also—simultane-ously—arrive. This would put a wholly uncharacteristic strain on the credulity of Shakespeare's audience.

Uninterrupted playing would, in this instance, substitute one muddled entrance for two clear ones. The Duke's entrance and his meeting with Angelo are moments spectacular and dramatic enough; Isabella and Friar Peter would only get in the way, to no discernible advantage. Likewise, if Isabella enters just before she speaks she immediately captures an audience's attention, by her very entrance. The Folio gives us the entrance of the Dike and Friar Peter, then Varrius, the exit of all three, the entrance of Isabella and Mariana, then of Friar Peter, then the exit of all three, within the space of a mere twenty-eight lines of dialogue: it thereby creates an impression of bustling preparations for the final long disentangling scene.[10] By getting rid of the scene-break as well as the act-break we would precede the Duke's entrance with a moment or more of mere waiting. Continuity weakens the Duke's return to Vienna, and we see no reason to assume that Shakespeare ever intended it, or that the scene-break between 4. 6 and 5. 1 represents a late theatrical adaptation.

Only Lucio remains as a serious candidate for unShakespearian elaboration. Dover Wilson and G. B. Evans both concluded that his role had been extensively expanded. But of all Lucio's appearances only the beginning of 1. 2 is extraneous: in his other scenes he must always have played essentially the same role that he does in the Folio. Moreover, unless the part had been prominent and popular to start with, it would probably not have been favoured with the special attention which the alleged addition in 1. 2 gives it. Very few of the words the Folio puts in Lucio's mouth can have come from any hand but Shakespeare's. His speeches, and the passages in which his presence are essential, are full of the features of vocabulary and word-formation most strongly associated with Shakespeare: compounds, words prefixed with *un-*, latinisms, nouns and adjectives formed from verbs, hapax legomena, and words or senses of words of which no earlier occurrence is recorded. And in our search of Middleton, we have found virtually no striking parallels between the language of these episodes and that of the suspected reviser of 1. 2. A detailed examination shows that almost all of Lucio's speeches are intrinsic to the development of the scenes in which they appear.

It will be convenient to begin at the end, with Lucio's role in the final scene. Isabella's story cues Lucio's introduction:

> I, (in probation of a Sisterhood)
> Was sent to by my Brother; one *Lucio*
> As then the Messenger.
>   *Luc.* That's I, and't like your Grace:
> I came to her from *Claudio*, and desir'd her,
> To try her gracious fortune with Lord *Angelo*,
> For her poore Brothers pardon.
>   *Isab.* That's he indeede.
>   *Duk.* You were not bid to speake.
>   *Luc.* No, my good Lord,
> Nor wish'd to hold my peace.
>   *Duk.* I wish you now then,
> Pray you take note of it: and when you haue
> A business for your selfe: pray heauen you then
> Be perfect.

[10] Most editors since Capell have called for 'ISABELL, *and Friar* Peter, *at their Stand*' at the beginning of 5. 1, thereby requiring their exit and immediate re-entrance between 4. 6 and 5. 1; G. K. Hunter in consequence conjectures that they never left the stage: 'Were There Act-Pauses on Shakespeare's Stage?' in Standish Henning, Robert Kimbrough, and Richard Knowles (eds.), *English Renaissance Drama: Essays in Honor of Madeleine Doran and Mark Eccles* (Carbondale, Ill., 1976), 15–35.

> *Luc.* I warrant your honour.
> *Duk.* The warrant's for your selfe: take heede to't.
> *Isab.* This Gentleman told somewhat of my Tale.
> *Luc.* Right.
> *Duk.* It may be right, but you are i'the wrong
> To speake before your time: proceed,
> *Isab.* I went
> To this pernicious Caitiffe Deputie.
>
> (TLN 2432–54; 5. 1. 72–88)

Both the beginning and the end of this passage are so integrally fitted in to the verse structure that it must have been original; it provides, moreover, the most logical point in the scene for introducing Lucio. This passage must be, in large part at least, original, and it confirms Lucio's presence in the original version of 1. 2, as also in 1. 4. Only lines 2444–8 ('Pray you . . . heed to't') could be an interpolation, but nothing suggests that they are.

Lucio's second intervention also arises naturally from the progress of the dialogue, and can hardly be removed:

> *Duk.* A ghostly Father, belike:
> Who knowes that *Lodowicke*?
> *Luc.* My Lord, I know him, 'tis a medling Fryer,
> I doe not like the man: had he been Lay my Lord,
> For certaine words he spake against your Grace
> In your retirment, I had swing'd him soundly.
> *Duke.* Words against mee? this' a good Fryer belike
> And to set on this wretched woman here
> Against our Substitute: Let this Fryer be found.
> *Luc.* But yesternight my Lord, she and that Fryer
> I saw them at the prison: a sawcy Fryar,
> A very scuruy fellow.
> *Peter.* Blessed be your Royall Grace:
> I haue stood by my Lord, and I haue heard
> Your royall eare abus'd: first hath this woman
> Most wrongfully accus'd your Substitute,
> Who is as free from touch, or soyle with her
> As she from one vngot.
> *Duke.* We did beleeue no lesse.
> Know you that Frier *Lodowick* that she speakes of?
> *Peter.* I know him for a man diuine and holy,
> Not scuruy, nor a temporary medler
> As he's reported by this Gentleman:
> And on my trust, a man that neuer yet
> Did (as he vouches) mis-report your Grace.
> *Luc.* My Lord, most villanously, beleeue it.
> *Peter.* Well: he in time may come to cleere himselfe;
>
> (TLN 2495–2521; 5. 1. 126–49)

Notably, Lucio here (as previously) speaks verse, and verse integrated into the structure of the surrounding lines. Lucio's part could not even be abbreviated without recasting the whole context, which has every appearance of authenticity. Moreover, Lucio here first expresses an opinion about the Friar, something he must do at some point in the scene. This passage must therefore be Shakespearian, and Lucio's second speech here confirms his presence in 4. 3.

Lucio's third intervention is prompted by Mariana:

> *Duke*. What, are you married?
> *Mar*. No my Lord.
> *Duke*. Are you a Maid?
> *Mar*. No my Lord.
> *Duk*. A Widow then?
> *Mar*. Neither, my Lord.
> *Duk*. Why you are nothing then: neither Maid, Wi-
> dow, nor Wife?
> *Luc*. My Lord, she may be a Puncke: for many of
> them, are neither Maid, Widow, nor Wife.
> *Duk*. Silence that fellow: I would he had some cause
> to prattle for himselfe.
> *Luc*. Well my Lord.
> *Mar*. My Lord, I doe confesse I nere was married,
> And I confesse besides, I am no Maid,
> I haue known my husband, yet my husband
> Knowes not, that euer he knew me.
> *Luc*. He was drunk then, my Lord, it can be no better.
> *Duk*. For the benefit of silence, would thou wert so to.
> *Luc*. Well, my Lord.
> *Duk*. This is no witnesse for Lord *Angelo*.
>
> (TLN 2544–64; 5. 1. 170–90)

All of Lucio's speeches here (and the Duke's replies to them) could be omitted. Lucio here speaks prose—but not until the context has slipped into prose. If the change to prose casts suspicion on Lucio's speeches it casts equal suspicion on what immediately precedes them; and if Lucio's helpful gloss 'Puncke' goes, then we should probably also omit the Duke's preceding speech, which clearly serves as a feed for the joke. This would leave us with:

> *Duke*. What, are you married?
> *Mar*. My Lord, I doe confesse I nere was married,
> And I confesse besides, I am no Maid,
> I haue known my husband, yet my husband
> Knowes not, that euer he knew me.
> *Duk*. This is no witnesse for Lord *Angelo*.

The Duke's first speech here completes a verse line; Mariana's speech answers the Duke's question; the Duke's reply immediately passes judgement on the riddling self-accusation of Mariana's confessions. Unlike all of Lucio's interventions so far, these could be cut without havocking the dialogue. On the other hand, Mariana's confession creates such an obvious opportunity for cynical interpretation that one would expect at least one irrepressible comment from Lucio. Diana, who plays a similar riddling role in the final scene of *All's Well*, is twice accused of being a prostitute (5. 3. 188, 286).

The authenticity of Lucio's interventions at 2552–3 and 2561 cannot be decided without reference to his next speeches, shortly after:

> *Duke.* Know you this woman?
> *Luc.* Carnallie she saies.
> *Duk*[.] Sirha, no more.
> *Luc.* Enoug[h] my Lord.
> *Ang.* My Lord, I must confesse, I know this woman,
> (TLN 2586–90; 5. 1. 210–14)

This could have been added, but nothing in particular casts doubt on its authenticity. Noticeably, both this and the preceding passage explain the Duke's growing impatience with Lucio. Without them, that impatience receives no expression for 180 lines before the Duke's exit; his last comment upon Lucio's interference would in fact have been favourable (TLN 2501–3; 5. 1. 131–3). This seems to us most implausible; consequently, one or both interventions must be original. Moreover, Shakespeare twice elsewhere plays on the innocent and sexual meanings of the verb 'know' (*Venus* 525, *Much Ado* 4. 1. 48). If the same joke here came from his pen, then the Duke's 'no more' rather strongly implies another intervention not long before. This passage therefore seems to vouch for at least part of the one which precedes it. And since both of the preceding interventions drag the dialogue—for the first time—into prose, the mere fact of prose cannot be taken as evidence against either's authenticity. The first and longest of the two suspect prose passages has a close parallel in *All's Well*, and inconspicuously manages the transition to prose by means of a series of short, ambiguously rhythmical speeches. It seems the least likely of the two to have been interpolated. Therefore, if we can suspect anything, it must be TLN 2561–3:

> *Luc.* He was drunk then, my Lord, it can be no better.
> *Duk.* For the benefit of silence, would thou wert so to.
> *Luc.* Well, my Lord.

We cannot prove the authenticity of this titbit; nor do we believe that an adapter would have troubled to add it, or see any reason to doubt that Shakespeare wrote it.

The rest of Lucio's part in this scene can hardly be doubted: his prose conversation with Escalus helps to cover the necessary interval between the Duke's exit as Duke and his re-entrance as Friar (TLN 2638–59), while his next major intervention leads to the Duke's all-important uncowling (TLN 2705–41); thereafter he remains predictably silent until the Duke turns to announce his punishment (TLN 2898–2923). These passages are necessary to the plot, essential to the staging, or demanded by the expectations of the audience; clearly Shakespearian in style, they cannot be easily disintegrated into authentic and unauthentic chunks.[11] Taking Act 5 as a whole, only 2444–8 and 2561–3 might reasonably be singled out as possible interpolations; yet nothing in either passage gives us good reason to doubt Shakespeare's authorship. Nor would the exclusion of either passage materially affect our view of Lucio's contribution in this scene.

Lucio's role in 5. 1 must be essentially original. But Lucio's penultimate appearance, in 4. 3, creates a passage in which Lever found signs of 'a hasty and rather careless rewriting . . . substituting Lucio's entry for the return of the

---

[11] Lever finds a parallel for Lucio's 'women are light at midnight' (TLN 2658–9) in *Mad World* 5. 1; but he also cites three other examples and describes the phrase as 'apparently a stock adage'.

Provost' (p. xxiii). The potential relevance of this claim to our own enquiry will be obvious. Lever, though looking at the text from a completely different viewpoint, found indications that (as Dover Wilson suggested) Lucio's part in the play has been expanded. Lever felt able to accommodate this conclusion to his own theory that Crane worked from Shakespeare's foul papers: he believed Shakespeare had revised the scene (p. xxiii). But if the end of 4. 3 was revised in a text elsewhere adapted, after Shakespeare's death, in such a way as to increase the prominence of Lucio's role, then the adapter may himself have conducted the revision of 4. 3.

However, Lever's arguments for revision are not compelling. The Duke announces that he will send letters to Angelo, and orders the Provost to return after delivering Ragozine's head to Angelo; Lever contends that Shakespeare must have originally intended the Provost to return to the Duke after his exit at 4. 3. 102 (TLN 2190) in order to collect the letters which he must take to Angelo. We see no such necessity. Indeed it would be dramatically awkward for the Duke to sit down and write letters while the Provost waited to deliver them; not only awkward but tediously predictable, in contrast to Lucio's intrusion upon the scene. As in 3. 1 Lucio functions primarily as an irritant to the Duke, a persistent and anarchic influence about which he can do nothing. The unexpectedness of his entry contributes to that dramatic function: the Duke cannot be rid of Lucio, who like 'a kind of Burre . . . shal sticke' (4. 3. 172; TLN 2270). The Duke's other concerns, not surprisingly, get temporarily swept aside.

Lucio also delays Isabella's departure. In fact she is provided with no exit direction in F; but missing exits are (as we have noted) common enough in the text. There is no mystery about why Isabella stays on stage: Lucio briefly addresses her before she leaves. Nor is it strange that she makes no reply to Lucio, for (as he observes) she is distressed. In the forty-six lines from her outburst on hearing of Claudio's death until Lucio's entry, she manages to utter a mere five limp words: 'I am directed by you' (4. 3. 133; TLN 2228); there are repeated references to her tears. Lucio's mixture of true sympathy and facetiousness requires no reply from Isabella other than a silent departure.

Little importance can be attached to the remaining puzzle, Lucio's greeting 'Good'euen' (4. 3. 145; TLN 2241) in a scene which evidently takes place in the morning. As Lever observed, at 5. 1. 134–5 (TLN 2404–5) Lucio affirms that his meeting with Isabella and the Duke indeed took place in the evening. Alice Walker pointed out that the 'dramatic clock' has simply moved forward, as it does by more than three hours between 4. 2. 96 and 101. 'Good'euen', she argues, is appropriate to any time after midday (p. 8).[12]

If Lucio did not appear in 4. 3 there would be a gap of well over 600 lines between 3. 1 and Lucio's crucial role in 5. 1—600 lines during which we hear little and see nothing of him. Lucio's recollection of the meeting in 4. 3 in a speech integral to the unfolding of 5. 1 bears independent witness to the integrity of the earlier episode. It is in 4. 3 that the Duke learns that Lucio has fathered a child by a prostitute, information he turns against Lucio in the closing moments of the play. If the scene has been rewritten, it is more likely that Shakespeare did so

[12] Even if Walker's explanation is rejected, there would be little justification in singling out this problem of time-sequence from the others, which Lever is content to ascribe to 'the usual' authorial inconsistencies and textual corruptions (pp. xvi–xvii).

before completing the play than that Middleton added the Lucio episode later. But Lever gives no convincing reason for believing that the episode was revised at all.

Lucio's speeches in 4. 3 are integral to the scene's development. Lucio enters with a greeting and asks the Duke where the Provost is—perhaps to explain his presence, perhaps merely to be provocative. His address to Isabella leads smoothly both to her exit and to his slanders on the Duke. Not a single speech of the ensuing dialogue can be subtracted without the dialogue collapsing. In the episode as a whole, only the opening greeting and exchange with the Duke could conceivably have been added after the rest, and they seem too perfunctory for an adapter to have bothered writing them.

The dialogue between Lucio and the Duke in 3. 1 lays the foundation for later developments in 4. 3 and 5. 1. Again the exchanges are so integrated into the scene that it is difficult to imagine individual speeches, or even parts of speeches, as additions. The only lines at all superfluous are Lucio's deprecations of the Duke just before he leaves, after his first farewell ('Farwell good Friar, I prithee pray for me': 3. 1. 174; TLN 1665–6). As he repeats the farewell at the end of the speech, the intervening lines might be regarded as a discrete and therefore possibly superimposed unit. But delayed departures occur often in the plays of Shakespeare and his contemporaries (and in life). More important, the Duke's soliloquy after Lucio departs follows the second farewell much better than the first. The soliloquy concerns 'Back-wounding calumnie' against the Duke himself, the exact substance of Lucio's words in the preceding lines; Lucio's attention before the first farewell moves from condemnation of Angelo to ironic praise for the Duke to a mitigation of Claudio's crime, and hence provides a less appropriate cue for the Duke's soliloquy.

Before his interview with the Duke, Lucio taunts Pompey as he goes to prison. Without this episode there would be no transition from the comedy with Elbow and Pompey to the episode with Lucio. The parallel between Pompey's progress to prison in 3. 1 and that of Claudio in 1. 2 has already been observed. Once again the dialogue has an internal coherence that does not encourage suspicion that any particular bits and pieces have been thrust in by a later hand.

Lucio's part in 2. 2 raises more serious doubts. Dover Wilson found it 'difficult . . . to avoid the conclusion that Lucio is an intruder in 2. 2 and robs the Provost, who is there by right, of most of his lines' (p. 99). We do not agree with this conclusion, but it deserves careful scrutiny.

At the end of 1. 4 Lucio parts with Isabella; he instructs her to go to Angelo, which she undertakes, and she sends him with a message of encouragement to Claudio. His presence in 2. 2, the scene in which Isabella first pleads for her brother's life, is therefore unexpected. Lucio is nowhere addressed in the scene, and his role is confined to encouraging Isabella in short, mostly single-line speeches. Some of these speeches are extrametrical. Dover Wilson was surely not justified in drawing the conclusion from this alone (or perhaps also from his distaste for Lucio) that those speeches are later additions. But in the light of the alleged expansion of Lucio's role in 1. 2, these facts do naturally arouse suspicions, suspicions heightened by a particularly close parallel between one of Lucio's lines and a line in a play usually attributed to the suspected author of the 1. 2 addition:

Thou'rt i'th right (Girle) more o'that
(2. 2. 132–3; TLN 887)

Th'art in the right, sweet wench, more of that vein
(Middleton, *Family of Love* 3. 2. 38–9)

The quotations themselves show that the resemblances are both verbal and situational; both are asides. As Eccles points out, 'vein' is a word Lucio uses elsewhere in 2. 2: 'I, touch him: there's the vaine' (2. 2. 73; TLN 821).

Lucio's speeches cannot have been entirely absent from 2. 2 in its original form. His first and longest speech urges Isabella to return to Angelo when she has apparently admitted defeat and is preparing to depart; Isabella's resumed pleading shows that she takes heed of the speech, and therefore must have heard it. Dover Wilson thought some of the speeches were originally spoken by the Provost. Middleton could have reassigned all but two of the Provost's speeches—the particularly pious ones—to Lucio, and filled out his part with further additions. Certainly the Provost cannot have applauded Isabella's observation that 'There's many haue committed' Claudio's crime (2. 2. 91; TLN 843–4); nor would we expect him to be particularly enthusiastic about Isabella's defence of 'fowle prophanation' (2. 2. 128–9; TLN 886–7) or particularly interested in the bad language of soldiers (2. 2. 130–2; TLN 888–90). These lines all seem designed for Lucio.

The content of Lucio's speeches suggests that they were written with him in mind; so does the context into which they are fitted. Just as it seems unlikely that innocent words spoken by the Provost should, by virtue of a mere change of speaker, acquire a sharp second edge of humorous irony, it would be equally strange if an adapter were able to add intrinsically neutral comments which would only sparkle through reaction with a context which was not designed for them. The humour of Lucio's exhortations is built into Isabella's speeches, which are themselves irreproachably Shakespearian.

This is a particularly acute aspect of a more general problem: the scene is simply better with Lucio than without him. He does not just scurrilously devalue the scene, but underpins the physical and erotic aspects of persuasion which Isabella, in effect but not intention, so devastatingly employs. The structure of the scene—a man and a woman in a dialogue leading to lust, observed and commented upon by other contrasting characters, one of whom takes a cynical view (and with some justification)—is thoroughly Shakespearian. It most strikingly resembles the flirtation of Cressida and Diomedes in *Troilus* 5. 2 (written c.1602), where the unseen observers include Thersites.

We doubt that the scene would be dramatically plausible with only one commentator and supporter of Isabella. The Provost in the scene as we know it is reticent and discreet, maintaining an outward neutrality. If he spoke even the bare minimum of Lucio's speeches, he would be required to intervene actively on Isabella's behalf. This is scarcely compatible with the duties of his office—of which, even when he conspires to save Claudio, he is conscientiously mindful. When at the beginning of 2. 2 he discreetly implies that Angelo may wish to change his mind about Claudio's fate, he is harshly checked and immediately apologizes; if the Provost is so obsequious in a private dialogue, he is scarcely likely to undermine his superior by encouraging a supplicant to challenge the validity of his decisions. Nor is Angelo likely to have let such flagrant interference pass unremarked and unrebuked.

Thus, though the case for Lucio's part being added by an adapter seems strong, the objections to it are even stronger. We must conclude that Shakespeare put Lucio in 2. 2. We may discount the extrametrical nature of some of the short speeches as deliberate prose interruptions of a verse dialogue: Lucio elsewhere speaks both prose and verse. The end of 1. 4 can be explained in terms of theatrical expedience. Isabella cannot leave with Lucio before seeing her mother superior; Lucio cannot accompany her; therefore they must part. A parting would be particularly necessary if, as Lever proposes, the nun Francisca stays discreetly onstage during Lucio's visit: Isabella would be required to retire with her. This particular difficulty may be wholly imaginary; it has not, after all, disturbed many readers or audiences.

It remains possible that Middleton added one or two of Lucio's speeches in 2. 2. We suspect he did not, though we cannot be dogmatic. Isabella's speeches so neatly set up Lucio's strongest comments that, if Shakespeare did not write them, he overlooked opportunities he had himself created. We are also influenced by a variant of the law of diminishing returns: the less an adapter could have contributed, the less likely he is to have contributed anything. Nevertheless, one must single out 2. 2. 132–3 (TLN 887), the line with the close Middleton(?) parallel, as particularly suspect. This speech and Lucio's next ('Art auis'd o'that? more on't.'—2. 2. 133; TLN 890) are the only ones to use the familiar second person singular, and Middleton liked the form *on't*. In Shakespeare *on't* is found just 125 times in the entire canon, and of these the majority (74) are in the late plays (*Antony* and after) or the parts of *Timon* attributed to Middleton. This leaves 51 occurrences in the remaining twenty-nine plays of the canon, an average incidence of less than two per play. By way of contrast, *on't* occurs 80 times in just three randomly selected Middleton plays: *No Wit* (28), *More Dissemblers* (18), and *Women Beware Women* (34).

Moreover, at least two Middleton plays contain parallels for the second of these speeches: 'Are you advis'd of that, my lord?' (*Mad World* 2. 1. 153) and 'art advis'd of that?' (*No Wit* 1. 3. 176). Against these parallels must be set Shakespeare's 'Are you avis'd o' that?' (*Merry Wives* 1. 4. 100). The variant of *advised* without the first 'd' in *Merry Wives* and *Measure* is probably a Crane spelling, as it occurs in no other Shakespeare play. More significant than either this or the abbreviated *o'* is the familiar second person singular verb-form 'art' shared with *No Wit*, which accordingly offers the closest single parallel with Lucio's line.

In the context of our argument that Middleton revised other passages of *Measure*, this evidence is sufficient to raise a suspicion that he interpolated the two lines in question. But it falls well short of demonstrating that they were indeed inserted by Middleton, especially as we cannot be sure that he even wrote the line parallel to 2. 2. 132–3 in *The Family of Love*. Jackson concludes that '*The Family of Love* may not be Middleton's at all' (*Attribution*, 109), and Lake, though less radical, also produces clear evidence of the presence of both Dekker and Barry in the extant text (*Canon*, 91–108). Whatever the play's original date of composition, it was clearly revised in 1605 or after, and may itself have been influenced by *Measure*. As we have seen, Shakespeare himself used *on't* over 100 times, and indeed 23 times in the four plays that would appear to be closest in date to *Measure* (*Twelfth Night*, *Troilus*, *Othello*, and *All's Well*). Isabella lapses into the second person singular when addressing Angelo in 2. 4; presumably Lucio can become colloquially informal through enthusiasm just as Isabella does through heated indignation. If Lucio was in Shakespeare's version of the scene, we can be sure that he must have had an effective role to play, and a role essentially identical to that he plays in the Folio text.

Looking back over the evidence so far accumulated, it should cause no surprise that there exists a scattering of parallels between Middleton's work and passages in *Measure* not suspected of revision. Eccles actually cites more such parallels between *Measure* and the works of Jonson, which in itself shows that the Middleton parallels in the play as a whole are unexceptional. Apart from the special case of Pompey's speech opening 4. 3 the parallels show no tendency to cluster outside 1. 2. Moreover, all of them can be matched with comparable examples in Shakespeare: with the possible exception of the similarity between 2.2.132–3 (TLN 890) and a line of *The Family of Love, the parallels are neutral and do nothing to demonstrate that Middleton rather than Shakespeare wrote the lines concerned. They differ strikingly, in both quantity and quality, from the parallels which suggest Middleton's authorship of the suspect passage in 1. 2.

Lucio is thus, with the exception of his appearance at the beginning of 1. 2, Shakespeare's creation; Middleton seems to have added little, and probably nothing, else. The Folio division into acts does not seem, with the exception of the beginning of Act 4, to have disrupted the original play. Pompey's one detachable solo number, in 4. 3, must be Shakespeare's. Outside the two major interpolations in 1. 2 and 4. 1, only one other passage—Escalus's short dialogue with the Justice, at the end of 2. 1—might be suspected as an unShakespearian intrusion.

INDEX